THE VATICAN GARDENS

A MAP OF THE MODERN VATICAN CITY

*A corresponding map appears at the opening of each chapter (excluding Chapter Nine)
and shows modifications undertaken during the period discussed in that chapter. Numbers in
the maps and captions refer to buildings and gardens, while letters refer to fountains.*

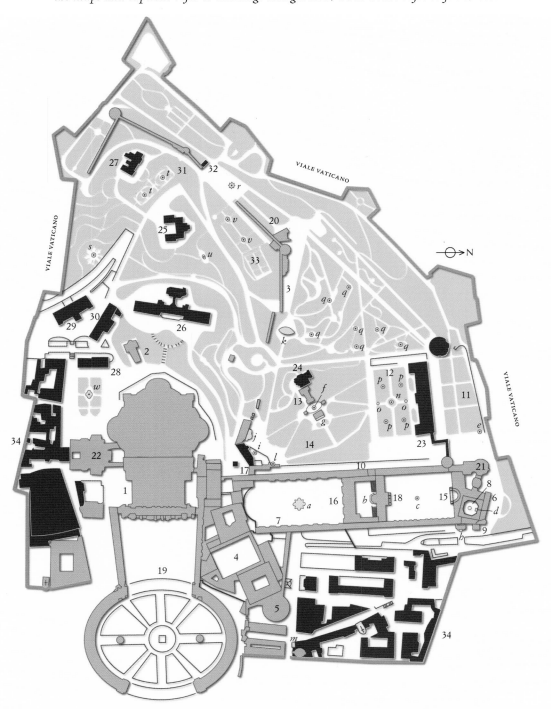

1. St. Peter's Basilica
2. Church of Santo Stefano
3. Leonine Wall
4. Vatican palaces with new additions
5. Tower of Nicholas V
6. Palazzetto del Belvedere
7. Loggias of Donato Bramante with exedra
8. Cortile of Michelangelo Simonetti
9. Spiral staircase
10. Loggias of Donato Bramante completed by Pirro Ligorio
11. Garden of Clement VII
12. Secret Garden of Paul III
13. Casina of Pius IV
14. The Giardino dei Semplici, converted into an English-style garden
15. Nicchione of Donato Bramante and Pirro Ligorio
16. Vatican Library
17. Wing of the Vatican palaces
18. Braccio Nuovo, Vatican Museums
19. The Colonnade of Piazza San Pietro
20. Chalet of Leo XIII
21. Museo Pio-Clementino
22. Sacristy
23. The Pinacoteca of Luca Beltrami
24. The expansion of the Casina of Pius IV
25. The Ethiopian College
26. The Palazzo del Governatorato
27. The radio tower
28. Palazzo di Giustizia
29. Train station
30. Mosaic studio
31. The Italian garden
32. Monument and grotto of Our Lady of Lourdes
33. Rose Garden
34. New buildings
a. Fontana del Belvedere
b. Nymphaeum of the Cortile della Biblioteca
c. The Fountana del Belvedere in the Cortile della Pigna, removed in 1846
d. Fontana di Cleopatra
e. Fontana della Zitella
f. Fountain at the Casina of Pius IV
g. Fish pond at the Casina of Pius IV
h. Fish pond of Julius III
i. Fontana del Forno
j. Fontana delle Torri
k. Fontana dell'Aquilone
l. Fontana degli Specchi
m. Fontana delle Api
n. The fountain in the Cortile della Pigna, moved to the Secret Garden of Paul III
o. Circular fountains
p. Wall fountains with sarcophagi
q. Fountains in the woods from the period of Benedict XV and Pius XI
r. Fontana delle Ranocchie
s. Fontana della Conchiglia
t. Fountains in the Italian garden
u. Fontana della Navicella
v. Fontana del Tritone and Fontana della Sirena
w. Fontana di S. Marta

THE VATICAN GARDENS

AN ARCHITECTURAL AND HORTICULTURAL HISTORY

ALBERTA CAMPITELLI

TRANSLATED BY CEIL FRIEDMAN

MUSEI VATICANI

LIBRERIA EDITRICE VATICANA

ABBEVILLE PRESS PUBLISHERS

NEW YORK LONDON

Front and back cover: Castel Gandolfo, the Belvedere Gardens created in the 1930s, with the cryptoporticus of the Villa di Domiziano to the right. See plate 255, pages 316–17.
Page 2: The Italian garden near the Palazzo della Radio, detail. See plate 224, page 272.

For the English-language edition
Editor: Austin Allen
Copy editor: Jacqueline Decter
Translation of quotations from the Latin: Jared Hudson
Production manager: Louise Kurtz
Composition: Angela Taormina
Jacket design: Misha Beletsky

First published in the United States of America in 2009 by Abbeville Press, 137 Varick Street, New York, NY 10013

First published in Italy in 2009 by Editoriale Jaca Book S.p.A., via Frua 11, 20146 Milano and Libreria Editrice Vaticana, Via della Posta, 00120 Città del Vaticano

First edition
10 9 8 7 6 5 4 3 2 1

Library of Congress Cataloging-in-Publication Data
Campitelli, Alberta.
  The Vatican gardens : an architectural and horticultural history / by Alberta Campitelli ; translated from the Italian by Ceil Friedman. — 1st ed.
    p. cm.
  Translated from Italian.
  ISBN 978-0-7892-1048-7 (hardcover : alk. paper)
  1. Gardens—Vatican City—History. 2. Gardens, Italian—Vatican City—History. I. Friedman, Ceil. II. Title.

  SB466.V3C236 2009
  712.09456'34—DC22
  2009019353

For bulk and premium sales and for text adoption procedures, write to Customer Service Manager, Abbeville Press, 137 Varick Street, New York, NY 10013, or call 1-800-ARTBOOK.

Visit Abbeville Press online at www.abbeville.com.

ILLUSTRATION CREDITS

All images are copyright © Archivio Fotografico dei Musei Vaticani, L. Giordano, including plates 103, 107, 108, 122, 126, 168, 177, 183–87, 194, 196, and 201–10, and with the exception of the following (all numbers refer to plates):

Archivio Fotografico dei Musei Capitolini: 5 (EM 253). BAMS photo by Basilio Rodella: 243. Biblioteca Apostolica Vaticana: 6, 27, 48, 49, 241, 242, 244. Biblioteca di Archeologia e Storia dell'Arte, Rome: 97, 101, 132, 133. Biblioteca Nazionale Marciana, Venice: 7. Bibliothéque de l'Arsenal, Paris: 8. Ministero per i Beni Culturali e Demoetnoantropologici, Rome: Catasto Gregoriano Urbano (ASR): 160, 161, 162, 165, 166; Archivio Cybo: 247, 248, 249, 250. Musée Royaux de Beaux Arts de Belgique, Brussels/Koninklijke Musea voor Schone Kunsten van België, Brussels (photo Cussac): 38, 42. Museo Biblioteca Archivio di Bassano del Grappa: 167. Francesco Radino: 239, 255–61. Soprintendenza Speciale per il Patrimonio Storico, Artistico ed Etnoantropologico e per il Polo Museale della Città di Roma/Museo Nazionale di Castel Sant'Angelo: 16, 42. Soprintendenza Speciale per il Polo Museale Fiorentino: 18, 26. Sovraintendenza ai Beni Culturali U.O. Musei d'Arte Medioevale e Moderna/Museo di Roma: 4 (MR 19848), 23 (MR 625), 25 (MR 1930), 28 (MR 1671-6), 50 (MR 625), 56 (MR 38022), 86 (MR 23293), 87 (MR 22271), 88 (MR 22670), 96 (GS 1126), 139 (MR 20292), 145 Pannini, 157 (GS 11530), 158 (GS 11530), 159 (MR 22985), 172 (MR 37005), 176 (MR 37455).

The maps at the beginning of each chapter were created by Daniela Blandino.

CONTENTS

Introduction

In the present-day expanse of greenery that covers some fifty-five acres (22 hectares)—half of the entire Vatican State—buildings alternate with gardens, fountains with groves, and monuments with panoramas: all evidence of a history that spans many centuries, a succession of patrons with differing personalities, and an evolving taste with regard to the art of gardens. The *viridarium* (garden), documented since the thirteenth century within the boundary walls built at the behest of Pope Leo IV, has been shown to be the oldest surviving garden in Rome. This extraordinary continuity over the centuries coincides with a complex stratification of building phases, the reconstruction of which has been possible thanks to a wide-ranging research endeavor that has revealed discoveries of great interest based on an abundance of previously unpublished documents.

The Vatican Gardens are world renowned, yet there are no specialized studies that address and investigate their history and evolution in a comprehensive way, starting from their thirteenth-century origins and concluding with the radical transformation that followed the Lateran Accords stipulated between the Kingdom of Italy and the Church in 1929. To be sure, many in-depth studies have been devoted to the Vatican's most important architectural nuclei, in particular the Palazzetto del Belvedere, the Cortile delle Statue, the Loggias, and the Casina of Pius IV. These, however, have been examined individually, not as elements within an extraordinary complex—and therefore not in relation to the garden spaces that surround them.

To fully comprehend the complexity of the Vatican Gardens, one must first consider the unique circumstance of the succession of popes from diverse regions and families, and therefore the discontinuity of patronage that occurred over such a long period of time. That the Vatican Gardens have belonged to the Church for centuries, without interruption, might seem to suggest a continuity analogous to that of certain aristocratic villas that have been in the same family for hundreds of years. One example in the environs of Rome is the Villa Borghese, where the same family has resided for four centuries, and where every modification undertaken by the descendants of Cardinal Scipione, the original patron, has aimed to exalt the continuity of the work of the forebears, in a process of purist emulation that has resulted in the harmonious, organic evolution of the gardens in spite of changing tastes.

Completely different, however, is the case of the Vatican Gardens, whose evolution stems from the patronage of numerous popes—often succeeding one another in the space of just a few years and each wishing to leave his individual mark in some way. Even if some projects in the gardens were characterized by a desire to maintain continuity with the work of a predecessor, the popes' differing political stances and family origins (many of the popes who succeeded each other were from rival houses) led them, in the majority of cases, to commission original works that were not always in harmony with the sites they had inherited. There were, in fact, instances of abrupt changes to projects that were already under way or just completed, and also of the utter destruction of valuable decorative elements. Among the most striking examples of discontinuity is the treatment of the Casina of Pius IV, an unsurpassed model of harmoniously coexisting Christian and pagan symbology. It was "moralized" for the first time, in accordance with the new Counter-Reformation climate, immediately after the completion of the work commissioned by Pope Pius V, and again in the early years of the nineteenth century by Leo XII, this time in the wake of radical changes in Church politics. Other substantial transformations were due, however, to the evolution of taste; for example, the late eighteenth-century exchange, at the behest of Pius VI, of the theatrical, Vignolian, rustic backdrop of the Fontana della Galera for a flat, banal wall with a fake ashlar finish, or the destruction of the splendid pergola in the Secret Garden of Paul III to make way first for ordered, symmetrical beds, then later for an irregular arrangement in keeping with English-style fashion.

An emblematic example of the periodic discontinuity that has characterized the Vatican Gardens is the Giardino dei Semplici, the Vatican botanical garden that was planted near the Casina of Pius IV in 1561 and destroyed in 1659. Initially, after its creation by the eminent naturalist Michele Mercati on behalf of Pius V, the Giardino dei Semplici enjoyed much care and attention, uniting beauty and scientific purpose through the incorporation of rare and exotic plants from the Americas. During the first decades of the seventeenth century, in a process traced for the first time in this volume, the fame and splendor of the Giardino increased under the direction of Johannes Faber, a distinguished member of the Academy of the Lynxes whose position was reconfirmed by five different popes, and who initiated international exchanges of valuable plants with the most important collectors of the day. Despite the illustriousness of this history, however, Alexander VII decreed its end in 1659 by transferring the Orto Botanico to the Janiculum Hill and depriving the Vatican Gardens of an attraction that had drawn erudite visitors from all over Europe.

Examples of continuity, on the other hand, include the

works of Donato Bramante, who, commissioned by Julius II, began the construction of the loggias that were consolidated and resumed under Paul III, and of the Cortile della Pigna, whose monumental Nicchione was later completed by Pirro Ligorio at the behest of Pius IV. Undoubtedly, it was much simpler to modify plantings, flowerbeds, or decorative elements than built works, which could generally be enlarged or embellished, and stamped with writings or inscriptions celebrating the new patron, but not destroyed. For the same reason, the monumental architectural fountains commissioned by Paul V remain on their original sites, while the simpler fountains have been taken away or moved, repeatedly, to accommodate the changing function of the courtyards or gardens.

The most striking transformation, however, dates to the last century and is directly linked to a radical change in the political scenario: after the Lateran Accords and the recognition of the Vatican City as a sovereign state, the entire area within the walls was involved in a massive renewal project that substantially, and irreversibly, modified its layout, with numerous new buildings distributed throughout the area. The result was the elimination of a fundamental characteristic of the Vatican Gardens throughout their long history: the coexistence of the pleasure gardens—originally situated near the Apostolic Palaces and then expanded to cover the entire area between the palaces and the Palazzetto del Belvedere—with the productive agricultural zones. Until recent times, in fact, the Leonine Wall served to delineate the two distinct sectors: on one side were valuable and spectacular flowers from faraway places, groves of citrus trees of every imaginable variety, pergolas, espaliers of roses and myrtle, and elaborate *parterres*, as well as fountains, statues, and ancient and modern embellishments; on the other were vineyards, cane fields, orchards, and vegetable plots, surrounded by rustic huts used as hay-barns, tool sheds, and dwellings for farmers. The cultivated terraces of the area behind the Basilica, contrasting markedly with the carefully tended flowerbeds of the gardens, are still visible in many fine photographs from the early twentieth century, confirming the divided functions of the two areas that archival documents record as having begun in the thirteenth century. Today nothing remains of the productive tradition, with the exception of the tiny vegetable garden near the Clarissan convent, which the nuns lovingly tend for the pope.

The most widespread images of the Vatican Gardens today are of twentieth and twenty-first-century arrangements, often spectacular revivals of much earlier patterns, whereas identification of the historical vestiges requires close examination and an understanding of the events that have transformed the Gardens over the centuries. The aim of this book is to reconstruct the historical process that has determined the Vatican Gardens' present-day appearance, to connect the various elements that comprise them, and to evoke those elements that are no longer visible but that have affected their evolution and, in many cases, left a mark on the history of the art of gardens. It is my hope that the reader, by retracing these centuries of history in such a complex context, will grasp the appeal of this site in which the life of Rome has been reflected, as has the patronage of those eminent personalities who have left such strong reminders of their own lives.

ALBERTA CAMPITELLI

Acknowledgments

I am indebted to many people who helped me in various ways both during the research that formed the basis for this book and during its writing. I thank, above all, my husband Gianni, an invaluable supervisor and critic; Alessandro Cremona, who contributed to the archival research; my friend Sofia Varoli Piazza, ever-generous with suggestions and materials; Elisabetta Mori, always ready to discuss my doubts; Chiara Stefanori, for her extremely detailed graphic reconstructions; and Anna Maria de Strobel, for her helpfulness in bringing documents of great interest to my attention. I also thank Antonio Pinelli for having once again shown me his friendship and esteem, and Christoph Frommel, Louis Godart, Francesco Colalucci, Giuseppina Lauro, Maria Angela San Mauro, Aloisio Antinori, Sandro Santolini, Lucia Tongiorgi Tomasi, Nicole Dacos, Ester Piras, Maria Lupoli, Barbara Steindl, Giuliana Ericani, David Freedberg, Cristina Pantanella, Simonetta Tozzi, Simonetta Sergiacomi, Mario Gori Sassoli, Camilla Fiore, and Lucia Calzana for giving me valuable materials, information, and advice.

I was able to conduct this research within a tight time-frame thanks to the generous help of the directors and staff of the Archivio Segreto Vaticano, the Archivio di Stato di Roma, the Biblioteca Hertziana, the Biblioteca Marco Besso, the Biblioteca and Archivio dell'Accademia dei Lincei, the Biblioteca dell'Archivio Storico Capitolino, the Biblioteca Casanatense, the Library of the British School in Rome, and the Library of the Swedish Cultural Institute.

The support and collaboration of Rosanna Di Pinto and Filippo Petrignani were essential. I am also grateful to Sante Bagnoli and Roberto Cassanelli for giving me the opportunity to take on such a fascinating and, in many of its facets, unexplored topic, and to return to the pleasures of research and discovery. Finally, my thanks to Francesca Belloni for her patience and professionalism throughout the editorial preparation of this book.

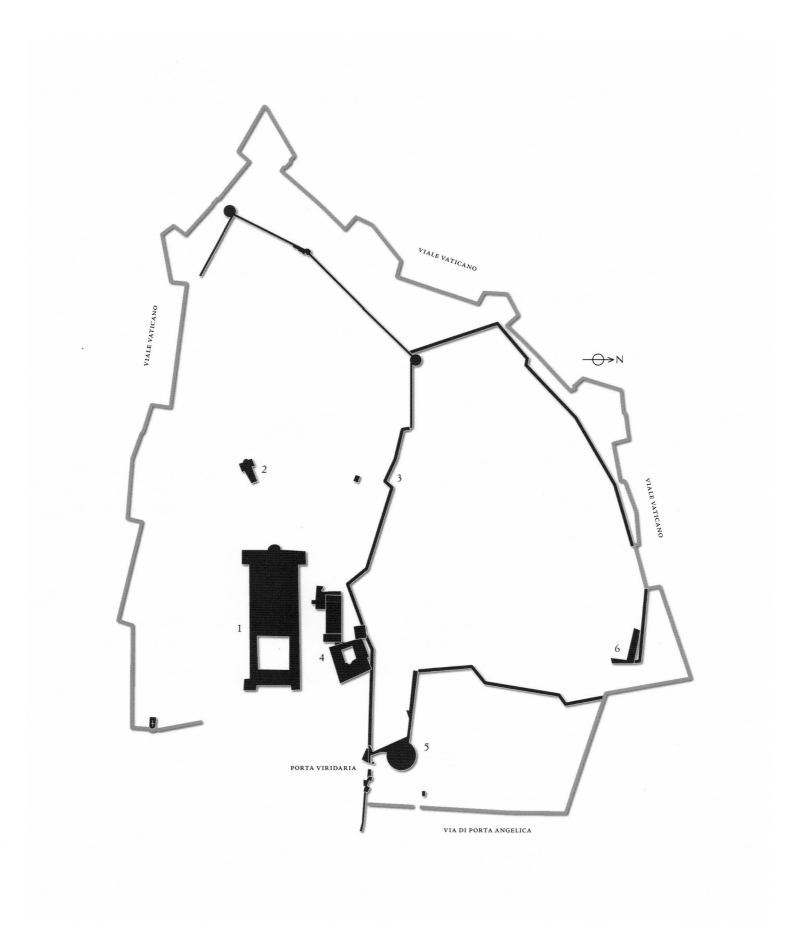

1. Constantine Basilica   4. Vatican Palaces
2. Church of Santo Stefano   5. Tower of Nicholas v
3. Leonine Wall   6. Palazzetto del Belvedere

VIALE VATICANO

VIALE VATICANO

VIALE VATICANO

N

PORTA VIRIDARIA

VIA DI PORTA ANGELICA

Modifications undertaken during the period discussed in this chapter are indicated in the map and captions above. For a complete map of the Vatican City and its major features in their present-day form, see page 2. Numbers in the map and captions refer to buildings and gardens, while letters refer to fountains.

ORIGINS AND FIRST DEVELOPMENTS FROM NICHOLAS III (1277–80) TO NICHOLAS V (1447–55)

The history of the Vatican Gardens is closely linked to the events surrounding the development of St. Peter's Basilica and the adjacent papal residences, as well as to the founding of what was originally called the Leonine City and, subsequently, Vatican City. Pope Leo IV (847–55) ordered the construction of the first boundary wall to protect the Basilica—hence the area's original name—and some sections of that wall are still visible in the gardens today. Innocent III (1198–1216) erected several buildings in the area north of the Basilica; of these, a small tower near the gardener's house remains (plate 1).[1] There is no evidence, however, of any particular contemporary arrangement of the green area within the Leonine Wall (plate 2). Innocent IV (1243–54) continued the expansion of the Vatican complex, and according to his biographer, the Franciscan Nicola da Calvi, in 1253, "at Saint Peter's, he had a palace, vaulted chambers, and a tower built, all of them very beautiful, and he had vineyards purchased there."[2] For the first time, in addition to information about the completed buildings, we have confirmation of the acquisition of land and the existence of agricultural practices within the Leonine Wall. Certainly, though, these were not yet garden arrangements, as the use of the word "vineyards" makes clear.

It is generally agreed that the origins of the Vatican Gardens can be traced to the work of Cardinal Giovanni Gaetano Orsini, a man of great culture and an expert in medicinal plants[3] who initially worked alongside Pope John XXI (1276–77) and was subsequently elected to the papal throne with the name Nicholas III (1277–80). Despite his brief papacy, this illustrious member of the Orsini family is credited with a major expansion of the Vatican territory, which grew to occupy an area almost the same size as it is today, extending well beyond the original Leonine Wall. To this end he purchased much land and many vineyards, primarily on the hill north of St. Peter's, the *Mons Saccorum*.[4] The result, in addition to the palaces and new structures, was a vast open area surrounded by walls that reached as far as the high ground where the Palazzo with the Cortile del Belvedere would later be built and encompassed meadows, gardens, vineyards, and woods. It is also well known that Nicholas III was the first pope to establish

1. (*below*) A medieval tower incorporated into the Casa del Giardiniere.

2. (*opposite*) The remains of the Leonine Wall and the radio tower.

his residence at the Vatican, abandoning the Lateran Palaces and paving the way for the realization of what would come to be known as the "palace in the form of a city."[5] After the loss of Jerusalem in 1244, Rome, in accordance with the pontiff's intentions, had to assume the role of sole capital of Christianity as well as that of "heavenly Jerusalem," seat of the Vicar of Christ, with the Vatican as its symbol. In this context a garden was essential, both to evoke Paradise and to represent on earth the Virgin Mary and her virtues through the indispensable presence of water, element of life and salvation.[6]

One document about the expansion of Vatican territory through land acquisition is of particular interest. Dated June 27, 1279, its reference to a small road, "pergens a porta viridaria" (extending from the garden gate), allows us to establish the existence, at that early date, of the Porta Viridaria, and thus to deduce that there was a *viridarium* (garden) nearby.[7] The Porta Viridaria, which disappeared during the period in which Bernini's colonnade was being built, is clearly documented in a number of plans, including Alessandro Strozzi's from 1447 (plate 3) and Leonardo Bufalini's from 1551. It was located near the great round keep (plate 4) built by Nicholas V,[8] still visible today along the walk from Porta Sant'Anna toward the Cortile del Belvedere. Mention of the Porta as early as the second half of the thirteenth century shows that there was certainly a *viridarium* in the Vatican area, and even if the term is somewhat generic, it confirms the existence of an arrangement of greenery with decorative as well as utilitarian characteristics.

The construction of the new boundary wall built at the behest of Nicholas III to enclose the palaces and gardens is clearly recorded in a lapidary inscription (plate 5), now in the Capitoline Museums, that reads: "In the second year of his papacy, he had the circuit of walls of this garden built…"[9] This first "palazzo-villa" nucleus was considered a kind of *domus aurea* (golden house), an association suggested, in part, by the proximity of the bygone Neronian circus and the naumachia.[10] It is not by chance that the first known depiction of the area—in the 1323 plan of Rome by Brother Paolino of Venice—evokes a circus: an elongated ellipsis containing buildings in open order along an imaginary axis and numerous animals scampering about freely, pursued by armed horsemen, in accordance with an iconography found in the hunting scenes on ancient sarcophagi (plate 6). The area depicted is located on the hill north of the basilica, which would later be occupied by the Belvedere, at the limits of the Roman countryside. A valuable description by Martino Polono (?–1278), made bishop by Nicholas III, further elaborates on the scope of the work carried out, in particular with regard to the *viridarium*. It

3. (*below*) Alessandro Strozzi, *Plan of Rome*, 1447, pen and ink. In the upper right corner is the Porta Viridaria.

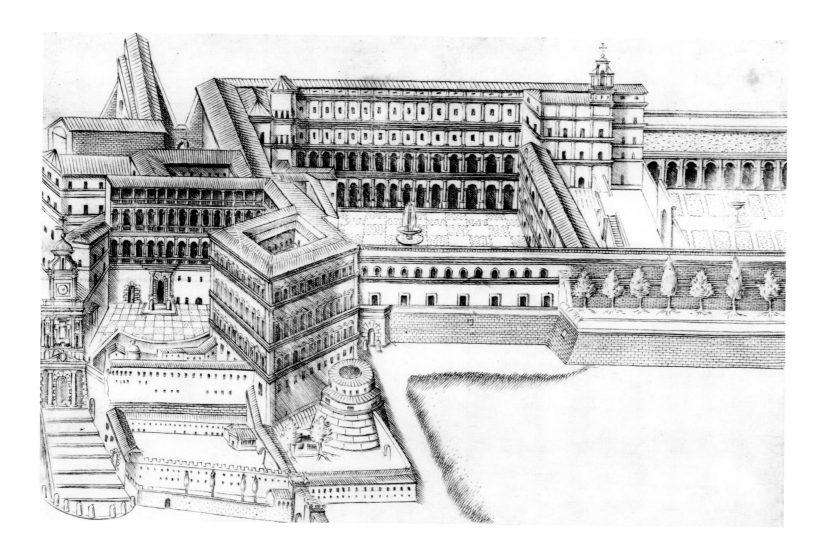

4. G. Lauro, *Vatican Palace*, early seventeenth century.
The keep built at the behest of Pope Nicholas v is visible
near the entrance to the Cortile del Belvedere.

relates, in fact, that "here [the pope] greatly expanded the palace of Saint Peter. And erecting many buildings, he enclosed a small lawn next to it, constructed a fountain that flowed from there, and fortified it with walls and towers, enclosing a large garden decorated with diverse trees."[11] This was, evidently, a *hortus conclusus*, a garden surrounded by walls according to medieval custom, and generally including an orchard and cultivated *semplici*, or herbs. The word *semplici* referred to medicinal herbs, but the denomination "Orto dei Semplici" also implied, in a broader sense, a kind of botanical garden. The *hortus conclusus*, according to the symbology of the period, was identified with the Virgin Mary—as is explicit in the celebrated verses of the Song of Solomon: "A garden inclosed [*sic*] is my sister, my spouse; a spring shut up, a fountain sealed"—but also with Paradise, a term defined in its Persian origin as an "enclosed site."[12] Albertus Magnus, in the chapter "De laudibus Beatae Mariae Virginis" of his *Opera Omnia*, also defines the *hortus conclusus* as the identification of the Virgin herself, and the plants and flowers as symbols of her virtues and God as gardener (plate 7).[13] This was, then, a site of enjoyment for the papal residence, but also a site rich with symbolic references to that "heavenly Jerusalem" referred to earlier.

The garden of Nicholas III contained a water supply; its meadow spaces alternated with areas containing various species of both decorative and productive trees, most likely citrus fruit trees; and it was most certainly of considerable size. Detailed information confirming the creation of this garden emerges from the accounts of the Camera Apostolica from the years between 1277 and 1279. Roughly thirty purchase and sale documents[14] attest to the acquisition of land situated beyond the Leonine Wall. Thus the Vatican's property was further extended to create space for the expansion of the papal residence and for the area that is variously referred to in the documents as *pomerium*, *viridarium*, and also *jardinum*,[15] lending additional credence to the idea of the coexistence of utilitarian and decorative functions. The acquired plots of land were mostly of modest size, ranging from 1 to 5 *pezze*,[16] were generally planted

5. (*below*) Inscription on marble commemorating the construction of the *pomerium* built under Pope Nicholas III in 1279. Capitoline Museums, Rome.

6. (*opposite*) Fra Paolino da Venezia, *Plan of Rome* with the "Vatican boat" populated with animals, 1323. Biblioteca Apostolica Vaticana (BAV).

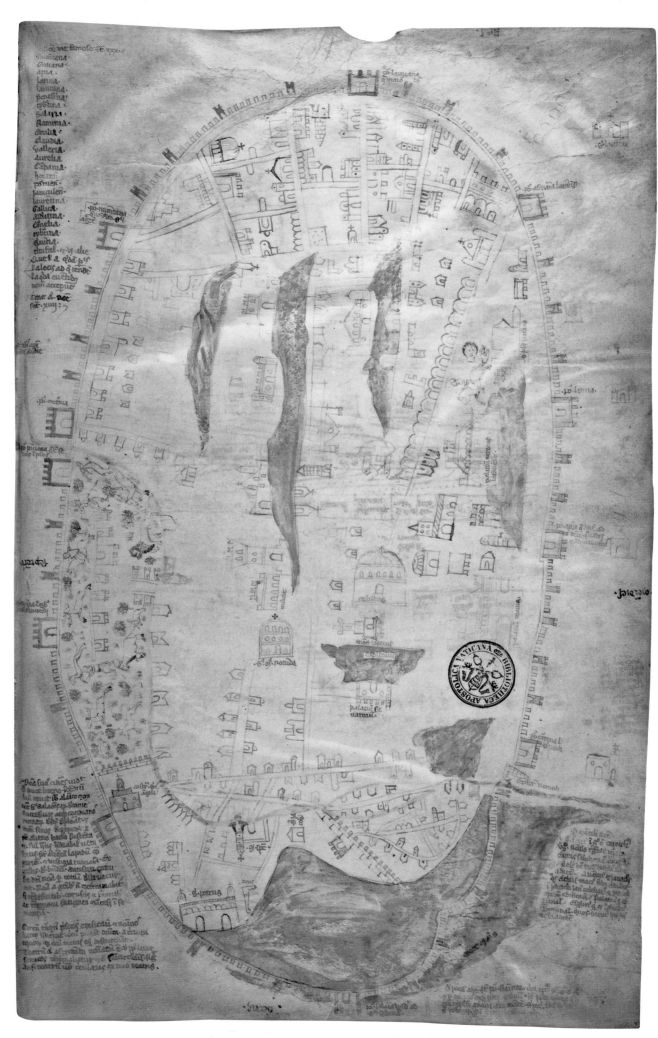

with vineyards, and often contained tanks and tuns, in keeping with the custom of making wine *in loco*. The expense books document the various phases of work for the cultivation of the vines, from the hoeing of the land to the pruning and harvesting of grapes, including the labor of *pueri*, or young boys, who removed worms from the new shoots.[17] The same records reveal that the rows of vines were shaded by trees, but the varieties are not specified. We can presume they were fruit trees, since "fruit-bearing and non-fruit-bearing trees" are cited.[18]

Other documents from the following years attest to the care the popes took with their "garden," used here to refer in a generic way to all of the various components of the unbuilt area within the walls. Between 1285 and 1286 the person in charge of the "expense facte…in iardino" (expenditures for the garden) was the *magister* Alberto da Parma, canon of St. Peter's Basilica, who had an administrative role. He was responsible for the production of wine (made for use by the curia, and certainly made at a loss); for the cultivation of such legumes as peas, broad beans, and chickpeas; and for the care of the fruit trees, including fig, apple, peach, pear, and walnut trees.[19] In the area within Nicholas III's walls there was surely a lawn, as the salaries of men hired to cut it appear in the accounts.[20]

The presence of Simone of Genoa,[21] a doctor and connoisseur of the therapeutic properties of plants, as well as chief papal physician at the time of Nicholas IV (1288–92), has been taken as confirmation of the cultivation of herbs in the Vatican, which many scholars have also interpreted as the beginning of a true botanical garden.[22] If this hypothesis is correct, we can assert that the first botanical garden on the Italian peninsula was created in the Vatican area, almost two centuries earlier than those in Padua and Pisa.[23]

The years of exile to Avignon (1309–77) inevitably led to a decline in interest in the Vatican residence. No important new projects were undertaken, but the complex of palaces and the adjacent gardens continued to receive care and attention. In fact, there are numerous documents from those years that attest not only to building maintenance but also to care of the vegetation in the gardens. The latter are cited in a letter from the bishop Angelo Tignosi of Viterbo, addressed to Pope John XXII (1316–34) on July 23, 1325, and again in a letter from Philippe de Chamberlhac of July 17, 1332, in which diligence "concerning the workshop of the basilica itself and concerning the guard of the palace and the papal gardens" is assured.[24] Interest in the gardens is also evident from some payments that refer to maintenance

and decoration. In 1353, under Innocent VI (1352–62), while a tower at the palace was being built and water was being brought to the kitchens, care of the *viridarium* is also mentioned.[25] In 1354 maintenance work was again carried out in the *viridarium* and mention is made of terraced *deambulationes* (walkways); afterward, vaguely identified "marbles" are transported, probably for decorative purposes, perhaps preceding those *antiquaria* that characterized courtyards and gardens for the entire fifteenth century.[26] Other unspecified tasks are mentioned in the years 1363–69, when attention to the *viridarium* is repeatedly documented in the expenses for maintenance of the residential complex, which intensify as the pope's return to Rome draws near.[27] Urban V's (1362–70) interest in the gardens, even while in exile, is documented in a long letter written from Avignon on November 13, 1365, and addressed to the bishop of Orvieto, in which he expressed his concerns as follows: "A reliable report has been made according to which our garden, near the Palace of St. Peter, and once abundant with a variety of fruit trees, is now in such a state of abandon as no longer to have the appearance of a garden, but rather that of an agricultural terrain full of twigs and thorns. As we wish that this garden again be properly cultivated, we enjoin your fraternity, once the twigs and thorns are uprooted and the boundary walls repaired where necessary, to cultivate this garden and fill it with good vines and fruit and decorative plants of various species."[28]

Again at the request of Urban V, in 1368 a "notebook" is put into use expressly to record the revenue and expenses for the *viridarium* and the vineyard. It includes a list of all those who worked there (at least ten men per day) and a description, albeit a brief one, of all the daily tasks that were carried out according to the seasons. The workers labored to plow the garden, dig it up, make a fish pond, hoe the vineyard, lay out the roads, irrigate, water the plants, "cut the grass and the plants," "plant cabbages and melons," and "water the trees."[29] Among the laborers in the garden were masons, carpenters, and marble workers, since the vineyard was surrounded by a stone wall covered in peperino and contained wood structures and stone decorations. One can thus imagine an area centered on the productive functions typical of a domestic garden, but in which embellishment and decoration also found space. In addition, to enhance the beauty of the site, plants were imported from

7. Gerard Horenbout, *The Immaculate Conception*, 1510–20, miniature, *Grimani Compendium*. Biblioteca Marciana, Venice. The *hortus conclusus* appears as a symbol of the Virgin Mary.

other countries. A document from 1368 refers to a shipment by sea—undertaken by three men from Portovenere—of trees whose variety is, unfortunately, not specified; they were to be planted in the *viridarium* of the Apostolic Palace.[30] However, we can assume that these were valuable plants, worthy of importation from afar because they were not available in the Latian area.

As evidence that Brother Paolino of Venice's depiction of animals in the park corresponded to fact, we have a 1367 document citing the gift to the pope of a leopard, which was brought to the Vatican residence.[31] For the entire duration of Urban v's papacy, there are repeated references in the documents to the presence of the garden and the care devoted to it—for example, to a "viridarium parvum" (small pleasure garden), then an "ortus parvus" (small garden) and an "ortus magnus" (large garden); the "vinea nostri pape" (vineyard of our Pope); a "pratum" (lawn), then "vine et piscarie" (vineyards and fish ponds); and to a certain Brother Guillermo, defined as a gardener, who is paid for having planted cabbages.[32] An anonymous chronicler of the time wrote that the pope, "near his Palace, had a large vineyard dug up and put in order, which, if properly cultivated and treated, could produce 300 casks of wine; in this he had planted, *ex novo*, many vines and fruit trees, which he had carried away from various and faraway lands and regions."[33] With his re-entry into Rome in sight (though it ultimately failed, in 1370), from his temporary residence in Montefiascone the pope authorized a payment of some 6,621 *fiorini* to Giovanni Cenci, clerk of the *Urbe*, who from 1368 to 1369 was charged with organizing the "vineyard and the fish pond" in the garden near the Palace of St. Peter.[34]

These are all further confirmations of the dual nature of the site, destined to produce food for the table of those who lived in the area, but also to embellish the adjoining residence. It should also be noted that some of the productive areas, such as the orchards, served both purposes; those trees that produced first splendid blossoms and then fruit were highly valued and often exhibited as collection exemplars.[35]

Pope Urban v's successors also continued to care for the garden. In 1376 a mason was paid to build the enclosure for a small *viridarium* that we can assume had the typical look of a medieval *hortus conclusus*, with the precious plants protected by walls from the bitter cold and from the animals that, apparently, were in the park.[36] Yet the *hortus conclusus* adjacent to the palace was probably not the only existing garden arrangement, given that there are often citations in the plural form, and it seems that as early as the reign of

Nicholas iii there were at least two gardens: a smallish one nearer the palace, and another, certainly much larger, in what would become the Cortile del Belvedere. The incidences of renovation and reorganization in the gardens, as we can see, become increasingly frequent as the papal re-entry from Avignon draws near. Of particular interest in determining how the gardens were laid out at the time, and further confirming that "delight" was one of their purposes, is a document from 1368 that testifies for the first time to the presence of citrus trees—planted and tended not only as a source of fruit but also for the beauty that their year-round, intensely green foliage and golden fruit lent to the gardens.[37] The citrus trees—lemon and sour orange—were watered and protected from the winter cold with "bark" and with true, removable "greenhouses." To build the latter, poles of chestnut wood and rush were purchased, and on these structures protective *stores*, or straw coverings in straw, were placed. These were usually removable, so they could be put on at night and taken away on mild days to allow the trees to soak up the light and rays from the sun.[38] The presence of these citrus trees also had symbolic value, not so much as an evocation of the mythic Garden of the Hesperides, the classical evocation destined to be embraced in the future, but rather because of their association with the Holy Land, and thus once again with the connotation of the Vatican citadel as Jerusalem.[39]

In subsequent chronicles we find few and fragmentary references to the Gardens. It is noted that Boniface ix (1389–04) pruned the vines himself,[40] while other sources tell us that Pius ii (1458–64), a nature lover, had a stone and wood pavilion built in the gardens, which he refers to in his *Commentari* as a splendid setting for official ceremonies.[41]

A genuine renewal of interest in the Vatican residence, and particularly in the gardens, arrived with the ascent of Nicholas v (1447–1455), son of a Pisan doctor, from whom he likely inherited a love of the natural sciences and of plants. Tommaso Parentucelli was considered the first "humanist" pope, initiating so many projects of urban embellishment that he became known as the "great builder" (also on the basis of his ties to Leon Battista Alberti, considered by many to be his inspiration)—even if recent analyses have cast doubt on the notion of a "marble Rome" existing at that time.[42] We know of the pope's undertakings from the biography written by Giannozzo Manetti (1397–1467), a Florentine gentleman who left the Medici court in

8. Giovanni Boccaccio, *The Decameron*, ms. 5070, f. 168r. Bibliothèque de l'Arsenal, Paris.

arespuissant il fait soy creindre des
plus riches. et ceste chose non mie du
tout mais en ptie appart en ma nou
uelle ensuiuant en la quele il me pla
ist retourner en nre cite florece de la q
le nous esloingnasmes moult en ces
six nouelles precedens. Tandiz que

nous parlasmes de diuerses choses en
nous remuant par diuerses parties
du monde.

Cy apres sensuit au long la xxxvij.
nouuelle coptee par emilie sur la .iiij.
iournee dont filostrate est roy.

En nre cite florence nague
res fut vne iouuencelle al
sez belle et gente selon la
condicion de son estat et
elle nommee symonne fut fille dun
pouure pere. combien qelle peust co
stariute gaigner son pain au labour
de ses propres mains et que en filad
laine elle gouuernast sa vie et four
nist soy de vitaille. Toutenoies symo
ne ne fut pas de si pouure couraige q
elle nosast receuoir et hosteler amo
en la pensee. amour longuemant a

uoit moustre soy vouloir entrer en
la pensee de symonne par les signes
et paroles dun iouuencel qui pas
nestoit de plus grant valeur quelle.
et le quel aux filereces portoit laine
a filer pour vng sien maistre dra
pier. Si tost que la fille ot receu a
mour en soy par le plaisant regart
du meune lhome qui icelle amoit et
qui auoit nom pasquin. elle mist
le desira. et sauz lui chaloit pou de
aultre chose a chascun fil de laine ti
lee. et a chascun tour de son fuseau.

1453 and moved to Rome, where he was employed by the papal curia. Among the episodes he narrates, which together convey the impression of a cultured pope with many interests, are references to the gardens and a clear description of an extensive area of greenery in the Vatican next to the palace: a "grand and splendid garden, rich with every kind of herb and fruit and irrigated with perpetual waters, which the pope ordered brought there from the top of the mountain, at great expense and through even greater technical skill, via subterranean pipes, for irrigation and for pleasure. In this enchanting paradise stood three splendid buildings of excellent workmanship."[43] Manetti also writes of another garden located to the west of the palace, where the Belvedere was later built. Facing this garden was a loggia, now gone, used for papal liturgical celebrations, a sign of the transformation of the garden over time from a place of retreat to the favored setting for the ceremonies of the court.[44]

Manetti often uses terms such as "splendid labyrinth" or even "magnificent paradise" to emphasize the delightful nature of the sites and also the complex symbolic value that the pope's garden assumed. The association of the garden with paradise is fully in keeping with a widespread tradition that originated in the Song of Solomon and was taken up again in medieval culture. It can be seen, for example, in the introduction to The Decameron (plate 8), in which Giovanni Boccaccio has the ten youths say, word for word, "If Paradise were created on earth, one would not know what form to give it but a garden."[45] The definition of labyrinth is also linked to the concept of a garden-paradise, in which the path of initiation and quest includes difficulties that the quester must overcome in order to arrive at the final prize. Overall, according to Manetti, the Vatican citadel owed its splendor to an image that included, in a modern sense, the entire surrounding landscape, and to the harmony between the cultivated and built spaces: "[It] was surrounded…by the urban walls, of truly extraordinary dimensions and robustness, sheltered and embellished everywhere by grand and splendid vines."[46]

The new image of Rome, and the major projects initiated by Nicholas v in advance of the Jubilee of 1450, were clearly perceived by a Florentine from the Rucellai family, who admired, above all, the magnificence of the papal residence: "The pope's palace, a beautiful residence…with great and small gardens, a fish pond, water fountains, and a rabbit hutch."[47] The importance and the role of the garden in Nicholas v's political strategy have been well analyzed by Marcello Fagiolo: "On a symbolic level, the Vatican garden could have been equivalent to the garden of knowledge, whose gardener was the pope, Vicar of Christ; on a political level it was the scene of government and of order. Nicholas v governed the Church from the height of a castle with strong walls and towers that protected the gardens, which were irrigated and rich with herbs and fruit. Here he could carry out with dignity the complex rituals of governing."[48]

The appearance of the Vatican citadel around the midfifteenth century, after the substantial changes made under Nicholas v, is documented in a fresco by Benozzo Gozzoli, held in the church of Sant'Agostino in San Gimignano and datable to 1465 (plate 9). In this view, the imposing nucleus of buildings comprising the basilica and the nearby palaces is depicted in the lower section, while in the upper part, within the walled area peppered with defensive towers, is a vast empty space painted a generic green. In the same view a second zone of greenery is visible in the area facing the porticoed palace, near the Porta Viridaria, and it contains visual evidence of great interest. One can see, for instance, a pyramidal pergola, a kind of vegetal pavilion with a fixed structure (probably of wood) and climbing plants all around. The presence of this pergola brings us back to the instructions from one of the first treatises on gardens, I piaceri della campagna (Ruralia Commoda), by the Bolognese writer Pietro de' Crescenzi (1233–c. 1320), who suggests the inclusion of a pergola, in the form of a house or pavilion, as an obligatory status symbol in the gardens of kings and lords.[49] The pergola-pavilion in the painting is surrounded by divisions of flowerbeds, one with a tree in the center. This is a formal layout, recalling the kind of geometric flowerbeds with a central tree—usually a citrus fruit tree—that were also common throughout the following century and typical of pleasure gardens.

The other area of greenery, perched on the hillside that would later be occupied by the Belvedere, seems less encumbered and is free of formal elements. We can suppose that it may have been used as a garden, orchard, and vineyard. From an analysis of the trades practiced at the court of Nicholas v, we know, in fact, that vineyards and gardens coexisted in the Vatican area. There were vinedressers, generally of Tuscan origin, as well as gardeners among the salaried workers.[50]

Nicholas' successor, Paul II, the Venetian Pietro Barbo (1464–71), expressed an interest in the subject of gardens, but directed it mainly toward the creation of the viridarium

9. Benozzo Gozzoli, View of the Vatican and the Surrounding Area, 1465, fresco. Church of Sant'Agostino, San Gimignano.

10. The palace and garden of Pope Paul II in Piazza Venezia.

adjacent to the family palace in Piazza Venezia (plate 10); thus began the tradition of richly decorated residences for papal families, and in particular for the cardinal-nephew, that became widespread in the following centuries.[51] Nevertheless, a few scattered bits of information prompt the presumption that he made some changes to the Vatican Gardens as well. On May 28, 1469, for example, documents show a payment for the construction of a "tentorio plumbeo" (lead covering) in the "jardino secreto palatii S. Petri" (secret garden of the palace of St. Peter).[52] It is the first time that the term "secret garden" appears— as an equivalent, essentially, to *hortus conclusus*—to designate an enclosed site with limited access.[53] In the same year, payments are documented to stonemasons for capitals and pillarets made at the "fonte jardini secreti palatii Sancti Petri" (fountain of the secret garden of the palace of Saint Peter).[54] We do not have other, more precise references to the presence of this fountain, but we can assume that it was located in the garden next to the palaces, the one with the pergola in Benozzo Gozzoli's fresco, and the lead covering might also have shared the same location.

From the information and descriptions available, we can conclude that in the mid-fifteenth century, the Vatican area contained at least two gardens: a small one near the papal palace and a second, larger one in the area that would later be occupied by the Palazzetto and the Cortile del Belvedere.[55] Both gardens were situated inside the imposing boundary wall that protected the entire complex, but certainly the smaller one, next to the palace, had an additional protective wall. There is no doubt that these contained *semplici*, or medicinal plants, but also flowers and fruit trees, including citrus varieties traditionally planted for their decorative value. It is probable that the gardens also contained other trees such as cherry, peach, and plum, because, according to a tradition followed until the last century, many fruit-bearing plants were considered ornamental and were cultivated in the flowerbeds of gardens. The green area near the palace must have had a layout closer to that which, in the modern sense, would be considered similar to the model of the pleasure garden: it contained geometric flowerbeds placed at regular intervals around a central pergola that probably served as a shaded resting area and also featured a fountain. The second garden, on the other hand, was primarily a *pomario*, or orchard, composed for the most part of fruit trees. In addition, within the boundary wall, and probably quite loosely arranged, were alternating lawns and vineyards whose rows were accented with fruit and other trees, placed both to offer shade and to create effects of perspective alignment.[56] The popes' interest in the gardens is further evidenced by the presence of salaried laborers and workers with specific roles. From the beginning of the fifteenth century, vine-dressers and gardeners appear regularly on the payrolls of the curia, as do distillers, who prepared perfumes, spirits, and medicines made with flower petals or plants such as wormwood.[57]

Thus emerges a fascinating image of the Vatican Gardens, which were decidedly ahead of their time in comparison with similar spaces designated for pleasure in the city of Rome. In fact, in the history of Roman gardens, the earliest evidence of the first planned gardens dates to the second half of the fifteenth century,[58] and only in the following century are spaces with decorative greenery near important residences documented.[59] The Palazzetto del Belvedere, completed before the end of the fifteenth century, also introduced an architectural typology directly connected to a garden layout, well before the creation of those pleasure villas that would come to characterize the city in the following century.

1. Constantine Basilica with new unfinished apse

4. Vatican palaces with new additions

7. Loggias of Donato Bramante with exedra

8. Cortile delle Statue

9. Spiral staircase

a. Fontana del Belvedere

b. Nymphaeum of the Cortile della Biblioteca

c. Fontana del Belvedere in the Cortile della Pigna

d. Fontana di Cleopatra

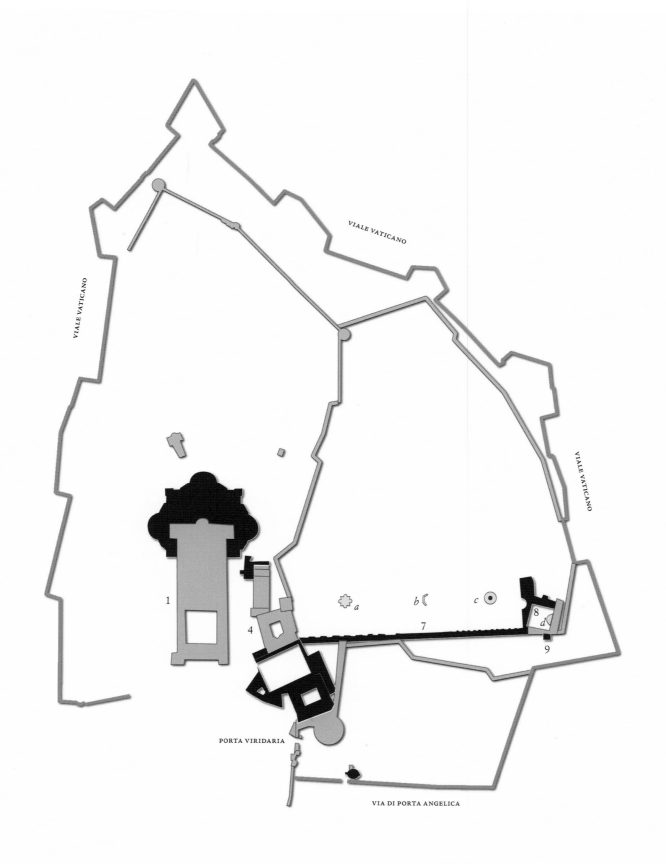

Modifications undertaken during the period discussed in this chapter are indicated in the map and captions above. For a complete map of the Vatican City and its major features in their present-day form, see page 2. Numbers in the map and captions refer to buildings and gardens, while letters refer to fountains.

CHAPTER TWO

THE BELVEDERE OF
INNOCENT VIII (1484–92)
AND THE COURTYARD-
GARDEN-THEATER
OF JULIUS II (1503–13) AND
DONATO BRAMANTE

Just after his election to the papal throne, Innocent VIII (1484–92) turned his attention to the Vatican residence, and by April 1485 he had acquired a vineyard to expand the garden and surrounding territory.[1] The following October he began construction of an extensive boundary wall to enclose and protect all the vineyards around the palace.[2] A payment to a stonemason of some five hundred gold *scudi* attests to the magnitude of this undertaking. It involved, as a passage from Vasari describes,[3] the consolidation of the existing *pomerium* (the area of consecrated, unbuilt terrain that ran along the walls of Rome) to make the structure he intended to build, the famous Belvedere, more dignified and secure. Innocent's name is linked, in fact, to the construction of the Palazzetto del Belvedere (so called for the splendid panoramas afforded by its position at a considerable distance from the Apostolic Palace), which marked the beginning of a project to reorganize the area that would conclude nearly a century later (plate 11).[4]

The Palazzetto (or Casino) del Belvedere, located on the summit of Monte Sant'Egidio, north of St. Peter's and the Apostolic Palace, has been defined by David Coffin as the first building in Rome with the characteristics of a Renaissance villa.[5] Obviously it was not the first building in a country estate to have the functions of a residence. There are earlier examples, such as the Casino of Cardinal Bessarione or the Villa Mellini at Monte Mario, and other more or less rustic summer houses designed for pleasure.

But the Palazzetto del Belvedere introduced a new model destined for imitation in subsequent decades, even if from an architectural point of view the structure itself was quite modest and clearly derived from houses in the Roman countryside that still featured such medieval details as crenellations (plates 12, 13). The architecture was characterized by a ground-floor loggia that opened onto the adjacent garden, creating a direct connection between interior and exterior. For this reason, more formal, ceremonial functions were assigned to the ground floor. It is this innovation that defines the *casino di villa* (garden house) model, which would become widespread in the decades to follow. Whereas in city palaces the more formal areas were located on the second floor—the so-called "piano nobile"—the *casino di villa* had the added value of its connection to the garden, through a loggia that was oftentimes frescoed in imitation of a pergola to further emphasize the continuity between indoor and outdoor space. The novelty of Innocent's building was clearly grasped by Pasquale Adinolfi, who described it as "small" in comparison to the Apostolic Palaces, "but most celebrated for the uses to which it was put," as it was destined to assume, over the course of the

11. (*below*) The Belvedere complex in the 1930s.

12. (*opposite*) The Palazzetto del Belvedere, detail.

13. The Belvedere complex, overall view with Donato
Bramante's loggias and the cupola of St. Peter's.

following centuries, increasingly ceremonial functions and a central role in the representation of papal power.[6]

According to the chronicles of Stefano Infessura, the pope "built the vineyard next to the residence, a palace called, for its view, Belvedere [literally, "beautiful view"], which cost 60,000 *ducati*."[7] Information about the building is extremely sparse, and its location is always mentioned in reference to the vineyard and adjacent garden—within the *pomerium* as restored for Nicholas III—atop Monte Sant'Egidio, from which there was a magnificent view of Monte Mario, Ponte Milvio and, on the horizon, Monte Soratte. Pilgrims who arrived in Rome, as well as corteges of visiting ambassadors and noblemen, passed directly beneath the Belvedere to enter into the Vatican, admiring its architecture and privileged, dominant position.

Little has survived of the original structure. Donato Bramante's subsequent construction of the Cortile delle Statue, which formed a connection to the oldest residence as part of what was called the Cortile del Belvedere, as well as the creation of the Museo Pio Clementino at the end of the eighteenth century, introduced many changes, making it difficult today, with the meager documentation available, to reconstruct the initial layout. According to the most recent studies, two construction phases took place under Innocent VIII (plate 14). In the first, a simple pavilion with a small apartment and a chapel was built. It was a

site for brief afternoon rests, and the cool air assured by its northern exposure and elevated position made it particularly pleasant. The ground floor was, essentially, an open loggia. The second phase consisted of the addition of a wing to the east, toward the city, and some new rooms, all of which transformed the pavilion into a true palazzetto. Even after the expansion, the connection to the outdoors and the garden was maintained; contemporary chronicles tell us that from the garden one could follow the mass celebrated in the small chapel.

The decorative program for the interior spaces was complex, with documented contributions by Pinturicchio and Andrea Mantegna. Although these rooms will not be examined here, it is worth noting that their decorative subject matter—landscapes, fields, seascapes, hunting scenes, and pastoral views—further accentuated the relationship of the interiors to the open space of the garden. Vasari's attribution of this building to Antonio del Pollaiolo has been questioned by recent studies suggesting the possible participation of Jacopo Cristoforo da Pietrasanta,[8] while at the same time confirming the "Florentine" layout of the project.

The two structures turned out to be asymmetrical, due to the different elevations of the ground on which they were built. Nonetheless, the architect managed to achieve—on the downhill side, which was more visible from the

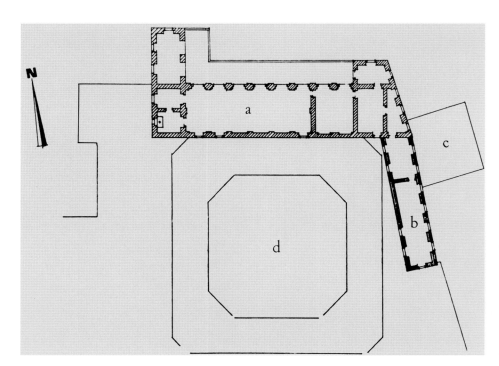

14. (*left*) Plan of the Belvedere with the various construction phases: a) oldest construction; b) added wing; c) tower designed by Donato Bramante with the "snail" staircase; d) the Cortile delle Statue, from D. Redig de Campos, *I Palazzi Vaticani*, 1967.

15. (*opposite*) Maerten van Heemskerk, *View of the Belvedere*, 1534–35, drawing.

city—a unified effect by constructing a high, sloping wall articulated with a series of arches. Subsequently, Donato Bramante designed on the eastern side of the Belvedere a monumental access staircase—the famous "snail," whose ramp was "an ascent so easy that the beasts of burden can climb it," according to Giorgio Vasari.[9] Once again, we see the introduction of a new model that would be imitated throughout the succeeding decades in many other garden houses, including the Villa Farnese in Caprarola, the Quirinal Palace, the Palazzo-Villa Barberini in Rome, and the Villa Aldobrandini in Frascati.[10]

According to some accounts, the palazzetto was surrounded by a garden with cypress trees; within the ample courtyard, citrus trees—most likely sour oranges—were cultivated around a fountain.[11] In both a drawing by van Heemskerk (plate 15), dated to around 1535, and a fresco from 1545 by Prospero Fontana (plate 16), the views of the palazzetto show numerous cypresses silhouetted against the walls, in confirmation of contemporary descriptions.

After the additions, the Palazzetto of Innocent VIII undoubtedly took on the aspect of a true residence, albeit a small one; yet it remained isolated on the top of the hill, separated from the Apostolic Palace by a vast area—probably cultivated with vineyards—that was not easily negotiable given the disparities of elevation. However, it allowed the pope a private space for *otium* (relaxation), without

taking him far from the *negotium* (business) that his role dictated.

The pope's fragile health had led him to seek cool air and rest not far from the Apostolic Palace. Documents of the time confirm that he rarely left the Vatican residence and that when he did, his movements were limited to brief visits to nearby Ostia or to the Villa della Magliana.[12] According to Francesco Serdonati (1540–1603), Innocent VIII also undertook the expansion and embellishment of the Apostolic Palaces, where he "added lovely and showy porticoes with delightful gardens," but this description has little documentary support.[13] There is no evidence that the pope, having completed the Belvedere building, undertook projects to connect it to the older, majestic palaces, or to rework the terrain to fill in or smooth over the more than 1,050 feet (320 meters)—with an 82-foot (25-meter) drop between a swampy valley and an irregular slope—that separated the two building nuclei. The layout of the area is clearly depicted in a view (plate 17) by Hartman Schedel—published in 1493 in Nuremberg in the *De Temporibus Mundi*—the overall design of which recalls the fresco by Benozzo Gozzoli, but features the addition of the Belvedere. In Schedel's work the turreted palazzetto, featuring an ample portico with arches and cross vaults on the ground floor, appears completely isolated on the summit of the hill. There is no connection to the Apostolic Palaces,

from which it is separated by a rather steep precipice, although the two areas are enclosed within the same boundary wall. The construction of a grandiose complex that would unify all of the various buildings within Nicholas v's walls, as part of an ambitious project to build a true papal citadel, was to begin some years later as a result of an encounter between two exceptional personalities: Pope Julius II (1503–13) and the architect Donato Bramante (1444–1514).

As soon as he was elected to the papacy, Giuliano della Rovere, nephew of Sixtus IV (1471–84), devoted his energy to returning Rome to a position of supremacy on both the political and artistic fronts after the weak and unscrupulous papacy of Alexander VI Borgia (1492–1503). After dealing decisively with Rome's disastrous economic and social situations, he set about using art and architecture, quite consciously, as instruments of propaganda and power. The heart of the *renovatio imperii* initiated by Julius II was the radical transformation of the Vatican to include a new, monumental Basilica; an expanded, regularized palace; and the interconnection of the pre-existing buildings—in particular the Palazzetto del Belvedere—to create a true court residence from which the new "emperor" could exercise spiritual and temporal power.

Julius II greatly cherished the Palazzetto del Belvedere; the chronicles of the time refer to his frequent use of the building, not only "for his pleasure" but also for events, such as the wedding—celebrated in the summer of 1504 with much pomp—of a niece to the brother of his great friend Agostino Chigi.[14] His interest in the gardens and the residence dated back, moreover, to his years as cardinal. In fact, during the same years in which Innocent VIII was building the Belvedere, the future Julius II, then Cardinal Giuliano della Rovere, built a summer house next to the church of the Santi Apostoli. It was a two-story structure, featuring a huge loggia with seven arches open onto the garden.[15] Unfortunately, the Casino della Rovere was radically modified and incorporated into the subsequent Palazzo Colonna; on the basis of available information we can only hypothesize about its resemblance to the Vatican Belvedere, with which it surely shared the layout of a building in close affinity with a garden.

Thus it is not surprising that when Julius II reached the papal throne, he showed great interest in the Belvedere and wanted to enhance it by including it in a major project. The heart of this plan was the reorganization of the area between the Belvedere and the palace, in order to fill the immense empty space while creating a structure that could

16. (*above*) Prospero Fontana, *The Cortile del Belvedere with scene of naumachia*, c. 1545, detached fresco. Sala dei Festoni, Castel Sant'Angelo, Rome.

17. (*opposite*) Hartman Schedel, *Perspective View of Rome*, from *De Temporibus Mundi*, 1493.

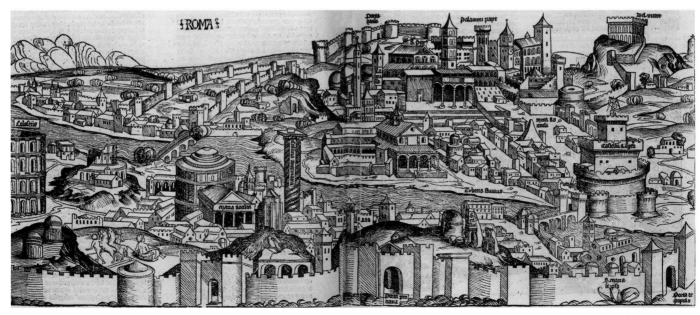

serve multiple functions. To this end, Bramante conceived a courtyard (plate 18) enclosed by two lateral wings with several levels that served as loggias; he employed, however, a completely new and original model. Laid out quickly (and completed many decades afterward), the great court-yard was in fact also a theater destined to host spectacular events, as later views attest. At the same time, it was a garden—the first "architectural" garden—with terraces, symmetrical flowerbeds, and fountains.[16] Finally, it was a museum in which the collection of antiquities belonging to the pope could find a worthy setting. As Alessandro Tagliolini has rightly stated, the construction of Bramante's Belvedere marked a new direction in the art of garden design: "The planned opening of the upper loggias allowed the garden to be projected outward and to merge with the landscape in an environmental continuity that incorpo-rated into the new architecture the vestiges of the spirit of ancient Rome."[17]

Vasari explains the genesis of the project in his narration of Bramante's life: "The fancy had taken that Pontiff to so transform the space that lay between the Belvedere and the Papal Palace, as to give it the aspect of a square theatre, embracing a little valley that ran between the old Papal Pal-ace and the new buildings that Innocent VIII had erected as a habitation for the Popes; and he intended, by means of two corridors, one on either side of this little valley, to make it possible to go from the Belvedere to the Palace under log-gias, and also to go from the Palace to the Belvedere in the same way, and likewise, by means of various flights of steps, to ascend to the level of the Belvedere."[18]

Well into middle age when he came to Rome from Milan in 1499, Donato Bramante[19] was struck by the magnificence of the ancient ruins that dominated the city's panorama, and by the discoveries that added to the understanding of their original grandeur; one need only think of the *Domus Aurea*, for example. These discoveries contributed on the one hand to the development of collecting, and on the other to the large-scale propagation of architectural models based on those illustrious examples. Indeed, Bramante's Cortile del Belvedere clearly reveals the sources that inspired him. As a means of connecting the Belvedere with the Apostolic Palaces and the Basilica, Bramante conceived a vast court, articulated on three levels linked by ample stairways and surrounded by a wall—some 92 feet (28 meters) in height—

18. Giovanni Antonio Dosio, *The Cortile del Belvedere*, c. 1560, drawing. Uffizi Gallery, Cabinet of Drawings and Prints, Florence.

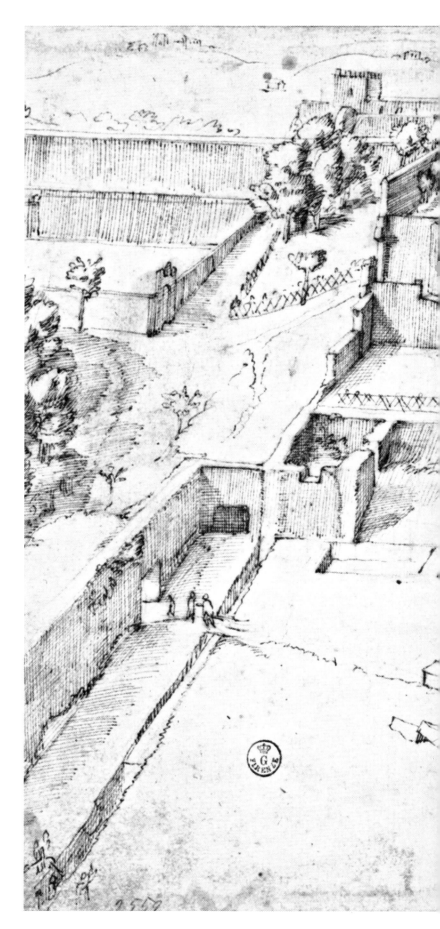

of exposed brick with decorative elements in peperino, along which ran loggias and arcades. This was an obvious evocation of the classical *deambulationes porticatae* (covered promenades) of the Imperial villas, cryptoporticuses (semi-subterranean covered passageways), and ancient circuses, while the terracing system had precise antecedents in the spectacular and scenographic layout of the Temple of Fortuna Primigenia in Palestrina, in the Villa of Domiziano in Albano, and in the *Horti Aciliorum* on Monte Pincio.[20] The evocation of the ancient world is also evident from the structure's dimensions: the Cortile del Belvedere was, in total, some 295¼ feet (90 meters) wide and 984¼ feet (300 meters) long. Not coincidentally, the Circus Maximus measured 328 by 984¼ feet (100 by 300 meters), and both Vitruvius and Alberti recommended a ratio of 1:3 for this kind of structure. The analogies between the Imperial palaces of the Palatine and the new Vatican residence have been widely noted, as confirmation both of the classical matrixes in Bramante's architecture and of the image of power that the pope-emperor wished to convey.[21] The brilliant solution adopted by Bramante[22] facilitated the connection of the two extremes of the papal residence, by filling the gap in elevation without interrupting the visual unity, and by allowing for various functions within the same monumental framework.

The structure has been considerably transformed over the centuries. Today, the three spaces are separate, each with its distinct, autonomous function, and it is difficult to imagine the original appearance. However, we are familiar with Bramante's project from the numerous contemporary depictions that have survived, an indication of the great impact that this innovative, complex project had at the time. The part of the structure closest to the palace and the Basilica, and still called the Cortile del Belvedere, was the largest (plates 19–21). Almost 459⅜ feet (140 meters) deep, it was conceived in part as the monumental entrance for those arriving from the Porta Giulia, but primarily as a theatrical space, with the connecting staircase on the upper level flanked by two towers, reminiscent of the proscenium of an ancient theater. The center of the space featured an antique fountain (plate 22) with a great granite basin taken from the baths of Titus.[23] On the sides of the central ramp were colossal stairs that could be used, during spectacles, as seating. Two fine etchings (plates 23, 24) by Antonio Lafrery (one a view from the extreme north, the other from the south) record the use of the court for a joust held on March 5, 1565, to celebrate the wedding of Annibale Altemps, brother of Cardinal Marco Sittico, and Ortensia

Borromeo, half-sister of Cardinal Borromeo, both of whom were related to Pope Pius IV (1559–65). In these views we see the tiers filled with crowds, while other spectators are seated in the semicircles at either end of the space. The same tournament is depicted in an anonymous (probably later) painting (plate 25), conserved in the Museo di Roma. Here the composition is the same as that of Lafrery's etchings, with a few variations and greater attention to such details as the multicolored drapes in the windows, the balconies, and the spectators' elaborate dress.[24] According to the frescoes visible in the apartments of Castel Sant'Angelo, painted around 1545 during the papacy of Paul III (1534–49) and attributed to Prospero Fontana, this part of the court could have been used, when opportunely filled with water, for spectacular naumachies, or mock sea battles.[25] Once again we have a revival of a Roman Imperial tradition, with an allusion, perhaps, to the lake at Nero's Villa.

The middle portion of the court was the smallest: only 98½ feet (30 meters) deep, with staircases connecting it to the lower and upper terraces. The upper backdrop featured a scenographic triangular staircase with double ramps, first divergent and then convergent, enclosing a small apsidal area carved out under the terrace, the walls of which were punctuated with a series of niches. This was an original construction, still visible today, albeit without many of its decorative elements.[26] Yet it was also a reprisal of a type common in ancient gardens: that of the grotto-nymphaeum, destined to be widely and successfully employed in aristocratic villas and gardens throughout the sixteenth century (plate 26).[27] The solution Bramante adopted to link the two levels alludes once again to the triangular, scenographic staircase of the Temple at Palestrina, in which there was an analogous apsidal space. The grotto-nymphaeum inserted between the staircases appears, in schematic form, in various depictions of the period, but can be seen in detail in a lovely etching by Domenico Parasacchi from 1647, when the library built for Sixtus V (1585–90), which separated the middle courtyard from the last, had already been completed. At the time it was richly decorated with tartars and fake rocks and adorned with dragons and eagles, emblems of the Borghese family. These were evidently added later, during the papacy of Paul V (1605–21). The jets of water that spurted from the mouths of the dragons inserted in the five niches flowed into a great,

19. (*opposite*) The Cortile del Belvedere today, with the Cortile della Biblioteca and Cortile della Pigna in the background.

20. (*opposite, top*) The Cortile del Belvedere at the beginning of
the twentieth century, view of the southern end of the garden.

21. (*opposite, bottom*) The Cortile del Belvedere at the beginning
of the twentieth century, view of the northern end of the garden.

22. (*above*) The Fontana del Belvedere, designed by Donato
Bramante, buried by order of Pius IV and reinstalled by Paul V.

23. (*below*) Antonio Lafrery, *Tournament in the Cortile del Belvedere*, 1565, etching, northern end. The pergola in the Secret Garden of Paul III is visible on the upper left.

24. (*right*) Antonio Lafrery, *Tournament in the Cortile del Belvedere*, 1565, etching, southern end. Visible on the upper right is the still incomplete cupola of St. Peter's.

Monstra della giostra fatta nel Teatro di Palazzo ridotto in questa forma dalla S.tà di N. S. Pio 4° come si vede nella stampa della pianta, con le sue mesure.

43

25. (*above*) Roman school, *Tournament in the Cortile del Belvedere*, first half of the seventeenth century, oil on canvas. Museo di Roma, Rome.

26. (*right*) Giovanni Antonio Dosio, *The Cortile del Belvedere*, 1560, detail with the nymphaeum. Uffizi Gallery, Cabinet of Drawings and Prints, Florence.

semicircular basin, open toward the garden. The terrace was, in fact, arranged like a garden, with two large, square flowerbeds, probably much like those on the upper level. The beds must have contained citrus trees, given that the above-mentioned etching by Parasacchi contains a reference to the "court of sour oranges," opposite the nyphaeum (plates 27, 28).

The last, and highest, terrace was around 328 feet (100 meters) deep and was a full-fledged garden, organized into large flowerbeds bordered by low boxwood hedges, and also containing citrus trees and a great central fountain fed by a subterranean hydraulic network that supplied water for the garden. This fountain, consisting of an austere gray granite basin, was removed during the papacy of Gregory XVI (1831–46) to make space for the base of the Colonna Antonina and reinstalled, with a new base decorated with the papal emblems, in the Secret Garden of Paul III, where it remains today.[28] The terrace, depicted in many views, was destined to become even more monumental when Pirro Ligorio created as its backdrop the *nicchione*, or great niche, later adorned with a spectacular bronze pinecone taken from the original Basilica of St. Peter, and with two splendid peacocks from the Basilica of St. John Lateran on the sides. Since that time, the terrace has been known as the Giardino, or Cortile, della Pigna (plates 29–30).

To hide the asymmetry of the edifice from Innocent's time, which loomed at the northern extreme of the vast space, and that of the last part of the courtyard, Bramante conceived as a backdrop for the terrace a great exedra (against which Ligorio would later set his monumental niche); in the middle space he created a courtyard to house the collection of antiquities belonging to Julius II. This space, called the Cortile delle Statue, was immediately considered one of the most ingenious and innovative works of the time, and was the first example of the garden-museum type that would proliferate in the decades to follow.[29] To house the antiquities collection of Julius II, begun when he was still a cardinal, Bramante designed a square court, opening on a garden, with a series of niches in which the most important statues in the collection were installed.[30] Other statues were placed at the four corners and at the center of each of the walls, while in the largely paved courtyard there were citrus and cypress trees, irrigated with water flowing through subterranean pipes into a fountain that further enlivened the site. The courtyard-museum was also accessible to the public from the outside, by means of the famous snail staircase that Bramante had set against

27. (*below left*) The nymphaeum in the Cortile della Biblioteca today.

28. (*below right*) The nymphaeum in the Cortile della Biblioteca, from D. Parasacchi, *Raccolta delle principali fontane dell'inclita città di Roma*, 1647.

29. (*opposite*) The Nicchione of Donato Bramante and Pirro
Ligorio with the bronze Pigna.

30. (*above*) The Cortile della Pigna seen from the Nicchione.

the eastern side of the Palazzetto del Belvedere. The possibility of visiting the collection independent of the building further underscores the architect's truly innovative plan. The high caliber of the statues exhibited in the courtyard has been amply demonstrated,[31] but equally important is the interpretation of the symbolic value of the site as "Venus' grove," which has been proposed in conjunction with the celebrated text by Francesco Colonna, *Hypnerotomachia Poliphili*, a comprehensive treatise on the analysis of the garden as an allegory of love, both religious and pagan.[32] An admiring description of the sculptures of Venus and the reclining Cleopatra (actually Ariadne), from whose breast water spouts, by Giovanni Francesco della Mirandola (nephew of the more celebrated Pico), as set in the "perfumed grove of lemons, paved in stone," allows us to identify an explicit parallel in a passage from Francesco Colonna's text in which he describes an analogous reclining nymph with spouting breasts. Starting from this analogy, Ernst Gombrich proposed an interpretation that attributes to Bramante—inspired by the equivocal religiosity of the *Hypnerotomachia*, which alluded to the *Sancta Venere*—the idea of creating an ideal grove symbolically centered on the figure of Venus as the synthesis of earthly and celestial love, and thus providing a further cause for reflection on the complex phenomenon of "Renaissance paganism."[33]

Just as the Cortile del Belvedere had introduced the type of the architectural garden, the Cortile delle Statue (plate 31) defined that of the garden-museum, or "garden in the antique style." This characteristic of the *hortus conclusus* was

perceived from its origins, emphasized in the contemporary descriptions,[34] and confirmed by the inscription on the entrance architrave, with its phrase taken from Virgil's *Aeneid*, Book VI: "Procul este profani" ("Away, you uninitiates!"), a clear allusion to the private nature of the site.[35]

Collections of antiquities already existed in fifteenth-century Rome,[36] but the innovative aspect of the Cortile delle Statue lay in its unification of the two functions of garden and open-air museum. For this reason, Bramante's creation would serve for at least a century as the model for many other gardens exhibiting valuable collections of antique statuary, the Giardino Cesi and the Giardino della Valle being among the earliest.[37] Another innovation that was destined to become a common motif in later gardens was the sleeping nymph inside a grotto-fountain, in the manner of the Cortile delle Statue's reclining statue (plates 32, 33). This was, in part, a revival of a typical element of classical gardens, that of the nymphaeum, and an evocation of Virgil, who in the *Aeneid* had described a "domus nymphearum" (nymph's dwelling) as a rustic grotto with dripping water. But it also constituted the conception of a new fountain model that united the natural setting of the grotto[38]—its jets of water, tartars, and aquatic plants—with the antique statue reclining in languid abandon,

31. (*below*) Reconstruction of the Cortile delle Statue before the eighteenth-century modifications.

32. (*opposite*) Francisco de Hollanda, *Ariadne*, 1539–40, etching.

presence of animals in the complex is confirmed by Francesco Albertini, who, when mentioning the Vatican in his 1510 description of Rome, wrote: "There are groves of animals and birds with gardens and greeneries."[41]

Another description of the site dates to 1510, during the residence of Federico Gonzaga of Mantua, whose parents had left him at the papal court as a hostage. In a letter sent by the Mantuan agent to Federico's mother, Isabella d'Este, he related that the youth was living in pleasant rooms with a loggia whose magnificent view justified the name Belvedere, as well as a garden, filled with orange and cypress trees, where musicians, singers, and jugglers entertained him daily.[42] A few years later, in 1513, the rooms of the Belvedere were occupied by another celebrated guest, Leonardo da Vinci,[43] in keeping with a tradition of hosting artists that would continue in the future. Because of its isolated and elevated position, which permitted the enjoyment of clean air, the Belvedere was also used as a refuge during the frequent episodes of plague that struck the city, as Baldassare Castiglione recounts in his letters. During the plague of 1521 Castiglione was in Rome as ambassador from Urbino, and he wrote to his mother from that refuge, with its beautiful garden, splendid antiquities, fountain, and running water.[44]

Of Bramante's project, however, only the central part with the three terraces and the conjoining staircases was completed. The side loggias were not finished, and structural problems soon emerged. The construction, begun in 1504, had been carried out with incredible speed, as Vasari relates: "…such was his eagerness as he worked, and that of the Pope, who would have liked to see the edifice spring up from the ground, without needing to be built."[45] Actually, only the terracing with the connecting ramps had been built in haste, permitting use of the court, while the loggias were completed only on the eastern side, as Vasari further explains: "Of this design, Bramante finished the first corridor, which issued from the Palace and led to the Belvedere on the side towards Rome, except for the upper loggia, which was to go above it. As for the opposite part, on the side towards the wood, the foundations, indeed, were laid, but it could not be finished, being interrupted by the death

thereby creating a marked contrast between rough and smooth surfaces, naturalness and artistic perfection.[39]

Innocent's original pavilion, now connected to the Vatican palaces by a majestic system of terraces, enriched with structures that regularized the layout, and endowed with a courtyard that constituted a true open-air museum, had acquired such beauty and importance as to become a source of glory for the pope, who not only used it as a private retreat but showed it off proudly to his guests. In fact, documents show that in 1509, while work on the complex was still under way, a *festa taurorum*, or bullfight, was held in the lower courtyard, and a small elephant given to the pope by the king of Portugal was left free to roam, perhaps with other animals, for the entertainment of the court.[40] The

33. (*overleaf*) Ariadne. Vatican Museums.

34. (*pages 52–53*) Nile. Vatican Museums.

35. (*page 54*) Apollo. Vatican Museums.

36. (*page 55*) Laocoön. Vatican Museums.

of Julius, and then by that of Bramante. His design was held to be so beautiful in invention, that it was believed that from the time of the ancients until that day, Rome had seen nothing better."[46]

Work continued at a slower pace after the death of the two protagonists and was definitively interrupted in 1521 with the death of Leo x (1513–21), successor to Julius II. Pope Adrian vi (1522–23), elected in 1522, showed little appreciation for the celebrated delights of Bramante's creation, and dismissed as too pagan the sculpture collection of Julius II;[47] he even refused access to the Venetian ambassadors, who succeeded in visiting the site only after insistent protests and recorded the sights they had admired in a vivid description.[48] This text, dated May 11, 1523, describes how the pope, in order to effectively limit access to the courtyard, had all of the doors walled up except one, accessible only from his rooms. The ambassadors, walking through the loggias, relate that they admired "on one side some meadows, some knolls, some groves, all enclosed by walls," while on the other side appeared a panoramic vista, over great balconies, of the "meadows of Rome," with a "very long view over the city, the hills, the river, and the Roman Forum, as well as many other beautiful things; for which it deserves the name Belvedere." Having reached the end of the loggias, the ambassadors entered the Cortile delle Statue, which they described as: "a beautiful garden, half of which is full of fresh grass and laurels, mulberries, and cypresses, the other half of which is paved with squares of terracotta laid on edge; and from the pavement in each square emerges a beautiful orange tree, of which there is a great abundance, arranged in perfect order. In the center of the garden are two huge marble men, one facing the other, twice life-size, reclining in the act of sleeping. One is the Tiber, the other the Nile (plate 34), most ancient figures; and from these spout two beautiful fountains." The description continues with admiration for the sculpture of Laocoön (plate 36) and the other statues, including those of Venus and Apollo (plate 35).

A few years later, another description confirms the layout of the courtyard-garden with its grove of golden apples surrounded by walls.[49] The abundance of citrus trees lent indisputable importance to the site and confirmed the tradition, dating back to the previous century, of cultivating those plants as a mark of particular dignity and distinction. The description of brick-paved areas alternating with neatly delineated flowerbeds conveys an image of the garden as a "built," architecturally conceived space (plate 37), confirming the innovative impact of Bramante's project.

While the Cortile del Belvedere, as mentioned above, soon underwent substantial modifications, the Cortile delle Statue remained unchanged for a long time, and we can presume that the painting (plate 38) by Hendrick van Cleve, dated 1560, mirrors quite faithfully its appearance at the end of the papacy of Julius II. The canvas offers a view of the Cortile delle Statue and the Cortile del Belvedere, seen from above and from the side of the Vatican hill, with the city clearly recognizable in the background. The perspective of the Cortile delle Statue appears slightly distorted and unrealistic, presumably to better show, arranged in succession, the monumental sculptures set up against the walls and in the center of the area. The entire space is subdivided into geometrical sections with flowerbeds surrounded by low hedges, probably of boxwood; among the trees we can make out the tall, subtle silhouettes of cypresses. The exhibition of the sculptures in the courtyard and in the adjacent gardens is visited and admired by figures in cardinal's robes, while numerous other people, in both curial and secular dress, stroll about. Only a small part of the Cortile del Belvedere is visible, the rest being covered by a grove of unidentifiable trees, but the layout of the flowerbeds in a rigorous geometric design is still clear. In the upper section, on the site of the exedra where Pirro Ligorio's gigantic niche would later be realized, is a fountain with a circular basin. The three orders of the loggias appear complete only on the side facing the city, while the internal side seems still unbuilt and has a haphazard, irregular appearance; the middle space is sprinkled with sculptures and small structures.

The courtyard was completed much later, during the papacy of Pius iv, under the direction of Pirro Ligorio, who was responsible not only for the great niche at the northern hemicycle but also for the completion of the side loggias and the creation of the hemicycle on the southern end. This is the appearance of the site as documented in Lafrery's etchings and in the anonymous painting in the Museo di Roma, which immortalize the configuration of the site in 1565, before the radical and irreversible transformation that Bramante's project would soon undergo with the construction of the library built for Sixtus v by Domenico Fontana. A further division of the courtyard, this time into three distinct parts with no connection among them, came between 1817 and 1822 under Pius vii (1800–23), with the construction of the so-called Braccio Nuovo, which definitively altered the brilliant creation of Donato Bramante and the humanistic dream of Julius II.

37. (*above*) The Cortile delle Statue today, with the eighteenth-century octagonal layout.

38. (*overleaf*) Hendrick van Cleve, *View of the Belvedere*, c. 1560, oil on canvas. Museè Royaux des Arts, Brussels.

1. St. Peter's Basilica

10. Loggias of Donato Bramante rebuilt under Paul III

11. Garden of Clement VII

12. Secret Garden of Paul III

a. Fontana del Belvedere

b. Nymphaeum of the Cortile della Biblioteca

c. Fontana del Belvedere in the Cortile della Pigna

d. Fontana di Cleopatra

e. Fontana della Zitella

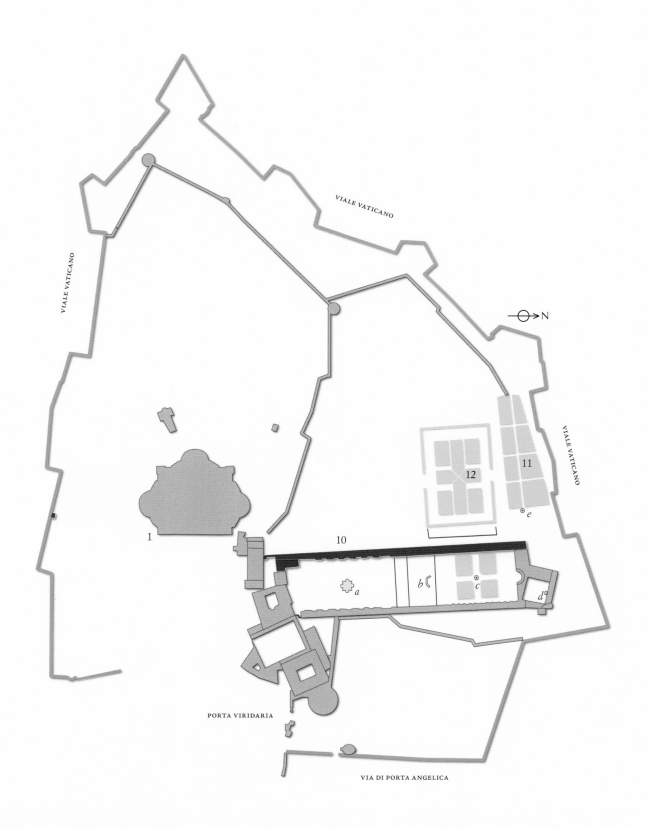

Modifications undertaken during the period discussed in this chapter are indicated in the map and captions above. For a complete map of the Vatican City and its major features in their present-day form, see page 2. Numbers in the map and captions refer to buildings and gardens, while letters refer to fountains.

CHAPTER THREE

THE SECRET GARDEN OF PAUL III (1534–49) AND THE CONTRIBUTION OF JACOPO MELEGHINO

The death of Julius III in 1513 and of Donato Bramante soon thereafter had left the great project of the Cortile del Belvedere unfinished. Work haltingly continued until the papacy of Leo X Medici and was definitively interrupted at his death, in 1521. The election of a second member of the Medici family, Clement VII (1523–34), to the papal throne brought a renewal of interest in the Vatican residence and the gardens in particular. The new pope resolved not only to complete what his predecessors had begun but also to create a new garden. It was to be distinct from the Belvedere but connected to it, and designed with the same goal of providing a spectacular view of the surrounding countryside—particularly of Monte Mario, which was dominated by the still-unfinished Medici family residence, Villa Madama.[1] Certainly it was no accident that Clement decided to favor a view toward the villa that he, as cardinal, had begun around 1517, calling in as architect the great Raphael.

The only evidence we have of this new garden is not documentary but iconographic: a 1574 plan by Mario Cartaro (plate 39) shows a beautiful formal garden marked with the letter K, which corresponds, in the legend, to the phrase "Garden of Pope Clement VII." This was a long, narrow space, located between the Secret Garden of Paul III (1534–49) and the rocky crag of the hill, facing toward Monte Mario.[2] It constituted almost a prolongation of the Palazzetto del Belvedere, a kind of secret garden set against the western facade where cypress trees once stood.

Completely surrounded by walls, it formed a spectacular panoramic terrace. Cartaro's plan indicates that it comprised a long, central path flanked by geometric beds bordered by hedges, probably boxwood. A row of tall trees running the entire length of the boundary wall served to separate it from the other gardens and shield the view somewhat, concealing and secluding the site. It seems to have been designed to allow the pope to enjoy a pleasant stroll while admiring a spectacular view, separated from the solemn rituals of the Belvedere, but at the same time close by. A small portion of the garden can be seen in the painting by Hendrick van Cleve from 1560 (plate 38). In the foreground some beds are clearly rendered; they are bordered by hedges, probably boxwood, and adorned with sculptures that are being admired by groups of visitors in a kind of idyllic extension of the Cortile delle Statue, visible in the background. On the inner side, atop the wall that borders Paul III's Secret Garden, is a walkway that would have allowed one to enjoy, from this privileged position, a view

39. (below left) Mario Cartaro, *True Rendering of the Stupendous Buildings, Gardens, Groves, Fountains, and Marvelous Things of the Belvedere in Rome*, 1574, detail.

40. (below right) Giovan Battista Falda, *Plan and elevation of the Belvedere Garden of the Papal Palace in the Vatican*, 1676, detail with the Garden of Clement VII along the bastions.

41. (opposite) The Secret Garden today.

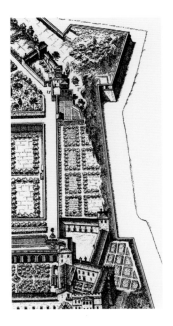

of both gardens as well as a panorama of hills in the distance. The garden is also well delineated in a 1676 plan by Giovan Battista Falda (plate 40).

According to Coffin, the idea of making a garden in this private location might have occurred to the pope during his forced retreat to the Vatican residence in 1524 and 1525, when an epidemic of the plague struck Rome.[3] A later date seems unlikely; the Sack of Rome in 1527[4] and its dramatic consequences certainly would have precluded the pope from devoting time to the gardens, at least until relative political and social stability had been reestablished. Today nothing remains of this garden, and the site is occupied by various new structures. The only remnant of the original arrangement is the Fontana della Zitella, so called because it is composed of a base with a large, water-spurting mask, on which rests a lovely Roman statue of a seated woman identified with Lucretia but popularly known as the *Zitella*, or "Spinster" (plate 43).

Paul III Farnese, while deeply attached to the splendid family residence in the Tuscia region and to the celebrated Horti Farnesiani on the Palatine Hill,[5] did not ignore the Vatican citadel. In fact, he devoted his attention both to the palaces and to the adjacent Castel Sant'Angelo, decorating the rooms of the ancient, austere fort with splendid frescoes.[6] His interest in art is further demonstrated by his establishment of the role of "Commissioner of Roman Antiquities," entrusted to the humanist Latino Giovenale Manetti; his enhancement of the Campidoglio (Capitoline Hill) with the prominent siting of the statue of Marcus Aurelius; and his resumption, after an interruption of more than twenty years, of the effort to transform St. Peter's Basilica, for which he summoned Antonio da Sangallo the Younger and then Michelangelo.

When Paul III reached the papal throne, Bramante's grandiose project for the Cortile del Belvedere was not only unfinished but partially in ruins, as a result of the acceleration of work that his predecessor, Julius II, had forced on the architect. The collapse of a section of the loggias on January 7, 1531, was prominently reported in the chronicles of the time, which recount how some 30 *canne*, or approximately 197–295 feet (60–90 meters), of wall crumbled from the top down to the foundation because the planned, necessary covering had never been put in place.[7] As previously mentioned, Vasari confirmed that Julius II was in such a hurry that he would have liked to see "the edifice spring up from the ground, without needing to be built," and this haste, perceived by Bramante, was "the reason that all his buildings have cracked, and are in danger of falling down,

as did this same corridor, of which a piece eighty braccia in length fell to the ground in the time of Clement VII, and was afterwards rebuilt by Pope Paul III, who also had the foundations restored and the whole strengthened."[8]

The Farnese pope's first undertaking was obviously the renovation of Bramante's work; he then turned to the further embellishment of the Cortile delle Statue, with the addition of new sculptures and decorations in a continuation of the work of Julius II.[9] Without a doubt, the most significant work he commissioned was a large Secret Garden created *ex novo*, surrounded on four sides by high walls with several openings and arranged in a formal layout that remained the same, in general terms, until the first decades of the last century. All the views of the Vatican from the period show the same arrangement of the garden. It was based on a division into four sectors, with two perpendicular central paths covered by a pergola that formed a cupola at the point of intersection. What can be considered the most important secret garden created in Rome[10] was isolated on the hill, far from any buildings. For this reason it

42. (*above*) Prospero Fontana, *View of the Vatican Belvedere with a Naumachia Scene*, c. 1545, detached fresco, detail with the Secret Garden of Paul III. Sala dei Festoni, Castel Sant'Angelo, Rome.

43. (*opposite*) Roman statue known as the *Zitella*, or "Spinster."

assumed even greater significance as a private site inaccessible to anyone on the outside, revealing its delights and pleasures only to those authorized to enter.

The greatest difficulty in the creation of the garden was the need to level a part of the hill in order to create a flat, uniform rectangular space of around 295¼ feet (90 meters) in width and 426½ (130 meters) in length. The exact position of the garden is visible both in the fresco (plate 42) painted in Castel Sant'Angelo in 1545 by Prospero Fontana, in which the walled enclosure can be seen clearly, and in the plan of 1577 by Étienne Dupérac (plate 45), where it is called "viridarium." Even clearer is the legend entry under the letter L in Mario Cartaro's 1574 plan (plate 44), which reads, "Secret Garden of Pope Paul III."[11]

Part of the garden is still visible, albeit with a much different layout than the original (plate 41). Two sides of the boundary wall are partially preserved, enough to give an idea of the site's design prior to the radical twentieth-century transformation.[12] Charged with this design was the Ferrarese architect Jacopo Meleghino (?–1550), but some sources have attributed the initial design to his teacher, Baldassarre Peruzzi.[13] Meleghino[14] was very close to the pope and active in the reconstruction of Frascati—both the city itself[15] and Villa La Rufina, better known as Villa Falconieri.[16] At the Vatican, having replaced Antonio da Sangallo as papal architect, he was primarily occupied with the fortification of the boundary walls that had been breached in 1527 by Charles v's lansquenets. Vasari writes that Meleghino was assisted in his work at the Belvedere by Jacopo Barozzi da Vignola, during his first stay in Rome, but his name does not appear among the payment documents found to date.[17]

Meleghino's participation in the construction of the Secret Garden is documented in numerous payment orders beginning in April 1537, when the first stage of work to level

the terrain was under way.[18] In fact, the first document attesting to the project's inception dates from November 1535, when the master builder Cristoforo Sbardiellini was paid for "work in the Belvedere to begin leveling the terrain where His Holiness wants to make a new garden."[19] And from January to December 1536, master Cristoforo completed the leveling job,[20] acquiring as necessary "shovels, pickaxes, and mattocks," and was paid by Giovan Battista da Sangallo (called "The Hunchback"), the papal accountant.[21] In 1537, in addition to payments to Meleghino for his work, payments are made for the planting of trees in the garden with the participation of gardeners, beginning with Romolo Lucerta (often written Lucertula) and Giovanni Aloisi.[22] On September 22, the latter went to Naples to get "bitter oranges and other citrus trees to plant in the new garden of the Belvedere." Then, on November 15, a load of "1,500 citrus trees from the Kingdom [of Naples] to plant in the new garden" reached Rome, and on December 15 Meleghino made an advance payment of 22.20 *scudi* to purchase "various trees…to plant in the aforementioned garden" and the equipment necessary to transport them.[23]

In 1538 the planting and espaliering of citrus trees continued, and again Meleghino was paid for "various fruit trees that he had bought to plant in the new garden," while another gardener, Antonio, worked to create "espaliers of bitter oranges, pomegranates, and laurels." Once again, Aloisi went to Naples to bring "trees for the new Belvedere garden," and on November 2 Lucerta "leveled the last

44. (*below, left*) Mario Cartaro, *True Rendering of the Stupendous Buildings, Gardens, Groves, Fountains, and Marvelous Things of the Belvedere in Rome*, detail with the Secret Garden of Paul III.

45. (*below, right*) Étienne Dupérac, *View of the Vatican*, 1577, detail with the Secret Garden of Paul III.

quarter of the new garden."[24] While trees were being planted and espaliered starting in February, Meleghino undertook the construction of an underground passageway to link the new Secret Garden built at the behest of Paul III with the pre-existing garden created by Clement VII. He was compensated for "work done to excavate the earth under the vault that goes from the new garden...to the old," while a few months later, evidently on completion of the masonry work, master Jacomo, a painter, received ten *scudi* "as payment for the painting that he is doing in the vault of the passageway that runs from one garden to the other."[25] The creation of the passage is also cited in a letter written by Meleghino to Cardinal Alessandro Farnese, in which he recounts that, "having finished the vault that runs from one garden to the other," work had been stopped for some months because payments were late.[26] The passageway, no longer extant, was documented by Coffin in an old photograph.[27]

From the end of 1538 to the end of 1540 the documentation concerning the work commissioned by Paul III is interrupted, and only beginning in 1541 is it possible to resume following the construction of the garden. In January Meleghino was busy replacing some trees that evidently did not take root with the first planting, and he was paid for "sixty trees bought to put in the new garden where the dead ones had been."[28] In October the usual gardener, Lucerta, took care of the garden, and bought "flower bulbs and other things for the Belvedere and to dress the espaliers of bitter oranges in the new garden and water them."[29] Again in 1543 "forty trees" were planted, and work was carried out to construct the espaliering trellises and, most importantly, to create the great pergola that covered the two central paths. Between June and July 1544, Lucerta worked in the garden, for which "1500 pairs of wooden rings...for use as part of the espaliers of bitter oranges in the new garden" were supplied; a "Bologna carpenter" attached these rings to the trees and trellises so that the trees would be trained to grow flat, creating the long walkway covered with greenery that can be seen in the views of the period.[30] At the same time, Meleghino saw to the water supply, working on the placement of a cistern and on the fountains' existing pipes, which required frequent repairs and extensions.[31] A review of the cited documents reveals that Meleghino was engaged on all fronts, both with directing the architectural part of the job and with overseeing every aspect of the garden plan, down to the choice of trees, in collaboration with the gardeners. What emerges is the image of a fascinating architect whose work for Paul III deserves further study.[32]

Unfortunately, we have only vague and fragmentary information about the plants and flowers that were cultivated in the garden, with the exception of the citrus espaliers. There were probably precious specimens, about which Paul III cared deeply, as a comment from his herbalist, Scipione, indicates: "Moreover, it was forbidden by Paul III, who was a lover of plants and of the natural world, that [the specimens] be sold anywhere, on account of their rarity."[33] Indeed, besides the gardeners Lucerta and Aloisi, the Vatican Gardens also had a *semplicista*, or herbalist, according to medieval tradition. Scipione Perotti, or Perotto da Benevento, must have been an important figure, as he was present in the Vatican Gardens for many years and was mentioned by botanists and garden experts, both local and foreign, who visited the gardens and to whom he showed the rare plants cultivated there.[34]

In the following years there is no evidence of any work in the Secret Garden apart from routine maintenance of the plants and the structures supporting the pergolas. The image of the garden that emerges from the written and iconographic documentation is that of a classical, Renaissance secret garden corresponding to the dictates of treatises of the period and to a codified design. The space was subdivided, as has been mentioned, into four sections, each composed of four beds with their corners rounded at the center to create a circular space where yet another bed, or perhaps a small fountain, was placed. The beds had a low border, probably of boxwood, and grass and some flowers in the center, as suggested by the supply of *cipolle*, or flower bulbs—most likely narcissus and anemones, the most favored at the time. There were also fruit trees, cited in a payment, but we do not know of what kind. A distinctive element was the imposing *cocchio* (plate 47), or covered walkway,[35] of the two intersecting paths that subdivided the garden. This pergola-like element was common in the gardens of the period and codified in the treatises. Consequently, we can reconstruct its appearance not only from the previously cited views but also from comparisons to similar structures. It was an installation, generally of wood, consisting of chestnut poles that supported a vaulted covering; citrus, pomegranate, and laurel trees were planted along its entire length, and their branches were trained as they grew to meet at the top, thereby forming completely shaded corridors.[36] To allow those strolling through to enjoy the outside view, window-like openings punctured the sides in imitation of an arcade. At the intersection of the two paths was a great cupola, supported by a wooden structure that opened in a series of arches to permit light and air to enter. It was modeled, undoubtedly, on various reproductions (plate 46) of this type of pergola contained in Francesco Colonna's *Hypnerotomachia Poliphili*, a celebrated text of the period.[37] An example of the spread of this decorative element can also be found in a drawing by Giovanni Colonna: a plan for the Garden of Paolo Ghinucci at the Quirinal Palace (plates 48, 49) that includes a detailed proposal for a wooden pavilion covered in greenery.[38] Baldassarre Peruzzi's participation in the design of the garden, at least in its initial phase, is likely confirmed by a drawing for an unspecified garden in which he proposed a four-part arrangement, with two paths forming an octagon at an intersection that we can imagine was covered with a cupola. The plan is definitely not for the Vatican Secret Garden, as it contains incongruous elements (there is, for instance, a building at one end, and one side of the rectangle is slanted), but the type and proposed layout are the same, and Meleghino was most likely familiar with his teacher's drawing.

The cross-shaped pergola in the garden can be seen clearly in Mario Cartaro's 1574 plan, but a part of the garden, with a very detailed rendering of the pergola, is also visible in an etching (plate 50) by Antonio Lafrery that depicts the tournament of 1565 in the Cortile del Belvedere. As already mentioned, the garden was enclosed on four sides by high walls (the highest abutted the hillside and

acted as an embankment); all along the walls were espaliers of citrus trees, and on every side were portals that can be seen in the various views of the period and that remained until the start of the last century (plates 51, 52). One of the portals (plates 53, 54) on the southern side is still in place, despite the radical transformation and reduction of the space, and leads into two staircases that descend to the level of the garden. It features two fine marble parastades, carved for use as candelabras, and an architrave decorated with reliefs of fruit and flower garlands and winged putti, with the inscription PIUS IIII PONTIFEX MAXIM. It is probable, as Coffin suggests, that this portal was built by Pius IV at the same time as Pirro Ligorio's Casina to underscore its relationship to the road that leads there. This interpretation lends weight to the notion that the garden of Paul III was considered a kind of continuation of the overall reorganization of the area.[39]

46. (*below*) Drawing of a *cocchio*, or pergola, from Francesco Colonna, *Hypnerotomachia Poliphili*, Venice, 1499.

47. (*opposite*) The *cocchio di agrumi*, or citrus pergola, in the garden of Cardinal Pio da Carpi, from Giovan Battista Ferrari, *Hesperides, sive de malorum aureorum cultura et usu*, 1644.

The previously mentioned connection between the new garden of Paul III and the old one of Clement VII answered the need to encompass the two sites in a single system of distinct, yet closely connected, spaces. In fact, when work on the new garden was nearly complete, the payment orders register numerous instances in which the destination "old garden" is clearly specified. This term surely refers to the Secret Garden of Clement VII. A payment to Lucerta for work on the "high road of the old Belvedere garden" dates to March 1541, and on November 26 there is another expenditure for "one hundred columns of wood, and forty-two crosspieces to fix parts of the frames of the espaliers of myrtle and rose in the old Belvedere garden,"[40] which clearly refers to the espaliers that covered the boundary walls. Other crosspieces and wooden columns for the espaliers of roses and myrtle were furnished on December 17 and December 26,[41] once again to repair the espaliers and, in particular, the *gelosie*—that is, the shuttered windows that were opened in the sides of the pergola, which, evidently, as in the "new" secret garden, had the

form of a *cocchio* or structured pergola covered with plants. Payments of substantial sums continued at regular intervals for all of 1542 and 1543; all were related to the making or remaking of espaliers and *gelosie* by adding, together with the usual columns and crosspieces, eight hundred *para de cerchi* or pairs of wooden rings to the canopy of the vault, with the help of both Lucerta and Hyeronimo the carpenter, called "el Bologna."[42] From the quantity of materials supplied, we can deduce that the pergola was quite long, probably extending the entire length of Clement VII's garden, and we can imagine how pleasant it must have been to stroll through it amid the sweet fragrance of roses and myrtle,[43] enjoying the view of the surrounding pastoral landscape from the openings along the route.

From what has been recounted so far, one has the impression that the projects commissioned by Paul III were concerned only with the pleasurable aspects of the gardens, and not with the agricultural endeavors that, as we know, were ongoing in the Vatican citadel. We can assume that in the area beyond the Leonine Wall the land continued to be

48. (*right*) Giovanni Colonna, Garden of Paolo Ghinucci on the Quirinal, detail, BAV.

49. (*opposite, left*) Giovanni Colonna, Garden of Paolo Ghinucci on the Quirinal, detail, BAV.

50. (*opposite, right*) Antonio Lafrery, *Tournament in the Cortile del Belvedere*, etching, 1565, northern end, detail with the pergola in the Secret Garden of Paul III.

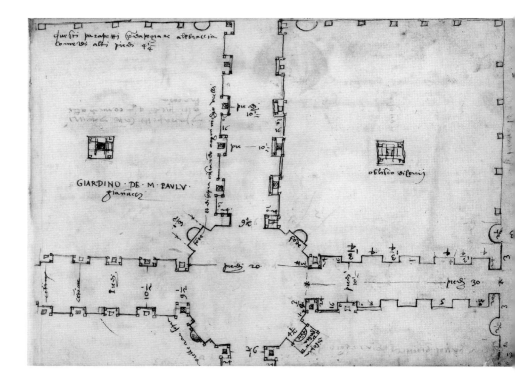

cultivated with vineyards and vegetable gardens, both for internal use and to supply the convents, as was the tradition. In addition, a careful reading of the documents reveals that even the pleasure gardens produced income from the perfumed waters, medicines, and liquors that were made from their flowers and plants. Many payments refer, in fact, to the purchase of charcoal and flasks for "the distilled waters" or "to distill roses,"[44] that is, to produce perfumed waters, perhaps also for sale. Peas were cultivated as well, and in the park outside the gardens, which were protected with "thickets of thorns," roe deer roamed freely.[45] Payments to Lucerta were made frequently for routine maintenance, such as cleaning the paths or watering the plants, with the help of two donkeys used for transport and, of course, several other gardeners whose names are cited at times in the payment logs.

A pope as cultured and passionate about art as Paul III certainly could not neglect the Cortile delle Statue, the garden-museum created by Bramante and exemplary not only for its admirable statuary collection, but also for its revolu-

tionary concept of space and function. Once again, we have the documentary support of payments that allow us to follow the arrival and placement of new sculptures (such as the Venus donated by the governor of Rome) and the decoration of the niches where the Apollo and the Laocoön group were installed. There are also records of payments for the maintenance of the jasmine plants and flowerbeds in the courtyard ("Make four small lawns in the statue court"), and the purchase and siting of an unidentified marble statue coming from the house of Nicolò de Polis.[46] We can infer that the Cortile delle Statue was by that time considered the symbolic site par excellence: a status symbol not only of power but also of a refined love and sensibility for art, in keeping with a taste for collecting that was by now widespread among the Roman aristocracy and that had, in Pope Paul III, a passionate supporter.[47]

An enthusiastic description of the gardens comes to us from the German jurist Johannes von Fichard (1512–1581), who during a trip to Italy in 1536 had visited the Vatican, and commented admiringly: "From the palace one enters

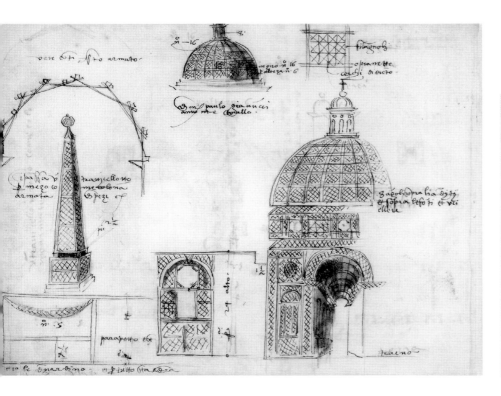

broad gardens, behind which is that well-known place, the Belvedere, which, in its buildings, walkways, fountains, ancient statues, location, and view is most elaborate and unequaled. It has a spiral staircase, by which we can climb all the way to the top, where the pleasantness and the view of the place is most clear to see; there is nowhere, I think, more pleasant."[48]

With Paul III's contribution, which constitutes a continuation and expansion of the work begun by Clement VII, the heart of the garden moves to an area that was previously either uncultivated or planted with grapevines by means of a progressive extension of its formal reorganization and, subsequently, of sites intended for pleasure. After the construction of the Palazzetto del Belvedere, the original garden next to the Vatican palaces was replaced by the area around Monte Sant'Egidio, now easily accessible via the

link that Bramante created through the Cortile del Belvedere, which was also largely devoted to garden space. Social and ceremonial life in the Vatican citadel was apparently divided between two distinct, if connected, locations. One was the old residence next to the Basilica, monumental and austere; the other was the new site, far more pleasant thanks to its elevated position and resemblance, in both its architecture and its surrounding gardens, to the pleasure villas that were starting to appear in Rome.[49]

51. (below) The Secret Garden of Paul III in an early twentieth-century postcard.

52. (opposite) The Secret Garden of Paul III after the transformations in the 1930s.

ROMA
Una Parte dei Giardini Vaticani

53. (*below*) The entrance portal to the Secret Garden in an early twentieth-century photograph.

54. (*opposite*) The entrance portal to the Secret Garden today.

1. St. Peter's Basilica under construction
10. Loggias of Donato Bramante completed by Pirro Ligorio
13. Casina of Pius IV

14. Giardino dei Semplici
15. Nicchione of Donato Bramante and Pirro Ligorio
16. Vatican Library
b. Nymphaeum of the Cortile della Biblioteca

c. Fontana del Belvedere in the Cortile della Pigna
d. Fontana di Cleopatra
e. Fontana della Zitella
f. Fountain at the Casina of Pius IV

g. Fish pond at the Casina of Pius IV
h. Fish pond of Julius III

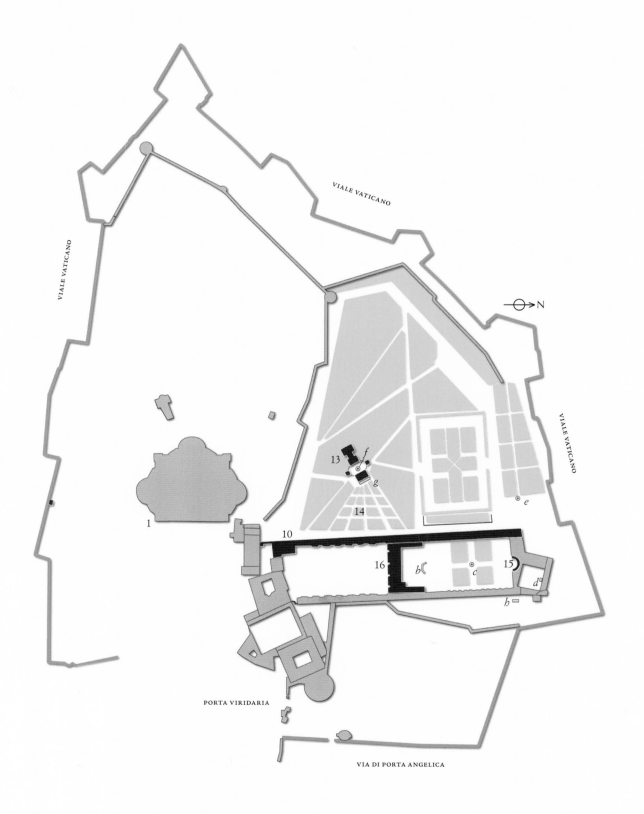

Modifications undertaken during the period discussed in this chapter are indicated in the map and captions above. For a complete map of the Vatican City and its major features in their present-day form, see page 2. Numbers in the map and captions refer to buildings and gardens, while letters refer to fountains.

CHAPTER FOUR

THE CASINA OF PIUS IV (1559–65) AND THE GIARDINO DEI SEMPLICI

The papacy of Julius III del Monte (1550–55), although brief, left us Villa Giulia, a paradigm of enormous importance in the development of pleasure residences thanks to the extraordinary contributions of Bartolomeo Ammannati, Michelangelo, Vignola, Giorgio Vasari, Prospero Fontana, Taddeo Zuccari, and other artists of lesser renown but equal talent.[1] Descriptions of the time testify to the grandeur of the complex (plates 56, 57), its revolutionary architecture, its fountains, and its magnificent gardens dotted with innumerable sculptures. The pope went to Villa Giulia whenever the affairs of government permitted. It was, indeed, his "true" residence, where he invested all his interests and passions.

Julius III's decision to build his "own" villa after election to the papal throne had a precise significance: the Vatican was no longer the privileged residence on which care and attention would be lavished or where official and private functions could coexist, complete with areas of the gardens that allowed the pope to retreat from court life without leaving its official seat. This arrangement, developed by his predecessors, was now interrupted. Rather than dedicate his energies to building new gardens and buildings (although the Vatican palaces did undergo important modifications during his papacy) to make the traditional papal residence and symbol of Christianity even more magnificent, Julius III chose instead to focus on a separate, private

site on the other side of the Tiber, where he could take refuge and affirm the clear separation between *negotium* (business) and *otium* (rest, pleasure).

Consequently, work in the Vatican Gardens at his behest was limited to the routine care of what was already there, including maintenance of the conduits that fed the fountains and irrigated the gardens, and the daily tasks carried out by the palace gardeners according to the seasons.[2] Some payment documents mention work at the "Belvedere vineyard and garden," but these are often grouped with those for Villa Giulia and, starting in 1553, refer exclusively to the latter.[3] Only one payment contains a precise reference to the Cortile delle Statue; in it, the famous fountain maker Curzio Maccarone is paid for work done on the rustic fountains, specifically the one featuring the sculpture of

55. (*below*) Mario Cartaro, *True Rendering of the Stupendous Buildings, Gardens, Groves, Fountains, and Marvelous Things of the Belvedere in Rome*, 1574, detail with the terraced garden of Julius III and the fish pond with rustic grotto abutting the Belvedere.

56. (*opposite, top*) Giuseppe Vasi, *View of Villa Giulia*, from *Delle magnificenze di Roma antica e moderna*, 1747–61, etching.

57. (*opposite, bottom*) Villa Giulia in a nineteenth-century etching.

Cleopatra.[4] Though archival documents identified to date do not offer support for this hypothesis, Julius III is credited with commissioning a small garden and a fish pond near Bramante's loggias on the side facing the city. The garden is shown in great detail in the previously cited plan (plate 55) by Mario Cartaro of 1574, in which the letters E and F correspond, in the legend, to the phrases "Garden of the fountain of Pope Julius 3" and "Fish pond of Pope Julius 3." The garden also appears in a less detailed rendering but with a similar layout in Étienne Dupérac's 1577 plan of the Cortile del Belvedere. A long, narrow rectangle in form, it is located on the terrace near the loggias and supported by the boundary wall that separates the Vatican from the city. It is divided into rectangular beds, which are themselves divided into smaller rectangles, with trees, probably citrus, espaliered against the walls of the loggias. At the end of the garden, bordering the Palazzetto del Belvedere and corresponding to the base of Bramante's famous snail staircase, is a large fountain composed of a rustic grotto with a large basin below (plate 58): the aforementioned fish pond. According to Ackerman and Marcello Fagiolo, the rustic grotto backdrop was built by Curzio Maccarone, almost certainly based on a design by Vignola and Girolamo da Carpi, and would thus constitute "the

first Vignolan example of a garden-fortress with a rustic grotto."[5] Little remains today of the original creation made for Julius III. Around 1620, during the papacy of Paul V (1605–21), the spectacular "Galera" (plate 59), a miniature vessel with a play of water jets, was added; under Pius VI (1775–99), at the end of the eighteenth century, the rustic backdrop was given a neo-classical look; finally, in more recent times, the garden was completely destroyed and replaced by roads.

Elements of continuity in the gardens' management from the period of Paul III through that of Julius III included the enduring, curatorial role of Scipione Perotto, or Perotti, as the *semplicista* or caretaker of the herb garden, and the

58. (*below left*) Étienne Dupérac, *View of the Vatican*, 1577, detail. At the bottom, the rustic grotto.

59. (*below right*) The Fontana della Galera after the eighteenth-century replacement of the rustic grotto with a masonry wall.

60. (*opposite, top*) Paul Marie Letarouilly, *The Cortile, the Loggia, One of the Two Propylaea, and the Casina*, 1882, etching.

61. (*opposite, bottom*) Paul Marie Letarouilly, *Section of the Casina of Pius IV Complex*, 1882, etching.

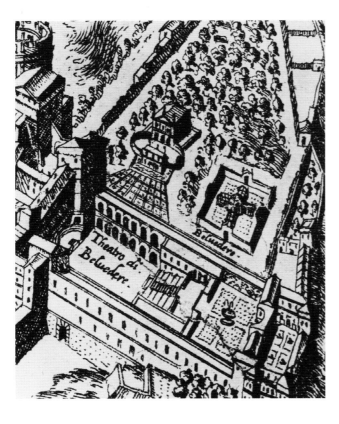

62. Paul Marie Letarouilly, *The Casina of Pius IV Complex
Seen from the Outside*, 1882, etching.

63. Paul Marie Letarouilly, *The Courtyard of the Casina of Pius IV with the Various Buildings*, 1882, etching.

practice of distilling flower petals and medicinal plants to make perfumed waters, which may also have been for sale. In some accounts from 1551 and 1552, in fact, a salaried distiller, Francesco Veniens, is mentioned as receiving rose petals from Perotto for this purpose, in keeping with a tradition that would be continued during the next two papacies.[6]

The successors of Julius III, Paul IV (1558–59) and Pius IV (1559–65), resumed the tradition of embellishing the Vatican Gardens, and they can be credited with commissioning and completing the masterpiece of garden buildings (plates 60–63): the Casina designed by Pirro Ligorio, a triumph of Mannerism and of a concept of art open to all possible variations, in both the material and symbolic senses. Paul IV Carafa turned his attention first to the completion of the papal apartments begun by Julius III, calling to his service at the papal court Pirro Ligorio (1513–83), with whom he shared Neapolitan origins. Subsequently he began the construction of the Casina, which is historically attributed to his successor, Pius IV. The first news pertaining to the construction of the Casina is contained in an *Avviso* of April 30, 1558, which announced that the pope "… has begun a structure in the woods that will be a fountain next to a loggia and some rooms, where he stops for two or three hours at a time, summoning there stonemasons and laborers such as a private [citizen] who builds."[7] In May of that year a Florentine ambassador also referred to the construction of a "fountain in the woods" and to "various rooms," again in the woods, with a clear allusion to the newly begun project.[8] The pope, old and in poor health, wished to have, as soon as possible, a private retreat in the middle of the woods, but not far from the papal seat.[9] The choice of an extremely out-of-the-way site was not made by chance. Far from both the oldest complex of palaces and from the Belvedere, it was in the center of what all of the contemporary views depict as a dense wood. According to documents cited, the original idea consisted of a fountain with a loggia and a few enclosed spaces for brief stops on summer afternoons.

Work was interrupted less than six months later, however, and resumed only under the new pope, Pius IV, who gave his name to the complex, immortalizing it in some twenty-five inscriptions and crests displayed everywhere. The new pope, a Medici from the Milanese branch,[10] earned the title of "builder" for the sheer quantity of buildings he completed or began, but the Casina in the Vatican Gardens was the one destined for immediate and long-lasting fame—an unparalleled example both in its architectural originality and in the incredible richness and

magnificence of its decorations. The character of the site is well summed up in a noted description by Burckhardt, who judged the complex "the most perfect retreat imaginable for a mid-summer afternoon."[11]

The payment documents attest to a limited period of time for construction: from August 1560 to November 1561,[12] when decorative work began, indicating that the structure must have been largely complete. The new pope confirmed Ligorio as papal architect, but the design of the Casina was probably modified in part, as indicated by a letter from Don Cesare Carafa, who visited the site in April 1561.[13] Pirro Ligorio,[14] an architect as well as a painter and archaeologist, was, according to scholars, heavily influenced by his teacher, Baldassare Peruzzi, with whom he shared an interest in the ancient world that can be seen beginning in his work on the world-renowned villa at Tivoli,[15] commissioned by Cardinal Ippolito d'Este.[16]

The Casina (plates 64–68) is often described in the documents as the "building in the woods," which could lead one to assume that it was closely connected to the surrounding wooded area. In reality, this is merely a topographical reference, as the building was, on the contrary, completely separated from the woods by boundary walls on the side facing the hill, with the trees behind it forming only a backdrop. The Casina, taking advantage of the uneven terrain, is set against the wood at the highest point, and opens on the level of the loggia, from which two staircases descend on either side and connect to the rear entrances.[17] The choice of this site at the edge of the woods was dictated by a desire for privacy, shared by both popes: while the Cortile del Belvedere was used as a ceremonial space par excellence and the Palazzetto of Innocent VIII was by then effectively a museum, Pius IV desired for himself and those close to him a secluded place, a few rooms immersed in the coolness of the woods, in which to stop and rest during hot Roman afternoons.

Before he was elected pope, Pius IV was particularly fond of his villa at Frascarolo, in Lombardy, and so as soon as he reached Rome, he followed the example of the building begun by his predecessor in creating a similar site for

64. (*opposite*) Detail of the facade of the Loggia facing the garden, with commemorative crests and inscriptions.

65. (*page 86*) Detail of the facade of the Loggia facing the fish pond.

66. (*page 87*) The complex of the Casina of Pius IV, seen from the outside.

XII.PONTIFEX.MAXIMVS.FRONTEM.HANC.RENOVAVIT.PONT.AN

PIVS·IIII·MEDICES·MEDIOLANEN·PONTIFEX·MAXIMVS·
INNEMORE · PALATII · VATICANI · PORTICVM ·
APSIDATAM · CVM · COLVMNIS · NVMIDICIS · FONTIBVS
LYMPHÆO · IMMINENTEM · E · REGIONE · AREAE ·
EXTRVXIT · ANN · SAL · MDLXI

67. The Loggia and, in the background, the Casina.

68. Another view of the Loggia with the Casina in the background.

himself, suited to frequent retreats with a small circle of companions whom he could join in convivial pleasures. The name Casina of Pius IV, or Villa Pia, generally refers not only to the Casina itself but also to the entire architectural complex arranged around the courtyard. Indeed, it is a true and complete villa (as its alternative name attests), comprising buildings, fountains, and greenery within a vast area of the Vatican Gardens.

All studies on the Casina to date have rightly focused on the large, elliptical courtyard, surrounded by buildings and furnished with benches all along its boundary wall, as evidence of its use as a gathering place. This central area constitutes a kind of open-air salon, while its form evokes the ancient naumachies, as is underscored by the pervasive presence of water—in the fountain that dominates the center of the oval, in the great basin at ground level near the eastern entrance, and in another basin downstream in the direction of the garden—as well as by multiple symbolic references and the use of "aquatic" material such as shells and tartars. The evocation of the naumachy and the presence of water are also explicit references to the "ship of the church," a codified symbol of refuge and salvation.[18]

Around the courtyard are the four structures that make up the complex. The main building, the two-story Casina, consists of a large vestibule leading to a long central section that culminates in two protruding wings: the smaller one, its size limited by the stairs, on the left and the larger one on the right, probably used as a chapel. Facing it is the loggia,

also two stories high: a splendid pavilion open on all sides, articulated with columns, and surrounded on three sides by a large fish pond that was originally quadrangular. On the sides are two vaulted aediculae that function as portals or propylaea, through which one entered the courtyard and then the building. The whole complex was governed by a rigorous symmetry, with the exception of the two slightly different wings in the Casina; this symmetry was subsequently altered by the construction of a rooftop belvedere at the left rear extremity, believed by some scholars to date to the second half of the seventeenth century.[19] The importance of the oval courtyard as the compositional center of the complex is emphasized by the curves of the facades of the two aediculae, echoing its elliptical shape. The "pictorial" treatment—the decorative elements shared by the external surfaces of all four of the buildings, the identical colonnades in the main building and the loggia, and the perfect correspondence between the two entrance portals—further confirmed the unified, rigorously coordinated conception of the project.

The innovative nature of Ligorio's plan to make the central, elliptical space the focal point of the complex has been justly emphasized, and a resemblance to the design of the oval in the garden of Baldassarre Peruzzi's Villa Trivulzio

69. (*below*) The nymphaeum of Villa Giulia.

70. (*opposite*) The Casina of Pius IV, detail of the mosaics.

·PIVSIIII
·PONTIF·
MAXIMV·

at Salone has also been suggested.[20] This comparison actually seems rather forced, but there is certainly a clear similarity to the splendid nymphaeum at Villa Giulia (plate 69): both spaces use diverse, polychrome materials and consist of open-air sites bounded by buildings. Both have a strong tie to water and are permeated by the same veneration for things ancient, even in their paganistic elements.[21]

In Ligorio's design the distinction between architecture and decoration was blurred even more than in the Villa Giulia nymphaeum. All of the surfaces[22] were uniformly covered in marble, mosaics, shells, tartars, inlays, stuccoes, and paintings, in a hodgepodge pushing the limits of a horror vacui (plate 70), and with a decorative effect that, unfortunately, has been greatly altered and reduced by various modifications through the centuries. The revolutionary significance of Ligorio's design lay in his decision to adapt techniques, materials, and decorative motifs previously reserved for interiors to the exterior. Although there had been some examples of decorative treatment of external surfaces in Rome, as at Palazzo Spada or Palazzo Branconio dell' Aquila, none could boast a richness of colors and materials comparable to the building facades of Pius IV's villa.

The sophisticated atmosphere of *otium* is underlined by the iconographic program that provided the setting for the pope's gatherings; Ligorio's own writings contain numerous interesting reflections on the "convivial life" to which he constantly alluded, with special reference to this project. In fact, the stucco work and mosaics that cover the walls depict mythological and allegorical themes serving as blatant reminders of the contemplative life and its virtues, next to other themes alluding to water, to the pastoral spirit of the site, to the symbology of the sun, and to the exaltation of the pope.[23]

Arranged on three levels on the main facade of the Casina (plate 72), next to Apollo and Hegle with their daughters, the Hours,[24] are reliefs depicting the Seasons as well as Pan and Cyparissus (the nymph who was transformed into a cypress tree), all evoking a rustic, pastoral atmosphere. The personifications of the rivers Tiber and Ticino exalt the element of water and associate the Roman seat with Pavia, where the pope had attended university.

71. (*right*) The Loggia, detail of the upper section.

72. (*page 94*) The facade of the Casina and the fountain by Giacomo di Casignola and Giovanni di Sant'Agata, c. 1560.

73. (*page 95*) The internal facade of the Loggia with the fountain in the courtyard.

PONTIFEX · OPTIMVS · MAXIMVS ·

Fame and Victory, along with the Medici crest and the large, celebratory inscription, acclaim the finished project and its commissioner.

Even more exuberant are the decorations of the loggia (plates 71, 73), distributed across its four equally visible facades. Today, the facade facing the garden appears the most altered with respect to the ornamentations that formed part of the original Ligorian scheme. Indeed, in about 1826, at the behest of Pope Leo XII (1823–29), many of the original sculptures were eliminated, particularly the four great, satyr-like caryatids that articulated the lower level. These were replaced by pilasters covered in pretty, polychrome mosaics with floral and bird motifs, held to be more in line with the spirit of the site than the mythological figures alluding to bacchanals and pagan triumphs. The four pilasters are perfectly aligned with the articulation of the facade in front of the Casina, in a play of transparencies and evocations that once again underscores the unified nature of the complex.

Even the large, originally rectangular fish pond surrounding the loggia on three sides was reduced in size and modified to assume a curvilinear form; the revised configuration has less visual impact than that documented, for example, in the view by Giovanni Maggi of 1615, in which the loggia looks almost like a fountain set amidst gurgling waters populated by marine creatures. The reference to water must have seemed so potent that a description from 1776 defines the complex as the "building in the midst of the water."[25] Actually, water is not as dominant an element here as it is at Villa d'Este, yet it is constantly alluded to in both the iconography and the use of materials. To evoke the fountain-nymphaeum model, for example, Pirro Ligorio made extensive use of surfaces worked with inlays of smooth river stones, shells, tartars, and irregular fragments of multicolored stones—all materials linked to water, sustenance,

and the spirit of the garden.[26] Dominating the central niche of the loggia, which appears almost suspended over the fish pond, is the seated figure of Cybele, while in the side niches are statues of Modesty and Youth, surrounded by elegant bas-reliefs of nymphs and graces. The upper story has a simpler, more linear structure, with ample openings framed by columns that permit a glimpse of the Casina in the background. Inscriptions commemorating both the work commissioned by Pius IV and additions by Leo XII are in evidence.

The richest facade (plate 71) of the loggia is undoubtedly the one that faces the interior courtyard and constitutes the pendant of the principal facade of the Casina. It is articulated on two levels, using the same scheme as the side facing the garden. The lower level has the customary four columns, flanked by two reliefs with festoons and the head of Medusa on the corner pilasters. The upper level is modeled after ancient sarcophagi: two huge marble slabs with bas-reliefs of the Muses being led in procession by Apollo and Bacchus, separated by a relief of Calliope, muse of epic poetry, on which the inscription PIERIS alludes to Mount Olympus, home of Jupiter and the Muses themselves; and at either end, depictions of Truth and Mnemosyne, the

74–77. (*below*) Paul Marie Letarouilly, *The Propylaea*, 1882, four etchings.

78. (*opposite*) The tree-lined avenue between the Secret Garden of Paul III and the Casina of Pius IV.

79. (*page 98*) The propylaeum on the southern side, exterior.

80. (*page 99*) The propylaeum on the southern side, interior.

81. (*page 100*) The propylaeum on the northern side, exterior.

82. (*page 101*) The propylaeum on the northern side, interior.

personification of Memory and also the mother of the Muses. The structure is capped by a triangular tympanum with a relief of Aurora driving the chariot of the Sun, flanked by Flora and Pomona, identifiable by their baskets overflowing with flowers and fruit.[27] On the right elevation are other fine reliefs depicting, again, Aurora, as well as Jupiter raised by the goat Amalthea.

The two propylaea (plates 74–77 and 79–82) have their own rich repertory of decoration. Their use of such varied materials as mosaics, stucco, and pebbles produces a highly original, polychrome effect. They have been compared to larariums, or small altars, some examples of which still existed; Ligorio was probably familiar with those in Villa Adriana and in Titus' baths. The interior walls are decorated with charming, multicolored mosaic compositions featuring fish, birds, and other animals, as well as garlands of fruit and little temples that strongly recall the decorations in the villas of Pompeii.[28] In the small barrel vaults, mythological stories of the triumphs of the gods are illustrated in elaborate stucco work. Marine themes with Galatea, Neptune, and Andromeda predominate, emphasizing yet again the relationship to water. Other decorations allude to the cycles of the seasons, again with obvious reference to the rustic atmosphere of the site (plate 78).

The complex symbology of the decorative themes has inspired several studies that have brought to light Pirro Ligorio's extensive knowledge of classical culture, along with his ability to translate it into works of great visual impact. For the privileged few granted admittance to the presence of the pope in this private space, the themes also represented an initiation into the temple of knowledge and learning—the *museion*, or house of the Muses.[29] The culmination of the iconographic program was the exaltation of the pope-client, celebrated in the repeated use of his personal crests and those of his family, in the multitude of inscriptions, and also in the allegories that alluded to his papacy as a return to the mythical golden age.

Overall, the iconographic program was classical and pagan, greatly influenced by a love of archaeology and classical culture that Ligorio and the pope himself shared. The clear emphasis on subjects far removed from religious references has been analyzed as contradictory to the client's role as the head of Christianity. In fact, in those years Pius IV was leading the Catholic church at the great turning point of the Counter-Reformation, decreed by the Council of Trent, which was heading toward conclusion. The love of a joyous culture, the cult of pagan antiquity, and the exaltation of contemplative *otium* as an exemplary

state of being must have seemed very far from the idea of a reformed church returning to its original, evangelical principles.

This contradiction became evident and unsustainable at the very time when the Casina was being completed and, with the architectural work concluded, execution of the internal decoration was set to begin. The change in the cultural climate found direct expression in the difference between the decoration of the interior and exterior spaces. Whereas it is difficult to identify evocations of Christian concepts, except in the broadest sense, in the profusion of themes depicted on the external facades, the interior rooms abound with biblical and religious episodes, albeit ones mixed at times with allegories and pagan myths (plates 83–85). The frescoes executed between 1561 and 1563 by Taddeo Zuccari, Santi di Tito, Federico Barocci, and Giovanni Schiavone, alongside elaborate stucco work, range from scenes of the Creation in the vestibule vault to a series of *sacre conversazioni* (Sacred Conversations) scenes in another section of the same vault to a depiction of the doctors of the Church, a religious repertory that culminated in the chapel with eight apostles and allegories of the Church and Peace. However, in counterpoint to the dominant religious themes, ancient sculptures were positioned all around, and an Ephesian Diana, executed with the skilled use of yellow river stones, was exhibited in the Casina's vestibule under the frescoed vault.

The ongoing changes that had, as we have seen, given the Casina a double, ambivalent character had also, necessarily, affected the life and habits of the pope and his entourage. Indeed, the pope's nephew, Carlo Borromeo, made cardinal by his uncle, had been at first the epitome of the hedonistic prince devoted to refined banquets and hunting expeditions, but was quickly forced to make such radical changes to his way of life that he would later attain sanctification.[30] Initially, the Casina in the woods represented for the young cardinal an ideal place to hold the cultured, jovial symposia of the academy he had founded in 1562: the *Noctes Vaticanae*, which brought together Cardinal Ugo Boncompagni (the future Pope Gregory XIII, 1572–85), Cardinal Tolomeo Gallio, and many other eminent figures united by a passion for secular literature and philosophy.[31] But in the

83. (*opposite, top*) Federico Barocci, *The Samaritan at the Well*, c. 1563, fresco on the vault of the Sala della Sacra Conversazione.

84. (*opposite, bottom*) Federico Barocci, *The Baptism of Christ*, c. 1563, fresco on the vault of the Sala della Sacra Conversazione.

wake of explicit criticism of his hedonistic and not particularly Christian way of life, the cardinal soon abandoned the customs and habits of a secular prince to become an active and resolute champion of the reformed church, obviously in close harmony with his uncle, the pope.

In this moralizing process, many of the pagan symbols of the Casina were redirected to Christian ends, in accordance with the idea that "everyone can be drawn to glory by our Savior."[32] This is the case, for example, with the water-related symbolism, which could refer to the pagan myths of the sea gods and the ancient naumachies but also to the baptism's power of salvation. This coexistence of meanings characterizes the complex as the last example of harmony between humanistic classicism and Christian spirit. Despite the intention to "moralize" the myth by placing it next to Christian iconography,[33] the result is a progression from the dominant "paganism" of the external decorations to the triumph of religion in the interiors. It marks the transition from the cultivated, pleasure-seeking, and carefree paganism of the Renaissance to the rigorous and severe Counter-Reformation culture that would be ardently affirmed by Pius v (1566–72), successor to Pius iv (1559–65), who immediately had the Casina stripped of those symbols that contrasted most obviously with the new religious climate.

Beginning in 1560, Pirro Ligorio acquired fifty ancient sculptures for the complex, which he installed here and there in no discernible order; very few remain today. An inventory from 1566 provides the precise number and, more importantly, the subjects of the statues, among them many depictions of Mnemosyne, the Muses, Diana, and Health. We know that by 1569, Pius v had begun to remove those that were clearly pagan, sending twenty-six of them to the Grand Duke of Tuscany, Francesco i.[34] Ligorio was forced to witness this pillaging of his creation, as he recounted in a discourse in which he stresses the relationship between the *coenationes* (conviviality) of the Imperial villas evoked in his architecture and that of the Casina of Pius iv: "It is not even inopportune [in this discourse] to mention that the statue of Mnemosyne, mother of the Muses, was found in the dining area of Hadrian's villa in Tibur, with a lyre atop her head, huge breasts, and a finely pleated tippet below. It was brought to Rome and dedicated by Pope Pius iv in the Vatican nymphaeum, and donated by Pope Pius v to others, as he wished to strip the site made by Pius iv, and begun by Pope Paul iv."[35] And in a passage from another

85. Federico Barocci, *Sacred Conversation*, c. 1563, fresco at the center of the vault of the Sala della Sacra Conversazione.

of his writings, Ligorio defended his creation with pride, lamenting the systematic dismantling under way: "Of the Casina in the Woods of the Sacred Palace…we took care in its design, and in its construction and decoration, which I happily agree to show as an antique model to curious men who love to see things from the past. But Pope Pius v of his own accord stripped every ornament from the ancient works."[36] The new pope's censorship of his predecessor's actions continued still further with the immediate dismissal of Pirro Ligorio from his position as papal architect.[37]

While still at work on the Casina, in 1562 Ligorio took on another demanding job: the definitive stabilization of the Cortile del Belvedere. First he further embellished Bramante's loggias by creating a corridor of statues, an extension of the Cortile del Belvedere that accentuated the museum-like character of the complex. Then he completed the northern end of the Cortile, which culminated

in a three-story exedra, by constructing a monumental niche. Finally, he added to the exedra an apsidal basin surmounted by a semicircular aerial loggia, completing the Cortile in dramatic fashion. At its southern end, by contrast, he introduced a kind of amphitheater with wide stone steps to accentuate the "theatrical" nature of the site. The result was impressive, as it struck an excellent compromise between the rigor and austerity of Bramante's original design and the elegance and attention to detail of Ligorio's additions.[38]

It is probable that the completion of these two very different, but complementary, projects—the retreat in the woods and the public site par excellence—spurred the

86. Giuseppe Vasi, *Papal Garden and Casina in the Vatican*, etching from *Delle magnificenze di Roma antica e moderna*, 1747–61.

pope to hold the spectacular tournament of 1565, which was celebrated in the chronicles of the day and immortalized in paintings and etchings. Discussing his etchings of the tournament, Antonio Lafrery commented on Ligorio's modifications, which had "transformed [the Cortile] into a Theater," such that "it is judged one of the most beautiful and noteworthy things done since ancient times, and one can call it the Atrium of Pleasure, which for any kind of celebration can easily accommodate 60,000 persons."[39]

The Giardino dei Semplici

It has been said that the Casina of Pius IV was conceived as architecture removed from the garden, with no relationship between the exterior and interior spaces (plate 86). However, in the area just in front of the Casina, and more

precisely between the loggia and Bramante's corridor, there was a spectacular garden that united beauty of design with a scientific concern unequaled in Rome at the time (plates 87, 88).

We know that by the Middle Ages, *semplici*, or medicinal plants, were cultivated for curative and scientific reasons within the confines of the Vatican Citadel. Beginning in the thirteenth century the entourage of the popes included the *simpliciarius*, who cared for these plants and was a figure quite distinct from the generic gardener or vegetable gardener, in that his job was scientific in all respects. A quintessential example is Simone of Genoa, who, in the service of Nicholas IV (1288–92) and his successors, distinguished himself through his scientific writings on

87. Francesco Piranesi, *View of the Belvedere in the Vatican*, late eighteenth century, etching.

medicinal plants.[40] Very often the role of *simpliciarius pontificius* coincided with a university position, such as botany professor, which was also awarded by the pope.[41] Rome was the first city to have a chair in botany; in his 1513 reformation of the University, in fact, Leo x instituted the chair "ad declarationem Simplicium medicinae" (for the teaching of medical simples, i.e., medical botany).[42] Yet the first report of the existence of a true Giardino dei Semplici, based on scientific criteria but also intended as a collection of rare and exotic plants,[43] dates to 1561, during the papacy of Pius iv, when Giacomo Boni of Ferrara "administered, under Pius iv, the Chair of Botany and the botanical garden."[44] Clearly, the two roles of teacher and curator of the garden are here combined, confirming the necessity of an approach to study that was closely tied to direct observation and experimentation in the field.

Pius v subsequently conferred this position on an exceptional personality: the eminent doctor and naturalist Michele Mercati (1541–1593), who, in a dedication to Gregory xiii of his small volume on plague remedies, wrote: "among the many graces, and favors, that I have received from Our Father, I was most content when Your Holiness confirmed me to care for the conservation and growth of the garden of *semplici*, because of the great desire that has always been in me to attain with effort and facility the acquisition of true knowledge of the qualities and virtues of many herbs."[45] The use of the term *confirmed* makes clear that his nomination to the post was made by the preceding pope, that is, Pius v.[46] In addition to his book on plagues, Mercati wrote another volume—titled *Metallotheca* and published in 1717 by Giovanni Maria Lancisi, a doctor—about the plan for a mineralogical museum he created, as well as a book on the obelisks of Rome, in which he writes of having created the Giardino dei Semplici in the Vatican.[47] Overall, references in his writings to his role at the Vatican are extremely brief and superficial, so in order to reconstruct the history of the garden he oversaw, it has been necessary to draw on a variety of sources.[48]

Mercati had come to Rome from San Miniato at the suggestion of Andrea Cesalpino,[49] who was his teacher in Pisa and considered him *discipulum praeclarissimum* (a most outstanding student). When he came to work at the Vatican, presumably in about 1570, he was still young but not in good health, as he complains in several letters that constitute valuable sources of information. Everything we know about his work to create and manage the Giardino dei Semplici in the Vatican comes from his correspondence with Ulisse Aldrovandi, particularly that dated between 1571

88. R. Wilkinson, *The Casina of Pius iv and the Gardens*, late eighteenth century, etching with watercolor.

and 1573, which documents not only his botanical experience and knowledge but also his relationships with authorities in the field. Herein we have proof that the enthusiastic exchanges of flower species considered typical of the following century were already widespread in the sixteenth.[50] Mercati's correspondence with Aldrovandi,[51] a renowned naturalist and a professor at the University of Bologna, confirms that the two men were close friends and that they frequently exchanged plants and seeds. In their letters, which, oddly, have received little attention or study, are numerous useful bits of information about the history of the Vatican Gardens, particularly about the size and organization of the Giardino dei Semplici. Aldrovandi's papers contain a very interesting list of the seeds he sent to Mercati in November 1570, which were evidently intended for the Giardino dei Semplici in the Vatican. In turn, Mercati had the plants that Aldrovandi desired sent to Bologna. In one of Aldrovandi's letters there is a reference to an exchange of catalogues of the "rarest plants" that existed in their respective gardens, which allowed them to compare and verify the holdings of each garden. Mercati lamented the loss of some valuable specimens in the Vatican Gardens due to the excessive Roman heat. Even more fascinating is a letter from November 1571, in which Mercati cites some plants he received from Aldrovandi, among these "rhodium-wood" (*Convulvulus scoparius* and *Convulvulus floridus*) and "dittany" (*Origanum dictamnus*) (plate 93), reciprocated with specimens of "alpine avens" (*Geum montanum*), "thyme-leaved savory" (*Thymus tragoriganum*), "golden samphire" (*Imula crithmoides*), "flax-leaved daphne" (*Daphne gnidium*), and "chamalea" (*Chamalea sive mezereum*).

From another letter we learn that Mercati cultivated some 470 varieties of plants in the Vatican Gardens, a truly impressive number for the time and proof that this was a full-fledged botanical garden,[52] stocked with plants cultivated for decoration and pleasure, not just for medicinal use and scientific analysis. Even more important information to be found in these epistolary exchanges concerns the contact that the pope had with other monarchs, in Europe and elsewhere, regarding the exchange of valuable plants, evidently through nuncios with seats in the various countries. At the beginning of 1572, the apostolic nuncio in Portugal sent to Rome some 160 specimens of extremely rare plants and flowers (probably from the Americas), which Mercati of course promised to share with his Bolognese friend. Mercati also writes of the passion for flowers cherished by Philip II, the king of Spain,[53] who had sent "a doctor to the Indies [the Americas]…expressly to bring back the rarest things"[54] to enrich his botanical garden, and who had also promised to send some to the pope, pleased that His Holiness delighted "in this subject of the plants." Mercati writes further that "living plants" were sent in two crates, with soil, from Barcelona, while two banana plants (*Musa paradisiaca*) arrived in Rome from Alexandria, Egypt, by way of Sicily, but in the city's cold climate did not take root. In a letter from May 1573, he informs Aldrovandi that he has sent to Bologna many "spleenwort fern" (*Asplenium hemionitis*) plants and a "garland-flower daphne" (*Daphnae cneorum*), and promises to send others as soon as the weather permits him to "go out and ride" to gather new exemplars. The lists of plants attached to the letters are also of great interest. They include many medicinal plants, but also many decorative species, including varieties from the Americas that were exceedingly rare at the time. Cited, for example, are exemplars of "Indian shot" (*Canna indica*) from South America; "nicotiana" (*Nicotiana tabacum*), a flower from the tobacco family (plate 91); "sunchoke" (*Helianthus tuberosus*), a plant similar to the sunflower (plate 90); "tomato" (*Solanum lycopersicum*); and "piper indicum" (*Capsicum annuum*), that is, peppers (plate 92)—all plants that came from across the ocean. Other species that appear on the lists include *argemoni*, similar to anemones (perhaps a Mexican variety), and tulips, an indication of the proliferation of those bulbs, which would become extremely popular a few decades later.[55] Many plants also came from Asian countries, including "hare's ear root" (*Bupleurum falcatum*), one of the most commonly used herbs in Chinese medicine, while "aloe" (*Aloe barbadensis* or *Aloe vera*) came from Africa.[56]

As has been mentioned, these documents are of great interest insofar as they help us reconstruct the appearance of the Giardino dei Semplici in the Vatican. They confirm that in addition to a rich collection of medicinal plants, the garden contained many rare and exotic specimens from the "Indies," both western and eastern, well in advance of those seventeenth-century collections that have had much more resonance and critical attention. Pius V, it seems, was particularly fond of the Giardino dei Semplici and appreciated Mercati's work there, as an order by Cardinal Michele Bonelli of March 10, 1571, attests: "To all the guards and others in the area, and to Portiano, not to disturb, but rather to assist Monsignor Michele Mercati, *semplicista* of our Lordship, who goes out to obtain supplies of medicinal plants and extract them from various places."[57] Pius V's

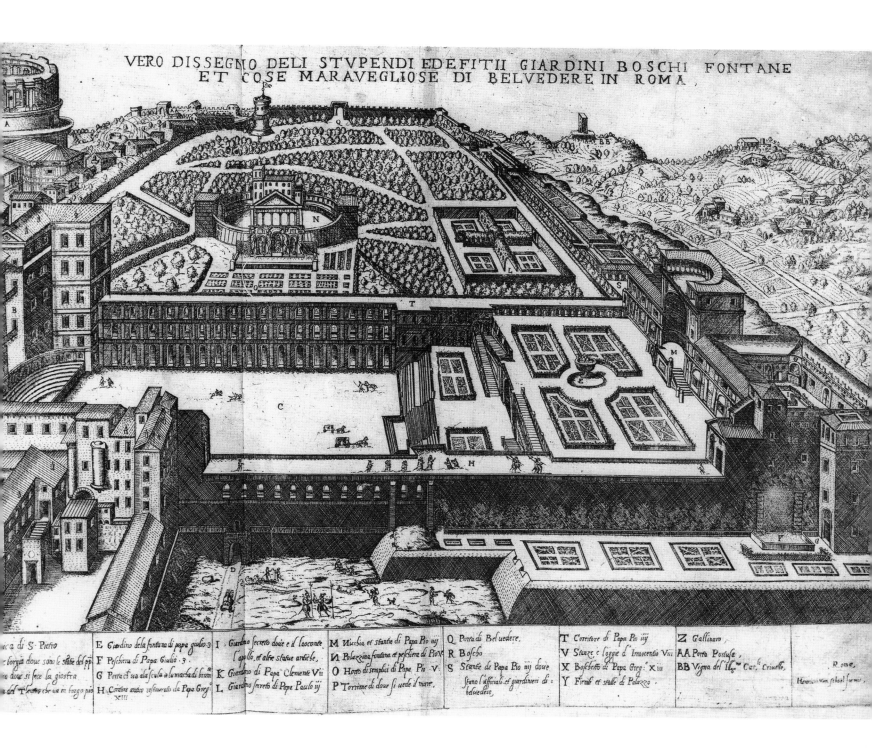

89. Mario Cartaro, *True Rendering of the Stupendous Buildings,
Gardens, Groves, Fountains, and Marvelous Things of the
Belvedere in Rome*, 1574, etching.

90. Sunflower (*Helianthus annuus L.*), *Erbario Aldrovandi*, Biblioteca Università di Bologna (BUB).

Helianthus annuus L.
l. c. 69. p. 228

Helianthus annuus L.
l. c. 75. p. 229

91. "Nicotiana" or tobacco (*Nicotiana tabacum L.*), *Erbario Aldrovandi*, BUB.

92. Pepper (*Capsicum annuum L.*), *Erbario Aldrovandi*, BUB.

Capsicum annuum *L.*
n. c. 48. p. 243

93. "Dittany" (*Dictamnus albus L.*), *Erbario Aldrovandi*, BUB.

Dictamnus albus L.
II, c. 258, p. 238

interest in botany and gardening is not surprising, as it was, at the time, commonly considered to be an "honest pleasure" particularly befitting representatives of the Catholic church. (The inevitable analogy was drawn between the gardener who cultivates flowers and the church pastor who cultivates souls.) He was a model of the virtuous, rigorous pope, removed from the tumult of the mundane, and a true exponent of the severe, Counter-Reformation culture that had by then replaced Renaissance hedonism.

To locate the Giardino dei Semplici within the Vatican citadel, we refer again to the 1574 view (plate 89) by Mario Cartaro—*True Rendering of the Stupendous Buildings, Gardens, Groves, Fountains, and Marvelous Things of the Belvedere in Rome*—the legend of which reads, under the letter O: "Herb garden of Pope Pius v." Thus Cartaro confirms, as does Mercati, the attribution of the garden's founding to the pope while giving us a precise indication of its location, which would remain unchanged until the eighteenth century, albeit with a different layout. Before the construction of the Casina of Pius iv, this site contained a wooded area that stretched to the limits of Bramante's loggias, as can be seen in the 1557 plan (plate 94) by Francesco Paciotti, which immediately precedes the transformation of the site. After the Casina was completed, Pius iv did not turn his attention to the reorganization of the surrounding green

area because his work was interrupted by his unexpected death in 1565, just before the abovementioned tournament in the Cortile del Belvedere was held to celebrate completion of the architectural work.

We can therefore suppose that the Casina stood in the midst of an unorganized space. Behind it lay the small wood that crested the hill and in front, in the direction of the Cortile del Belvedere, a flatter area of no particular distinction. As Mercati affirms, Pius v loved the gardens because he perceived them as an occupation befitting his status,[58] and so it seems plausible that he decided to impose a formal organization on the space in front of the Casina used for cultivating herbs and rare, exotic plants. Pius iv's 1561 appointment of the Ferrararese Giacomo Boni as *simpliciarius pontificius* was in keeping with medieval tradition and does not prove that he was responsible for the layout of the garden in front of the Casina, since, in that year, construction of the complex was still under way.

94. (*below left*) Francesco Paciotti, *Plan of Rome*, 1557, detail with the area of the Vatican, before the construction of the Casina of Pius iv.

95. (*below right*) Étienne Dupérac, *Plan of Rome*, 1577, detail with the area of the Vatican.

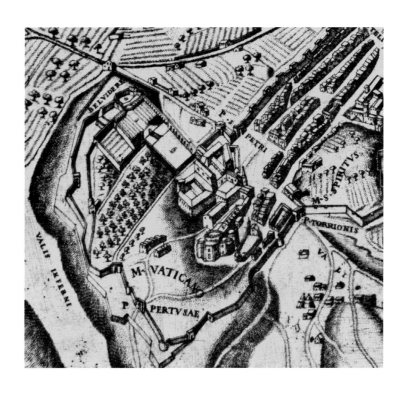

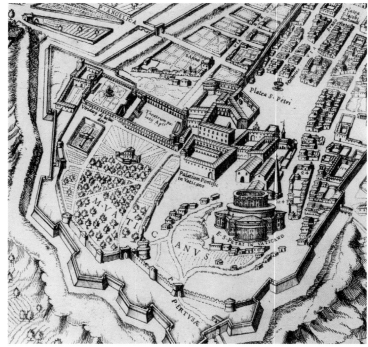

In Cartaro's plan the garden, visible only in the part nearest the Casina, is divided into a series of rectangular beds arranged in rows, and is located between the large fish pond and the walls of Bramante's loggias. In later views, such as those by Étienne Dupérac of 1577 (plate 95), Antonio Tempesta of 1590 (plate 96), and Giovanni Maggi of 1615 (plate 97), the beds are arranged more elaborately, in rectangles divided internally into four other beds with a fifth, circular bed in the center. Furthermore, whereas in Cartaro's plan it seems that only low plants were cultivated—probably flowers or medicinal herbs—the later depictions show small trees at the center of the beds. These were probably citrus fruit or other fruit trees, as was common at the time. Only in Maggi's plan of 1615 does the Giardino dei Semplici appear larger, extending to the area between the Casina of Pius IV and the Sacramental Fountain. Three large rectangles with geometric divisions are designated "Hortus herbarum salubrium" (a garden of salutary herbs). This enlargement was due, in all probability, to the later modifications made by Johannes Faber.

Michele Mercati cared for the Giardino dei Semplici until 1587, when, still young, he left the job, perhaps because of the precarious state of his health, which led to his death in 1593 at just over fifty years of age. For several years he was succeeded by Castore Durante, author of *Herbario Nuovo*,

published in Rome in 1585,[59] and from 1590 until 1600 by Andrea Bacci,[60] who was known for having published a useful tract on the medicinal properties of herbs.[61] Mercati, in any case, deserves credit for having organized the Giardino dei Semplici, which certainly existed in the preceding centuries but had no definite layout or stable location. After Mercati, the Giardino dei Semplici was always situated near the Casina of Pius IV, and despite the modifications introduced by his successors, it remained a distinguishing element in the history of the Vatican Gardens until at least the mid-seventeenth century, contributing to the development of botanical studies in close connection with university teaching.

We have no indication that Pius V's successors took an active interest in the Vatican Gardens. It seems they preferred to spend their leisure time in the summer months in

96. (*below left*) Antonio Tempesta, *Plan of Rome*, 1590, detail with the area of the Vatican.

97. (*below right*) Giovanni Maggi, *The Vatican Temple of St. Peter, Most Famous in the Entire World: Accurately Delineated, Together with Adjoining Papal Quarters and Gardens; All of Which Pope Paul V Has Expanded and Decorated in Many Parts*, 1615, etching, detail with the Casina of Pius IV and the Giardino dei Semplici.

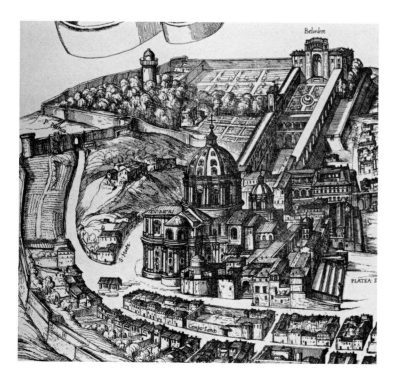

their suburban villas. Gregory XIII (1572–85) was among the first to favor Frascati, where Cardinal Altemps had built a splendid villa called, in the pope's honor, Mondragone,[62] an obvious allusion to the heraldic dragon of the Boncompagni family. Sixtus V (1585–90) adored, in addition to his estate at Torre in Pietra,[63] his splendid Villa Montalto,[64] built when he was still a cardinal and residing in a vast area near the Basilica of Santa Maria Maggiore. According to contemporary chronicles, he enjoyed spending his free time caring personally for the family garden. He also resided often at the Quirinal, rather than in the traditional Vatican residence.[65]

The project for which Sixtus V is best remembered, in conjunction with the Vatican Gardens, has nothing to do with botany. Rather, he commissioned the construction of the magnificent Vatican Library, designed by Domenico Fontana and built in the Cortile del Belvedere.[66] Although unanimously recognized as a splendid work both for its architecture and its pictorial decorations, the library was subjected—by Pope Paul V (1605–21),[67] for example—to criticism and even to plans for demolition because it substantially altered the spatial configuration of the Cortile del Belvedere. The plan for the library's construction, begun by Gregory XIII and resumed and modified by Sixtus V, was published in an *Avviso* (Announcement) of May 13, 1587: "The dismantling of the stairs of the Theater of Pius IV at the Belvedere has begun and on that site rooms for the Library of the Vatican will be built."[68] The decision was not well received, particularly in learned circles, as a letter of May 30, 1587, from Attilio Malegnani, agent of the duchy of Mantua, attests: "His Holiness has dismantled the stairway commissioned by Pius IV…and the fact that he has ruined this Theater built at great expense has displeased the entire court, especially because he has ruined the view and the Belvedere, and in particular [the view] of the creations of Pius IV."[69] Built across the courtyard in a position corresponding to the ramp between the first and second terraces, the library effectively took the place of the theatrical exedra-proscenium, interrupting the visual unity of the courtyard and destroying the essence of Bramante's project,

which was based on the idea of combining three different functions—theater, garden, and museum—in an open, continuous space articulated with architectural elements that served as partitions.

During the brief papacy of Gregory XIV (1590–91), we have evidence only of some maintenance work on the fountains. A certain "Valerio, gardener," is cited, as are the woods and the Giardino dei Semplici, which continued to be cared for and maintained.[70]

Clement VIII Aldobrandini (1592–1605) was very fond of the villas commissioned by his nephew, Cardinal Pietro: the first, in the city, was near the Quirinal residence that Gregory XIII had begun building and using; the second, a grandiose villa in Frascati, was completed just months before his death.[71] In any case, during his papacy the Vatican gardens and fountains were not neglected. Payments show constant attention to the irrigation of the plants and maintenance of the water conduits; to the espaliers of citrons and bitter oranges, whose crosspieces and joists were replaced; and to the protective coverings that were carefully repaired after removal in order to be ready for use the following winter.[72] Mention of repair work to a trellis allows us to presume that at the time the lovely pergola structure in the Secret Garden of Paul III was still extant and being used. Additional maintenance work or modifications involved the buildings, such as the Casina of Pius IV—referred to as the "Palazzina del Buschetto"—where "stucco work" was done, while the sculptor Taddeo Landini repaired an unspecified fountain. The payment orders also show that the garden was put to productive use, as it contained a hen house, an aviary, a rabbit hutch, and a courtyard with capons. From the mention of a roe deer that had fallen into a well, we can deduce that there were free-roaming animals in the woods, as was also the case at Villa Borghese, in the area appropriately called Parco dei Daini, or Deer Park. Finally, it must be recalled that it was Clement VIII who wanted Johannes Faber, recently arrived from Bamberg, to take charge of the Vatican Gardens, thus opening a new chapter of great significance not only for the history of the site, but also for the history of botany in general.

98. The Vatican Library.

1. St. Peter's Basilica completed under Paul v
17. New wing of the Vatican Palaces

i. Fontana del Forno
j. Fontana delle Torri
k. Fontana dell'Aquilone
l. Fontana degli Specchi

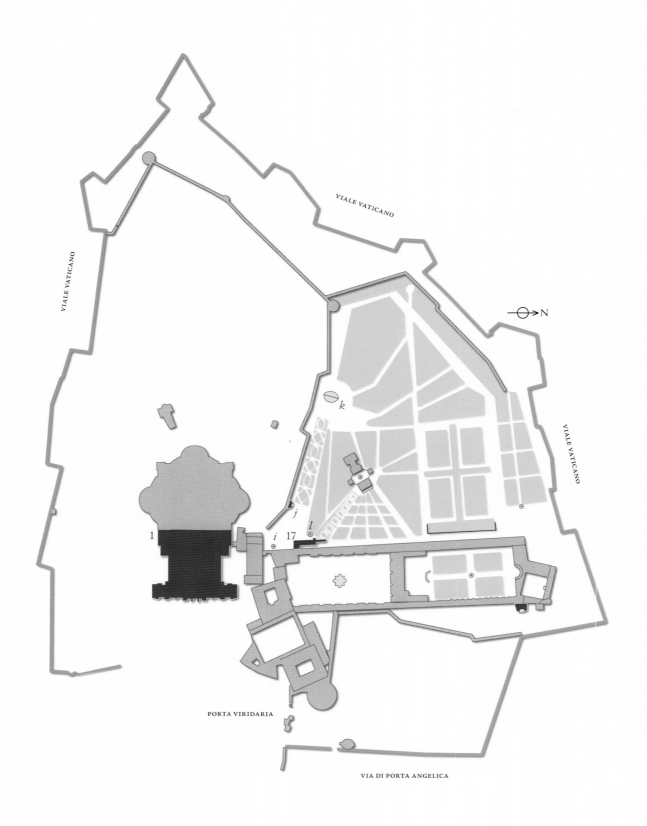

VIALE VATICANO

VIALE VATICANO

N

VIALE VATICANO

k

j

i 17

l

1

PORTA VIRIDARIA

VIA DI PORTA ANGELICA

Modifications undertaken during the period discussed in this chapter are indicated in the map and captions above. For a complete map of the Vatican City and its major features in their present-day form, see page 2. Numbers in the map and captions refer to buildings and gardens, while letters refer to fountains.

THE FIRST DECADES OF THE SEVENTEENTH CENTURY: THE FOUNTAINS OF PAUL V (1605–21) AND JOHANNES FABER, "GARDENER" EXTRAORDINAIRE

The first decades of the seventeenth century were extremely important for the Vatican Gardens, from both the architectural and botanical (plate 100) points of view. The construction of the Acqua Paola, along with the related addition of some splendid fountains at the behest of Pope Paul v, led to substantial changes in the paths and perspectives near the palaces and the Basilica. Untouched for centuries, this area was wooded and had no particular design or organization. At the same time, having so prestigious a figure as Johannes Faber as curator placed the Gardens at the center of the vast network of exchanges among enthusiasts and collectors of rare and exotic flowers taking place throughout Europe.[1] And with the introduction of splendid, valuable exemplars, the Gardens became a destination for admiring visitors, on a par with the sculpture collections and works of art.

The Papacy of Paul v Borghese:
The Construction of the Acqua Paola and the New Fountains

Pope Paul v Borghese, over the course of his lengthy pontificate, left important evidence of the passion for art that he shared with his cardinal-nephew, Scipione Caffarelli Borghese. Besides having overseen the completion of the facade of St. Peter's Basilica, he was responsible for substantial changes to a sector of the Vatican Gardens into which his predecessors had never ventured—that is, the area nearest the Palaces and the Basilica itself, where the original gardens had been located before the construction of the Palazzetto of Innocent VIII. His interest in gardens was not limited to the Vatican, however, and he played a major role in other important commissions of the time. For instance, he can be credited with substantial modifications to, and the creation of numerous fountains in, the Quirinal gardens.[2] Through the cardinal-nephew, he ordered the construction of the Villa Borghese di Porta Pinciana (plate 99),[3] status symbol of the family, and various villa residences in Frascati, a true Borghese city.[4] Paul v spent a good deal of time in all of them, and in the summer months Frascati was transformed into a little Rome, the

99. (*below*) Heinz the Younger, *Villa Borghese*, 1625, oil on canvas. Collection of Prince Scipione Borghese.

100. (*opposite*) Garden with rocaille.

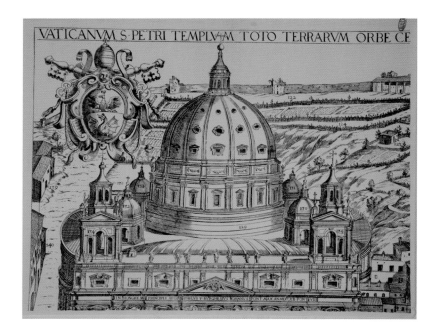

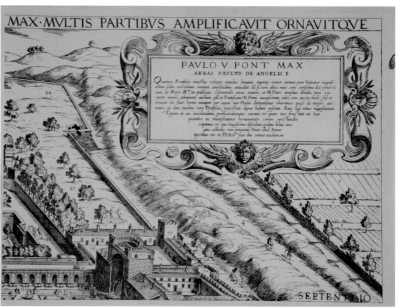
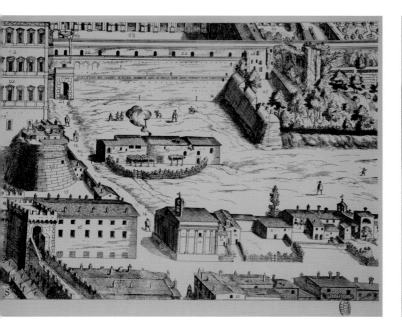
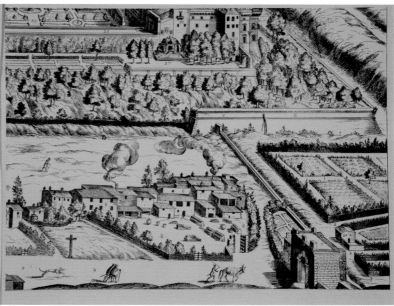

101. Giovanni Maggi, *The Vatican Temple of St. Peter*, 1615.

venue for important visitors and spectacular entertainments for the court, which was installed there.

The pope's decision to move the central axis of the Vatican Gardens from the Belvedere to the area of the palaces and the Basilica was followed immediately by the addition of a new wing to the oldest nucleus of the residential buildings. It included a staircase that created an autonomous and direct link to the gardens below, or "through which there is easy access from the Pope's innermost chamber into the lowest gardens," as one writer described.[5] The entrance and the staircase were built between 1607 and 1608, as confirmed by some payments to the stonemasons Arminio De Giudici and Francesco De Rossi for "work on the stairs in peperino that lead from the pope's rooms to the Belvedere gardens."[6] They are still visible today, with an inscription on the portal commemorating the pope, near the small, unusual Fontana degli Specchi and in the direction of the grandiose Fontana delle Torri, or Fontana del Sacramento, at the head of the path that leads visitors past the creations Paul V commissioned.

The projects credited to the Borghese pope in the Vatican are recorded in both documentary and iconographic sources. In addition to the multitude of payments conserved in the archives of Rome,[7] which allow us to trace all phases of the work, there is a reliable biography written three years after the pope's death,[8] as well as many etchings that illustrate the completed fountains. Essential to understanding the appearance of the Vatican citadel around 1615, after the pope's building program had largely been fulfilled, is the large view (plate 101) by Giovanni Maggi, published by Giacomo Mascardi and titled *The Vatican Temple of St. Peter, Most Famous in the Entire World: Accurately Delineated, Together with the Adjoining Papal Quarters and Gardens; All of Which Pope Paul V Has Expanded and Decorated in Many Parts*.[9] In it, the entire expanse of the citadel, from the Basilica to the Belvedere, is illustrated with great precision and attention to detail. The salient sites are marked with numbers corresponding to a legend that describes them and their functions clearly.[10] The Basilica, visible in the foreground, shows the finally completed facade with its inscription celebrating the pope's achievement. Also clearly visible are the buildings at either end of the courtyard—the two nuclei of the palaces annexed to the Basilica itself and the Belvedere complex—and the green areas within the boundary wall are meticulously rendered, showing geometric beds alternating with more natural groves and areas cultivated with vines or vegetables. The demarcation line between the ornamental gardens—that is, the

beds and groves—and the *pars rustica* (rustic part) cultivated for productive purposes follows the course of the Leonine Wall, with the towers of Nicholas III and Nicholas IV and some service buildings, including a warehouse and a hay barn, attached to it.

An essential condition for implementing Paul V's grand program to beautify the Vatican Gardens was an adequate water supply. The capacity of the Acqua Felice, built under Sixtus V, was not sufficient to feed the spectacular monumental fountains, complete with surprising and playful jets of water, that represented the ideal backdrop for scenographic perspectives, according to the Baroque taste of the day. Thus the pope's first undertaking for the improvement of the gardens was to pipe in abundant water, which he did by diverting a branch of the city's water source, the Acquedotto Paolino, to the showy spectacle of the Fontanone del Gianicolo.[11] This accomplishment was described as follows by the biographer Bzovius: "By means of the conduits of the Acqua Alsietina [actually the Acqua Traiana], originally built by Augustus, almost destroyed and then restored by Pope Adrian I but then again reduced to ruins because of age, Paul V, with work underground and on the arched course made according to the plan of Martino Ferrabosco, the greatest hydraulic engineer who ever lived in Europe, restored those conduits and took water from the lake, the Bracciano territory, and other most salubrious sources, bringing it to Rome along a course of 35 miles, adding other mains [along the way]...the gardens, made more agreeable with fountains and fish ponds built here and there and with a magnificent view, distribut[ed] the water brought from the Bracciano territory extensively, at great expense."[12]

The name of Martino Ferrabosco, defined by Bzovius as an *aquilegius*, literally "plumber," occurs often in the archival documents pertaining to the fountains in the Vatican Gardens, next to those of other well-known personalities who worked for the Borghese family—among them Flaminio Ponzio, replaced at his death in 1613 by Giovanni Vasanzio; Carlo Maderno; Giovanni Fontana; and Giulio Buratti—making it difficult to establish each man's role with certainty. It is not clear, at the present stage of research, whether Ferrabosco was involved only with the execution of the conduits and maintenance of the fountains, or with their design as well, nor is the scope of his position as "superintendent of the fountains of Borgo and of Belvedere" well defined.[13]

102. Bronze Pigna (Pinecone) within the Nicchione.

The first years of Paul v's papacy saw a whirlwind of activity in the gardens as new conduits were laid and existing ones repaired or modified. A legion of workers, including tinsmiths, masons, and diggers, were busy under the direction of Flaminio Ponzio, designated "Architect of His Holiness and of the Palace."[14] On November 4, 1609, work was nearly finished, and in the *Avvisi di Roma* this comment was published: "Monday after lunch His Holiness went to the little house of Pius v, where he was shown, near the site called the Crucifix, a test of the Acqua Pavolina, which is brought here from the Bracciano, and which will be finished in spring; and various drawings were made of the monumental fountains that they want to create."[15] The project proposed substantial innovations made possible by the supply of water from the Acqua Paola, but also foresaw the upgrading and repair of the existing network. In a kind of ideal evocation, the water mains laid during the papacy of Julius II would be reactivated and Bramante's walls strengthened and cleared of the fig and ivy plants that had overrun them.[16]

One of the first modifications commissioned by Paul v, dated near the beginning of his papacy in 1606, aimed to impart even greater dignity to the upper part of the Cortile del Belvedere. To embellish Bramante's Nicchione, completed by Pirro Ligorio, the pope installed the splendid bronze Pigna, or pinecone (plate 102)—previously sited in the quadriporticus of the Basilica of Constantine—flanked by two bronze peacocks and set on a finely carved marble base. The Pigna, from which the Cortile derived its name (still in use today), was transformed into a fountain and relocated: "Under Pope Paul v, in order to erect the facade of the church, the aforementioned pinecone was moved from its location and transferred to the Vatican gardens."[17] It is said that Paul v also intended to tear down the library built by Sixtus v, which had disrupted the unity of Donato Bramante's plan for the Cortile del Belvedere. An *Avviso di Roma*, in fact, reported the popular belief that, at the pope's will, "the Vatican Library will be torn down, and the site where books are now held will be given over to fountains, scenic views, and other beautiful things in the Theater of Pius IV."[18] This was, evidently, only conjecture, as the library remained where it had been built. However, the pope's desire to restore the original spacial configuration of Bramante's design is confirmed by the completion of the niche in the double-ramped staircase abutting the terrace between the first and second Belvedere courtyards. The niche, which in drawings documenting Bramante's project appears free of decorative elements, is depicted in a fine

1647 Domenico Parasacchi etching covered with tartars and mosaics, along with five small niches that contain eagles and dragons (Borghese family emblems) spouting jets of water. The apsidiole in the uppermost part of the niche, carved in the form of a double shell, held another eagle, and at the top of the arch a Borghese crest with symbols of the papacy confirmed the identity of the client. It is obvious that the embellishment of the niche, transformed into a splendid nymphaeum,[19] made sense only if positioned in a perspective that the limited space of the Cortile certainly did not afford, closed off as it was by the transverse wing of the Biblioteca Sistina (Sistine Library).

Another alteration made to return the Cortile to its original form involved restoring the lovely fountain (plate 103) that Bramante had placed on the lowest level (still called the Cortile del Belvedere) and that Pius IV had buried in order to convert the space into a theater. Paul v, capitalizing on the abundance of available water, decided, as his biographer recounts, to dig up "the biggest basin of Numidian marble that exists in Rome, which at one time Julius II had excavated from the ruins of the baths of Titus and Vespasian and placed on a base in the theater of the Vatican Palace; he [Paul v] brought it to light after forty years of burial, restored it, decorated the base, and, by placing it in the middle of a pool, made an admirable fountain that shoots water at least 20 cubits into the air with violent force. From the pool, the water erupts from four pipes, reaching the edges of the basin."[20]

This information is confirmed in numerous payment orders. In October 1608 work was under way "to cover with lead the bolts of the basin installed in the ground"; in June 1609 work was done on the "big basin" of the "fountain of the Theater"; in September lead pipes were laid down, again for the "fountain of the Theater"; and in December payment was made for "hollowing out openings for the fountain of the Belvedere."[21] Further confirmation comes from the previously cited view by Maggi, which contains the following phrase corresponding to the fountain: "Insignis magnae aquarum copiae Theatri fons cum scatabris a Paulo v" ("the fountain of the Theater, remarkable for its

103. (*opposite*) Mario Cretoni, *The Belvedere Fountain*, c. 1853, decoration on the armoires in the Gallery of Urban VIII. Vatican Library.

104. (*page 130*) Ranuccio Semprevivo and Cesare Rossetti (attributed), *The Belvedere Fountain*, c. 1610, fresco. Sala dei Paramenti Piemontesi, Quirinal Palace.

great abundance and jets of water, [was constructed] by Paul v"). The fountain's octagonal base, designed by Carlo Maderno, was decorated with travertine dragons and eagles—emblems of the house of Borghese—in keeping with the usual practice of "signing" the restoration, which is also documented by inscriptions recalling the difficult task.[22] At the time of Pius XI (1922–39) a smaller marble basin was placed atop the great antique basin, altering the fountain's proportions; fortunately it was removed in 1987, returning the fountain to its original harmony. [23]

The creation of the new fountains in the Vatican Gardens is celebrated in two fresco cycles illustrating the pope's undertakings. The first, recently identified in the Quirinal Palace, was painted between 1609 and 1610, perhaps by Ranuccio Semprevivo and Cesare Rossetti, in the Sala dei Paramenti Piemontesi, as it was named after the Savoyan modifications that concealed the previous decorations.[24] Among the rediscovered lunettes, set within elaborate frames decorated with putti and allegorical figures, the fountains of the Vatican Gardens appear next to larger structures. The first lunette contains the restored Fontana del Cortile del Belvedere (plate 104). The second shows the Fontana del Forno (oven) (plate 105), or Fontana della Panetteria (bakery), with its multilobed basin and three smaller, tiered basins, situated at the foot of the graded ramp that leads to the gardens. The third depicts the apartments that Paul v added to the Vatican Palaces next to the Fontana degli Specchi (mirrors) (plate 106); in the background is the Fontana delle Torri (towers), or Fontana del Sacramento (Sacrament), and in the foreground a simple

fountain with a large bottom basin and two smaller basins above, each supported by carved figures that are not clearly identifiable. A second cycle celebrating the works of Pope Paul V can be found in the Sala Paolina of the Vatican Library; it is attributed to Giovan Battista Ricci and dated 1611–12.[25] Two lunettes in this cycle are also devoted to the Vatican Gardens. Depicted in the first are four fountains, rendered with much perspective license. The Fontana delle Torri predominates. The Fontana degli Specchi is on the left and the Fontana dell'Aquilone (large eagle), or Fontana dello Scoglio (rock), on the right; in the foreground is a fountain (plate 107) that is no longer extant but closely resembles the one depicted in the Quirinal fresco, and can probably be identified as the one for which the sculptor Niccolò Cordier made a marble group with Neptune and

105. (*page 131*) Ranuccio Semprevivo and Cesare Rossetti (attributed), *The Apartments of Paul V, the Fontana degli Specchi, a Lost Fountain, and the Fontana delle Torri*, c. 1610, fresco. Sala dei Paramenti Piemontesi, Quirinal Palace.

106. (*opposite*) Ranuccio Semprevivo and Cesare Rossetti (attributed), *The Fontana del Forno*, c. 1610, fresco. Sala dei Paramenti Piemontesi, Quirinal Palace.

107. (*above*) Giovan Battista Ricci, *The Fontana del Forno*, c. 1612, fresco. Sale Paoline, Vatican Library.

108. (*overleaf*) Giovan Battista Ricci, *The Apartments of Paul V, the Fontana degli Specchi, a Lost Fountain, the Fontana delle Torri, and the Fontana dello Scoglio*, c. 1612, fresco. Sale Paoline, Vatican Library.

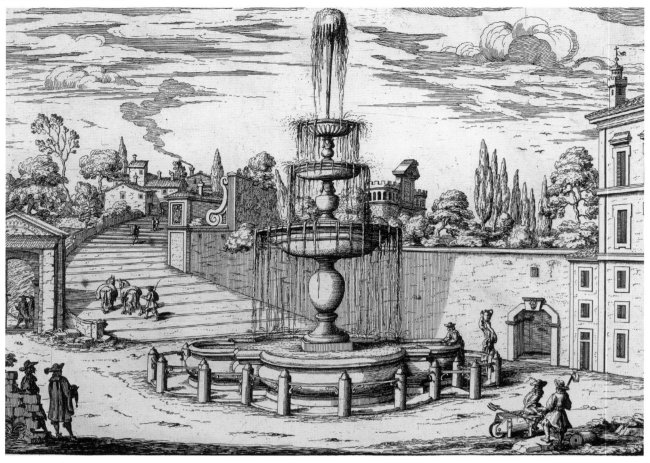

dragons.[26] The second view shows the Piazza del Forno (plate 108), or Piazza della Panetteria, with the eponymous fountain in the foreground, while in the background, partially hidden by the boundary wall of the buildings and staircase, is the upper tip of the Fontana delle Torri. To the right another project of Paul v is illustrated: the great avenue (still called the Viale dei Giardini) that links the palaces with the Belvedere, running on one side along Bramante's loggias and on the other along the gardens, in the direction of which a fine portal opens. The differences between the depictions in the two cycles are due almost exclusively to the few years that elapsed between them; at the time of the first the Fontana dello Scoglio had not been started and consequently could not appear in the fresco.

The first wholly new fountain constructed under Paul v, even before the channeling of the Acqua Paola was complete, was the one placed at the base of the graded ramp in the direction of the *panetteria* (bakery), also called the Piazza del Forno. Besides being represented in the frescoes in the Sala dei Parati Piemontesi of the Quirinal and the Sala Paolina of the Vatican Apostolic Library, this fountain was included in Domenico Parasacchi's and Giovan Battista Falda's (plate 109) respective volumes on the fountains of Rome, with an attribution by Falda to Carlo Maderno.[27] In all of the depictions it appears to be situated at the base of the new wing of the Vatican palace, in which the arch leading into the great Avenue of the Gardens opens up. It consists of a low, multilobed basin and three carved pillars, each supporting a basin of decreasing size. A powerful jet of water shoots up from the smallest basin at the top. Its construction, begun in March of 1608 with the preparation of conduits "for the new fountain that is being made for the

Piazza della Panetteria," continued in April with the installation of the "big basin" and in November with work to "fuse with molten lead the marble around the fountain opposite the bakery, that is, around the great basin,"[28] while in October two basins and two carved balustrades were acquired from the Oblate nuns in Tor de' Specchi. We can assume that these, too, were used in the composition of the fountain.[29] No payment document allows us to confirm the attribution of the project to Carlo Maderno, as proposed by Falda.

The fountain is still in place (plate 110), although it looks very different from its depiction in the fresco cycles and in the etchings by Parasacchi and Falda, as it is missing the two upper basins, which were removed at some indeterminate date. It is a model sixteenth-century fountain, with a classical, linear form and without the striving for wondrous effects typical of the incipient Baroque taste that would characterize the fountains Paul v built in the Vatican Gardens over the next few years.[30]

Many Roman fountains that survive today, and that date to the early seventeenth century or before, belong to this same type: for example, the one built at the Villa Borghese

109. (*opposite, top*) Giovan Battista Falda, *The Fontana del Forno*, c. 1676, etching.

110. (*opposite, bottom*) The Fontana del Forno.

111. (*below left*) Giovan Francesco Venturini, *Fontana Oscura at Villa Borghese*, 1684, etching.

112. (*below right*) Giovan Francesco Venturini, *Fontana della Vela at Villa Borghese*, 1684, etching.

for Cardinal Scipione, called Fontana Oscura (plate 111) for its placement in a shadowy grove and composed of a simple basin on the ground surmounted by two smaller basins; or the Fontana di Piazza Scossacavalli, now at Sant'Andrea della Valle; or the fountains in Piazza San Pietro.[31] Indeed, no extant examples of fountains that imitate a natural grotto predate the Fontana dello Scoglio in the Vatican and the Fontana della Vela (plate 112), or Fontana del Mascherone, in Villa Borghese,[32] both Borghese commissions begun in 1611. In reality, however, we have reliable evidence that even in Rome, starting in the first decades of the sixteenth century, spectacular fountains of a revolutionary type existed. An example of a fountain formed with tartars and rocaille, situated in the villa of Monsignor Giovanni Gaddi at Celio, is described by Annibal Caro in one of his letters,[33] in which he praises the invention of a cavern made with spongy tufa and set up in a "certain disorderly order," with cavities in which "herbs" were planted and water oozed everywhere. Even more detailed is Claudio Tolomei's description, in a letter of 1543, of the fountain in the Belluomo Garden, in which he praises the "ingenious artifice" of mixing art with nature such that it was impossible to distinguish one from the other.[34] This fountain was made of the spongy stone from Tivoli, the so-called "tartars" or calciferous incrustations "produced by the waters and returned to the service of the waters" with extraordinary hydraulic contrivances that, as Tolomei writes, "guide, separate, direct, beat, break, and cause the waters to rise and fall." Tolomei praises the

incredible effects of the water acrobatics, which surprised visitors with their unexpected jets, creating great entertainment; he also refers to the "music" produced by the waters, first resembling a light rain, then a downpour, as they spouted in jets or thin streams, trembling or bubbling up and evoking amazement. Unfortunately, neither of the fountains described survive, even in depictions that would help us better define their appearance and type.[35]

Yet the descriptions above could apply perfectly to the Fontana dello Scoglio (plates 113–19), built in the Vatican Gardens in an area previously occupied by woods or vineyards. In Maggi's aforementioned view the fountain is clearly reproduced, and the legend defines it as *Celeberrimus atque admirabilis magnae aquarum copiae fons rusticus* ("a rustic fountain most famous and marvelous for its great abundance of water"). Numerous payment orders attest to the execution of the work beginning in the autumn of 1611, with the participation of architects, sculptors, and stonemasons.[36] In October "large lead" conduits were laid down,

113. (*below*) Giovan Francesco Venturini, *Fountain Called "lo Scoglio" in the Belvedere Garden of the Papal Palace*, c. 1684, etching.

114. (*opposite*) Fontana dello Scoglio or dell'Aquilone, detail.

115. (*pages 140–41*) Fontana dello Scoglio or dell'Aquilone.

116–18. (*pages 142–45*) Fontana dello Scoglio or dell'Aquilone, detail.

attesting to the substantial quantity of water used for the "huge fountain with the water show in Belvedere," and including a conduit "that scoops up the forced water and takes it to the top of the rocks."[37] Meanwhile, blocks of travertine were taken from Campo Vaccino—that is, the Roman Forum—and used to sculpt decorative dolphins and putti for the basin.[38] A variety of craftsmen worked on the fountain: the sculptors Stefano Maderno and Santi Solaro made the putti and the dolphins, Carlo Fancelli was charged with carving the rocks and dragons,[39] the stucco workers Stefano Fuccaro and Dario Simone interceded numerous times to perfect the rocks,[40] and the architect Giulio Buratti signed the work reports.[41] The result was magnificent. The fountain, called dello Scoglio and also dell'Aquilone for the imposing heraldic eagle on top of it, was effectively a monumental display of the Acqua Paola—the foil, in rustic style, to the Fontanone del Gianicolo, where Paul v had triumphantly shown off his successful restoration of the aqueduct. The mountain of rocks that forms the grottoes and arches looms over a large basin, in which little putti and marine figures bathe as bubbling jets descend from sinuous recesses; water spurts from the mouths of dragons set in the niches and from the bugles of dolphin-riding tritons. The center is dominated by a complex and elaborate system of waterfalls located inside the largest grotto, which create a spectacular effect. The entire basin is surrounded by a course of water that descends and gurgles among the rocks, forming little waterfalls.

The type of the rustic fountain—of which the Fontana dello Scoglio, which also conformed to the model of a grotto-nymphaeum, is the most celebrated example—was adopted in the gardens of innumerable Roman villas throughout the entire seventeenth century and the centuries following. One need only think of the previously mentioned Fontana della Vela at Villa Borghese (destroyed at the end of the eighteenth century), or the Fontana del Diluvio and Fontana della Pioggia on the Quirinal, or the rustic fountains at Villa Mattei and Villa Pamphilj, which led to the great proliferation of fountains with rocaille in many gardens of the first decades of the twentieth century.[42]

The "great theater of rocks" rose at the end of an avenue originating at the palaces and was preceded along the route by another marvel: the Fontana delle Torri (plate 120), also called the Fontana del Sacramento for the configuration of its central jets of water, which resembles a monstrance. In this case as well, the architecture is, to say the least, original and unusual. The defensive structures of the Vatican citadel were transformed into a fountain with two towers crowned by battlements, flanking a rustic niche (plates 121, 122) topped by a pediment with the papal crest and the

119. (*opposite*) Fontana dello Scoglio or dell'Aquilone, detail with waterfall.

120. (*below*) Giovan Francesco Venturini, *Fontana delle Torri*, c. 1684, etching.

inscription: PAULUS V PONTIFEX MAXIMUS AD AUGENDUM PALATII PROSPECTUS ET HORTORUM DECOREM FIERI IUSSIT PONT. ANNO IV ("In the fourth year of his pontificate, Pope Paul V ordered that [this] be built so as to augment the view of the palace and the splendor of the gardens"). The Borghese family's heraldic emblems, dragons and eagles, reinforce the commissioner's identity, and the fountain clearly conveys the message of the power of the church led by Paul V. The recourse to turrets in the medieval mold has been interpreted by Federico Zeri as a sign of the neofeudal involution typical of Counter-Reformation art,[43] but the use of types garnered from other building models is common in many fountains of the period.

The first documents that refer unequivocally to the construction of this fountain date to September 1610, when the mason Battista Rossi is compensated for having "placed the turrets in the fountain in the gardens of the Belvedere." The

following year, in November, the dragons were placed on the summit and the conduits that bring the water "from the fish pond to the spray" were completed; finally, in the month of December, other conduits create the spouts "at the great fountain of the Turrets."[44] The names of other artisans do not appear, but it is probable that Martino Ferrabosco's contribution is included among the many generic payments for work on the Vatican fountains that follow, without interruption, from 1608 until 1619.[45] By the same token, Flaminio Ponzio and Carlo Maderno,[46] because they were salaried, are not cited for each and every

121. (*above*) The Fontana delle Torri or del Sacramento.

122. (*opposite*) Mario Cretoni, *The Fontana delle Torri*, c. 1854, decoration on the armoires of the Gallery of Urban VIII. Vatican Library.

job, but may well have participated in the project. Even less specific are the expenses for the channeling of the water; payments are made to tinsmiths and masons, who lay out and install pipes and reservoirs, without specific reference to one fountain or another.

After the great rustic spectacle that seemed to have borrowed its appearance from nature, and after the architectonic Fontana delle Torri, Paul v commissioned another amazing fountain. The Fontana della Galera (galley) (plates 123–27) was raised on the site where Julius III had earlier established a fish pond: at the back of the terraced garden overhanging the wall that separated the Vatican citadel from the city at the foot of the Palazzetto del Belvedere. In Maggi's view it is called "Fons rusticus ad Bramantis scalam a Paulo v instauratus atque ornatus" ("a rustic fountain near Bramante's staircase installed and decorated by Paul v"), and it appears to be a rustic cave with a reclining figure inside. But the basin is empty; the astonishing Galera is not depicted. In fact, if we accept the dating of Maggi's view, the Galera, which is believed to date to 1620,[47] had not yet been positioned in the great basin of the fountain. We can presume, therefore, that work was carried out in two stages. The first involved the creation of the rustic setting, the second the installation of the miniature Galera, a realistic metal reproduction of a warship—symbol of the ship of the Church, which safely navigates the waters, but also of the power of the pope's fleet, which was very actively defending the coasts of the Vatican State.

In the archival documents, work at the "fish pond," as the fountain of Julius III was called, begins in 1610, and in 1612 more payments are documented for unspecified work at the "old fish pond." A payment to Orazio Censore, a noted metalworker of the time, for work "done and to do" on the Vatican fountains, could suggest that he worked on the Galera. Certainly his skill as a craftsman was already known to the Borghese family: he had "cast in lead" the beautiful statue of Narcissus for the fountain that was removed from the rear courtyard of Villa Pinciana at the end of the nineteenth century.[48] In addition, although the payment referred to work done in the years 1608–09,[49] long before the siting of the Galera in the fish pond, we cannot exclude the possibility that Censore himself cast the spectacular ship and that it was put in place later. We know of no other works in metal made for the Vatican fountains in this period that could have required the involvement of such a renowned craftsman, and it seems hard to imagine that others could have executed a work as complex and precise as the Galera, which was presumably conceived by an architect—Cesare D'Onofrio proposes that it may have

123. (below) Giovan Francesco Venturini, *The Fontana della Galera*, c. 1684, etching.

124. (opposite) *The Fontana della Galera*, etching, from Domenico Parasacchi, *Raccolta delle principali fontane dell'inclita città di Roma*, 1647.

125. The Fontana della Galera.

126. (*above*) Mario Cretoni, *The Fontana della Galera*, c. 1854, decoration on the armoires of the Gallery of Urban VIII. Vatican Library.

127. (*opposite*) The Fontana della Galera.

been Giovanni Vasanzio[50]—noted for his particular skills in the decorative arts.[51] In his fine description from the years 1622–27, Ferdinando Caroli presents the fountain as follows: "A mountain that opens at its base in a vast cave with rocks everywhere, dripping water, welcomes the Old Man of the Waters, who reclines in the native moss. Amid the swells the enormous lake keeps a lead trireme safe and sound despite the shaking of the storms. This, with its wondrous imitations of cannons, and simulated firings, and raining flames…is admirable for the pleasure it gives."[52] The miniature Galera, made of copper and lead, is rendered in every detail, from the sails, shrouds, bridges, and masts to the figurehead and the cannons, which fire powerful jets of water, as do the trumpets blown by a trumpeter hoisted atop the poop deck. It is an extraordinary *divertissement*, about which Maffeo Barberini, the future Pope Urban VIII (1623–44), dedicated some verses.[53] These verses are today inscribed on a tablet next to the fountain: BELLICA PONTIFICUM NON FUNDIT / MACHINA FLAMMAS SED DULCEM / BELLI QUA PERIT IGNIS AQUAM ("The war engines of the popes dispense not flames but sweet water, by which the fire of war does perish"). The singularity of the fountain is perhaps connected in some way to the pope's ambitious plans for the expansion of the port of Civitavecchia, executed under the direction of the architect Giulio Buratti from 1608 to 1611, as well as to the plans for supplying the papal fleet with a new galley in addition to the five it already possessed.[54]

To complete the survey of the fountains commissioned by Paul V, we must examine the small, often overlooked Fontana degli Specchi (mirrors) (plate 128), located near the entrance created by the pope to link the new wing of the apartments to the garden below. It is a fountain of modest size, but so richly decorated as to be described by Chattard as "superlatively marvelous" and "lovely beyond measure."[55] It has the appearance of an aedicule supported by gray marble pilasters and ancient green columns, between which is a deep niche covered in colorful mosaics. Its apse is decorated with a bird-filled pergola and twelve tondos that once held the mirrors for which the fountain is named. At the center of the niche is a rustic waterfall that flows into a small basin. The design is rigid and schematic, in marked contrast to the rustic naturalness in favor at the time, and thus must have been executed later. The small barrel vault is also richly ornamented with colorful mosaics depicting grotesques, including the usual Borghese emblems of eagles and dragons as well as the papal tiara. Even the tympanum that crowns the aedicule is topped with a heraldic eagle. On the right, free side (the left abuts the building) is a small niche, also adorned with a mosaic of small stones and tiles that probably once held a small statue. Gilded mosaics with the Borghese emblems cover the bases of the columns, but the fairly unrefined quality of the work suggests a recent restoration.

According to Belli Barsali, the Borghese emblems must be a later addition, as she believes that the fountain is decidedly sixteenth century and perfectly in keeping with the decorative models of the Casina of Pius IV.[56] Countering this argument are the depictions of this fountain in the Quirinal and Vatican Library frescoes celebrating the accomplishments of Paul V, as well as some payment documents that clearly attest to decorative works executed during his papacy. In the years 1613–14, for example, Martino Ferrabosco is paid for mosaics for an unspecified fountain, while between September 1614 and March 1615 the stonemasons Agostino and Bernardino Radi[57] receive a payment for work on the "little fountain newly made at the foot of the stair in the Belvedere garden." In the latter case, both the size and the location seem to leave no doubt that the reference is to the Fontana degli Specchi. Finally, in 1619, Ferrabosco is again paid for "two statues placed at the fountain at the foot of the stair that goes down into its garden from the Vatican palace"; once again, the reference must be to the Fontana degli Specchi, which still stands next to the entrance.[58] It seems certain, therefore, that under Paul V important decorative additions were made to the fountain that are not depicted in the Quirinal and Vatican Library frescoes, which show within the aedicule a simple, rustic backdrop with a spout of water and small basin. In the Quirinal fresco water also spouts from a heraldic eagle, but neither representation shows a trace of the polychrome mosaics, which leads us to exclude the possibility that they date to the papacy of Pius IV. Nor does the decorative program of the little fountain seem in keeping with that of the Casina from a stylistic point of view: the former uses, essentially, the classical mosaic technique, while the latter relies on the use of various materials and the mixing of techniques.

However, one element that poses some problems in the attribution of the fountain to the time of Paul V is its architectural style. In its architectural line and harmony it is, indeed, a typically sixteenth-century structure, quite different from the fantastical garden decorations that became widespread in the seventeenth century. An even

128. The Fontana degli Specchi abutting the apartments of Paul V.

more problematic issue is the position of the fountain, which abuts the apartment built by Paul v and is therefore closed off on one side by the building. This last element suggests that the small structure was initially designed with a niche on either side and was thus intended for a site where both sides would have been visible; it also suggests that the papal apartments were built up against one side at a later date. The mosaic decorations present dating problems as well: those in the apse and in the small barrel vault are clearly different and belong to two distinct phases. The first (plate 130), depicting the pergola, present a decorative solution that recalls analogous works of the period, all commissioned by the Borghese family, such as the "painted garden" of the Quirinal[59] or the decorations (plate 129) of the Villa Borghese Aviary.[60] They have, in fact, the same *grillage*, and the carefully and realistically rendered depictions of birds are very similar. The mosaics in the small barrel vault (plate 131) are less refined: the palette is flat and dull, while the decorative scheme is more banal and limited to grotesques alternating with the family emblems.

We believe, therefore, that an aedicule was already in place on this site, dating perhaps to the time of Pius iv, and that Paul v decided to decorate it further, enhancing its importance both in connection with the entrance to the apartments and as the starting point of the garden path he had conceived. It is very likely that the mosaics were executed in two phases: those on the apse must date to

the first years of his papacy, while those on the small vault, referred to in payment orders, were probably carried out at a later date, when work was nearing an end. All of our sources record that the pope's death impeded the completion of the fountain, and this fact likely explains the subsequent creation of the incongruous "waterfall." We can thus conclude that Paul v embellished the pre-existing fountain in two phases, decorating it with his own emblems, but did not finish the work, which underwent modifications long after he died.

Given the abundant water supply, the little fountains that adorned the beds of the Giardino dei Semplici,[61] in front of the Casina of Pius iv, could not be neglected. Their upkeep was entrusted to Ferrabosco, who also added mosaics to the niche containing a fountain and the reclining Cleopatra in the Cortile delle Statue.[62]

The installation of new fountains in the gardens had created new vistas and modified some paths. From the entrance to the palaces near the Fontana degli Specchi, two great avenues were created. The first, on the left, passed in front of the Fontana delle Torri and reached the clearing dominated by the Fontana dello Scoglio, behind which the most natural, wooded part of the garden began. The second avenue, on the right, led to the Casina of Pius iv and the

129. (*below*) Annibale Durante, *Pergola with Birds*, 1616, fresco. Uccelliera di Villa Borghese.

130. The Fontana degli Specchi, detail of the mosaics.

131. The Fontana degli Specchi, detail of the mosaics.

beautifully ordered beds filled with precious and exotic flowers. A third, wide avenue, the Viale dei Giardini, was created along the Bramante corridor. It led up to the Belvedere, where it intersected with the Viale della Giostra, or della Zitella (now Viale dello Sport),[63] near the garden built for Clement VII. The layout of this area remained essentially unchanged until the nineteenth century, but new twentieth-century constructions altered it substantially.

Johannes Faber, simpliciarius pontificius (1600–29)

Johannes Faber (1574–1629), born in Bamberg but a resident of Rome from 1598 on,[64] is known chiefly for having been a member of the Accademia dei Lincei (Academy of the Lynxes), that extraordinary assembly founded in 1603 by a group of friends who shared a passion for all the natural sciences, and centered around the Duke of Acquasparta, Federico Cesi.[65] He was also a surgeon at the Santo Spirito hospital, a zoologist, a professor of botany at La Sapienza University, and, from 1600 to 1629, Semplicista Apostolico—that is, director of the Giardino dei Semplici or Vatican Botanical Garden.[66] Faber remained in this role under five popes: Clement VIII Aldobrandini (1592–1605), Leo XI Medici (1605), Paul V Borghese (1605–21), Gregory XV Ludovisi (1621–23), and Urban VIII Barberini (1623–44), all passionate garden enthusiasts remembered for having commissioned, either directly or through their cardinal-nephews, celebrated villas in Rome and the Roman countryside.[67] Faber himself recalls the beginning of his work in the Vatican Gardens in one of his writings from 1607: "While nevertheless this is now the third Pope of Rome under whom I take care of the pontifical Vatican Gardens."[68] Yet despite being integral to the history of the gardens, Faber's life and work have not, to date, received due consideration or been adequately documented.[69] Of his enormous number of surviving papers, many contain references to his botanical interests, and while they are not always clearly or directly linked to his service to the popes, new information could certainly emerge from further study.[70] Faber took the place of his teacher, Andrea Bacci, who had in turn replaced Michele Mercati, the originator of the Vatican Botanical Garden. Like Mercati, Faber enjoyed a special permit to circulate in the gardens, granted on April 11, 1603, by Clement VIII's house steward, patriarch of Jerusalem Fabio Biondo, who entreated the guards not only to leave him undisturbed while he was gathering herbs

but even to "nurture him and give him every comfort, so he may do his work with greater passion."[71]

Unfortunately, no pictorial document allows us to ascertain how the Vatican Botanical Garden was laid out, nor is it clear whether Faber's responsibilities were limited to the so-called "scientific" part—that is, the plants commonly defined as "semplici" and cultivated for study or medicinal purposes. In views of the Vatican Gardens a "Giardino de' semplici," as the Botanical Garden was referred to at the time, is often indicated near the Casina of Pius IV with an arrangement in small, regular compartments, very different from the other areas of the park, in which formal beds alternate with groves. In particular, in the previously cited view by Maggi (plates 132, 133) there are multiple formal gardens: facing the Casina of Pius IV are some quadrangular beds, bounded by low espaliers and trees at the corners. Each quadrangle is subdivided into four sections with another, circular bed in the center, in which a single tree is inserted. These beds are marked with the number 57, which in the legend corresponds to *Hortus herbarum salubrium*, thus defining the "medicinal" part of the garden. Not far from the Casina, in the direction of the Fontana delle Torri, are two more compartments, surrounded by fences and marked with the numbers 102 and 105, which correspond to *Areola herbarum salubrium*, again a reference to cultivations with medicinal properties. The beds are rectangular and decidedly less elaborate than those in front of the Casina.

In the vast garden area there are other plots of land laid out in geometric patterns. The Cortile della Pigna has a formal organization, with its lovely central fountain and smaller fountains at the center of four compartments, subdivided in turn into four beds bordered by trees. The middle courtyard, enclosed on one side by the Sistine Library and on the other by the double-ramped staircase with the nymphaeum, is also subdivided into beds. According to the legend, both of these courtyards were used as "citrus gardens" and are defined, respectively, as "Intimum pomarium malorum aereorum cum scatabris et fontibus, a Paulo V" ("Inmost orchard of bronze-colored fruits, with water jets and fountains, by Paul V") at no. 39 and "Pomarium inferum malorum aereorum cum suis aquarum fontibus, a Paulo V" ("Lower orchard of bronze-colored fruits, with its water fountains, by Paul V") at no. 63. The distribution of the citrus trees[72] must have extended to other areas of the Vatican Gardens, as suggested by the numerous espaliers attached to the boundary walls—for example, the one below the loggia facing the city, which borders the long, narrow terrace containing the Fontana della Galera and a regular arrangement of beds that could have been admired from atop the walkway. The presence of citrus trees in the gardens is confirmed by some payments for the piping in of water to irrigate the "espaliers of citrons."[73]

The Secret Garden of Paul III was also bounded by walls covered with espaliers, presumably of citrus trees, and is no more than partially visible in Maggi's plan, which contains a reference only to its entrance door, identified by no. 71. Its configuration appears very different here than in plans of a few decades earlier. The imposing pergola that covered the two intersecting paths is no longer depicted; we can make out only geometric beds with low fencing and regularly spaced trees. One could presume that in this view the pergola was simply left out, as it was built by a predecessor of the pope whom the author aimed to glorify, or that because only part of the garden is shown, the projection of the boundary wall hid the pergola from view. Some references to the pergola in documents from the time of Paul V lead us to hypothesize that this element, although distinctly sixteenth century, was still present. In 1608 a carpenter is paid for generic work on the *cerchiate* (wooden rings) of the pergola without the location being identified, while another payment, again from 1608, clearly refers to the "Cortile delle Statue," where *cerchiate* are made in the four beds with "laurel trees."[74] There is another reference to the presence

of *cerchiate* in the "new avenue" leading from the Casina of Pius IV to the Secret Garden,[75] but the Maggi view provides no iconographic confirmation of it, unless it, too, is situated in the part obscured by the boundary walls.

The organization of the vast green space into a multitude of gardens with varying characteristics, as outlined by Maggi's view, along with the lists of plants among Faber's papers, leads us to presume that the Vatican also had flower gardens—as was the custom in the seventeenth century—and included, in particular, numerous varieties of flower bulbs.[76] The so-called *cipolle* (literally, onions) were very fashionable at the time and fetched exorbitant prices. Many varieties recur time and again in Faber's papers. For example, appearing in an undated list of plants, under the rubric "planted in the Vatican," are many ornamental, non-medicinal flowering plants, including tulips of various species, geraniums, foxglove, rattan, and gentian, all of which suggest the existence of a flower garden (plates 134–38).[77] In fact, the term "Giardino dei Semplici" was often used in reference both to gardens with medicinal plants and those

132, 133. (*below*) Giovanni Maggi, *The Vatican Temple of St. Peter*, 1615, etching, detail.

134. (*opposite*) Snake's head (*Fritillaria persica L.* and *Fritillaria Imperialis L.*), *Erbario Aldrovandi*, BUB, vol. I, c. 79, p. 229 and c. 78, p. 229.

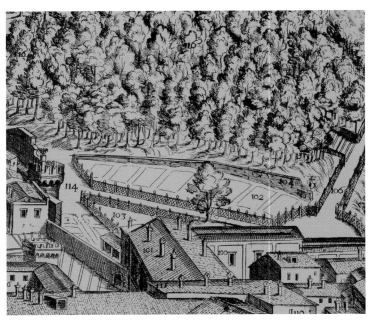

Fritillaria persica L.
1. c. 78. p. 229

Fritillaria imperialis L.
1. c. 79. p. 229

containing plants and flowers of a decorative nature. For example, the Casabona Codex, which describes a Giardino dei Semplici, has a depiction of a tulip on the opening page.[78] Giorgina Masson, too, maintained that the term *semplici*—particularly in Italy—referred to both medicinal and ornamental plants.[79] Recurrent tasks typical of flower cultivation are cited in the archival documents as being carried out in the Vatican "Giardino de' semplici," surely at Faber's behest, and for the entire period between 1608 and 1615 work was repeatedly undertaken to make compartments (that is, flowerbeds) in the garden.[80]

From the papers that have come down to us, it appears that on botanical matters Faber was in constant contact with other scholars and collectors, including the renowned herbalist and botanist Enrico Corvino, who supplied him with plants, especially bulbs.[81] In a note sent in December 1621, a "list of plants given to…Corvino for the garden of B. videri [sic]," and thus clearly destined for the Vatican, includes absinthe, rue, psyllium, mallow, camomile, chaste-tree, nicotiana (*nicotiana tabacum*, a flower similar to the tobacco plant, very rare at the time because it came from the Americas), foxglove, varieties of ranunculus, iris, so-called Peruvian hyacinth (probably Peruvian squill), and trachelium, a fashionable plant also called *Lobelia cardinalis*, both for its lovely vermilion color and in homage to the flower-loving Cardinal Francesco Barberini.[82] That the plants on the list were destined for the Vatican Gardens is certain, as is the fact that there were both medicinal and decorative plants, presumably for different sectors, confirming that Faber was in charge of the entire garden complex. A letter, unfortunately not dated, allows us to intuit how Faber used his position to extend his reach to every aspect of the gardens, far beyond the requirements of scientific interests. In this letter, addressed to the pope and written in his own hand, Faber argued: "…for order to be established within it, the Giardino dei Semplici needs many seeds and various plants, some of which I will find myself, as I have in the past, and others which, if you see fit to give written orders to the apostolic nuncios in France, Spain, Venice, and other places for which this speaker has given you the lists, are found there in quantity and will be supplied you, and thus you will fill the Garden without expense. I implore you again to order that the garden be fenced in while it is being built, as the propriety of the site requires, and I promise to maintain it with every diligence so that Your Holiness will be satisfied."[83] In another volume of Faber's papers,[84] not directly connected to this letter, are detailed lists of plants, each headed by a country

name. One can easily assume that these were the lists he had prepared for the apostolic nuncios, with the respective requests included. There are, in fact, lists for Spain, Flanders, France, Venice, Constantinople, Naples, and Egypt, indicating Faber's vast medical and botanical knowledge and his ability to identify, for each country, the rarest and most precious varieties found there—including, for example, even pineapples and plants that are colorfully named but hard to classify, such as the "sad arbor of India."[85] Yet again, these are plants that must have been destined not just for the Giardino dei Semplici in the strictest sense, but also for other gardens in the Vatican territory; after all, in addition to rare and exotic examples of flowering plants, there are trees of considerable size. We don't know whether Faber's ingenious idea for obtaining the rarest plants at no expense succeeded, as no information has been found in the documents examined to date about the participation of the nuncios in the enrichment of the Vatican Gardens. This was, however, a common practice, as the earlier experience of Michele Mercati attests; he had already used the pope's representatives to replenish his supply of precious plants, particularly from Spain, which at the time was the go-between with the Americas.[86] The continuation of this practice in the seventeenth century is documented by the shipment of precious bulbs from Cardinal Guido Bentivoglio, papal nuncio in Brussels, to Cardinal Scipione Borghese, the pope's nephew, for the gardens he was creating in his Villa Pinciana.[87] Additionally, a payment order, dated October 26, 1613, and found amid the reams of archival documents pertaining to the work in the Vatican Gardens during the Borghese papacy, clearly attests to the arrival of flower bulbs from Flanders and Constantinople.[88] Unfortunately, the specific plants are not indicated, but coming from Constantinople and Flanders, in particular, they were most likely tulips. Indeed, tulips were extremely popular at that time and were exchanged and sold in innumerable varieties, thanks to crossbreeding and unscrupulous experiments, paving the way for the "tulip mania" that would shortly cause an extraordinary rise in the price of bulbs—and bring Flanders to the brink of economic collapse once the bottom fell out of the market.[89]

In addition to requesting plants from all over Europe, Faber attended personally to the collection of specimens for planting in the pope's gardens; we have news of his travels

135. Narcissus (*Narcissus tazetta L. ssp. tazetta*), *Erbario Aldrovandi*, BUB, vol. VII, c. 115, p. 246 and vol. VIII, c. 98, p. 248.

Narcissus tazetta L. ssp. tazetta
VIII, c. 115, p. 246

Narcissus tazetta L. ssp. tazetta
VIII, c. 98, p. 248

for this very reason to Naples in 1608[90] and Ostia in 1609.[91] An excursion to Monte Gennaro, near Tivoli—organized by Federico Cesi on October 12, 1611, with Faber, Teofilo Muller, Enrico Corvino, and Giovanni Schreck; recorded with much fanfare in the chronicles of the Academy of the Lynxes; and alluded to by Faber in one of his letters—describes the purpose of the trip as providing for the *plantarum collatione* (collection of plants) and mentions his role as *simpliciarius pontificius*.[92]

At the root of Faber's activity as papal "gardener" was the trading network that he had organized with Roman, and farther-flung, collectors. We have already mentioned his relationship with Enrico Corvino,[93] many of whose letters, conserved among Faber's papers, refer to the supply of flowers (particularly bulbs) destined for the Vatican Gardens. Equally interesting is Faber's correspondence on botanical subjects with Ferrante Imperato,[94] Theofilo Muller,[95] Carlo Faccaro, and such illustrious garden owners as Ferdinand of Bavaria, the count of Furstenberg, Princess Polissena of Venosa, Monsignor Capponi, Cardinal Francesco Barberini,[96] and Alessandro Rondanini, whose Roman garden must have been of great interest, judging by the plants cultivated there.[97] Faber probably lent his expertise as "gardener" to some private Roman gardens, as implied by his copious correspondence with Alessandro Rondanini and an interesting list of plants sent to Cardinal Lanfranco Margotti, owner of the splendid villa near the Colosseum, now known as Villa Silvestri Rivaldi.[98]

Obviously, Faber could not be ignored in the writings of Giovan Battista Ferrari, whose treatises constituted a fundamental reference for all botany enthusiasts of the day.[99] Ferrari mentions Faber as papal herbalist and member of the Academy of the Lynxes, but his reference to the Vatican Gardens, where Faber worked, is very brief, especially in comparison to his commentary on other Roman gardens.[100] Ferrari describes his work as follows, grouping him with the Quirinal gardeners also employed by the pope: "In the Quirinal, and in the Vatican, the two Gardens of the Popes are bursting with majestic blooms, planted there to relieve [the popes] of pastoral cares; thus the appearance of the gardens is no less majestic than the works they perform."[101] True, Ferrari published his first treatise in 1633, after Faber's death, and perhaps the difficulty of gaining access to

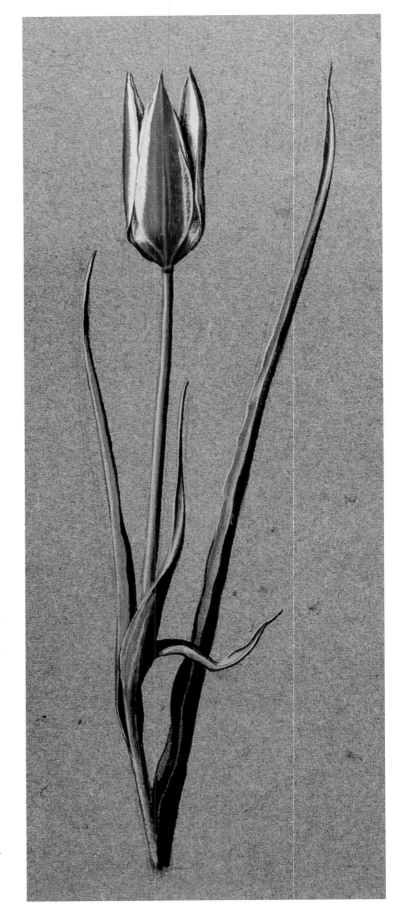

136. (*right*) Tulip (*Tulipa clusiana*), BAV, Barb. Lat. 4326, sheet 24.

137. (*opposite*) Ranunculus (*Ranunculus asiaticus L.*), BAV, Barb. Lat. 4326, sheet 70.

70.

the Vatican Gardens explains this strangely brief nod, which surely does not convey any sense of the gardens' beauty and variety at the time.

In 1627 Faber still appears on the payrolls of the court of Urban VIII, in the list of "major officials," as herbalist,[102] but there is no subsequent mention of his activity. After his death in 1629, Faber was succeeded in his position by Pietro Castelli, who was active for only a few years before he chose to move to Messina to become curator of the local botanical garden. A document from 1637 attests to his presence on the papal payrolls under the pseudonym Tobia Aldini,[103] listed among the "minor officials" as herbalist and "superintendent of Belvedere."[104] Despite their shared interests and both men's friendship with Enrico Corvino (Castelli's brother-in-law), it seems that the relationship between Faber and Castelli was dreadful, so much so that the latter wrote in a letter of 1626: "A certain Io(hannes) Faber did not dare join battle with me."[105]

With Paul V at the helm and Johannes Faber as gardener, the Vatican Gardens experienced a period of splendor and innovative fervor. The gardens were greatly enriched, both botanically and architecturally, and assumed a configuration that would endure more or less unchanged for over two hundred years. No other pope in the subsequent centuries would introduce as many embellishments and innovations; Paul V's successors simply managed the gardens as they were, making limited modifications dictated by changing taste.

138. Marigold (*Tagetes erecta L.*), *Erbario Aldrovandi*, BUB, vol. IV, c. 312, p. 239.

167

Tagetes erecta L.
II, c. 312. p. 239

8. The Cortile delle Statue transformed into the octagonal Cortile of Michelangelo Simonetti

18. Braccio Nuovo, Vatican Museums

19. The Colonnade of Piazza San Pietro

m. Fontana delle Api

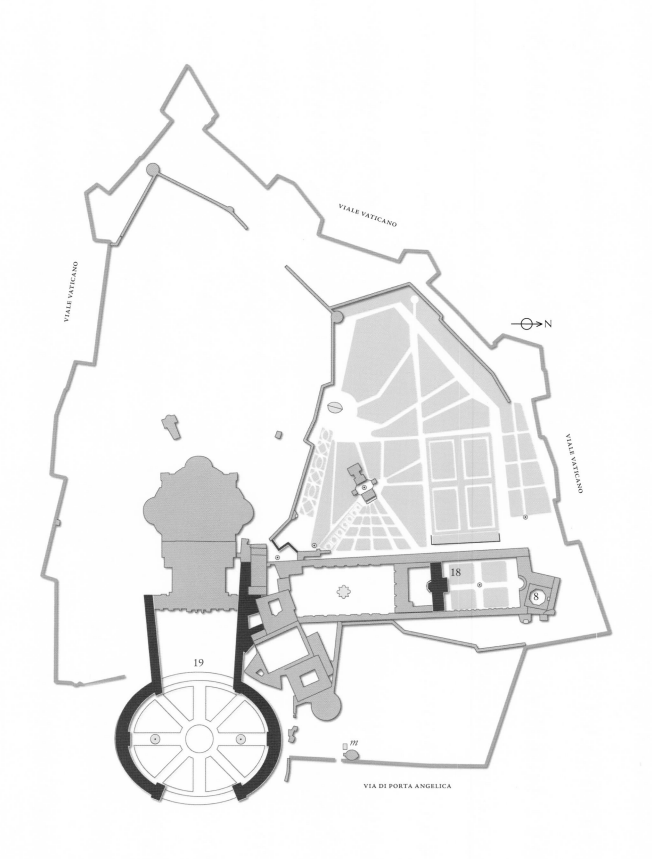

VIALE VATICANO

VIALE VATICANO

VIALE VATICANO

N

18

8

19

m

VIA DI PORTA ANGELICA

Modifications undertaken during the period discussed in this chapter are indicated in the map and captions above. For a complete map of the Vatican City and its major features in their present-day form, see page 2. Numbers in the map and captions refer to buildings and gardens, while letters refer to fountains.

THE SEVENTEENTH AND EIGHTEENTH CENTURIES: GARDEN PRACTICES AND BOTANICAL INNOVATIONS

The great era of the Vatican Gardens came to an end with the works commissioned by Pope Paul v Borghese (1605–21). No subsequent pope would undertake such substantive new projects; in fact, the involvement of Paul's successors was limited either to the partial modification of existing elements or to the introduction of modest embellishments that favored the Quirinal residence to the detriment of the Vatican. In the summer months, the popes moved to suburban villas in the surrounding countryside, often the property of their own families, which offered not only a cooler climate but also diversions and the opportunity to withdraw from the pressures of governing. Only after Italian unification in the nineteenth century would the Vatican citadel again become the permanent papal residence and the gardens the focus of renewed attention; by that time, however, the era of grand endeavors was definitively over. The work that was actually executed had little impact on the existing layout; it was primarily concerned with the areas that had remained in a rural state.

After the brief papacy of Gregory xv Ludovisi (1621–23), who devoted his attention almost exclusively to the family villa—completed in 1624, when Urban viii (1624–44) rose to the papal throne; located on the site of the antique Horti Sallustiani; and unfortunately destroyed at the end of the nineteenth century[1]—the gardens were divided into four distinct sectors, each with its own appearance and characteristics. These were clearly evident in Giovanni Maggi's beautiful view of 1615, which immortalized an arrangement that would endure for many decades to come. Beginning from the northern rise of the Belvedere, the first area shown is the garden with trees, espaliers, and beds around the Fontana della Galera on the long terrace supported by the city wall. Next are the gardens inside the Cortile del Belvedere and the Cortile delle Statue, which, despite their transformation into museums, had preserved their layout of geometric beds and citrus trees. Between the Casina of Pius iv and the boundary wall facing Monte Mario lies a series of formal gardens, beginning from the north with the terraced garden of Clement vii, followed by the completely walled-in Secret Garden of Paul iii, and ending with the regular beds of the Giardino dei Semplici in front of the Casina. The entire hillside in the background, up to the summit bounded by the bastions, is covered with woods. This was the only area of the park that had not undergone important changes in the course of the two preceding centuries. Beyond the division formed by the ancient Leonine Wall, but still within the Vatican walls,

lie some plots that were most likely planted with vineyards and vegetable gardens.

Urban viii, at the time Maffeo Barberini,[2] was a renowned garden enthusiast and an expert collector of rare and exotic flowers. The gardens of his family residence, the palazzo-villa near the Quirinal, were among the most celebrated of the time, and the subject of admiring and learned accounts.[3] He is responsible for instigating the creation of what would become the papal summer residence par excellence, the Villa at Castel Gandolfo.[4] In 1614, while still a cardinal, he had in fact acquired land and begun restoration work on a *casino*, or summer house, of modest dimensions but featuring a garden. It seems he began spending time there in 1618 on the advice of his doctors, who suggested that the climate in Castel Gandolfo was more suitable for his health than that of Rome. Even after his election to the papal throne, he continued spending long stretches of time in that residence until 1637, when his declining condition no longer permitted him to leave Rome.[5]

Despite these clear preferences, a sign of his activity in the Vatican Gardens can be found in the small but graceful Fontana delle Api (bees) (plates 139, 140), which recalls another, more celebrated fountain, the Fontana del Tritone, built by Gian Lorenzo Bernini in the Roman piazza that carries the pope's family name. The little Vatican fountain, initially placed on the ramp leading from the Cortile del Belvedere to the gardens and commissioned by the pope as drainage for an open spring on that site,[6] was recently moved to the area near the Porta Sant'Anna entrance to the Vatican complex. The conception of the fountain was attributed to Gian Lorenzo Bernini by his son Domenico,[7] although it was executed by Francesco Borromini, who in 1626 received 112 *scudi* for a "shell with five bees, three of which spout water; two big laurel trunks, which spout water from two branches, arising out of the sides of a mound; an inscription with the sun above, and around it, two cartouchelike festoons and a mask."[8] Indeed, the fountain consists of a simple, curved basin attached to the wall, surmounted by a marble slab on which are carved rocaille, laurel branches, garlands of fruit, and five bees (the heraldic symbols of the Barberini family), three spouting water. In the upper section is an inscription within an elaborate cartouche topped by a carved sun, another emblem generally associated with Urban viii. The fountain attracted the

139. *Fontana di Belvedere* (*Fontana delle Api*), etching, from D. Parasacchi, *Raccolta delle principali fontane dell'inclita città di Roma*, 1647.

Fontana di Bel'uedere

attention of John Evelyn during his visit to the gardens in about 1640. In his detailed description of the jets of water spouting from the bees' proboscises, Evelyn also mentions the inscription, still visible today, which consists of a verse that was probably written by a poet in the pope's entourage: "Why do you marvel at the Bee, which drinks honey from the flowers, / If it pours honeyed water for you from its gullet?"[9]

In addition to the fountain commissioned by the reigning pope, Evelyn praised the sculpture collection, the great Pigna, and the numerous other fountains in the gardens, particularly the one with the marble basin from the baths of Titus that adorned the Cortile del Belvedere. He went on to laud the grottos, the plays of water, the waterfall at the site of the Galera, the innumerable spectacular inventions, the terraces, the walkways, the fruit trees, and the views over the city. Evelyn's visit and written account attest to the Vatican Gardens' inclusion in the grand tour given foreign visitors, and therefore to their status as true open-air museums, worthy of visiting not only for the works of art they contained but also for their layout and the precious plants cultivated there.

Although there is no conclusive documentary evidence to this effect, Pope Urban VIII must have had a close relationship with the *simpliciarius pontificius* who had been in charge of the Vatican Gardens for some time: Johannes Faber, a member of the Academy of the Lynxes with ties to the scholarly circle of which Urban had been a member since his years as cardinal. We can assume that many of Faber's endeavors—especially the introduction of rare and precious flower specimens, bulbs in particular—were requested or encouraged by the pope. Again, however, documentary support is scant, as Faber's papers are largely undated and thus difficult to place chronologically.[10]

In the course of his lengthy pontificate Urban VIII did not add any other embellishments to the Vatican Gardens, yet they must nevertheless have remained splendid during that time. In a few years, however, many changes, and not positive ones, would take place. Urban VIII's successor, Innocent X Pamphilj (1644–55), was primarily interested in ensuring the visibility of his own family, which he accomplished through the creation of the splendid city residence in Piazza Navona, the suburban villa outside Porta San Pancrazio,[11] and that anomalous "principality," San Martino al Cimino, in the territory of Viterba, the homeland of his powerful and influential sister-in-law, Donna Olimpia Maidalchini.[12] He seems to have paid little attention, however, to the Vatican residence, which we can assume remained unaltered.

In 1659, with the papacy of Alexander VII Chigi (1655–67), a major change did occur. The celebrated Vatican Orto Botanico—that is, the Giardino dei Semplici cared for by illustrious persons who had introduced rare and exotic plants—was replaced by a new and larger Orto Botanico on the Janiculum Hill.[13] With this move, the Vatican Gardens lost the scientific association that, along with the charm of the site, had made theirs the vanguard model since medieval times. Gone forever was that preeminent characteristic of a place where one could observe plants never before seen in Rome, carry out botanical and medical studies in connection with the university, undertake experiments, and investigate those naturalistic interests pursued with such enthusiasm by the Academy of the Lynxes just a few decades earlier.[14] In the second half of the eighteenth century it seemed that the experience of this earlier Vatican Orto Botanico would be revived, but it was only a brief window fated to close forever, marking the end of all scientific inquiry there. The gardens fell once again into the hands of unremarkable personalities, no longer linked to the university or the world of research.

Pope Alexander Chigi was responsible for two major projects in the Vatican citadel, and at St. Peter's in particular—Gian Lorenzo Bernini's great colonnade and restoration of the Scala Regia—but in the area of the gardens it seems he did nothing. The Chigis, too, possessed splendid estates in Rome: in Tuscany, their region of origin, and in Ariccia, near Rome, where they owned a magnificent property with a palace set in an enormous park.[15] In addition to using these family residences, the pope spent long stretches of time at Castel Gandolfo.

Dating to the years immediately after the Chigi pontificate is a truly merciless description of the Vatican Gardens written by a French traveler who, on a visit to Rome in 1676, comments on the city's charm as well as its limitations. This guide, published only recently,[16] clearly reveals the traveler's French origins, as the Vatican Gardens are unfavorably contrasted with the splendid creations of Le Nôtre and such famous French sites as Versailles, the Tuileries, Chantilly, Vaux, and Sceaux. When compared to the majestic and carriage-friendly avenues, elaborate flowered parterres, and spectacular waterfalls of those gardens, the "little paths" of the Roman gardens seemed rather paltry to the visitor, and he found intolerable the heat that punished both people and plants, permitting the cultivation of only a limited variety of flowers. While other Roman gardens

140. The Fontana delle Api.

of the time, such as those of Villa Montalto or Villa Pamphilj, had been adapted to French taste, the Vatican Gardens had remained much as they were in the early seventeenth century. And so, the anonymous visitor concluded, "in the Vatican Gardens, despite their fame, you will find nothing that will elicit the wonder of those who are used to seeing the gardens, even the most ordinary ones, around Paris." Such a judgment seems ungenerous toward the Vatican Gardens, which, even if not in the latest style, still must have had much of interest to offer.

In the same year as the unidentified French tourist's visit, Giovan Battista Falda published two etchings[17] that allow us to verify how and how much the gardens had changed since Pope Paul V Borghese's reign, and to see that they had, in any case, an interesting layout. The etchings consist of a plan (plate 141) and a perspective view (plate 142), which, taken together, make it possible to "read" the garden design with a certain accuracy. Whereas the plan reproduces the full extent of the Vatican citadel and distinguishes the boundary between the area for relaxation and the rustic zone, the perspective is limited to the gardens alone, rendered with great precision and detail and accompanied by a legend of "noteworthy things."[18]

The most prominent feature of the garden area is the continued presence of both formal and informal areas. As in Maggi's view, drawn more than half a century earlier, the geometric beds, bordered by rectilinear paths, alternate with groves traversed by winding paths. The gardens themselves appear clearly bounded by the Leonine Wall, beyond which extends the agricultural area with vineyards and plots for vegetables—a division that was, as we have seen, a constant in the Vatican Gardens. In Falda's plan, there is no trace of pleasure gardens in the vast area behind the Basilica; instead cultivated plots alternate with huts, as can also be seen in Maggi's view. The most obvious changes appear in a few specific sections of the gardens: the beds around the Fontana della Galera have been replaced by groves, while the Giardino dei Semplici in front of the Casina of Pius IV no longer has beds aligned in various rows; it is now arranged in a pattern of radiating paths, a layout that would remain popular throughout the next century. This pattern is also echoed in the wooded area beyond. The design of the beds seems more elaborate, as can be seen in the perspective view, in which they appear in the foreground. Within the areas bordered by boxwood hedges we can make out intricate patterns of flowering plants and trees, including palms, the presence of which is emphasized and depicted here for the first time, although

we have written confirmation from a visitor in 1600 that multiple varieties of palm tree already existed in the gardens then.[19] The beds occupy not only the flat part of the terrain but also the rises to the sides, which, despite the substantial slope, are divided into geometric areas, probably planted with flowers and bordered by rigorously squared-off hedges. Next to these is a fountain that appears to consist of a basin on the ground and another, smaller one above, a configuration that recalls the nearby Fontana della Panetteria. Number 13 on the legend attached to Falda's plan calls it "Fontana de gli Specchi," the same name as another fountain that we know was located nearby but that had a decidedly different appearance. The path leading from the Fontana delle Torri to the Fontana dello Scoglio

141. Giovan Battista Falda, *Plan of Rome*, c. 1676, etching, detail with the Vatican.

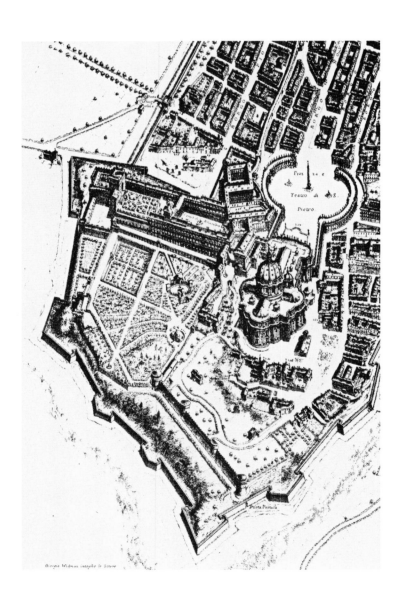

(numbered 11 and 12, respectively, in the plan) is marked by a long, narrow compartment of beds with elaborate rhomboid and circular designs, perhaps achieved through a knowing manipulation of the hedges according to the precepts of topiary. The garden of Paul III once again looks different. If in Maggi's view the central pergola had been replaced with regular beds, each with a tree at its center, in Falda's plan there are only four large beds, bordered by trees—probably citrus—yet the site retains the name "Secret Garden." The Cortile del Belvedere features a garden layout on the two upper terraces (the present-day Cortile della Pigna and Cortile della Biblioteca), while the lower, much larger courtyard contains only the monumental fountain restored by Pope Paul V.

Falda's view and plan are commonly dated to 1676; starting from the next year, the registers of the Computisteria Apostolica (Apostolic Accounts) include special notebooks entitled "Rincontro dei Giardini" (Garden Accounts), in which all of the work carried out in the Vatican Gardens is meticulously recorded, month by month and year by year, until 1740. Although the numbering of the registers continues uninterrupted, no payments are noted from that year until 1795; in 1795 they resume in a regular fashion until February 13, 1798, at which point they stop completely, this time not by chance. The French had entered Rome, proclaimed the Roman Republic, and taken the pope hostage; consequently it was no time to be concerned with the gardens.[20] However, a glance through the pages that for more than a century—albeit with one substantial interruption—recorded the life of the gardens permits us to retrace their

142. Giovan Battista Falda, *Plan and Perspective View of the Belvedere Garden of the Papal Palace in the Vatican*, c. 1676, etching.

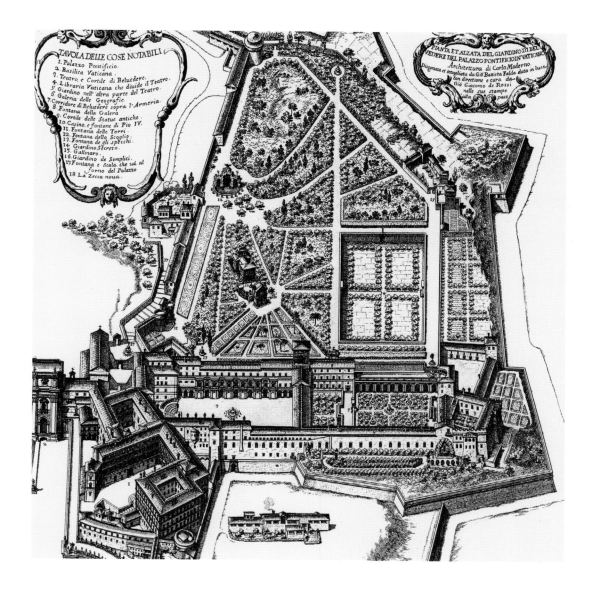

history and extract much useful information, both about the plants introduced and the cultivation techniques employed.[21] This important documentary source is supplemented by descriptions of the ornamental gardens, vegetable gardens, and vineyards, written when they were turned over to a succession of gardeners and vinedressers beginning in 1677 and continuing through the first half of the following century.

The first point of note that emerges from these documents is the abundance of citrus trees in the gardens. These were attached to the walls with espaliering trellises (plate 143) and planted either in large pots or directly in the ground. The many varieties of fruit included bitter oranges (plate 144), sweet oranges, citrons, bergamots, limes, and Calabrese oranges, all of which received constant care. In addition to watering, pruning, and cleaning, all operations necessary to protect the plants at the change of seasons were regularly carried out. When the cold set in, normally in November, the potted trees were moved to orangeries, while the espaliers were protected from the rigors of winter by a complex system of coverings. The gardeners tied mat coverings made of straw to the wooden structure of the espaliers, which consisted of "crosspieces" of chestnut with smaller timbers above, and to which the trees were attached, in order to create a covered, protected tunnel known as a *cocchio*. These coverings could be raised on mild days and during the warmer hours to allow the sunshine to reach the plants. On the coldest nights, when the protection of the mats was insufficient to ward off frost damage, braziers with burning coals were placed inside the structure to temper the inclement night air.[22] This technique was widely used in citrus gardens and had even been codified in the 1644 treatise devoted to these fruits by the Jesuit priest and expert botanist Giovan Battista Ferrari.[23] The care lavished on the citrus trees was an indication of their importance at the time, which stemmed in large part from their symbolic value as a continuation of a tradition dating back to the origins of the Vatican Gardens. Not only did the existing citrus trees receive painstaking care, but new specimens were sometimes acquired as well, perhaps to fortify the existing espaliers, as in the winter of 1679, when various trees had become "dead because of the frost" in spite of the protective coverings.[24] Payments are registered for the acquisition of citrus trees in 1686, and again in 1723 and 1725.[25]

During the papacy of Clement XI Albani (1700–21), modifications to embellish the gardens were carried out at a cost of some 323 *scudi* under the supervision of such

renowned architects as Carlo Fontana and Giovan Battista Contini.[26] Payments were made to stonemasons for the execution first of thirty-four and then of twenty-six travertine pedestals to support equivalent numbers of potted citrus trees intended for the Secret Garden—a term that no longer referred to the garden created by Paul III, but rather to the Cortile della Pigna, as another document makes clear.[27] Each pedestal was carefully carved by the master stonemason Giuseppe Luraghi, and the papal emblems— two stars and three mountains—were carved alternately on their four sides. An additional eight pedestals, similar but larger in size, were made to be placed around the fountain in the center of the garden. This work is confirmed in another document, in which Clement XI's undertakings are summarized;[28] mention is made of the construction of the bases for the pots of citrus trees in the Secret Garden, where, in addition, a "fine antique pedestal with bas reliefs" was placed beneath the "great metal pinecone where the ashes of Emperor Hadrian are preserved."[29] And, in the same Secret Garden, after Clement XI's workers had "restored the walls," "beautiful scatterings of boxwood in the French style"—in other words, elaborate parterres— were made. These were documented in contemporary etchings, including one by Francesco Pannini that shows the Pigna atop a decorated pedestal in front of the great *nicchione*, with pots of citrus trees all around and the arabesque-shaped beds in the center (plate 145). The same document credits Clement XI with repairing the Casina of Pius IV, including the frescoes and mosaics; restoring Andrea Mantegna's paintings in the Belvedere Palazzetto of Innocent VIII; and, lastly, making some improvements to the Cortile delle Statue, including the relocation of the Apollo to the interior rooms and the restoration of other statues. We can deduce that a payment from 1706, when "all of the sections in the new secret garden of the Belvedere" had been planted with boxwood from the villa of the Pamphilj prince, refers to the creation of the parterre in the Cortile della Pigna, evidently called the "secret garden" at the time.[30] Some years later other boxwood plants are purchased to "restore the arabesques and divisions and make new ones," most likely, once again, for the Cortile della Pigna.[31]

The "Rincontri dei giardini" also reveals that the gardens contained flowers, including jasmine, roses, lilies of the valley, tuberoses, carnations, jonquils, and numerous pots whose locations and contents were not specified. Among the plants mentioned in 1693 are nineteen boxes of tulips,

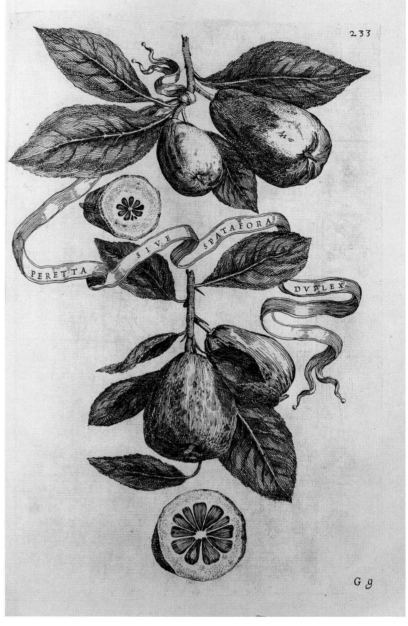

143. The citrus espaliers, from Giovan Battista Ferrari, *Hesperides, sive de aurearum malorum cultura et usu*, 1644.

144. Citrus fruit, from Giovan Battista Ferrari, *Hesperides, sive de aurearum malorum cultura et usu*, 1644.

evidence of the bulb's undiminished popularity since the first decades of the century, as well as jasmine, in flower boxes with *Lilium convallium*, or lilies of the valley; boxes of "Persa," as marjoram (*Majorana hortensis*) was called because it came from the Orient; and "Madonna lilies" (*Lilium candidum*), plants with clear religious symbolism.[32]

There were also abundant fruit trees, especially pear (three hundred are purchased to make a "planting") and peach, which were often brought from Florence. The park also housed a full-fledged farm, as evidenced by the presence of chickens, vineyards (with salaried workers who tended them regularly), plots of beans, chickpeas, broad beans, and an olive grove in which eight hundred trees are planted in 1744, at a cost of 360 *scudi*. The pope and the Curia must have been particularly partial to strawberries, because every year, with great regularity, tens of thousands of strawberry plants were cultivated and lavished with care and water. Besides the head gardener, who was paid 6 *scudi* per month, there were workers of various specialties. Mentioned in particular are "workers with scissors," "shovelers," "hedge trimmers," and "espalier maintenance workers," who used specially-made wooden *castelli*, or scaffolds, to trim the high espaliers. Every May, on the day of the Feast of Corpus Domini (Corpus Christi), all of the gardeners gathered large quantities of flowers and leaves to scatter during the ceremonial procession.

The Dominican pope Benedict XIII (1724–30), of the Orsini family, did not care for spending holidays in the villas and resided permanently at the Vatican. We have no information about modifications to the gardens during his papacy, but we can assume that he spent a lot of time in them, as the registers show frequent orders to clean the paths where His Holiness strolled.[33] Under Benedict XIV (1740–58), of the Lambertini family, buttresses were added to the east wing of the Cortile del Belvedere, and on the southern side, toward the palaces, a masonry exedra with a central, niche-shaped aedicule was built, thus definitively altering the theater conceived by Pirro Ligorio. As Chattard relates: "The said Theater being steep in parts, particularly in the seating and stair areas, in the year 1755…it changed in form and shape."[34] We do not have any documentary support, but from an interesting collection of garden drawings that recently came to light, it seems that the pope had a splendid villa in Pianoro, near his native city of Bologna, and that Antonio Scardin, the man responsible for its gardens, came to Rome in 1746 to offer his services in the Vatican Gardens.[35]

145. Francesco Pannini, *The Cortile della Pigna*, etching,
late eighteenth century.

A detailed document that allows us to verify the layout of the gardens during the pontificate of Benedict XIV is a plan (plate 146) by Giovan Battista Nolli, published in 1748, the accuracy of which has been amply demonstrated.[36] Nolli, too, confirms the division of the gardens into two sectors: the garden proper, comprising the area between the Leonine Wall and the bastions toward Monte Mario—called the "Papal Garden"—and the agricultural area occupying all the space between the apse of St. Peter's Basilica and the boundary wall separating the Vatican from the city. This area, traversed by a carriage road (the Vicolo Scaccia, known to us through various histories), was subdivided into the "Garden of the Building of St. Peter," the "Vineyard of the Reverenda Camera," and the "Vineyard of Santo Spirito," while the ample, unnamed band near the bastions is filled in with the crosshatching that in the Nolli plan generally indicates vegetable gardens or cane fields. Outside the Leonine Wall, against which many rustic constructions lean, the garden is divided into various distinct sectors. On part of the hillside is a dense planting of trees that gives an idea of what is meant by a *boschetto*, or grove. Farther down we can identify the Fontana dello Scoglio, with its large elliptical basin. Next to it is the quadrangular garden of the Casina of Pius IV, with its woods in back and its formal layout of radiating rectilinear paths and beds arranged as parterres in front. Right next to this garden, entirely enclosed by walls, is the Secret Garden of Paul III, subdivided into sixteen regular beds, all with parterres in arabesques. Here we can make out two structures, probably the sheds mentioned in the documents, where numerous pots of citrus trees from all over the gardens were stored. The spaces that were once the gardens of Clement VII (located on the terrace facing Monte Mario) and Julius III (near the Fontana della Galera) have irrevocably lost their subdivisions into beds and are filled with various trees.

The two upper terraces of the Cortile del Belvedere—more precisely, the Cortile della Pigna, tellingly referred to by Nolli as the "Giardino della Pigna," and the smaller Cortile della Biblioteca—are also characterized by a garden layout with beds in geometric and arabesque configurations. Confirmation of the arrangement documented by Nolli can be found in the perspective views by Francesco Pannini (1725–post-1794) and Giovan Battista Piranesi (1720–78) of the garden in front of the Casina of Pius IV, each of which depicts the elaborate swirls in the beds, suited to the contemporary taste for the "French style," but with a few differences. The beds in Piranesi's etching,

the earlier by at least a couple of decades, have a border in relief and blossoms in the center, while in Pannini's etching, simple, low bands of boxwood form the elaborate pattern.

In the following years some changes were introduced in the gardens to accommodate the construction of new buildings that expanded the museum spaces at the expense of garden areas. In fact, in 1771, under Clement XIV (1769–74), construction began on a new museum wing in the upper area of the gardens next to the Belvedere, on the site partially occupied by the garden of Clement VII. This structure was completed by Pius VI (1775–99) and called the Museo Pio-Clementino. The Cortile delle Statue, too, lost its Renaissance aspect during the papacy of Clement XIV, when it was redesigned by the architect Michelangelo Simonetti and took on an octagonal, decidedly neoclassical form, featuring an arcade articulated with columns. This project was completed in 1774, as an inscription still visible today recalls.[37]

After the hiatus from 1740 to 1795, the garden registers[38] resume without major changes. The names of the gardeners are different, but the salary of the head gardener is still six *scudi* per month; there are now "piazza workers," or laborers called in occasionally for specific tasks, but there are still "espalier maintenance workers" and "shovelers." Fruit trees, including *bricocole*, or apricots, continue to be planted and grafted; the citrus espaliers are covered and uncovered with the seasons, and thousands of strawberry plants are cultivated. The only prominent novelties are the presence of pineapples, then a rare and exotic plant (first introduced to Italy in the eighteenth century), and a substantial reforestation of the woods with young holm oaks. Indeed, two important acquisitions of "large oak trees to fortify the woods" (108 in 1796 and another hundred in 1797) are recorded.

Amid this apparent continuity, an event of great import took place in the Vatican Gardens around the late 1780s: the formation, for the second time, of a very interesting Orto Botanico, or botanical garden. We have already seen that starting in 1659 under Alexander VII Chigi, the Orto Botanico on the Janiculum[39] was built on the land directly behind the great Fontana dell'Acqua Paola, resulting in the abandonment of the Vatican Orto, which had been so important in the sixteenth century and the first half of the seventeenth.[40] Beginning in about 1788, the Reverend Filippo Luigi Gilii (1756–1821), an extremely interesting figure in the history of botanical culture in Rome and an active collaborator with Gaspare Suarez, took a new initiative.[41]

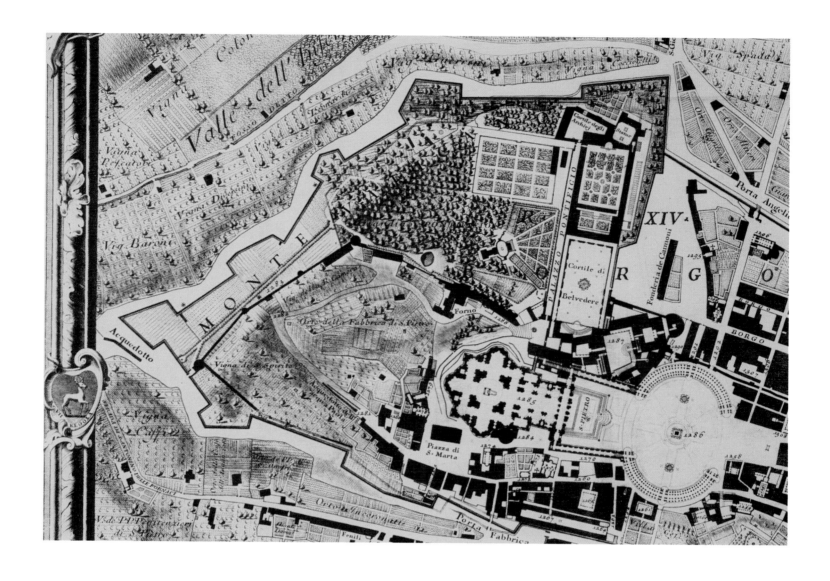

146. Giovan Battista Nolli, *Plan of Rome*, 1748, detail with the
Vatican.

147. (*above*) Francesco Pannini, *The Casina of Pius IV*, watercolor,
late eighteenth century. Private collection.

148, 149. (*opposite*) Francesco Pannini, *The Casina of Pius IV*,
watercolor, late eighteenth century, details. Private collection.

Gilii was the first person in Italy to appreciate the Linnaean system and classify plants according to it.[42] He conducted experiments regarding the nature and properties of specimens from other geographical regions—the Americas in particular—on his land at the foot of the Janiculum, until he was granted the opportunity to move his research to a plot of land placed at his disposal in the Vatican Gardens. He wrote of this experience himself: "The elegant form of our present garden, due to the acquisition we have made of a larger and better-situated area on the eastern slope of the Vatican hill, the absolute property of the Reverenda Fabbrica of St. Peter, we owe to Mons. Giovanni Bufalini, who in his role as custodian of the same Reverenda Fabbrica, is pleased to allow us at our instigation to render it thus, by removing some partially rundown buildings that are good for nothing except taking up space and depriving the garden of that pleasing expansiveness that we have now returned to it; and since a garden, that is, *orto*, of this nature is completely dedicated to botanical observations, it deserves to be known by a particular name. And so we have chosen to distinguish ours with the name Orto Vaticano-Indico, having considered that its location is by many minds celebrated and that the plants we cultivate within it are mostly from the Indies, both eastern and western."[43] The new botanical garden had nothing in common with its antecedent. First, it was devoted to the cultivation and study of non-Mediterranean plants, and second, it was in a completely different location from the site—next to the Casina of Pius IV—of the first Vatican botanical garden made famous by Michele Mercati and Johannes Faber.

From Gilii's description, we can deduce that the new botanical garden was located in the rural area behind the Basilica that in Maggi's plan of 1615 and Falda's of 1676 appears occupied by huts and cultivated plots. Unfortunately, we do not have any iconographic evidence of the garden's layout, and information about it is extremely scarce. Gilii's garden was studied only once, by Monsignor Giuseppe Lais,[44] who, in the last years of the nineteenth century, discovered some papers of great interest in the Biblioteca Apostolica Vaticana, in Gilii's hand.[45] At the time of Monsignor Lais's study, there was still one palm tree and some traces of a *viridarium* on the site once occupied by Gilii's garden—residual evidence of that brief episode. Fortunately, among the papers left by Gilii, Monsignor Lais found some truly exceptional materials: the complete lists from 1794 of all the plants that were cultivated in the Vatican-Indico Botanical Garden. Included in these lists,

which are arranged in alphabetical order and provide both scientific and common names, are 658 specimens of mostly exotic and rare flowers and trees. Gilii's decision to devote the garden to Indian plants, Western and Eastern, is reflected in the lists he compiled, which include many important species from the Americas, some of them being planted in Rome for the first time. Among them we discover *Bignonia catalpa*, *Melia azedarach*, *Annona squamosa* (plate 150),[46] *Myrica cerifera* (plate 151), *Schinus molle*, *Albitia julibrissin*, *Gleditschia triacanthos*, *Liriodendron tulipifera*, *Lippia americana* (plate 152), *Kalmia angustifolia* (plate 153), and the spectacular *Bromelia pinguin* (plate 154), all quite rare.[47] We know that the same plants were introduced, at this very time, in Cardinal Giuseppe Doria Pamphilj's Villetta Doria (situated in the area occupied today by the Galoppatoio, or dirt horse track, of Villa Borghese near Porta Pinciana), and that the extraordinary "gardener" responsible, Francesco Bettini,[48] had imported them from France with great difficulty. The general reaction to these novelties among the Romans was exceedingly negative, largely because they lacked the scientific knowledge needed to appreciate such new and original specimens.[49]

Gilii's garden comprised many exotic plants already widespread in the seventeenth century—indeed, the pride of that era's flower gardens. Many came from the Americas—among them *Scilla peruviana*, marigolds, yucca, aloe, *Canna indica*, various kinds of cactus, *Nicotiana tabacum*, and *Mirabilis jalapa*—but there were also many plants from the Orient and precious Middle Eastern bulbs such as *Fritillaria imperialis*. Some of the specimens included in the lists were clearly from Central and South America and have colorful or obscure names such as "Huacamaya ruste della Habana," "Lengua de vaca," "Arrayán," and "Marilopez." According to Monsignor Lais, Gilii and his collaborator,

150. (*opposite*) *Annona Squamosa*, from Filippo Luigi Gilii and Gaspare Suarez, *Osservazioni fitologiche*, 1792.

151. (*page 188*) *Myrica Cerifera*, from Filippo Luigi Gilii and Gaspare Suarez, *Osservazioni fitologiche*, 1792.

152. (*page 189*) *Lippia Americana*, from Filippo Luigi Gilii and Gaspare Suarez, *Osservazioni fitologiche*, 1792.

153. (*page 190*) *Kalmia Angustifolia*, from Filippo Luigi Gilii and Gaspare Suarez, *Osservazioni fitologiche*, 1792.

154. (*page 191*) *Bromelia Pinguin*, from Filippo Luigi Gilii and Gaspare Suarez, *Osservazioni fitologiche*, 1792.

IV.

Annona Squamosa

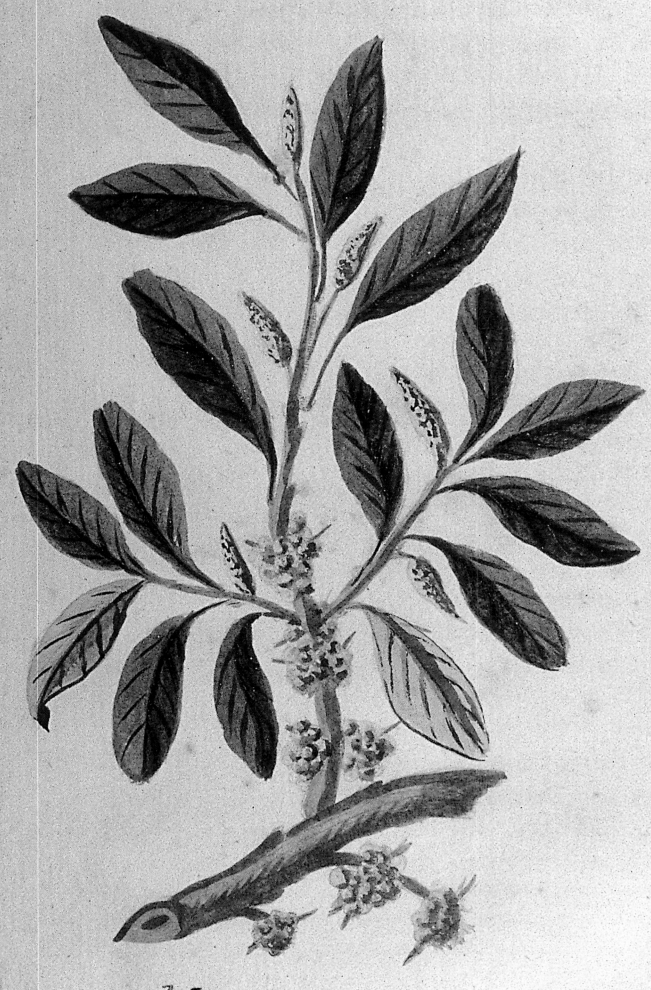

Myrica Cerifera

Lippia Americana

III

Kalmia Angustifolia

II

Bromelia Pinguin

Suarez, had obtained quantities of exotic plants from the Peruvian botanist Hipolito Ruiz Lopez,[50] mostly from South America, and with the help of Father Cesare Majoli, drawings of many of them were made and published in the literary periodicals of Rome. Another of Monsignor Lais's great contributions was the discovery of a splendid, rich herbarium—also the work of Gilii, and comprising some 1,200 specimens supplied by the Vatican Botanical Garden—which must have formed the basis for the creation of a museum of the natural sciences.[51]

The existence of the Vatican-Indico Botanical Garden must have been very brief, and it was probably interrupted by the political events surrounding the French occupation of 1798, which created more than a few problems in the Vatican. What is astonishing is that within a very few years this garden was completely forgotten, as a note sent to Cardinal Ercole Consalvi, Secretary of State to Pope Pius VII, leads us to understand. It is undated, but most likely written during his years in office, and therefore about 1815. In this "memo," also unfortunately unsigned, the creation of a botanical garden within the Vatican gardens is proposed, and the site described as the most suitable place in which to increase "the delights and magnificence of the sovereign palace."[52] To support his argument, the anonymous author completely ignores the more recent experience of Filippo Gilii and refers instead to the first botanical garden, particularly the work of Johannes Faber. He writes of how Faber, in the service of popes Clement VIII, Leo XI, and Paul V (omitting Gregory XV and Urban VIII), had been "engaged with great zeal" in increasing the number of specimens in the garden, especially those of marine plants, and how he had planned the publication—unfinished because of his untimely death—of the botanical codices held in the Vatican Library, in accordance with a project later taken up by Gilii.

Before the political situation worsened, Pius VI had introduced elements of neoclassical style into the gardens. First, in 1779, as an extant inscription records, he radically transformed the backdrop of the Fontana della Galera: the rustic grotto—created under Julius III and given greater importance under Paul V with the installation of the spectacular metal Galera in the fish pond below—was replaced by a severe architectural facade with masonry facings and a central niche, which featured a relief with the personification of a river. A long inscription[53] and a large papal crest in travertine top the facade. Nearby, at the start of the path

that leads to the Fontana della Galera, a portal was erected (plate 155), also in linear, neoclassical style and with a papal crest on the architrave. A second portal (plate 156), consisting of two simple pilasters with an inscription commemorating its commissioner, was positioned atop the hill to separate the woods from the rural area, creating a boundary that would subsequently lose its significance with the changes commissioned by Pius XI in the 1930s.

The Vatican Gardens, and in particular the complex of the Casina of Pius IV, could not have been omitted from the corpus of drawings dedicated by Charles Percier and Pierre-François Leonard Fontaine to the villas of Rome, which they visited and surveyed during their stay in the city in the years around 1784. In the collection, published in 1809,[54] a lovely watercolor etching depicts the Loggia and the Casina with the sixteenth-century decorations that survived the destruction under Pope Pius V and documents the state of the site before the moralizing modifications that took place a few decades later (plate 157). A second etching shows the floor plan of the architectural structures immersed in a wooded setting without a trace of parterres, clear evidence of a kind of "naturalization" that was replacing formal layouts (plate 158).

The French occupation of the Vatican citadel, which occurred on February 16, 1798,[55] caused substantial damage to its artistic heritage, and the occupants' pillaging of works of art from the museums and palaces is well known. The gardens, too, suffered the consequences, as reported in a chronicle of the time, dated April 22, 1798: "From the Gardens of the Vatican all of the pots have been removed, and the Jew Coen himself has shown up to purchase them. The rooms where the tools were kept for working in said gardens have been destroyed. Never has a plundering like this been seen. A sack lasting several days or a barbarian invasion would have caused far less damage than that of our generous liberators, who come here into our peaceful home to eat, to clothe themselves, and practically to go on holiday."[56] Pastor states the situation more concisely in his summary of the events leading to the exile of Pope Pius VI, referring to the "capricious devastation that took place in the Vatican gardens and collections."[57]

The eighteenth century ended with these tragic events, which initiated a period of instability and political upheaval that would absorb the full attention of the popes. Only after the Restoration of 1815 would it again become possible to attend to the gardens.

155. (*top*) The portal near the Fontana della Galera.

156. (*bottom*) The portal leading to the woods.

157. (*above*) Charles Percier, Pierre-François Leonard Fontaine, *Overall View of the Casina of Pius IV*, c. 1809, watercolor. Museo di Roma.

158. (*opposite*) Charles Percier, Pierre-François Leonard Fontaine, *Plan of the Casina of Pius IV and of Part of the Surrounding Gardens*, c. 1809, ink and watercolor. Museo di Roma.

20. Chalet of Leo XIII

21. Museo Pio-Clementino

22. Sacristy

c. The fountain removed in 1846

n. The fountain in the Cortile della Pigna, moved to the Secret Garden of Paul III

o. Wall fountains with sarcophagi

p. Circular fountains

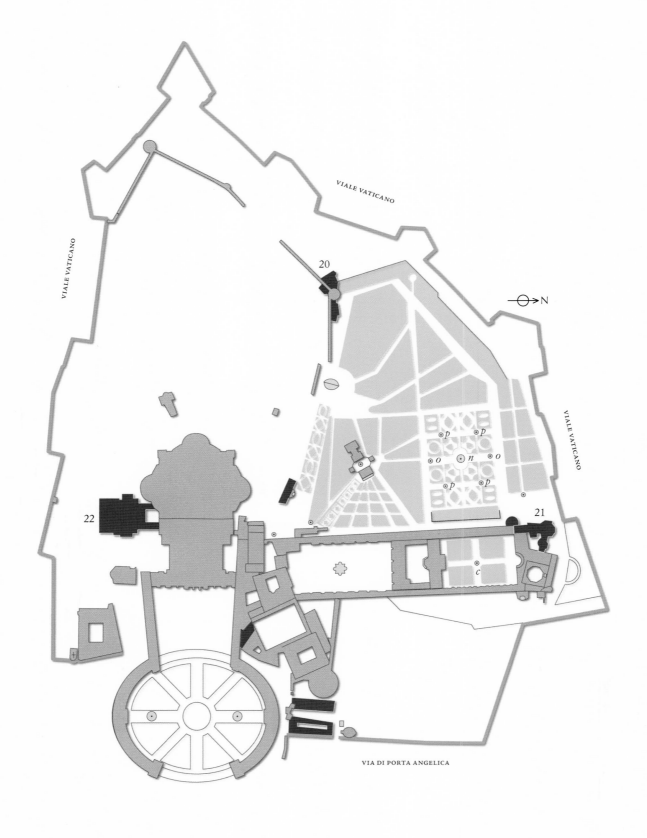

Modifications undertaken during the period discussed in this chapter are indicated in the map and captions above. For a complete map of the Vatican City and its major features in their present-day form, see page 2. Numbers in the map and captions refer to buildings and gardens, while letters refer to fountains.

THE NINETEENTH CENTURY: THE FRENCH OCCUPATION, ENGLISH STYLE, AND THE "GARDENER POPES"

Pius VII's (1800–23) triumphal return to Rome on July 3, 1800, opened a new era of projects in the Vatican Gardens. Over the course of the century, modifications were made in keeping with evolving tastes, as well as to repair the devastating damage wrought by the social upheaval that overwhelmed the city during the French occupation (1798–99), the Roman Republic (1848–49), and finally the years preceding the 1870 proclamation of Rome as the new capital of the Kingdom of Italy. The latter event definitively separated the city from the Vatican citadel, which withdrew into its confines. Consequently, the nineteenth was a difficult century for the gardens, with periods of lavish attention alternating with years of neglect and abandonment. Little research has been done on the Vatican Gardens in this period, during which at least two papal personalities, Gregory XVI (1831–46) and Leo XIII (1878–1903), left considerable evidence of their interest in the gardens.

At the start of the century, the gardens still had the appearance established at the time of Paul V (1605–21), albeit with a few limited innovations, such as the arabesque patterns in the planted beds of the Cortile della Pigna and in the garden in front of the Casina of Pius IV (plate 160). The clear division between the agricultural areas and those used for pleasure persisted. The demarcation line was still formed by the Leonine Wall: in the area to the north was the Casina of Pius IV with its formal beds, as well as the

Secret Garden of Paul III, modified in its floral design and now lacking its pergola but with its overall layout intact. The highest part of the hillside (plate 159) was dominated by the *boschereccio*, that is, the area densely planted with oaks and other trees; the steeper area to the south, between the Leonine Wall and the Basilica, contained alternating vineyards and vegetable gardens, along with such functional buildings as hay barns, chicken coops, stables, and wine cellars.

A clear and direct confirmation of the dual use of the unbuilt area within the Vatican walls can be found in the accounting books of the Sacri Palazzi Apostolici, in which everything that took place in the complex, including the gardens, was recorded. The accounts pertaining to the gardens make clear that even the pleasure areas were considered important for their productive potential, whereas references to flowering plants with solely decorative value are rare. Only once, in 1806, is there an entry for the purchase of flowers alone (one hundred pots for a sum of eight *scudi*).[1] The decorative needs at the Vatican were essentially

159. (*below*) Jacques Prou, *View of the Vatican Hill Behind St. Peter's Basilica*, c. 1680, etching. Museo di Roma.

160. (*opposite*) Borgo, the 14th historic district of Rome, Gregorian Cadastre, detail with the Casina of Pius IV. Archivio di Stato di Roma.

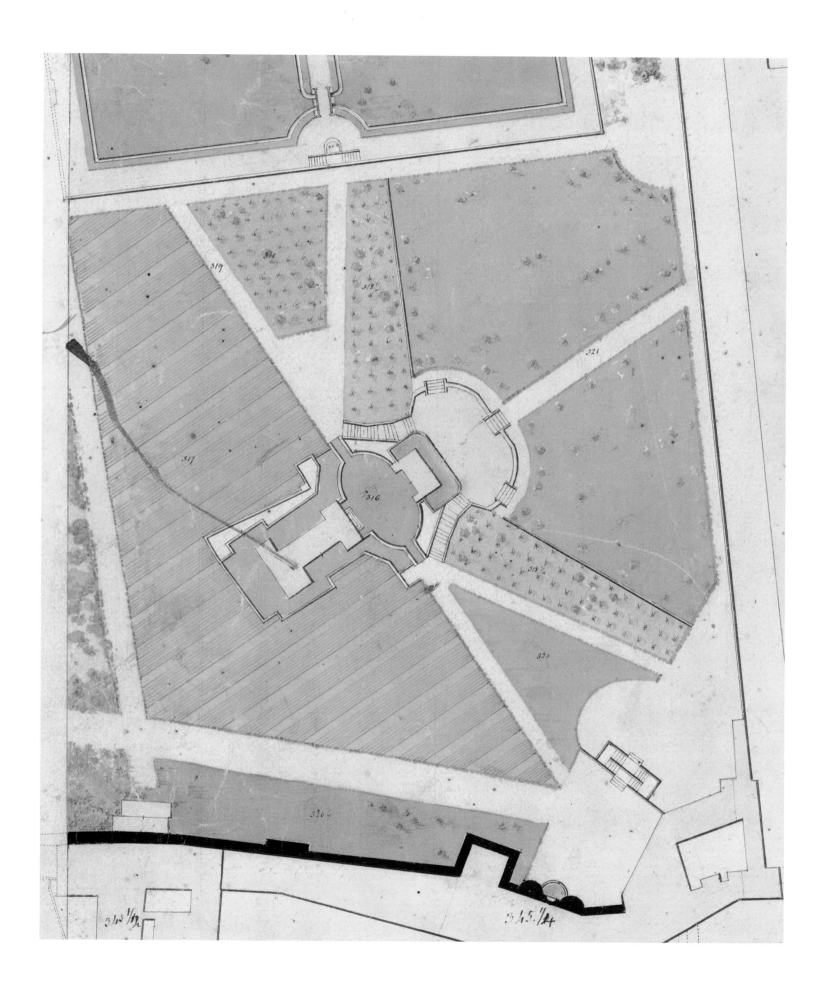

fulfilled by potted or espaliered citrus trees. Not only were these beautiful to behold, the regular sale of their fruit also produced income. This approach to the plants is confirmed by the accounts reported year after year starting in 1803, when the balance sheet shows that expenses had reached a total of 2,592.74 *scudi*, but that the revenue had covered more than half of that sum: a total of 1,451.74 *scudi*, earned from the sale of vegetables, citrus fruit, cane, and wine.[2] It is curious to note that the wine produced in the Vatican was sold, while fine wines from other regions were acquired for the table of the pope and the Curia. The vegetable garden supplied produce for internal use as well as for sale and included, depending on the season, artichokes, broccoli, lettuce, cauliflower, turnips, celery, various salad greens, legumes, *gobbi*,[3] peppers, eggplant, tomatoes, onions, garlic, and fennel. The olive trees in the gardens yielded some thirty-five jugs of oil[4] each year. Even the fruit trees, in addition to supplying the papal table, furnished products for sale: as in the seventeenth and eighteenth centuries, thousands of strawberry plants were cultivated, not all of which, surely, were intended for internal consumption. The citrus trees received the usual care: as cold weather approached, those in pots were moved to special sheds, while the espaliers were protected with mats laid over wooden structures that in many cases also had a little tile-covered roof. Citrus trees were highly valued, given that each year several thousand fruits of different kinds were brought to market. A look at the accounting books indicates that the management of the garden areas was more or less identical to that of the previous century. The same plants were cultivated and the same cleaning, pruning, and watering routines were carried out, as was the traditional gathering of "greens" for the "scattering" of leaves and flowers during the solemn procession for the annual Feast of Corpus Christi (Corpus Domini).[5]

One innovation is worth mentioning. In the first decades of the century, due to the recurrent political instability, the Vatican Gardens were repeatedly rented out to private individuals under onerous contracts designed to produce income. A snapshot of the state of the Vatican Gardens after the seating of Pius VII—and a comparison with what the register books tell us—is provided by a detailed description written on January 21, 1801, in connection with the consignment of the complex to a renter named Filippo Frigiotti, who had the obligation to "maintain, conserve, and, finally, return [it] after his tenancy in the [same] form as the…description and not otherwise."[6] The document, titled "Description of All of the Buildings, Fountains,

Basins, Open Pipes, Doors, Iron Gates, Walls, Plants, Pots of Citrus Trees, and Everything Else that Exists in the Gardens of the Vatican Palace, Known as Belvedere," is an invaluable source for understanding the gardens' layout and contents at that time, and allows for comparison with the situation at the time of Paul V Borghese, when the last major changes—immortalized in the plan by Giovanni Maggi's view of 1615—were made.

Once again we have confirmation of the area's division into pleasure gardens and agricultural fields, but this document also highlights the presence of numerous fences, each with its own gate, enclosing the various zones and cultivations.[7] Vineyards and "vegetable gardens" still occupied the entire area behind the Basilica and within the Leonine Wall, the summit of the hill near the bastions, and the lower areas next to Porta Sant'Anna. The area between Fontana della Galera and the palaces was subdivided into various cultivated plots, in which the main decorative element consisted of potted or espaliered citrus trees. There was a shed used specifically for sheltering the numerous potted citrus trees distributed throughout the gardens; it was located not far from Bramante's "snail" staircase and near the garden called "the semicircle," which had been carved out of one of the bastions at the foot of the Palazzetto del Belvedere.

The garden of Clement VII, which once occupied the terrace along the wall facing Monte Mario, also had a citrus espalier, and nearby was the "Gallinaro" and the cellar for storing the barrels of wine produced from the vineyards. Adjacent to this was the "Bosco de' Leccini," the wildest, most natural part of the park, where an "animal reserve" was situated among the expanse of oak trees. There were also many aviaries, but all were empty and abandoned. In the vineyard stood a remnant of earlier hunting traditions: a *paretaio*, or little tower, that must have been used by the men who lay in wait during the bird season. There was no longer any trace of the geometric beds around the Casina of Pius IV in the Giardino dei Semplici, but the espaliers of citrus trees endured here as well.

The two areas that had best preserved the look and feel of pleasure sites were the Cortile del Belvedere and the former Secret Garden of Paul III, both enclosed by walls and clearly separated from the rest of the park. The upper section of the Cortile del Belvedere—that is, the Cortile della Pigna—was separated from the other two terraces by another large shed for sheltering the citrus trees. (A few years later the so-called Braccio Nuovo, an extension of the museums, would be constructed on this site, definitively dividing Bramante's courtyard into three areas.) According to Gaetano Moroni, this shed was built during the papacy of Benedict XIII (1724–30) to "shelter the pots of citrus trees and flowers,"[8] and is described in the 1801 document as crammed with "big stools," on which pots of citrus trees were placed, as well as numerous "ancient inscriptions, tablets, and tombstones."[9] The courtyard space contained pedestals onto which the citrus trees were placed in warm weather; also employed in warm weather were large planters, "for the use of herbs and flowers." Additional wood structures supported other pots of flowers, and in the center of the garden was the lovely fountain dating to Bramante's time. Next to this courtyard was the Cortile della Biblioteca, bordered on its four sides by the above-mentioned shed, the Biblioteca Sistina, and the two loggias. Here, too, all the boundary walls were covered with espaliers of citrus trees; against the library wall, within "four false arches," were "four ancient marble urns full of earth, in which flowers [were] planted."[10] The four rectangular divisions of the garden, designed as parterres, were adorned with pots of citrus trees on peperino and travertine pedestals. The Secret Garden of Paul III, also surrounded by walls on all four sides, is called the "Low Garden," as it sits at the foot of a forested hill. It is described as having a fine marble portal "with bas-relief arabesques, capitals above, an architrave, frieze, and cornice," situated between two masonry walls and leading to the garden level by means of a double-ramped staircase, as can still be seen today. Following custom, the containing and enclosure walls were covered with continuous citrus espaliers, which were protected with straw mats from the winter cold. Only pedestals for supporting pots of citrus trees are described as occupying the center of the garden, and there is no indication of a division into beds. The part of the garden that in 1929 would be occupied by the Pinacoteca, or art gallery, designed by Luca Beltrami, contained another masonry shed for sheltering the citrus trees.

The description of the gardens' monumental fountains indicates that they were in a precarious state of conservation. The big Fontana dello Scoglio, or Fontana dell'Aquilone, was notably "missing many tartars and other [elements] from the niches, grotto, figures, and dragons, and the front parapet is almost completely devastated and crumbling." The Fontana degli Specchi was in even worse condition; the document states that "it is dilapidated in many parts and missing mosaics and other [ornamentation]."[11]

The overall impression created by this document is one of gardens in disrepair, with no particular attraction and a general air of neglect and poor maintenance. The payment orders registered in the Computisteria dei Palazzi, or palace accounts, show that the productive rather than decorative functions of the Vatican Gardens prevailed. Vegetable gardens now supplanted many areas that had been filled with strictly decorative arrangements in the seventeenth century, including the garden of Clement VII, the one near the Fontana della Galera, and the area next to the Casina of Pius IV. The only exceptions to this expansion of agricultural cultivation were the citrus trees along the boundary walls, which served a dual purpose: the lovely, shiny green leaves and the fruits' warm tones of yellow and orange lent beauty to the sites, while the lemons, citrons, and oranges themselves provided an important source of income, being sold on the open market in addition to supplying the Vatican table, as the regular purchases by merangolari (fruit sellers) attest.

The lease to Filippo Frigiotti lasted only two years, from 1801 to 1803, after which the gardens were again entrusted to a group of salaried gardeners headed by Rocco Moriani.[12] From October 1812 to October 1814 they were leased again,[13] a direct result of the Napoleonic decree of August 4, 1812, which gave the French possession of the Vatican citadel and gardens.[14] The rental contract, dated October 1812, contains a new, interesting, and comprehensive description of the tasks essential for the maintenance of the vineyard, the vegetable garden, and the gardens in general. From this description we can extract additional information about the condition of the sites, which seems improved in comparison with the beginning of the century. In fact, the number of fruit trees and flowering plants increased, greatly enhancing the sites. In front of the Casina of Pius IV was a garden with 250 pots for flowers, espaliers of laurel and boxwood, and some 125 fruit trees of various species, including pear, apple, apricot, plum, almond, fig, peach, quince, and pomegranate. Another 481 fruit trees included, besides those already cited, 139 olive, hazelnut, fig, and service trees in the "cordoned vineyard." In the "Low Garden"—that is, the Secret Garden of Paul III—all of the boundary walls were covered with espaliers of lemons, citrons, and sweet oranges, with their wood "armature" and "tile coverings" to protect them from the winter cold. In the center were 160 pots of various citrus trees, including bergamot oranges.[15]

However, at the end of the French occupation, despite the detailed instructions for the care of both the pleasure gardens and the productive areas—and despite documents in October 1814 showing that the leaseholder saw to the planting of lavender, carnations, various unspecified flowers, and citrus trees[16]—when the pope returned, the state of the gardens was so unsatisfactory that the majordomo, Monsignor Naro, lamented in a letter that they "needed urgent restoration."[17] Indeed, in order to fulfill this need, from 1816 to 1822 teams of *forzati*, or convicts, worked in the gardens under the supervision of guards.[18]

A memorandum from the years immediately following the return of Pius VII—unsigned and undated, but traceable to about 1815 and addressed to Secretary of State Cardinal Ercole Consalvi (1757–1824)[19]—harshly criticizes the conditions of the Janiculum Orto Botanico, which it describes as "incomplete, of little use to public instruction, and indecent for Rome." It proposes the transfer of the Orto to the Vatican Gardens[20] with an eye toward resuming the illustrious tradition of the era of Johannes Faber, *simpliciarius pontificius* from 1600 to 1629.

According to the anonymous writer, the presence of a scientific institution of this kind, through its "contiguity with the Museum," would have made "the passage from . . . the enchantments of art to those of Nature smoother, and thus Nature would appear more splendid, its materials perfected and its products enriched, the former enlivened by the industrious chisel, the latter by planned, lovely, and regular vegetation." For this project, "a more advantageous or dignified setting could not be found than the Pontifical Garden in the Vatican," which would not only contain all of the plants and auxiliary equipment necessary for such a garden, but also "constitute the delight and magnificence of the Sovereign Palace." The author demonstrates familiarity with the activities of the Academy of the Lynxes—that is, of the close linkage of art with science—through the project, begun by Michele Mercati and continued by Faber, of joining aesthetic contemplation with scientific study of the gardens; he also reproposes the old idea of gathering and publishing the many precious botanical codexes of the Biblioteca Vaticana. In addition, the document includes a proposal to entrust the new Vatican Orto Botanico to Antonio Sebastiani, who directed the Janiculum Orto Botanico from 1815 to 1820 and was also a professor of botany at La Sapienza University.[21] The memorandum, however, did not prompt any action, as we know for certain that no botanical garden was created in the Vatican Gardens after the one planted in Filippo Gilii's short-lived experiment of about 1788, and that the city's botanical garden remained on the Janiculum Hill until it was moved in 1818 to its new location next to Palazzo Corsini alla Lungara, where it remains to this day.[22]

Some notations in the payment documents reveal that in the first decades of the nineteenth century, the gardens still contained, probably in the Cortile della Pigna, the parterres visible in the eighteenth-century views. In fact, in 1816 we note the acquisition of "pozzolana [volcanic ash] to color the arabesque," that is, to create contrasts of color between the earth and the plants, and the following year "strings are stretched to design the arabesques," according to the customary procedure for executing that kind of composition.[23] This is a confirmation of the persistence, in Roman gardens, of the formal models that had been supplanted some years earlier in France and England by so-called English-style layouts, which were based on a notion of nature as free and spontaneous and no longer to be forced into rigid geometric forms. A concession to the English-style garden, however, can be found in the plan (plates 161, 162) of the Giardini del Catasto Gregoriano (Gardens of the Gregorian Cadastre), dated 1818, and thus contemporary with the cited documents, in which some winding paths can be seen in the wooded zone—evidence of an eclectic incorporation of both models.[24]

Just after the seating of Leo XII (1823–29) following the long, difficult pontificate of Pius VII, another description of the Vatican Gardens, written by an expert agronomist, was given in a *motu proprio* dated November 24, 1824, issued to "turn over [the gardens] to the respective gardeners."[25] The document contains a detailed list of all of the plants in the garden areas, comprising the gardens proper, the tracts of land cultivated with vegetables, and the vineyards. This description is confirmed by the aforementioned detailed plan of the Catasto Gregoriano[26]—created just a few years earlier, in 1818—which supplies, in its attached *brogliardo*, or legend, a precise list of the gardens' contents and arrangements. An analysis of these documents makes it possible to draw some important conclusions about the transformation and condition of the gardens. The Cortile della Pigna (plate 165) was subdivided into thirty-five squares, bordered by low boxwood hedges arranged in elaborately designed parterres, while all around were brick planters laid "on edge" directly in the ground and filled with seasonal flowers. Around the edges and in the centers of the squares, some 140 travertine bases supported pots

161. (*opposite*) Borgo, the 14th historic district of Rome, Gregorian Cadastre, detail with the woods. ASR.

162. (*pages 204–5*) Borgo, the 14th historic district of Rome, Gregorian Cadastre. ASR.

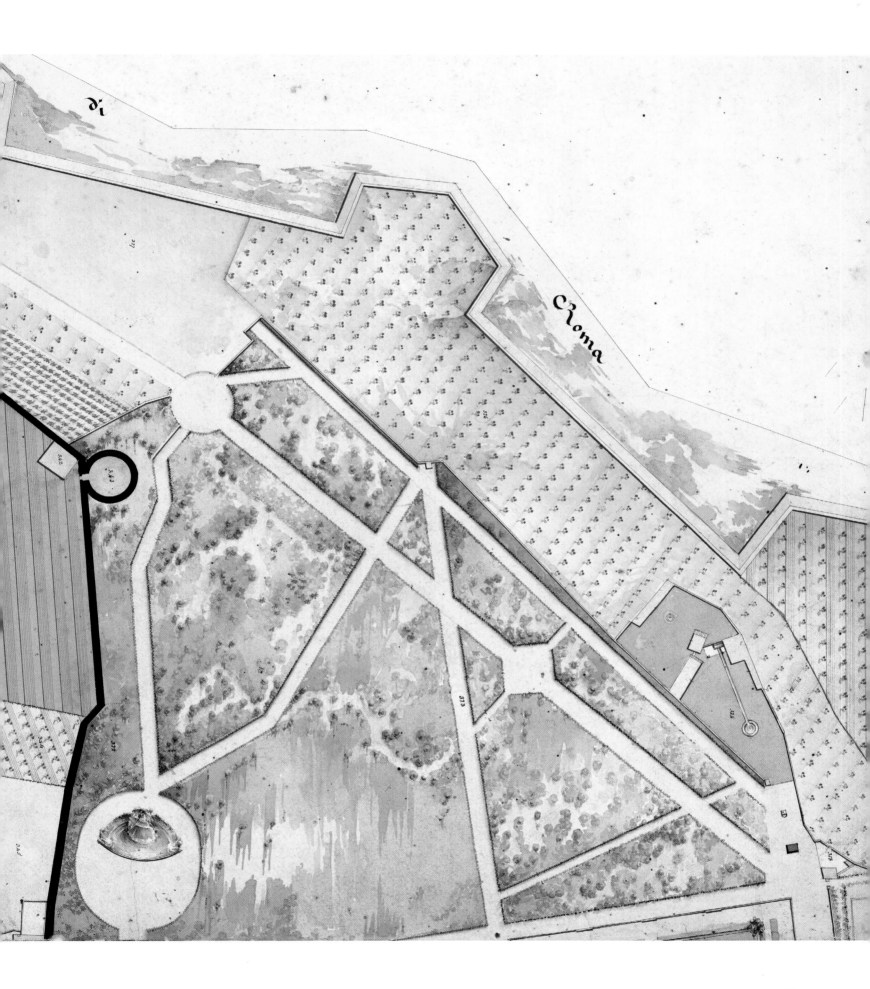

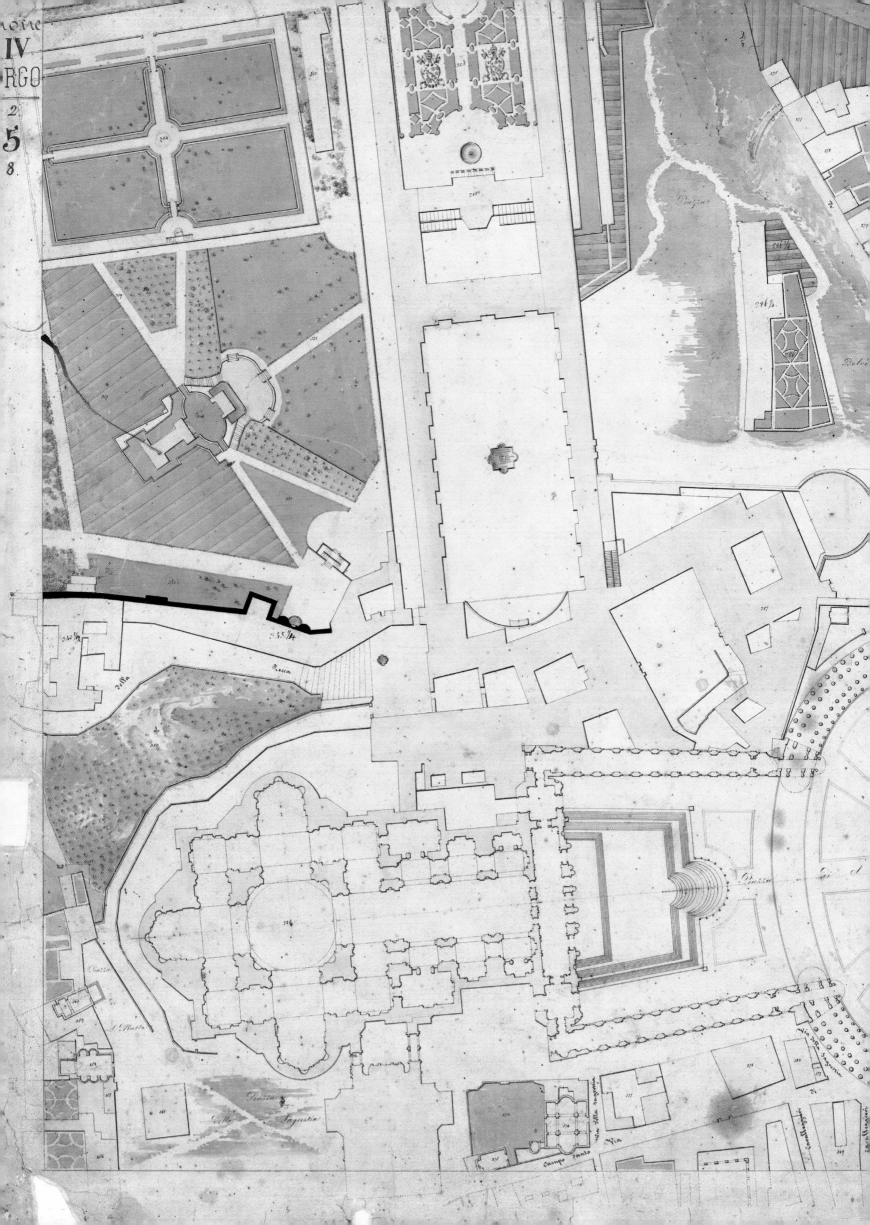

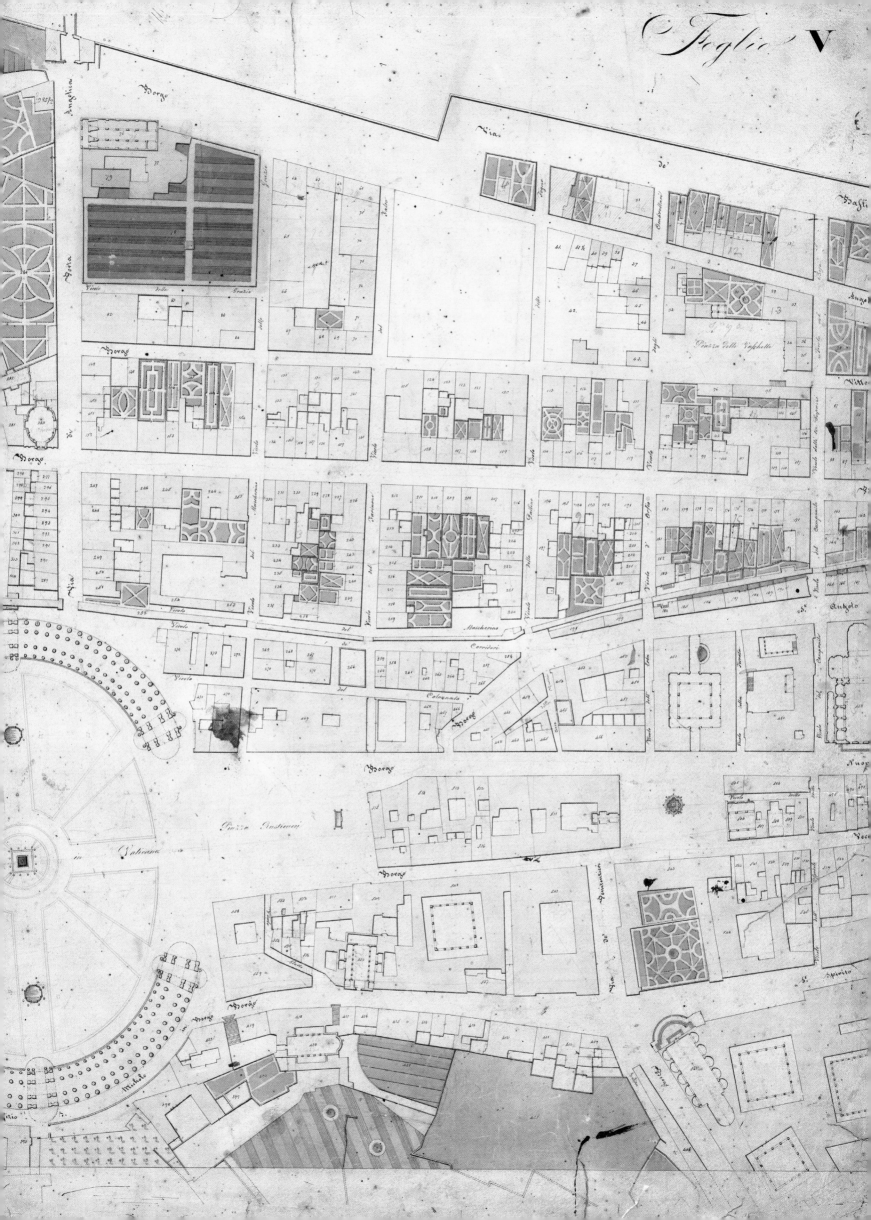

of various kinds of citrus trees. In the garden of Julius III, on the site of the Fontana della Galera, the walls were covered with the usual espaliers of citrus trees, supported and protected by a wood armature, while on the other side of the avenue was an espalier of myrtle. Here, pots of citrus trees lined the route, and an area designed as a nursery sheltered 372 small orange trees; a long strip of land contained a vegetable garden, fruit trees, and planters of yucca. Beyond the gate that divides this area from the fountain is a particularly interesting site that appears here for the first time in the history of the gardens and contains an original creation. It is the so-called "semicircle" (plates 163, 164) beneath the high, sloping wall of the Belvedere (plate 166), overlooking its bastions. It, too, was adorned with espaliers of citrus trees and flower planters—the dramatic layout of which radiated around a central structure, perhaps a pool—and it was designated a "pleasure site." Beneath the bastion the terraced area was cultivated and referred to, in the Catasto Gregoriano, as an "irrigated garden on a slope with trees."[27] The entire terrace of the garden of Clement VII was dotted with pergolas and espaliers of citrus trees, while the central area was used as a vegetable garden. The Secret Garden of Paul III, here called "Garden Below," was still bordered by walls covered with espaliers of citrus trees and divided into four large, boxwood-bordered beds, each with citrus trees at the corners and a central fountain with a circular basin; in the Catasto this is called a "pleasure garden with trench enclosure and fountains."

The Casina of Pius IV appears in the Catasto plan as "pleasure house" and in the description as "View of the Caffeaus" ("caffeaus" being a structure used for brief stops and refreshment). In the garden, defined as "productive terrain," there were sixty citrus trees and eighty-six fruit trees of various other kinds; the paths leading to the Garden Below, or Secret Garden of Paul III, were densely lined with oak trees that formed shaded *cocchi*—in other words, arcades created by the intertwined crowns of the trees. Two tracts of land that branched out from the stairs on the sides of the Casina were used as "artichoke beds with trees," again confirming the intermingling of production and pleasure.[28] The entire area in front of the building is called a "pleasure site with trees," but it was probably an orchard that, in this case as well, united the ornamental and the productive. The area behind had citrus groves and various trees, as well as a vegetable plot.

Our overall image of the gardens in these first decades of the century is that of a large orchard filled with impressive numbers of citrus trees, both potted and espaliered. The

163. The "semicircular" garden.

164. (*overleaf*) Another view of the "semicircular" garden.

laborious upkeep of this arrangement required the gardeners not only to water, fertilize, and prune the plants but also to protect them from the cold through such strategies as placing braziers with burning coals inside the *cocchi* on freezing nights.

We have no evidence of specific alterations to the gardens under Leo XII, who is remembered, however, for having "moralized" the Casina of Pius IV by removing profane sculptures, such as the four satyrlike caryatids, from the facade of the loggia facing the fish pond. This intervention was part of a substantial restoration of the entire monumental complex, which had sustained some damage as a result of the changing political tides, but which in the course of the restoration also endured the loss of some of the characteristics of Ligorio's plan, among them the contrast in the loggia between the rustic base and the classical, ethereal upper section.[29]

The pope, a passionate hunter in his youth, was also responsible for the resumption of the hunting tradition in the park. To this end, in 1824 he ordered the construction of an aviary with a copper covering,[30] and in 1825 set up a pheasant farm to which the king of the Two Sicilies contributed four hundred eggs and sent an expert gamekeeper to look after the brood. Later, in 1828, fifty pheasants arrived from the royal reserve of Capodimonte, thereby establishing a custom that is documented as continuing until 1858.[31]

A painting of the gardens (plate 167), dated 1825, allows us to verify this "natural" and slightly rustic, rundown image. Its artist, Roberto Roberti (1786–1837), chose the Belvedere as a most unusual vantage point for his work.[32] It depicts the great Viale dei Giardini (Avenue of the Gardens), created between Bramante's loggias and the gardens at the behest of Paul V Borghese and connecting the Belvedere with the Basilica and the palaces. At the end of the

165. Borgo, the 14th historic district of Rome, Gregorian Cadastre, detail with the Cortile della Pigna. ASR.

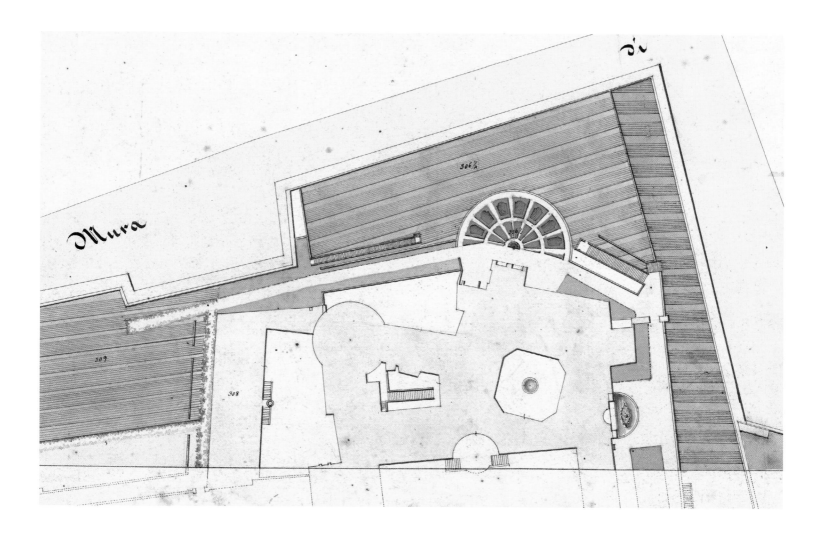

avenue the asymmetrical construction that the pope had built to create a link to the gardens can be seen near the Fontana degli Specchi. The portal that marks the end of the avenue opens onto the Piazza del Forno, which features the classic fountain that was also built under Pope Paul v. In the background is the majestic Basilica, seen from its apsidal facade, and right next to it is the beautifully designed Fontana delle Torri, or Fontana del Sacramento. Flanking the fountain, a multitude of huts with utilitarian functions are lined up along the length of the wall. These would be eliminated a century later. In the central zone is a rather plain area—a clearing with a few trees—evidence of the transformation and decline of the garden in front of the Casina of Pius IV. This area, which from the sixteenth to the eighteenth century had been characterized by elaborate formal beds filled with specimens of rare and exotic flowers, had by now lost every decorative element of value, and all traces of the design that had been documented until the mid-eighteenth century had disappeared.

The next pope, Gregory XVI (1831–46), by contrast, was very interested in the gardens and directed substantial energy and resources to their care. He introduced innovations inspired by the English style that was taking hold in Rome, albeit much later than in the rest of Europe.[33] A fine contemporary report about the work undertaken in the gardens during his papacy was written by Gaetano Moroni.[34] He attributes to the will of the pope, whom he calls an "expert in the natural sciences and especially in herbs,"[35] a general "refurbishing" of all of the boundary walls, but principally the new design by the papal gardener Sebastiano Rinaldi for the Secret Garden of Paul III (plate 169).[36] This new design is documented, and corresponds precisely with Moroni's description, in a watercolor drawing by Rinaldi's son (plate 168) that is dedicated to the pope

166. Borgo, the 14th historic district of Rome, Gregorian Cadastre, detail with the "semicircular" garden and the Palazzetto del Belvedere. ASR.

and titled *Part of the Vatican Papal Garden Newly Orna-mented and Decorated by Order of the Holiness of Our Father Gregory XVI Optimus Maximus.*[37] In the foreground the Secret Garden is depicted with geometric beds, and the coat of arms of the reigning pope is formed out of the flow-ers.[38] Pots of citrus trees border all of the paths (we know from Moroni that there were some 224 of them), and citrus espaliers line the walls. In the middle of the garden is a monumental fountain with a circular basin, a high base decorated with the papal emblems, and a gray marble basin above, still in place today. Four smaller, circular, ground-level fountains are visible at the intersections of the paths, and another two are carved into the facades set against the enclosing walls. It appears that two ancient sarcophagi are inserted into these two fountains. The large central foun-tain (plate 170) came from the Cortile della Pigna, where it had been sited by Donato Bramante in the sixteenth cen-tury; it had subsequently been removed in 1835 to make way for the base of the Colonna Antonina, which had been near the Fontana della Zitella.[39] In the distance, we can identify the Casina of Pius IV between a dense wood and an area with straight paths. Here, too, there is no trace of the geometric beds of the sixteenth-century Giardino dei Semplici, which had been documented until the mid-eighteenth century. Behind the Casina and the Secret Garden we can make out the beginning of the freer, more natural part of the park, described by Moroni as a "most surprising, wooded garden,"[40] while the area toward the city is bordered by a wall running along the Viale dei Giardini opened by Paul V, which separates the gardens from the long loggia building dating to Bramante's time. Along the course of the boundary wall the pope had ordered the open-ing of a monumental portal (plate 173), as the inscription on the architrave attests: GREGORIUS XVI PONT MAX / ADITUM AD HORTOS VATICANOS / NOVO OPERE EXORNAVIT / ANNO MDCCCXXXI SACRI PRINCIPATUS I (In the year 1831, the first year of his sacred principate, Pope Gregory XVI adorned the entrance to the Vatican Gardens with new work).

Moroni relates that there were also "two hothouses of pineapples" in the Secret Garden. They are not visible in the drawing, but they may have been on the side that is not depicted, or more precisely on the site where the Pina-coteca would later be built and where we know that there had previously been a shelter for the citrus trees. Even the wooded hillside in the background, according to Moroni,

167. Roberto Roberti, *View of the Vatican Gardens*, 1825, oil on canvas. Museo Civico of Bassano del Grappa.

168. Francesco Rinaldi, *Part of the Vatican Papal Garden
Newly Ornamented and Decorated by Order of the Holiness of
Our Father Gregory XVI Optimus Maximus*, c. 1840, drawing
with watercolor on paper. Vatican Museums.

was radically transformed—"reduced to an English garden with paths, groves, and rose beds," enriched with other flowers and plants, and adorned with marble stones, busts, and statues, "not to mention false remnants of buildings" (that is, fake ruins). Fountains and marble benches were also added, and there was even a man-made lake with a small bridge and, nearby, an open loggia from which one could "see the view of the Roman countryside."

Again according to Moroni, the pope ordered that the terrain that had been used for some time for vegetable gardens, and that had been extended into the monumental area beyond the traditional boundary of the Leonine Wall, be recuperated and returned to its original function as a pleasure area. He recounts, in fact, that Michele Mercati's sixteenth-century Giardino dei Semplici had been so neglected over the years "that neither vestige nor memory remains,"[41] but that "in 1836 the tract in front of the Casina of Pius IV was turned into a garden; and then behind the building it was decorated with orange plants, groves, and flowers."[42] Even in the site around the Fontana della Galera, "the *orto* was reduced to a garden [in 1844]: the upper part was decorated with marble busts, statues, and monuments with charming paths; the lower part was closed with three iron gates, and had a travertine staircase, a copious number of succulents with parterres of flowers and boxwood arabesques, and two beautiful fountains; and near the bastion of Paul III the magnificent greenhouse or hothouse for pineapples was built. This is made entirely of cast iron for the armature and covered with glass, length 70 *palmi*, width more than 21, and above in marble is the papal coat of arms."[43] On the site today are various structures built beginning in the 1930s, but there is no trace of the "magnificent greenhouse," which was not large—about 55¾ × 16½ feet (17 × 5 meters)—but probably resembled the hothouses for exotic plants that were being built in Roman villas of the time, for example at Villa Borghese, Villa Torlonia, and Villa Pamphilj. In addition, Moroni relates that at the foot of the Belvedere walls, "where people played ball games and bowled," the *sottoforiere* or superintendent of construction at the Vatican Apostolic Palace, Filippo Martinucci, had made a public promenade lined with trees. The Cortile della Pigna (plate 172) had been further embellished with the installation, supervised by the architect Gaspare Salvi, of the great decorated base of the Colonna Antoniniana (plate 171), which had previously stood in front of the Fontana della Zitella.[44] Many exotic plants had been placed in the gardens, along with decorative elements from the warehouses.[45] A detailed inventory of the gardens, dated

169. (*above*) The Secret Garden of Paul III.

170. (*opposite*) The fountain transferred from the Cortile della Pigna to the Secret Garden of Paul III, with the coat of arms of Gregory XVI.

January 1, 1841, allows us to retrace all of the construction mentioned above and confirms the presence of citrus trees, fruit trees, groves, and formal garden arrangements without adding any information to what we know from previous descriptions, except for a few select details of interest.[46] We learn, for example, that the grove on the hill was covered for the most part with holm oaks, common oaks, laurel, pine, and boxwood, and that it was essentially designed in the English style, with its numerous decorative elements including a reflecting pool, not large but with a small wooden bridge, and—scattered among the paths—urns, herms, and stones; some fifteen statues, both fragmentary and intact; columns "solid and broken"; "ornamental fragments"; and myriad inscriptions. As Moroni also recounts, there was even a fake temple ruin. Many statues and ancient fragments were distributed here and there in the Secret Garden of Paul III, while statues and small marble pyramids adorned the piazza in front of the Casina of Pius IV.

What emerges is a complete inversion of the tendency of the previous decades: a reduction of the productive areas in favor of the pleasure grounds—particularly where the monumentality of the sites was incompatible with the cultivation of garlic and onions—accompanied by the introduction of eclectic decorative elements, in keeping with the new fashion of art in gardens. In confirmation of the renewed allure of the gardens, Moroni writes that in order to limit the number of visitors, an entrance ticket—already a widespread custom in other Roman villas, such as the Villa Borghese[47]—had been instituted, while noble guests were admitted on request, as numerous letters in the archives confirm.[48]

Even the rural area, newly delimited by the Leonine Wall, was subject to modification. The vineyards were arranged *a cordoni*, that is, in cordons, on terraces created by great excavations of earth; the aviaries were enlarged, repaired, and populated with pheasants and peacocks; and the "hunting site," as Moroni calls it (we can deduce that it was the *paretaio*, or bird trap, on the hill), was restored.[49] The previously cited inventory of 1841 mentions "a marble balustrade with two small, equal pyramids" next to the *paretaio*, which shows that even in the rural area ornament was not overlooked. Confirming the renewed interest in hunting, which was limited to birds, is the documented arrival in 1841 from Lombardy of 1,500 chaffinches and three falcons.[50]

The innovations introduced in the Vatican Gardens during the papacy of Gregory XVI could not escape the notice of such an expert traveler and garden lover as Louis Eustache Audot, who in 1839 and 1840 toured the principal cities of southern Italy, including Rome, and left vivid descriptions of the gardens he visited.[51] He found the Vatican Gardens much improved (perhaps in comparison to an earlier visit) and well maintained. Once abandoned and impenetrable woods had been transformed by the gardener Sebastiano Rinaldi into cool, pleasant sites with well-planned paths and ancient marbles. The pope had received compliments from his French guest, whom he told of his passion for flowers and for the gardens, where he strolled every day despite his advancing age. He also told him that he had commissioned seven fountains,[52] in addition to those that already existed, and listened with interest to Audot's account of the activities of the Société Royale d'Horticulture of Paris, to which the Frenchman promised to present a report on the gardens he had observed and on his conversation with the pope.[53]

The years to come were again marked by a difficult political situation, and Pius IX (1846–78) was not able to attend to the embellishment and care of the Vatican Gardens during his papacy. Shortly after his election, in fact, he was faced with the events of the second Roman Republic, which

171. The Cortile della Pigna with the base of the Colonna Antonina, c. 1862, albumen print.

172. Paolo Cacchiatelli, Gregorio Cleter, *The Cortile della Pigna,*
c. 1845, etching.

173. (*overleaf*) Portal with inscription commemorating
Gregory XVI.

involved the Vatican citadel directly, and in particular the battle of April 30, 1849. In July, after order was restored, the *sottoforiere* Filippo Martinucci presented Marquis Sacchetti, pro-prefect of the Sacred Apostolic Palaces, with a detailed memo describing the damage to the Vatican palaces and gardens.[54] Almost all of the windows of the greenhouses were broken, and many of the drain covers were damaged; an espalier of citrus trees had been burned, and the walls were punctured by cannon fire in many places. In addition, the gardens were dotted with little huts built by the occupying soldiers for shelter out of the beams that supported the espaliers, which were consequently damaged and in need of reinforcement. The pheasants had been stolen from the aviary, and some 164 trees—more precisely, 58 elms, 15 holm oaks, 85 mulberries, 3 cypresses, and 3 pines—had been cut down. Finally, throughout the park there were remnants of barricades, with mounds of earth to be removed and trenches to fill. One can only imagine the great effort and commitment necessary to return the area to its previous state, much less contemplate innovations or embellishments.

Pius IX did not have family residences at his disposal and visited the villa in Castel Gandolfo only rarely, when the political situation permitted, between 1851 and 1869.[55] During his forced seclusion in the Vatican he almost always took a daily walk in the gardens, usually around midday, and allowed the visitors who happened to be there to approach and speak with him.[56] About 1869 he commissioned the architect Virginio Vespignani to design a monument to the First Vatican Council. This was intended to be built on the Janiculum Hill and to consist of a tall marble column, topped with a bronze statue of St. Peter by Filippo Gnaccarini (plate 174), and a square marble base adorned with the depiction, in low relief, of the story of the council executed by Pietro Galli. The political events of 1870 delayed the project, and only in 1885 was the monument finally erected, not on the Janiculum but inside the Vatican citadel, in the Cortile della Pigna. However, in the 1930s it was dismantled and moved to a site near the Gardener's House, where some elements of it are still visible (plate 175).

The tradition of "gardener pope," which had produced so many interesting innovations under Gregory XIV, was to be repeated during the long papacy of Leo XIII Pecci. By the start of his reign, Leo XIII was already an established resident of the Vatican, but he was originally from the nearby town of Carpineto and nurtured a great love for nature and the Roman countryside, which had inspired him

to write this couplet: "Quam felix flore in primo, quam laeta Lepinis / Orta jugis, patrio sub lare, vita fuit" ("How fortunate was life in first bloom, how happy it was, begun in the Lepini Mountains, in my ancestral home!"). The gardens' condition at the time of his seating is clearly captured in a fine watercolor etching by Félix Benoist (plate 176), part of the series of views called *Rome dans sa grandeur*, published in 1870. The view of the Vatican Gardens, as seen from the cupola of St. Peter's, depicts the whole area of the gardens proper except for the rural zones. In the foreground are the palaces and the Piazza del Forno with its classic fountain; next to these is the newly begun Leonine Wall, which is partially obscured by the irregular constructions abutting it. Beyond the wall we can see the grand Fontana dello Scoglio, behind which the woods extend as far as the summit of the hill. In the flat area between the woods and Bramante's loggias are the gardens around the Casina of Pius IV and the Secret Garden of Paul III, both clearly bounded by walls covered with espaliers of citrus trees. The gardens around the Casina appear much more decorous and better cared for than in depictions from the first half of the century, yet the original division into beds has been completely lost. The garden paths are arranged in a radial pattern and covered with pergolas; the hedges are pruned and geometrically aligned. The Secret Garden of Paul III retains the layout it had after Gregory XVI's modifications: a division into sixteen beds, with the lovely Bramantesque fountain in the center and the four fountains placed at intersections of the paths. The coat of arms of the reigning pope has been rendered in an artful composition of flowers, and on one side is a building that was probably the above-mentioned shelter for citrus trees and exotic plants. The barely visible Cortile del Belvedere is now divided into three sections, the first of which is organized into beds.

The Pecci pope's unusual and passionate relationship with the Vatican Gardens has been described in two very lively texts, which are interesting primarily because they relate episodes of daily life reported by people who were eyewitnesses to his papacy. The first is the fine book by Silvio Negro, *Vaticano minore*, published in 1936, at a time close enough to the pontificate of Leo XIII to include direct sources. The second, *I Papi in campagna* (*The Popes in the Countryside*), by Emilio Bonomelli, was published in 1953 and is based on original, previously unpublished documents to which the author had direct access in his position as head of the papal gardens.

When Leo XIII came to the Vatican, he found the gardens in a general state of disarray and neglect, which extended to such celebrated sites as the Cortile of the Belvedere Library. According to Negro's description: "In that old, forsaken place the grass grew so tall in the fissures that sheep were brought in to graze on it; chickens scratched about and ducks dove in the sixteenth-century fountains."[57] To remedy a situation that was certainly not in keeping with the dignity of the residence of the head of the Catholic Church, renovation work quickly began, and the courtyard, no longer paved, was made into a garden. However, the love and care lavished on the gardens was foiled by the expansiveness and magnanimity of the pope, who opened them indiscriminately to pilgrims, with the result that "those gatherings in the middle of the beds were anything but appropriate for the preservation of the flowers or the cultivation of vegetables."[58] To enable the pope to climb the hillside in a carriage, the grand avenue that still hugs the Vatican walls on the side toward Monte Mario was created. It is lined with plane trees and holm oaks and affords a

splendid view of the surrounding countryside, which was still rural at the time. The carriage road undoubtedly altered the "natural" character of the woods, but it attested to the pope's desire to enjoy the entire expanse of the gardens, which, in his forced seclusion, constituted his only "holiday destination." It is not by chance that the definition of the Vatican Gardens as "our little Castel Gandolfo"[59] is attributed to Pope Leo XIII, as the gardens took the place of the summer residence into which no pope, from 1869 until 1934, set foot.[60]

Both of the authors cited are highly critical of the Vatican Gardens, in sharp contrast to their broader reputation;

174. (*below left*) Filippo Gnaccarini, *Saint Peter*, 1869, bronze statue, once part of the monument to the First Vatican Council.

175. (*below right*) Remains of the monument to the First Vatican Council.

French writer Émile Zola, for instance, called them "the most beautiful garden in the world."[61] Bonomelli stressed that they had, at the time, "a heterogenous and fairly run-down appearance,"[62] because, as Negro specified more precisely, "each pope who took an interest in the low hillside added to it what best corresponded to his temperament, and the result was something between a garden and a park, between the shady promenade of a convent among the many chapels and statues and the flowery embankment of a fortress through the solid ramparts that surround it."[63] Undoubtedly, the irregularity of the terrain impeded the "harmonious unity (of the gardens) of other regal palaces," but the defining characteristic of the Vatican Gardens was indeed "a strange mixture…a bizarre alternation of architectural views and little vegetable gardens planted with cabbage and lettuce."[64]

One element of disorder, apart from the eclecticism of the layouts, was the rustic section bordered by the Leonine Wall, which, as can be seen in some prints of the period, "was all a tangle of planters, vegetable plots, and little vineyards, with a big mill and a road that was little more than a country lane."[65] The garden of Paul III, by contrast, was appreciated by the two authors, who referred to it as the "Secret Garden" or "citrus garden." They approved of the changes made under Gregory XVI, whom they also praised for the English-style transformation of the woods surrounding the Casina of Pius IV.[66] It seems clear that both writers preferred formal gardens with geometric beds, in keeping with the revival of the Italian garden style that was in vogue at the time of their respective writings, but that during the pontificate of Leo XIII had yet to come and would only enter the Vatican citadel with Pius XI (1922–39).

In Rome during the last decades of the nineteenth century, rustic taste still dominated, and the reigning pope, a great enthusiast of the georgic side of the gardens, contributed to the growth of their rusticity. Although he delighted in botany and loved flowers, so much so that he is said to have picked whichever ones struck his fancy during his frequent strolls, Pius's true passion was the vineyard. To look after them, he summoned from Padua a "singular and bizarre personage," Don Condeo, considered an expert in the care of vineyards. The pope was convinced that he had created a model vineyard, for which he had imported vines from the Burgundy region of France, and he closely followed the seasonal operations of pruning and grafting

176. Félix Benoist, *View of Rome in All Its Splendor*, 1870, etching.

and introduced innovative cultivation techniques. He even advised priests who lived in the countryside to study and apply these novel agricultural practices as an occupation befitting their status. According to Bonomelli, however, the results of such efforts were less than dazzling, as the wine produced was of such poor quality that it found no buyers and was generally given away to communities and convents.[67] There were really three distinct vineyards: the first, and largest, toward the bastions of Sangallo; the second—and the pope's favorite—near the tower of Nicholas v; and the third, on a small plain that is occupied today by the railroad station.[68] During his daily walks in the garden, the pope chatted with the head gardener, Cesare Balzani, discussing botany and showing off his knowledge of Latin scientific terminology.[69]

The pope's habit of receiving visitors in the garden is immortalized in a fine micro-mosaic (plate 181) by Biagio Barzotti, mosaicist of the Fabbrica del Mosaico di San Pietro,[70] roughly datable to the 1880s. It shows the seated pope welcoming some cardinals on the terrace at the foot of the Palazzetto del Belvedere, near the portal built under Pius VI, which opens onto the path running past the Fontana della Galera. Plants in vases, agaves in particular, decorate the piazza, and in the background the city, with the unmistakable silhouette of Castel Sant'Angelo, can be seen.

Leo XIII's rural origins and his youthful love of the hunt led him to build a *roccolo*,[71] a snare for catching birds, in the upper part of the woods (where the Madonna della Guardia can be found today), bending the crowns of trees in such a way that they formed a net. Bonomelli saw the vestiges of this trap and, remembering those times, asked himself what had become of the registers of the catch—"kept day by day with meticulous precision, with indications of the weather and the winds"—that the pope "consulted with his trusty fowler, to draw comparisons and auspices from other hunting experiences."[72] For the "rustic" sector, the pope also wanted a new cowshed and an enclosure for the does, roe deer, gazelles, ostriches, and pelicans given to him in 1888 by Cardinal Lavigerie, the archbishop of Carthage, on the occasion of his sacerdotal jubilee.[73]

Because of his forced seclusion in the Vatican complex, during the summer months the pope went from time to time to the Casina of Pius IV, which was equipped for brief stays only and did not have views or clean air. To create a semblance of a holiday residence, in 1890 the large keep situated along the Leonine Wall was restored. Its dominant position with a fine view of the gardens below was perfect for the pope's summer stays. Following a design by the architect Costantino Sneider,[74] who was in charge of the Sacred Apostolic Palace after the death of Virginio and Francesco Vespignani, the single large space of the upper floor of the keep—a circular room (plate 177)—was decorated in such a manner as to minimize the imposing presence of the fortress walls and luxuriously appointed with inlaid furniture and crystal lamps. Decorated panes of glass filtered the light as it entered the windows, and on the ceiling the artist Ludovico Seitz (1844–1908) painted the vault a celestial blue, ornamented with the constellation Leo in homage to the pope. Many tiny electric light bulbs were lit in imitation of stars, creating the illusion of open sky.[75] In order to receive the pope's retinue and host his audiences, a small brick chalet crowned with crenellations—almost a small fort—was built next to the keep. The tract of the Leonine Wall between the keep, with its annexed chalet (plates 178–80), and the next tower had crumbled some time earlier; to rebuild the link, a futuristic metal walkway—a kind of elevated viaduct—was built.[76]

By now, the pope's advanced age made his habitual strolls in the garden increasingly difficult. However, on June 1, 1902, at the venerable age of ninety-two, Leo XIII returned to the gardens after a year's absence to inaugurate the still-unfinished monument to the Madonna of Lourdes. That same year he had a row of holm oaks planted along the road near the keep and the chalet, where he had spent some afternoons, though he was aware he would not be able to witness the slow growth of the trees. In 1903, a few days before his death, he was able to return once again to the garden he had so loved, where he had been immortalized in numerous photographs during events celebrated in his personal "holiday residence."

177. Leo XIII's room in the radio tower, from *Illustrazione Vaticana*, no. 19, 1931.

178. (*below left*) The chalet built at the behest of Leo XIII, in an early twentieth-century postcard.

179. (*below right*) The chalet in a photograph from the 1930s.

180. (*opposite*) The chalet with the radio tower and the Leonine Wall.

181. Biagio Barzotti, *Leo XIII in the Gardens*, c. 1880, micro-mosaic. Collection of Gianni Giordani.

12. The Secret Garden of Paul III, reduced after the construction of the Pinacoteca

14. The Giardino dei Semplici, converted into an English-style garden

23. The Pinacoteca of Luca Beltrami

24. The expansion of the Casina of Pius IV

25. The Ethiopian College

26. The Palazzo del Governatorato

27. The radio tower

28. Palazzo di Giustizia

29. Train station

30. Mosaic studio

31. The Italian garden

32. Monument and grotto of Our Lady of Lourdes

33. Rose Garden

34. New buildings

q. Fountains in the woods from the period of Benedict XV and Pius XI

r. Fontana delle Ranocchie

s. Fontana della Conchiglia

t. Fountains in the Italian garden

u. Fontana della Navicella

v. Fontana del Tritone and Fontana della Sirena

w. Fontana di S. Marta

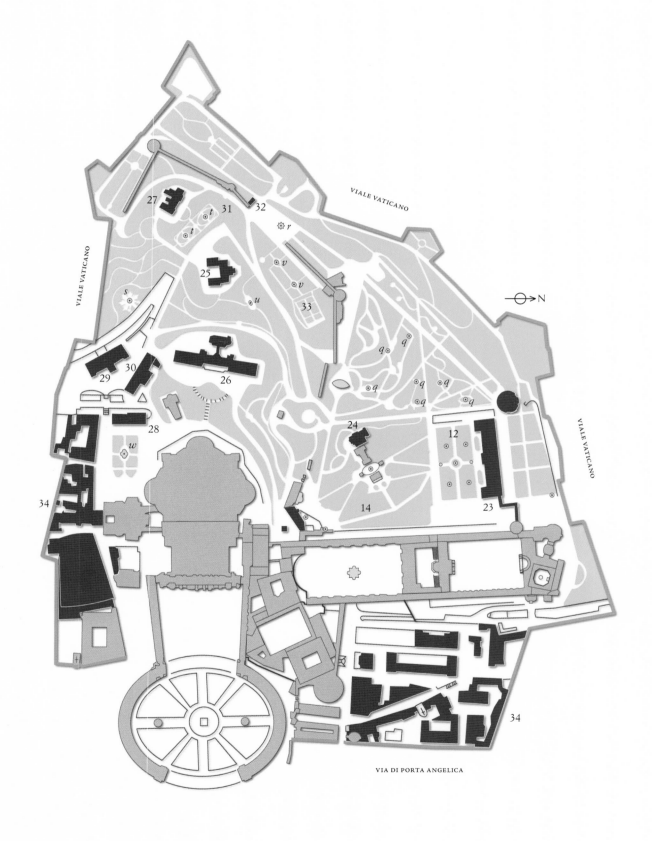

Modifications undertaken during the period discussed in this chapter are indicated in the map and captions above. For a complete map of the Vatican City and its major features in their present-day form, see page 2. Numbers in the map and captions refer to buildings and gardens, while letters refer to fountains.

CHAPTER EIGHT

THE NEW IMAGE
OF THE CITY-STATE,
1900–1930 AND BEYOND:
GARDENS, FOUNTAINS,
BUILDINGS, AND MONUMENTS

After the lengthy pontificate of the "gardener pope" Leo XIII, the twentieth century (plate 182) opened with Pope Pius X Sarto (1903–14), who, accustomed as he was to the unlimited horizons of the Veneto country-side, did not care for the confined, reduced space at his disposal and called the Secret Garden of Paul III, which Gregory XVI had embellished with statues and fountains, a "cemetery," because it was enclosed within walls and geometrically ordered.[1]

Pius X was responsible for the construction of the underpass that leads directly from the Cortile del Belvedere to the gardens, as well as for the transfer of the *Specola vaticana*, or Vatican observatory, from the Torre dei Venti to the keep with the chalet where Leo XIII "vacationed." In addition, at his behest the fake grotto containing the Madonna of Lourdes was completed with an overlaid, neo-Gothic construction for use as a chapel. It was demolished in the 1970s (plates 183, 184).

Pope Benedict XV (1914–22), although not particularly enthusiastic about the gardens, visited them every morning in his carriage to pay homage to the Madonna della Guardia, the monument donated in 1917 by his native city, Genoa, as a replica of the sanctuary of the same name overlooking that city's port. Nevertheless, certain modifications did take place in the gardens during his pontificate, including the creation of some wide roads (plate 185) as well as the channeling of water to feed three new rustic fountains and a lively addition to the site known as the *boschereccio*: a spectacular composition of rocks crisscrossed with numerous little streams and waterfalls (plates 188, 189).[2] The first-constructed of the three fountains (plate 190) has a travertine wall abutted by an embankment and a central pool surmounted by a large water-spouting mask. Above the latter is a pediment composed of the papal crest surrounded by volutes, garlands, and the inscription BENE-DICTUS XV PONT. MAX / PRISTINAM HORTORUM AMOENI-TATEM REVOCAVIT AUXIT ANNO II ("In his second year, Pope Benedict XV renewed and increased the former pleasantness of the gardens"). Completing the decoration are two travertine basins at the summit and a large terra-cotta vase at either end of the wall. The second fountain, at the center of a shady clearing dotted with fragments of sculpture used for seating, has a quadrilobed pool in a cross-shaped apron of cement mortar, as well as a small basin with a high central spout surrounded by five others that spray water out of the pool (plate 191). This is a rustic construction, made with such inexpensive materials as mortar and rocaille. Its design is simple, perhaps conceived by the garden laborers themselves. There is no sense, in fact, of its having an architectural plan; it certainly cannot be compared to the spectacular seventeenth-century fountains designed for Pope Paul V by Carlo Maderno, Giovanni Vasanzio, Flaminio Ponzio, and Martino Ferrabosco. The third fountain, while modestly sized, was the only one with a monumental or architectural aspect made during the papacy of Benedict XV. It consists of a mixtilinear, six-lobed pool with a central, cylindrical turret surrounded by little arches and topped by a small basin with a central spout. The upper edge of the turret contains an inscription commemorating the pope-commissioner and the year of the fountain's execution, 1920 (plate 192).

A lovely photograph (plate 186) records the gardens as they appeared during the papacy of Benedict XV. In the foreground the Secret Garden of Paul III still has the regular beds designed at the time of Gregory XVI, only now they are traversed by little paths and adorned with palm trees and flower compositions recalling the "mosaic-cultivation" technique,[3] also used in the center of the garden to form the coat of arms of the reigning pope and that of his immediate predecessor, Pius X. In the middle ground, we can clearly see the tunnel that Pius X ordered built from the Cortile del Belvedere to the gardens and then to the Casina of Pius IV, surrounded by an eclectic grove of palm, pine, and cypress trees and two *cocchi*, or covered walkways, of holm oaks. In the background, along the walls, we can recognize the seventeenth-century Fontana delle Torri, or Fontana del Sacramento, followed by a row of utilitarian buildings. Farther back, next to the majestic apse of the Basilica, we can discern the beginning of the agricultural area. A description of the gardens by a certain Bechnick, translated into Italian from its original German and dating to the years of Benedict XV's papacy, suggests that by this time there were no longer citrus trees in the gardens: Bechnick mentions orchards, but makes no reference to espaliers, *cocchi*, or potted plants. In addition, this obscure writer, who refers to an official position connected to his profession, declares that the "maintenance…leaves much to be desired" and laments the fact that more is not being done to beautify and preserve the gardens.[4]

During the pontificate of Pope Ratti, Pius XI (1922–39), the layout of the Vatican citadel was truly revolutionized. The way the gardens look today derives largely from the developments that took place during the last ten years of this papacy—developments involving not only the

182. The Vatican Gardens in the twentieth century.

184. *(top)* The Gothic chapel seen from above, from *Illustrazione Vaticana*, no. 1, 1933.

185. *(above)* An avenue in the woods, from *Illustrazione Vaticana*, no. 5, 1932.

183. *(above)* The Grotto of Lourdes with the Gothic chapel, from *Illustrazione Vaticana*, no. 10, 1931.

186. (*above*) The gardens in an early twentieth-century photo taken from the Belvedere.

187. (*above*) The gardens in an early twentieth-century photo taken from the cupola of St. Peter's.

188, 189. Fountain with small cascades
from the period of Benedict XV.

BENEDICTVS·XV·PONT·MAX·
PRISTINAM·HORTORVM·AMOENITATEM·REVOCAVIT·AVXIT·ANNO·II

190. Fountain with inscription commemorating Benedict xv.

191. *(below)* Fountain with jets.

192. *(opposite)* Turret-shaped fountain with inscription commemorating Benedict xv.

transformation of the existing design but also the conspicuous recovery of the rural sector for use as pleasure grounds, with the creation of new, eclectic, and highly original arrangements of the garden areas.

At the start of Pius XI's papacy, the garden area of the citadel, by now definitively separated from Rome, held little appeal. The agricultural sector was subdivided into various plots, and there were numerous small functional buildings of no aesthetic value. The Secret Garden of Paul III and the Cortile della Pigna retained their formal designs, but in general the garden areas had become more "naturalized," taking on the appearance of a rustic park punctuated with some spectacular vestiges of history, such as the Casina of Pius IV, the remains of the Leonine Wall, and the monumental or curious fountains from the epoch of Paul V. A fine photograph from the start of the century (plate 187), taken from the cupola of St. Peter's, shows the layout of the sites before the transformations commissioned by Pius XI. In the foreground we see the series of buildings abutting the Leonine Wall, the expanse of vineyards and vegetable plots, and beyond the wall the historical garden with the Casina of Pius IV and the two pergola-covered roads leading to the Secret Garden of Paul III. Visible beyond this is the expanding city, which would soon replace the numerous brick buildings whose chimneys still dominate the landscape.

The first years of the Ratti papacy did not bring major innovations, but to allow for strolls in the garden on rainy days, Pius XI had two long sheltered promenades built along the sides of the Leonine Wall;[5] they were subsequently removed, but are remembered in an inscription: PIUS XI P.M. / AMBULATIONEM AB IMBRIBUS TUTAM / FIERI IUSSIT ANNO III ("In his third year, Pope Pius XI had a promenade built, safe from the rains"). He then had some fountains built in the same style as those commissioned by his predecessor. These, too, were made of cement mortar and rocaille and may have been the work of the same laborers. In the woods, several modest, rustic fountains were installed, each featuring three spheres and an eagle—elements of the reigning pope's coat of arms—in plain view. The first of these fountains consists of a round basin abutting a rocky crag, against which the papal coat of arms, fashioned from cement mortar, stands out as a decorative element. A cylinder with three spheres in relief supports the heraldic eagle, crowned by the papal tiara. The second fountain, made of the same materials and similar in style, also has a circular basin, at the center of which is

a mound supporting the spheres, the eagle, and a two-tiered circular element, which in turn supports a group of "candle holders" spouting jets of water (plate 193). A third fountain, again made of the same rustic materials, has at its the center a kind of chunky candelabrum of five branches, each with a gushing spout (plates 194, 195).

The condition of the sites until 1929, before the major modifications that would revolutionize the Vatican Gardens and the entire citadel, is documented with great precision in a finely detailed plan (plate 196) and description by Count Federico Paolozzi, dated 1924 and dedicated to the pope.[6] The plan is watercolored and reproduces exclusively the area of the gardens bordered by the Leonine Wall, beyond which the "fields cultivated with vineyards" are labeled.[7] The gardens are divided into six sectors, identified by letters, and for each sector there is a detailed legend listing all of the objects of interest to be found within: fountains, portals, benches, pots, busts, statues, amphoras, urns, small obelisks, monuments, architectural fragments, columns, and capitals—a total of some 166 elements. The image conveyed is that of a garden replete with sculptural decorations, many undoubtedly added during the nineteenth century in keeping with the fashion of English-style gardens. In particular, the Secret Garden of Paul III and the woods (divided into two sectors, marked by the letters B and C) behind the Casina of Pius IV appear to be crisscrossed by winding paths and sprinkled with myriad statues, busts, and fountains, as well as the "remnants of a little temple with columns and capitals"—in other words, a fake ruin. The woods also included a small lake with an irregular outline, around which are various ancient marble fragments used for seating. The statues and busts in the gardens are generally ancient and depict such mythological figures as Jupiter, Flora, Ceres, Apollo, Minerva, and Bacchus, along with Roman emperors, warriors, and orators. Some of the subjects are not identified, and it is striking how many of the statues are headless, primarily those located in the area near the Casina of Pius IV. The woods also included sentry boxes, two aviaries—identified in the plan by drawings of variously colored birds—and some greenhouses. Four of the latter are aligned in the Secret Garden of Paul III, against the boundary wall, on the site where the Pinacoteca would later be built; others are near the so-called semicircle, the garden beneath the Palazzetto

193. Fountain with "candle holders" and the coat of arms of Pius XI.

194. *(below)* Fontana del Candelabro (candelabrum), from *Illustrazione Vaticana*, no. 1, 1933.

195. *(right)* Fontana del Candelabro.

196. *(pages 246–47)* Federico Paolozzi, *New Plan of the Vatican Gardens with a List of the Monuments Held There*, 1924, drawing with watercolor. Vatican Museums.

New map of the Vatican Gardens with the list of the monuments held there, executed by Count Federico Paolozzi and dedicated by him with filial devotion to the Holy Father Pius XI, happily reigning in the year of our Lord MCMXXIIII

LEGEND

A-1 Large fountain composed of a round basin above a pedestal decorated with the coats of arms of Gregory XVI

A-2 Roman emperor in the act of speaking

A-3 Jupiter with thunderbolt

A-4 Roman warrior

A-5 The aged Augustus with horn of plenty and swagger stick

A-6 Roman urn with effigy of a married couple and small fountain

A-7 Shelf with small putto and ornate bases of [...]

A-8 Bust of a Roman man

A-9 Roman statue of Flora

A-10 Fountain with head of a lion

A-11 Roman statue of a female water-bearer

A-12 Niche with little statue of a woman with amphora on a small shelf

A-13 Bust of Benedict XV

A-14 Portal in the style of Sansovino with inscription honoring Pius IV

A-15 Roman bust above an arch

A-16 Bust of a Doctor of the Church

A-17 Statue of Lucretia seated and adjacent fountain with head of a lion and water of Saint Damasus

A-18 Roman bust of a man above a door

A-19, 20 Two earthenware pots with embedded pedestal

B-1 Bust of a Roman with drapery of pink marble over a capital, above a base with a gorgon's head

B-2 Small obelisk above a base with the head of a woman

B-3 Another of the same above a base with the head of a woman

B-4 Statue of a semi-nude emperor in the act of speaking

B-5 Earthenware pot from which bath water runs out

B-6 Seat with coat of arms

B-7 Seat with frieze of a lion devouring a goat

B-8 Seat with fragment of a female statue

B-9 Seat with memorial stone

B-10 Bust of a Roman above a decorated column

B-11, 12 Two pieces of similar decorated columns

B-13 Roman bust on a base with female head

B-14 Shattered capital with vase

B-15 Monument to a child on granite column

B-16 Fountain in the form of a Greek cross

B-17 Pedestal amphora

B-18 Monument with various friezes and coat of arms of Urban VIII

B-19 Oblong fountain basin with shelf

B-20 Statue of a woman

B-21 Capital

B-22 Niche fountain built at the behest of Benedict XV

B-23 Amphora

B-24 Seat with sarcophagus fragment

B-25 Small obelisk on a capital

B-26 Coat of arms of Innocent VIII

B-27 Seat with column fragments and laurel friezes

B-28 Capital on a base

B-29 Remains of antique walls

B-30 Large earthenware pot with cover on high pedestal

C-1 Bench with coat of arms of Urban VIII

C-2 Fountain with little dolphins and shell

C-3 Decorated vase on pedestal

C-4 Remainder of small temple with columns and capitals

C-5 Amphora, capital, and sarcophagus fragment with effigy of a married couple

C-6 Seated statue of Apollo Citharist

C-7 Bench with head of a woman

C-8 Statue of Ceres on round pedestal

C-9 Large fountain with two tritons built at the behest of Paul V

C-10 Column with jar

C-11 Amphora on iron pedestal

C-12 Little kneeling man with stick

C-13 Memorial stone bordered with friezes and laurel leaves

C-14 Large earthenware pot with cover on pedestal

C-15 Decorated vase on pedestal

C-16 Well with fragmentary inscription and piece of a cover

C-17 Earthenware pot with cover on pedestal

C-18 Bust of Minerva

C-19 Column with capital and vase on base with bas-relief head

C-20 Bust of a man

C-21 Fountain built at the behest of Benedict XV with inscription, coat of arms, little obelisks, and fountain spout in the form of a mask

C-22 Fountain with magnificent urn above a historiated pedestal

C-23 Group of various fragments of sarcophagi and columns

C-24 Large vase on pedestal

C-25 Statue of orator

C-26 Headless statue

C-27 Roman bust on a column

C-28, 29 Front of an urn with griffons and lions' heads

C-30 Column with capital on base with bas-relief head

C-31 Bronze group depicting St. Alpino and Attila the Hun

C-32 Headless statue

C-33 Capital

C-34 Column with capital and ball above base bordered by leaves

C-35 Piece of a column

C-36 Large earthenware pot with cover and round base

C-37 Jupiter seated among columns and capitals

C-38 Small fountain with coat of arms of Innocent VIII

C-39 Small altar on high pedestal

C-40 Small obelisk

C-41 Madonna with small, niche temple offered by the Genovese to Benedict XV, called "della Guardia"

C-42 Seat with frieze and coat of arms

C-43 Seat with coat of arms

C-44 Seat with sarcophagus fragment

D-1 Marble statue of semi-nude Roman warrior on a pedestal

D-2, 4, 5, 7 Head of a woman in northern entrance of the nyphaeum of Pius IV

D-3 Bust of a Roman woman in the same location

D-6 Bust of a Roman man in the same location

D-8 Fountain with two putti, dolphins, and shells in the middle of the courtyard of the nymphaeum

D-9, 10 Truncated statues above sea-horses in the same courtyard

D-11 Headless statue of an orator in the loggia of the nymphaeum

D-12 Semi-nude, headless statue of an orator in the same location

D-13 Headless statue of a female declaimer in the same location

D-14 Headless statue of a man in the same location

D-15, 16 Two identical basins with decorations and friezes with the coat of arms of Pius IV

D-17 Headless bust at the south entrance of the nymphaeum

D-18 Bust of a Roman man in the same location

D-19 Headless bust in the same location

D-20 Headless bust in the same location

D-21 Damaged bust of a man in the same location

D-22 Bust of a Roman woman in the same location

D-23 Headless statue of a woman in the pronaos of the Casino

D-24 Another, similar artifact in the same location

D-25 Large headless statue of a woman holding a book and seated on a capital in the same location

D-26 Headless statue of a fat, hairy man in the same location

D-27, 28 Two identical oval basins with decorations and coat of arms of Pius IV in the same location

D-29, 30, 31, 32 Roman busts of men on colored marble columns in the first room of the Casino

D-33 Statue of a male child over the south entrance door of the nymphaeum

D-34 Statue of a female child over the north entrance door of the nymphaeum

D-35 Large statue of a seated woman with a tower on her head above the external basin of the nymphaeum

D-36 Statue of a seated woman on one side of the nymphaeum

D-37 Statue of a seated woman on the other side

D-38 Large earthenware pot with cover on a high pedestal

D-39 Fontana delle Torri built at the behest of Paul V

D-40 Unfinished small grotto with marbles and mosaics built at the behest of Paul V, called the Fontana degli Specchi

D-41, 42, 43, 44, 45, 46 Small obelisks, all similar

E-1 Monument to Saint Anstremonio, the first bishop of Alvernia

E-2 Small figure of a man embedded in the wall

E-3 Piece of monumental stone embedded in the wall

E-4 Small bas-relief embedded in the wall

E-5, 6 Two columns of equal dimensions

E-7 Bronze monument to Urban II

E-8 Small fountain with head of a lion built at the behest of Benedict XV

F-1 Bust of a Roman woman above an arch

F-2 Bust of a Roman woman on a shelf

F-3 Bust of a Roman man on a shelf

F-4 Headless bust on a shelf

F-5 Rectangular peperino basin

F-6 Upside-down capital with altar on wall

F-7, 8 Similar small obelisks on wall

F-9 Headless statue in a niche

F-10 Statue of Bacchus in a niche

F-11 Bust of a Roman woman

F-12 Bust of Marcus Aurelius

F-13 Urn-shaped fountain with spout in the form of a mask

F-14 Fountain with coat of arms of Pius VI above a ball

F-15 Decorative vase

F-16 Copper galley after a drawing by Maderno

Key to Symbols

_ Arched doorway

V Decorative vase

Y Fountain with ornamental spout

Z Basin with central upright spout

P Decorative ball on doors or balustrades

- Stair and smaller stairs

L Built structures in wood

S Greenhouses and storage areas for flowers or citrus trees

G Cages

O Niches

... Artificial rocks in tufa-stone

Key to Colors

LIGHT GREEN = lawns and flower-beds

BRIGHT GREEN = vegetable gardens and vineyards

DARK GREEN = woods and timberland

LIGHT BROWN = wooden structures

DEEP BROWN = boundary walls, called "of Belisario"

DARK BROWN = Leonine Wall

LEMON YELLOW = streets and avenues

YELLOW-ORANGE = papal museums and galleries

RED = masonry structures

LIGHT BLUE = fountains and basins

SKY BLUE = glass greenhouse

GRAY = courtyards and stone pedestals

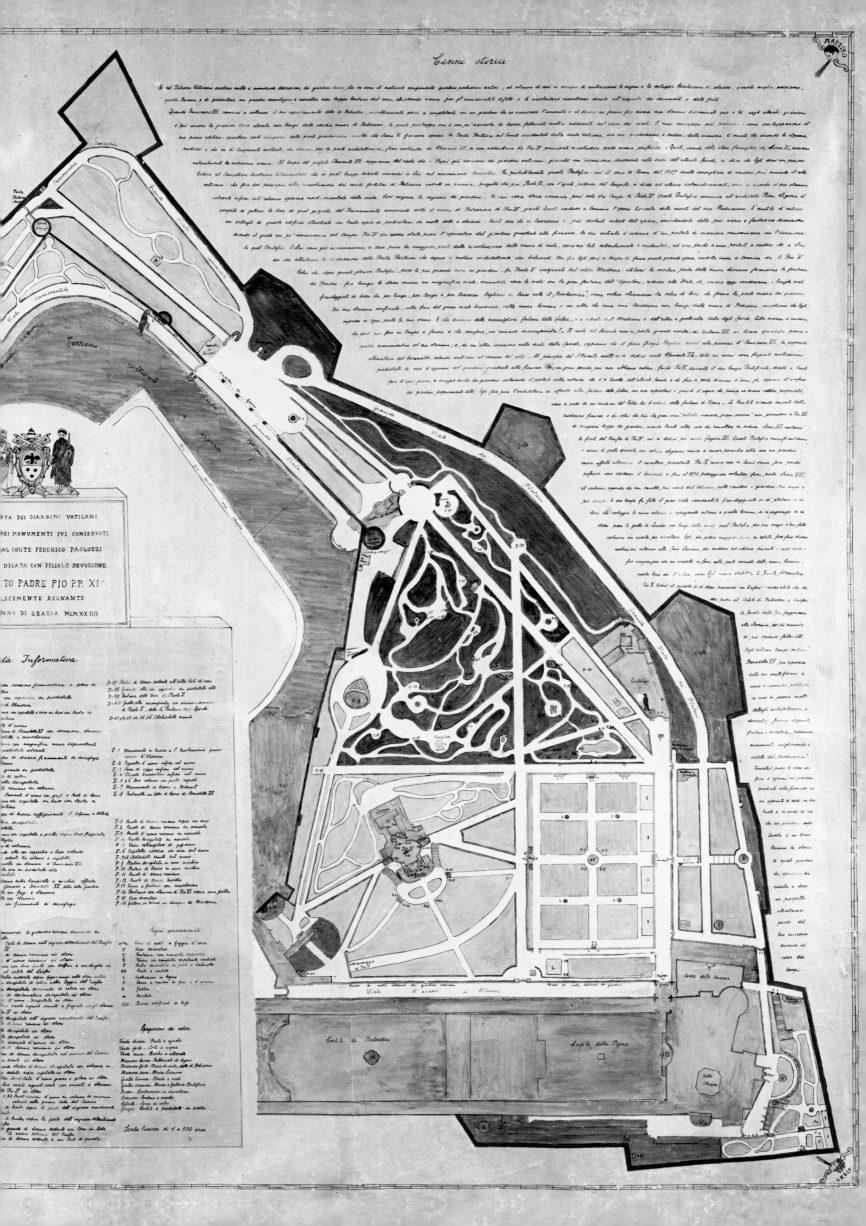

del Belvedere. There are also sacred monuments, generally gifts from religious communities, the number of which continues to increase rapidly to this day. At the time, besides the previously mentioned Madonna of Lourdes and Madonna della Guardia, the list included the monument to Urban VIII, in the wooded area behind the Secret Garden of Paul III; the bronze group with St. Alpino and Attila, also in the woods; and the bronze monuments to Urban II and St. Anstremonio, both in the high part of the garden beyond the woods. Additionally, in a number of places, there were coats of arms of the various popes and a bust of Benedict XV.

From these documents we again derive an image of the gardens as divided into the same basic zones that had endured since the time of Paul V, albeit with a few concessions to English taste, including the transformation of the beds, which by then had lost the geometric arrangement of the formal gardens, and the woods, which were so filled with sculptural elements as to become almost an open-air museum (plates 197–200). The presence of utilitarian, rural structures and of the agricultural areas beyond the Leonine Wall gave the Vatican citadel the picturesque look of the "Roman countryside," which the expansion of the city on all sides now rendered anachronistic.

February 11, 1929 saw the signing of the Lateran Accords, which sealed, decades after the "Porta Pia breach," an agreement between the Kingdom of Italy and the Holy See that recognized the latter's territorial sovereignty over the Vatican State and the Villa of Castel Gandolfo. In compensation for the territories and property taken by force in 1870, a substantial indemnity was awarded to the new state; this was used immediately for the construction of buildings to house the administrative and operative functions, thus initiating a radical transformation of the entire area. Indeed, the years immediately following the Lateran Accords witnessed an unprecedented building campaign, with an impressive proliferation of new edifices concentrated in the 109 acres (44 hectares) of Vatican City. The mammoth renewal project, which included the gardens, also created numerous jobs for the many unemployed victims of the Great Depression, and thus contributed to the amelioration of a substantial social problem.[8] A chronicle at the time

197. (right) An avenue in the woods.

198, 199. (pages 250–51) Views of the woods.

200. (pages 252–53) The woods with ruins of a small temple.

reported that "the creation of the Vatican Gardens was prompted by a crisis that had battered the entire world and that resulted in the painful aftermath of unemployment."[9]

Work on the gardens began in March 1930 and was completed four years later. The scope of the project was vast, encompassing the renovation of the existing gardens and the transformation of some thirty-two acres (13 hectares) of terrain that had been used for vineyards and vegetable plots into an ornamental, richly decorated space (plates 201–8). The entire vast area between the Leonine Wall and the back of St. Peter's Basilica lost, once and for all, its centuries-old agricultural character, and even the shape of the terrain was modified by massive excavations of the clayey or sandy layers. To complete the new layout of the area, water drainage channels were created and palisades built to reinforce the terracing and the uneven terrain. These were connected to escarpments that reached an incline as steep as 40 percent. According to the previously cited chronicle, more than one million cubic meters of material were excavated, resulting in the demolition of the huts along the Leonine Wall. A clear sense of the scope of these transformations emerges from an examination of two plans of the Vatican citadel, one from 1874 and the other from

1933 (plates 209–10), which are compared in an article about the work undertaken during the papacy of Pius XI.[10]

The design of the administrative, jurisdictional, and institutional buildings for the new state was entrusted to the architect Giuseppe Momo (1875–1940), a personal friend of the pope, who had named him Architect of the Reverenda Fabbrica di San Pietro and president of the Commission for Public Works.[11] Momo is responsible for the design and construction, beginning in 1930, of the Palazzo del Governatorato, or Government Palace (1931), distinguished by the aedicule-like loggia at its summit; the railway station (1931); the Vatican radio station (1933); and the post office (1933). The seminary building was renovated for use as a courthouse (1931), while the Casina of Pius IV, remodeled to house the seat of the Pontificia Accademia delle Scienze (Pontifical Academy of Sciences), was substantially enlarged by an addition at the back of the original Pirro Ligorio building. The new seat was inaugurated with great pomp by Pius XI on December 17, 1933, and defined as a place to promote the interaction between faith and scientific culture.[12] All of the

201–204. The agricultural area before the transformations, from *Illustrazione Vaticana*, no. 1, 1933.

buildings designed by Momo have a homogeneous look; neo-Renaissance in style, their monumentality is due to the liberal use of the colossal order, hewn stone, and travertine, as well as loggias and aedicules. These buildings arose, in large part, on what was previously agricultural land, and all around them gardens, perhaps designed by the same architect, were laid out to beautify the sites.

The new entrance to the gardens, created near the Arco delle Campane (Arch of the Bells), connects to the dramatic layout at the start of the visitors' route. On the incline between the railway station and the Palazzo del Governatorato is a kind of fan-like design created out of boxwood hedges and flowers, with a central fountain—made of humble materials (mortar painted white to imitate marble), but very effective visually—in the shape of a huge shell, with open valves from which water spouts (plate 211). The fountain was designed by the sculptor Guarino Roscioli (1895–1974).[13] Ornamental evergreen trees, primarily conifers and pines, are planted all around, while the sides of the road leading to the higher part of the gardens are embellished by a rocaille facing in which many varieties and species of flesh-leaved plants, succulents, and flowering cacti were planted and acclimated (plates 213–17). Between the Palazzo del

Governatorato and the apse of St. Peter's, the design of the flowerbeds and boxwoods forms the coats of arms of the reigning pope and the Vatican State (plate 212); next to these are specimens of a rare and exotic plant, the *Nolina longifolia*. The grassy lawns that cover the slopes are dotted with *Canna indica* bushes, which produce spectacular, bright red and yellow blossoms. Behind the Palazzo del Governatorato, not far from the building that houses the Collegio Etiopico (Pontifical Ethiopian College), is another graceful fountain, also made of cement mortar painted to imitate marble. It has a round basin on the ground, in the center of which is a small boat borne up by two dolphins

205–206. *(below left)* The new buildings under construction, from *Illustrazione Vaticana*, no. 1, 1933.

207–208. *(below right)* The new Pinacoteca, from *Illustrazione Vaticana*, no. 1, 1933.

209. *(page 256)* Plan of the Vatican citadel in 1874, from *Illustrazione Vaticana*, no. 1, 1933.

210. *(page 257)* Plan of the Vatican citadel in 1933, after the transformations, from *Illustrazione Vaticana*, no. 1, 1933.

PIANTA TOPOGRAFICA DEL VATICANO

NELL' ANNO 1874

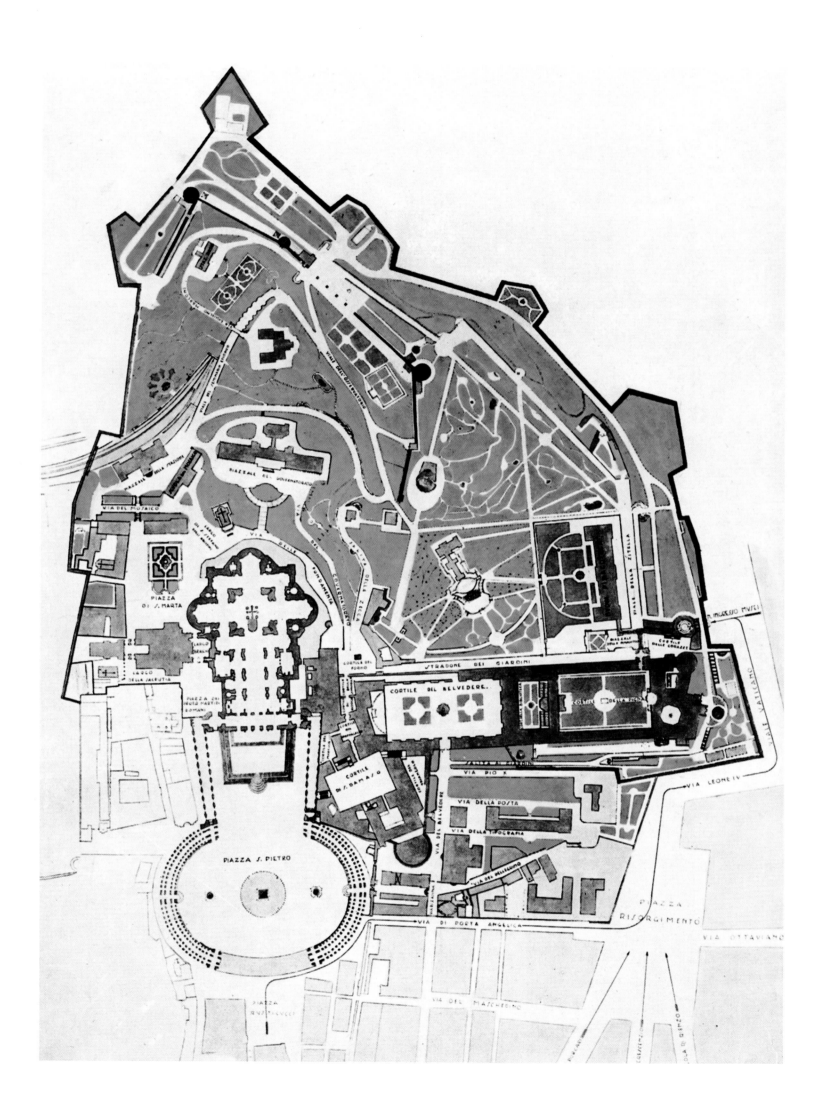

PIAZZALE DELLA STAZIONE

VIA DEL MOSAICO

PIAZZA DI S. MARTA

VIA DELLE

PIAZZALE DEL GOVERNATORATO

CORTILE DEL FORNO

CORTILE DEL BELVEDERE.

STRADONE DEI GIARDINI

CORTILE DI S. DAMASO

VIA DEL BELVEDERE

VIA PIO X

VIA DELLA POSTA

VIA DELLA TIPOGRAFIA

PIAZZA S. PIETRO

VIA DI PORTA ANGELICA

PIAZZA RISORGIMENTO

VIA LEONE IV

VIA OTTAVIANO

VIA DEL MASCHERINO

257

211. (opposite) The hill surrounding the Fontana della Conchiglia (conch shell).

212. (above) Papal coat of arms rendered with boxwood in front of the Palazzo del Governatorato.

213–217. (pages 260–65) Views of the gardens in the twentieth century.

218. (*above*) The Fontana della Navicella (small boat).

219. (*opposite*) The Fontana della Navicella, detail with the Rose Garden in the background.

and a pedestal with Baroque volutes topped by the insignia of the reigning pope, the heraldic eagle, and three spheres (plates 218, 219). In this fountain, which harkens back to earlier models, we can read an evocation of the traditional symbols of the Church, such as the little ship of salvation and the dolphins. All around it are oleanders, groups of banana trees, calla lilies, and other aquatic plants, as well as some bitter oranges, which recall the historical, imposing presence of citrus trees in the Vatican Gardens (plates 220, 221). In 1936 some of the sculptures that formed the Monument to the First Vatican Council, originally set up in 1885 at the behest of Pope Leo XIII in the center of the Cortile della Pigna, were placed not far from this fountain, near the gardener's house. In addition to the bronze statue of St. Peter, set on a low column, there are reliefs by Pietro Galli and some sculptural fragments scattered on the lawns (plate 222).

The most interesting of the many gardens created during this phase is located near the Palazzo della Radio (radio station building). It constitutes the reintroduction of an Italian-style garden (plates 223–25), with regular, geometrically framed beds and an abundant use of boxwood, in keeping with a revival that was sweeping the entire country in those years and producing an excessive number of gardens in this style.[14] It was believed, in fact, that Renaissance gardens, lacking flowers, were severe and rigorous and heavily dependent for decorative effect on the artful combination of hedges and bushes, manipulated according to the precepts of topiary or the varying shades of green of the plants in the designs. The new garden, located on a broad, level terrace, consists of two large, rectangular, symmetrical beds bordered by low boxwood hedges. In the center of each bed is a fountain with a circular basin on the ground

220. (top) Citrus trees in the garden.

221. (left) Banana trees in the garden.

222. (opposite) Sculptural fragments by Pietro Galli, 1869, from the monument to the First Vatican Council, now sited near the Casa del Giardiniere.

223. (overleaf) The Italian garden.

224, 225. (pages 272–73) The Italian garden, detail.

226. (page 274) The coat of arms of Pius XI, sited above the Italian garden.

227. (page 275) View of the gardens.

and a simple spout in the middle. A pattern created out of boxwood, squared off or with spherical forms at the corners, is repeated in mirrorlike fashion in the two beds, alternating curved and broken lines and forming a hint of a labyrinth. Planted around the Italian-style garden, next to cedars, cypresses, firs, and pines, are numerous varieties of palm trees, such as the *Chamaerops humilis*, or dwarf palm; the Butia; the Washingtonia; and the Livingstonia. At one end of the garden is a splendid beech tree (*Fagus selvatica*), a species that normally takes root at an altitude of over 3,281 feet (1,000 meters). One of the short sides of the garden is bordered by the high enclosure of the Leonine Wall, which bears the travertine coat of arms of Pope Pius XI, who thereby put his "signature" on the spectacular creation (plate 226).

In those same years, a demanding project was carried out on the upper slope of the hill, beyond the Leonine Wall and next to the Grotto of the Madonna of Lourdes. It involved the entire area occupied by a garden dating to the papacy of Leo XIII, who, as mentioned previously, had built a chalet there for his "holiday sojourns." To supply the small state with an adequate supply of drinking water, an enormous underground tank was installed in the flat area between the gate created by Pius VI at the edge of the woods and the Grotto of the Madonna of Lourdes. The tank was waterproofed and connected to the conduit from Lake Bracciano. Above the tank, which was covered with two feet (60 centimeters) of earth, a simple, geometric garden was designed, with squared-off beds, boxwood hedges, plantings of flowers both in the ground and in pots, and some particularly valuable trees—of which the cinnamon (*Cinnamon canphora*), native to China and Japan, stands out among specimens of magnolia, cycas, and cedar—as well as bushes with lovely flowers, such as buddleia and lagerstroemia (plate 227). An avenue lined with olive trees recalls not only the setting of the passion of Christ but also the original, agricultural use of the site (plate 228). At the center of the area is the simple, elegant Fontana delle Ranocchie (Fountain of the Frogs). Its low, circular, travertine basin, filled with flowering, aquatic plants and an antique amphora that spouts water in the middle, features several bronze frogs seated on the edge (plates 230, 31).[15]

228. *(top)* The avenue lined with olive trees.

229. *(bottom)* The fir grove.

230, 231. *(pages 277–79)* The Fontana delle Ranocchie (frogs).

232. The Rose Garden.

233. Another view of the Rose Garden.

234. *(above)* The Fontana del Tritone (triton) in the Rose Garden.

235, 236. *(pages 284–85)* The Fontana della Sirena (siren) in the Rose Garden.

The wood below, in a sorry state at the time, became the object of great attention and care. Some 150 of the area's 200 large trees underwent phyto-surgical treatments, while 100 new specimens were planted to replace those that had died. Despite the introduction of some exotic plants, the wood has preserved its chiefly Mediterranean character, with a predominance of holm oaks and other oak varieties, along with maples, poplars, acacias, and plane trees. The undergrowth is filled with boxwood, viburnum, and privet, among which iris, primulas, acanthus, crocus, and narcissus bloom in the spring. Additionally, on the slope to the north, toward Monte Mario, a new wood of fir trees was planted (plate 229), "including about 200 varieties, from dwarf to procumbent, shrub, and arborous."[16] In this regenerated wood many sculptures remained, disposed in eclectic arrangements that, as documents from 1925 describe, juxtapose pagan subjects with Christian ones. Many of these sculptures are still in place today.

Near the Leonine Wall, in a level space on the summit of the hillside that was previously used for vineyards and vegetable gardens, a spectacular *roseto*, or rose garden, was created. A geometric design divides the space into regular beds, with boxwood borders and splendid roses of all kinds in the center. A sequence of arched trellises covered with jasmine and climbing roses frames fine views of the cupola and the surrounding landscape (plates 232, 233); two lovely fountains in imitation marble make the garden even more evocative: at the center of two low travertine basins, resting on a kind of four-part shell, are a triton (plate 234) and a siren (plates 235, 236), each holding a Roman trumpet that spouts a high jet of water.

To complete the work, new greenhouses were built on the site of the sixteenth-century garden of Clement VII—in other words, along the terrace with a view of Monte Mario and near the historical Fontana della Zitella. These modern greenhouses, erected to replace the old orangeries, were equipped with all the latest technology, and in addition to facilitating the breeding of garden plants, they supplied fresh flowers in every season for the altars of the Basilica and for the other churches in the Vatican.[17]

The labor-intensive creation of the new gardens did not, however, preclude work on the existing ones, which were all in need of restoration or renovation. Thus, within the framework of the ambitious projects carried out in the 1930s, changes were also made to the only gardens that had

237. The Secret Garden of Paul III after the construction of the Pinacoteca.

preserved the layouts of past centuries: the garden in the Cortile della Pigna and the Secret Garden of Paul III (plate 237). The former was essentially cleaned up and put in order, without specific modifications apart from the installation of the monument to the First Vatican Council. The latter, however, was completely redesigned, following the construction of the Pinacoteca building. In the area toward the boundary wall, in the direction of Monte Mario—formerly the site of the underground passage that led to the terraced garden of Clement VII, and later of the shelters for citrus plants and precious flowers—a new, monumental building was erected to exhibit the Vatican's painting collection. The design of the new Pinacoteca was entrusted to the elderly and esteemed architect Luca Beltrami (1854–1933) with the instruction that it "not venture too far from the predominant line and character of the sixteenth-century buildings, from the Vatican's ambience."[18] The architect,[19] already active in the Vatican for some time, did not need to be reminded to respect the context in which he was working, and the Pinacoteca he designed, with its heavy use of travertine and brick, fit harmoniously with the preexisting edifices. However, the Secret Garden of Paul III was gravely marred by the subtraction of a substantial amount of terrain and the loss of its axial layout. It therefore became necessary to move the Bramantesque fountain that had come from the Cortile della Pigna and that Gregory XVI wanted in the center of the garden, and to lay out new paths that were no longer aligned with the fake portals in the wall toward the wood. The new beds were no longer filled with elaborate multi-color floral compositions, but instead with simple lawns bordered by boxwood hedges with potted trees at the corners. The result was an impoverished garden with no remaining connection to its predecessor, which, although changed over time, was always a distinctive space that had preserved its original boundaries for centuries.

The last of the series of projects that revolutionized the appearance of the Vatican citadel was the reorganization of the Piazza di Santa Marta, which included the installation of a new fountain consisting of a circular basin on the ground, a base ornamented with the coat of arms of Pius XI, and another circular basin above.[20] This fountain bears a striking resemblance to the sixteenth-century fountains, in particular those set up by Donato Bramante in the Cortile del Belvedere, but the use of cement mortar in place of marble clearly reveals its modernity.

As a result of all of these modifications, during the last years of the papacy of Pius XI the configuration that the Vatican Gardens had assumed in the seventeenth century, and maintained with only minor alterations for some three hundred years, was radically changed. Whereas the "historic" part of the gardens diminished in importance and character and was reduced and reapportioned to make room for the new buildings, new gardens were created in the area traditionally used for agricultural production. A vestige of the traditional presence of vegetable gardens exists today near the Fontana dello Scoglio, or Fontana dell'Aquilone, in the form of a small, modest plot of earth where the Clarisse nuns of the nearby Mater Ecclesiae Convent cultivate the vegetables for the pontiff's table (plate 238). Most surprising is the almost total disappearance of citrus trees, except for a few specimens planted in pots or directly in the ground. There is no trace of the espaliers that, until the nineteenth century, covered the walls, or of the *cocchi*, or pergolas, that once received so much attention and care. The citrus trees also disappeared from other important Roman villas, such as Villa Borghese[21] and Villa Pamphilj,[22] where the ornamental uses of the "golden fruit" are traceable only until the nineteenth century. It is likely that the high costs of maintaining the citrus trees led to the abandonment of their cultivation in favor of simpler arrangements, which had, however, less decorative and symbolic value.

This new configuration of the gardens has endured until our time, with a few limited modifications owing to the practice of installing monuments donated to the popes by various religious communities in the garden areas, thus creating an assortment of paths filled with sacred imagery. The appeal of the Vatican Gardens today lies primarily in the spectacular and scenic twentieth-century arrangements rather than in the historical remnants, the image and memory of the originals' grandeur having largely been lost. A few visible vestiges remain, however, allowing us to retrace the evolving organization of the *Vaticanus Mons*, or Vatican Hill, over the period from the Middle Ages to the first decades of the last century, during which the form of the Vatican Gardens reflected the distinctive personalities and inclinations of the reigning popes.

238. The papal vegetable garden.

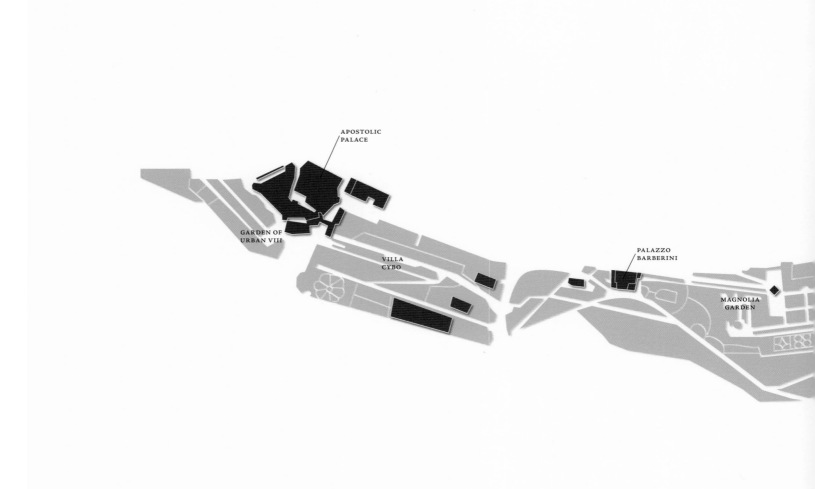

APOSTOLIC
PALACE

GARDEN OF
URBAN VIII

VILLA
CYBO

PALAZZO
BARBERINI

MAGNOLIA
GARDEN

CHAPTER NINE

PAPAL HOLIDAYS AND THE VILLA IN CASTEL GANDOLFO: THE MIDDLE AGES TO THE TWENTIETH CENTURY

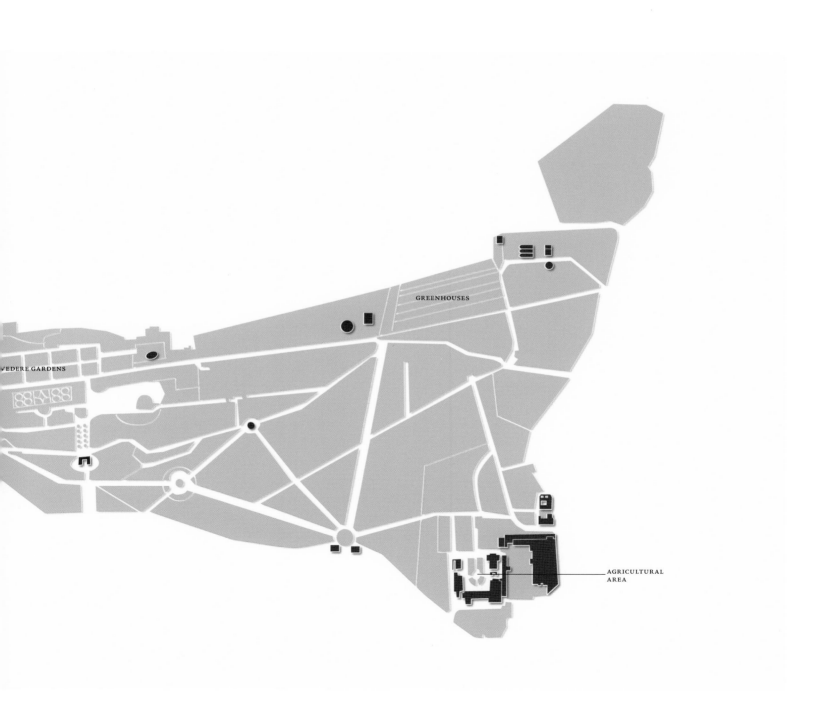

GREENHOUSES

VEDERE GARDENS

AGRICULTURAL AREA

The papal custom of spending holiday periods, short or long, far from Rome is documented at least as early as the eighth century,[1] when Paul I (757–67) died in the monastery of St. Paul Outside the Walls, having gone there to escape the summer heat.[2] Gregory IV (827–44) had a residence near the port of Ostia, with porticoes and terraces[3]; Damasus II, elected in 1048 and originally from Bressanone, settled, "to escape the city heat,"[4] in Palestrina, where he died after only twenty-three days as pope; Eugene III (1145–53) had a small palace built in Segni, to which he went frequently and which other popes subsequently used.[5] Stays in the city during the summer months had become increasingly unhealthy, in part because of the progressive abandonment of the countryside for the residential area of Rome, and therefore in the thirteenth century the custom of spending several months in hillside cities, such as Anagni, Subiaco, Viterbo, Orvieto, and Perugia, was established. During that century, the popes' leave-taking followed a regular pattern: the departure took place between May and June and the return between October and November, often in conjunction with a liturgical holiday of particular importance.

There is evidence that the institutionalization of this practice began with the pontificate of Innocent III (1198–1216). In contrast with his immediate predecessors, who had never left Rome, Innocent sojourned elsewhere some fourteen times during his eighteen years on the papal throne.[6] A thirteenth-century chronicle confirms that summer sojourns had become customary; in it, the official papal residence at the Lateran is defined as the *hiemale palatium*, or winter palace, to distinguish it from the summer seat.[7] Hygienic and health considerations were surely at the root of these seasonal moves, and the chroniclers did not hesitate to emphasize that the popes would leave Rome because of *romani aeris suspecta conditio* (the dubious condition of the air at Rome) or *estatis incendia* (summer heat).[8] The basic assumption was that the popes should maintain their good health in order to guide Christianity and transmit an image of serenity, equilibrium, and composure, as a tract from the period prescribed.[9] The practice of the *recreatio corporis* as a recognized necessity was substantiated by the presence in the thirteenth century of a "papal physician," to avoid circumstances in which the pope's weak health might negatively impact the life of the Church. Gradually, along with the practical considerations, the concept of pleasure and of the enjoyment to be found in immersing oneself in beautiful, welcoming natural surroundings began to

surface—albeit in a veiled way, as evidenced by a chronicle written by a cardinal in the entourage of Innocent III. In describing the pope's sojourn in Subiaco from August to September 1202, the cardinal writes enthusiastically about the landscape, stressing that water, a source of beauty and pleasure, also has salvational and purifying properties.[10]

Staying in Rome during the summer months was discouraged not only because of the suffering caused by the heat, but also—indeed, primarily—because of the frequent epidemics of plague and other infectious diseases that regularly overtook the city. Until the fifteenth century, Rome had just over 30,000 inhabitants concentrated in the bend of the Tiber, living in dwellings that lacked water and toilet facilities, as documented in numerous edicts of the Maestri di Strada,[11] who presided over urban cleanliness and repeatedly reminded the public to respect the most elementary rules of hygiene. In the presence of pestilence, which occurred frequently, prescriptions for remedies multiplied, as did the search for the cause of these infections, but the most effective precaution remained staying far away from infected areas. However, some opposition to the pope's leaving Rome in times of plague arose in the fifteenth century; this was based on the belief that his proximity to the suffering faithful was essential to their healing. Martin V (1417–31), for example, was praised because "he did not leave the nidus of the pestilence" that had struck Rome in 1430, although on other occasions he had often gone to family properties in Genazzano, or to the Colli Albani or Sabina.

Of all the cities close to Rome, Viterbo was the most frequented for summer and other holidays, so much so that it was called the second Rome. The primary reason for this preference was the abundance of thermal waters there. Throughout the fifteenth century there are chronicles of papal sojourns made for the purposes of taking cures, and it is noted that Nicholas V (1447–55), an assiduous visitor to the thermal baths that still bear his name, favored their development but did not pass up trips to the nearby and cooler Soriano nel Cimino or the more distant Fabriano, which offered greater guarantees of safety in case of pestilence.[12]

The regular alternation between summer holidays in a city in the Lazio region and the return to the Vatican or Lateran in the cooler months required complex organization,

239. At Castel Gandolfo, a curtain of cypress trees and an equestrian statue of Septimius Severus.

in part to ensure that certain institutional functions would not be neglected, as the pope's mobility at times took on a political dimension. In fact, for the entire thirteenth century the pope was also a feudal seigneur, and his travels were at times linked to the interests of his family of origin. It is well known that Boniface VIII (1294–1303) took advantage of the movements of the Curia to visit the Caetani family property in Lazio,[13] and that in 1208 Innocent III went to various cities in the Lazio region in order to "stabilize the affairs of the Kingdom."[14] Pius II (1458–64) mixed business with pleasure: when he went to Tivoli he did so not only to breathe the clean air but also to observe the unstable political situation firsthand.[15]

During the fifteenth century the popes' travel to other cities did not keep them from staying in places within Rome besides the official Vatican and Lateran residences. Martin V had a family palace with a secret garden in the Piazza Colonna, while Paul II (1464–71) loved to stay in the monastery in Aracoeli, where he had his own apartments. It is well known, too, that Paul II enlarged the palace in San Marco, in which he had lived as a cardinal, adding a garden and transforming it into his usual holiday destination.[16] Even Sixtus IV (1471–84), who did not look down on sojourns outside of Rome, in 1481 and 1482 stayed in the urban residence of Cardinal Francesco Gonzaga, near Sant'Agata dei Goti, situated on the Quirinal hill and therefore in an elevated, healthy location.[17]

Pope Pius II, known for his humanistic interests, visited Viterbo and other cities in the Lazio region with regularity, but loved spending long periods in Tuscany, his native land, and made frequent trips to Siena and the thermal sites in that region. Pius's writings help us to understand how the new humanistic culture altered the concept of vacationing and helped establish a precise ideology of "villa life." His *Commentarii* include numerous descriptions of the landscapes he traversed or contemplated, often accompanied by meditations about the pleasure that the beauty of nature afforded. An important innovation is attributed to this widely traveled pope: the practice of travel as an end in itself, without justification in terms of health or politics. This was a sign of the newfound affirmation of such personal exigencies as the need for rest and solitude. The chronicles of his travels contain frequent, repeated references to *relaxandi animi* (relaxation of the spirit) and *lieti conversari* (pleasant association), according to the classical concept of *otium* that many humanists had embraced for some decades, although care was always taken to emphasize

that the pope, even when far away from the seat of government, continued to attend to the interests of the Church. We cannot credit Pius II alone with the introduction of a conscious culture of "villa life," but the cultured pontiff undeniably contributed to creating the practice of *otium*, and to recapturing the harmony between man and nature, by conferring authority on the theories of such noted exponents of humanistic culture—both curial and secular—as Jacopo Ammannati, Poggio Bracciolini, Gaspare da Verona, Guarino Veronese, Bartolomeo Platina, and Leon Battista Alberti, who reprised themes and concepts already expressed by Cicero or Pliny in a pure evocation of the classical age.[18]

The new relationship with nature had engendered the idea of constructing country residences at high elevations, both to afford sweeping views of the landscape and to enable the structures to be admired from afar and express dominance over the territory. However, all the fifteenth-century writings focus on the beauty, the healthiness, and the pleasant nature of the sites, and do not contain references to specific types of residences. Moreover, the popes did not generally own vacation residences; rather, they used those put at their disposal by cardinals or monasteries, and only at the end of the fifteenth century, with the construction of the Palazzetto del Belvedere in the Vatican at the behest of Innocent VIII, did this type of villa building appear in the area of Rome. Even though Paul II, as mentioned above, preferred his Roman residence near the Basilica of San Marco (in contrast to his predecessor, Pius II, who traveled often), by the end of the century the custom of papal vacations had become institutionalized, as can be inferred from an instruction written in 1485 by Johannes Burchard, master of ceremonies of the Curia: "On the fourth of July, general vacations were announced, from this day until the Kalends of October exclusively."[19] The use of the term "general vacations" (*vacationes generales*) and the fixing of the dates leads one to presume that this was the regulation of a custom that was already commonly observed and accepted.

The habitual summer interruption of the *negotium* and the usual departure of the pope from Rome led the cardinals to follow the same practice. As early as 1464, during the conclave that would conclude with the election of Paul II, the cardinals had requested a country residence where they could escape from the Roman heat. The future pope had promised to satisfy their request, but once elected did not keep his word.[20] As a result, in the conclave of 1484, the cardinals insisted upon a written act from Innocent VIII (1484–92) with the following wording: "I swear and promise that each of the lord Cardinals, both current ones and those to come, is to govern, hold, and possess, with full jurisdiction, with all revenues and yields accruing to that Cardinal, one estate or castle in a nearby place, as above, including a fortress, if it should have one, so that these lord Cardinals too should have some special place, to which they may betake themselves freely, either to avoid plague, or for the sake of their own recreation."[21]

The first nucleus of a residence, built near Rome, that was destined to accommodate papal sojourns for nearly a century dates to the pontificate of Pius II. Used primarily as a hunting lodge, the Villa della Magliana, situated along the via Portuense only eight miles from Rome, was—before Castel Gandolfo (plate 239)—the "villa of the popes."[22] During the papacy of Sixtus IV, his nephew Girolamo Riario organized magnificent hunts at the villa that were celebrated in the chronicles as society events beyond compare. Innocent VIII (1484–92) enlarged the existing structure, giving it the look of a little crenellated palace, and made frequent trips there, not only for personal diversion but also to host ceremonial functions in a charming setting, as on September 13, 1486, when he entertained representatives of the king of Spain.[23] The expansion of the Villa della Magliana was contemporaneous with Innocent's modifications in the Vatican, where he commissioned the Palazzetto that still bears his name. In both instances, a building type was introduced that, despite such medieval vestiges as battlements and fortlike elements, would have considerable influence on the character of the villas built in the Roman area.[24]

According to the diary of Stefano Infessura, Innocent's successor Alexander VI (1492–1503) rarely went to the Villa della Magliana, in part because of its proximity to Ostia Antica, the home of his archenemy, Cardinal Giuliano della Rovere, later Julius II (1503–13). Julius II was behind the construction of the first architectural structure conceived in direct relationship to the landscape—the beautiful loggias designed by Donato Bramante to connect the Vatican palaces and St. Peter's Basilica with Innocent VIII's Belvedere—a structure that would become the archetypical union between the evocation of the antique and innovation in architectural, landscape, and functional terms.[25] Although by that time Julius II had an adequate official seat at his disposition within the Vatican citadel, complete with gardens and places for *otium*, he showed

great enthusiasm for the Villa della Magliana. "We have by the will of Our Lord…built in the Magliana a great edifice." Thus did Cardinal Alidosi refer to the transformation of Innocent VIII's *palazzetto* into a splendid villa—by will of Julius II and after a design by Giuliano da Sangallo, with the subsequent contribution of Donato Bramante, who also designed the garden. The pope made frequent sojourns to Magliana, arriving on horseback. The villa was often a stopping-off point along the route to his castle in nearby Ostia Antica, another residence to which he went frequently, even if only for a few days.[26] In the Villa della Magliana, called a "pleasure site," the pope devoted himself to *otium* but did not neglect affairs of state. In fact, in July 1509 he held a consistory there and in 1510 hosted a delegation of ambassadors.[27] The papal sojourns did not stop even after pirates sacked the villa on September 30, 1511, causing considerable damage, and came to an end only a few months before the pope's death.

His successor, Leo X (1513–21), used the villa even more frequently, and not just during the summer months. An avid hunter and outdoorsman, the pope often moved ceremonial functions to the villa, turning it into a true second residence, as is amply documented in the biography by Paolo Giovio. The contemporary chronicles commented that the pope made frequent visits to the villa to devote himself "to the usual pleasures," but also to "purge himself." It seems evident that, by this time, the hygienic-salutary motivations that had induced popes to leave Rome were all in the past. The right to pleasure, to the *relaxandi animi*, was now accepted, and Leo X's habit of purging himself was part of his personal health regimen, the same one that prompted him to travel to Magliana on horseback or by foot. To satisfy the pope's passion for hunting, a proper reserve was created with the requisite structures, expert gamekeepers, and numerous assistants tasked with organizing frequent shoots. But the pope also loved music, and the accounting ledgers include repeated references to the organization of concerts in the villa during the summer months and in spring. Confirmation of the popes' custom of leaving Rome in any season and at their pleasure, without seeking justifications such as the heat or the explosion of an epidemic, can be found in the account of the pope's death: on the evening of November 24, 1521, Leo X was at Villa della Magliana when news reached him that the French attempt to regain Lombardy had failed. During the subsequent celebrations, the pope caught a chill that in the space of a few days led to his death.[28]

Another papal vacation destination was Tivoli, close to Rome and rich in thermal waters. Pius II sojourned in the Franciscan monastery that would be transformed a century later into the splendid Villa d'Este, but at the time it was uncomfortable and full of mice.[29] Sixtus IV also stayed there in 1473, but it was the humanist cardinals such as Bibiena, Bembo, and Carafa who most loved the town, not only for its cool climate and the beauty of its sites, but also for its classical antiquities. Paul III Farnese (1534–49) went there occasionally and appointed his nephew, Cardinal Alessandro Farnese, governor of Tivoli, hoping to develop it into a vacation site. This project, however, was abandoned due to the unrest of the inhabitants.

While still a cardinal, the pope loved to stay in the paternal estates in the Viterba region, particularly Capodimonte and Bisentina Island in Lake Bolsena, which was considered the ideal retreat for studying in peace.[30] In the same period, he had an airy, frontal loggia added to the severe ancestral fortress of Capodimonte, thereby lightening and refining the massive structure so much that it was referred to as a villa. This was an ideal holiday site, enriched by the splendid view of Lake Bolsena and the island with the Farnese sanctuary, where even Pope Leo X had stayed several times as the guest of his friend Cardinal Alessandro Farnese. Together, they indulged in the pleasures of hunting in the surrounding hills and fishing in the lake, forgetting obligations and formalities. To be sure, the area of Lake Bolsena, and the town of Montefiascone in particular, had been a favorite of the popes for centuries; Urban V (1362–70), during his Italian period, 1367–70, spent the summer months there because, said the chronicles, it was *ubi aer purus est et sanus* (where the air is pure and healthful).[31] Alessandro Farnese, even after his election to the papal throne, retained his love for the family properties, where he spent his holidays, and referred to Capodimonte as "my dear little peninsula."[32] The convivial banquets he organized there were so renowned that Pastor wrote that one could "relive the sybaritic life of the Farnese, all entertainment, banquets, and rowdy hunts, in which one saw elegant cavaliers and ladies, poets, jesters, actors, and musicians."[33]

Paul III was also responsible for the creation, starting in 1542, of the world-famous Horti Farnesiani (Farnese Gardens) on the Palatine Hill, which were in wonderful harmony with the site's classical ruins. The pope often went to Frascati as well, where he would stay in the Villa Rufina,[34] but while in Rome he also spent time in the Vatican Belvedere, the Vigna Carafa on the Quirinal Hill, and the Torre Paolina (Tower of Paul III) on the Capitoline, built for him in 1535 and connected by covered passageway to the summer residence of the Palazzo di San Marco. But despite his declared passion for holiday sojourns and travel, during his papacy he did not participate in the tradition of building magnificent villas that was begun by his predecessors in the Medici family with Villa Madama and continued by his successor, Julius III, with Villa Giulia. In part this was because of the traumatic events of the Sack of Rome, which had debilitated the city.

Under Julius III (1550–55) the papal commissions of country villas reached their apex with the swift construction of one of the most splendid and stately complexes in the area of Rome: Villa Giulia, situated along the via Flaminia not far from the Porta del Popolo. According to chronicles of the time, the pope suffered from gout and, after having fruitlessly sought a cure in the thermal baths of the Viterba region, had given up traveling because it caused him too much discomfort. Instead he dedicated himself to his villa, which he reached by crossing the Tiber in a boat and then continuing in a litter along a tree-shaded path, as depicted in a contemporary etching. Villa Giulia had been conceived to rival the Medici's Villa Madama, which faced it almost directly on the opposite bank of the Tiber, and construction proceeded at a rapid pace until the pope's death, with contributions from the most famous architects and artists of the day, including Michelangelo, Bartolomeo Ammannati, Vignola, Giorgio Vasari, and Taddeo Zuccari.[35] The pope visited the site frequently, staying in the Villa del Poggio, which had been incorporated into the property, while work proceeded. In addition to following the building's progress, the pope cured his gout with the pure, restorative waters of the Acqua Vergine, which had been piped into the nymphaeum, and received ambassadors and other dignitaries, all without neglecting the pleasures of the table or the traditional peasant dances and festivities. The pope's passion for his "Villa Julia" was such that Panvinio remarked, "For those gardens it seemed he went crazy," and Muratori added, "He wanted to outdo Nero in his gardens outside Porta Flaminia."[36] Indeed, his entertainments with music and song became infamous and are even evoked in the frescoes by Prospero Fontana, who depicted them in the *Banquet of the Gods* on the vault of one salon. It was here, in his favorite residence, that Julius died, leaving behind a masterpiece that, although used by his successors to host important guests, was quickly stripped of its finest appointments and fell into decline.[37]

Paul IV (1555–59), who had links to the Theatine order, had founded the monastery next to the church of San Silvestro on the Quirinal, using it often as a retreat and to escape from the heat, while the members of the Curia were housed in the villas on the hill. Among the latter was a nephew, Cardinal Carlo Carafa, who, unlike his uncle, greatly enjoyed the leisure of villa life, as did the pope's other nephew, the duke of Paliano. The contrast between the religious rigor of the pontiff and the unchecked hedonism of his nephews was so great that it induced him, in the end, to banish them from Rome. Nevertheless, it is to Paul IV that we owe the origins of the Casina, that splendid building in the Vatican Gardens, destined to pass into history with the name of his successor, Pius IV (1559–65), and to stand as a model of pagan joie de vivre.[38]

Pius IV, while still a cardinal, was known for his great appreciation of villa life, and his sojourns in his Lombardy residence in Frascarolo were cited as examples of *otium* by Bartolomeo Taegio in his treatise.[39] In Rome, the pope had rented the Villa Pucci, on the Janiculum Hill, near the Villa Lante,[40] but was renowned for moving continually from one residence to another. The chronicles of the time narrate how he would have lunch at San Marco and sleep in the monastery in Aracoeli that same day, or go first to the Palazzo dei Santi Apostoli, then to the Villa Giulia, again to the Vatican, and finally to the Quirinal. The pope owned a small vineyard near the Quirinal and in 1564 purchased the palace and garden in Piazza Santi Apostoli, which had belonged to the Colonna family, for his nephew Carlo Borromeo. But the residences at his disposal in the city or nearby were truly numerous, and he used them all: Villa Giulia, the Torre Paolina on the Capitoline, Palazzo di San Marco, Palazzo dei Santi Apostoli, and, in his last years, the Vatican Casina. He also made frequent trips to Tivoli, Villa Magliana, Ostia, and Frascati.[41]

With the election of Pius V (1566–72) the change in papal habits was abrupt and absolute. In the first years of his papacy the severe head of the Inquisition and incorruptible interpreter of the Counter-Reformation chose to remain close to the Vatican, except for brief sojourns in the Torre Paolina on the Capitoline, in the garden of Cardinal Ferrara on the Quirinal, or in the monastery of Santa Sabina on the Aventine, where he had been a Dominican monk. Among his favorite destinations was the Villa Giulia, but always for brief stays, as holidays were considered incompatible with the religious rigor that he preached and practiced. The chronicles of the time reported, not coincidentally, that he

had ordered his nephew, Cardinal Alessandrino, not to leave the Vatican without his permission.[42] Nonetheless, Pius V's name is linked to the history of a suburban residence situated near the via Aurelia Antica, less than two miles from the Vatican, as attested by the family crest on the portal of the terrace overlooking the valley. It is a rustic country dwelling with various plots of land purchased beginning in 1565, when he was still Cardinal Ghisleri. The property, still known as the Casaletto di San Pio V, is on an elevated site, and its conception has been attributed, albeit without documentary support, to Nanni di Baccio Bigio.[43] It is an imposing rural structure without decorative or superfluous ornamentation. And although the interior courtyard is harmonious and elegant, the architectural structure seems fully in keeping with Pius V's inflexible, rigorous lifestyle. The pope took advantage of its proximity to the Vatican, going there often to enjoy the cool air of the site and share frugal meals with a few intimates; the only documented event organized there was a hunt in October 1571.[44]

After the moralist pause imposed by Pius V, the tradition of holidays and the culture of the villa resumed vigorously during the papacy of Gregory XIII (1572–85), with the bold creation of a new nucleus of illustrious residences in Frascati. Its proximity to Rome, pleasant climate, surrounding woods, and reacquisition as a property of the Camera Apostolica—carried out in 1537 under Paul III, who also ordered its reconstruction—all lay behind the development and new role of Frascati. However, an element that cannot be overlooked was the recollection of its history, evoked by the still-visible ruins of the classical age. Tellingly, the medallion commemorating the work of Paul III in Frascati bears an image of the Villa Rufina, the first modern residence built there, as well as the phrase "Tuscolo rest(ituita)," suggesting an idealized connection with the ancient Tuscolo—site of the villas of Cicero, Cato, and Lucullus.[45] Gregory XIII moved around frequently, often making last-minute decisions that wreaked havoc on the organization of the court. While in Rome, he loved to stay in San Marco, the Quirinal, and the villa of the cardinal of Ferrara, but he also often visited the nearby villas of his cardinals in Caprarola, Bagnaia, and Tivoli, as well as the Roman villas of the Medici and Cardinal Montalto. But his favorite retreat was Frascati, where Cardinal Marco Sittico Altemps, a nephew of Pius IV, had put a new stamp on the area's development, first with the purchase of Villa Angelina from the Farnese family, which later became Villa

Tuscolana, and then with the creation, attributed to Martino Longhi between 1573 and 1575, of the first nucleus of Villa Mondragone—so called in homage to Gregory XIII, whose family crest included a dragon—located near the ruins of Villa dei Quintili. The future pope, while still a cardinal, had been a frequent guest of Cardinal Altemps, and he was apparently responsible for the suggestion that Altemps expand his holdings in Tuscoli, as he preferred the hospitality of his friend to having his own residence. His physicians had recommended Frascati as the perfect place to rest following his efforts to reorganize the Church after the Council of Trent; the town also held for him—former jurist that he was—a great fascination, given its history as the place where Cicero had written and set his *Tuscolanae Disputationes*. Moreover, his frequent sojourns in Frascati attracted his friends and collaborators. The cardinals Tolomeo Galli and Antonio Carafa built villas in Frascati, while some religious orders, such as the Capuchins, the Jesuits, and the Oratorians, had seats there. These were, in fact, among the orders most involved in the reform of the Church.[46] Finally, it was the pope's custom during his country sojourns to deal with political affairs, receive and entertain important dignitaries, and hold audiences, to such an extent that in Frascati he instituted a Sacred Congregation to address relationships with the Eastern churches, and in March 1582 issued the papal bull that sanctioned the reform of the Julian calendar.[47]

In his free time Pope Boncompagni took long excursions on foot or on horseback and often went as far as the ruins of Tuscolo or the Capuchin monastery. The beauty of the gardens of the Tuscolan villas—Villa Rufina in particular—as well as daily life there are vividly narrated by Camillo Sighellio, who was a guest in 1578.[48] His letters give a good idea of how the days were spent in outings on horseback, admiration of the classical ruins, and lively conversations at the dining table. The Villa Mondragone, where the pope had his own apartments connected to a secret garden, was a coveted destination for the personages associated with the papal court, and over the years, in addition to its value as a place for recreation, it assumed increasing importance as a symbol of social and political power.[49] Beginning in 1582, when the pontiff sojourned there on some twelve occasions, his relationship with Cardinal Altemps started to deteriorate. Various chronicles of the day allude to the difficulties that the cardinal began to pose, including calculating the costs of the papal sojourns, acting less hospitably than in the past, and finding other

pretexts to prevent long stays.[50] Consequently, in the last two years of his papacy, Gregory XIII reduced his sojourns in Frascati considerably and turned his attention to the Quirinal residence that belonged to Cardinal d'Este, who, by contrast, preferred his villa in Tivoli. A longed-for plan for a residence on the Quirinal Hill—renowned for its healthy air and home to small villas belonging to celebrated humanists since the fifteenth century—had been in the works since 1573, but was always put off because of the costs it would have incurred. Only in 1583 was there an announcement of an allocation of 23,000 *scudi* to begin construction of a dwelling that, according to estimates, would cost some 50,000. The work, under the direction of Ottavio Mascherino, was begun promptly, and by the end of 1584 the pope was able to reside there—but only for brief periods, and without the problem of ownership having been resolved, as the property still belonged to the Carafa family and was rented to Cardinal d'Este.[51]

With the election of Sixtus V (1585–95), the holiday periods in Frascati ceased completely. The new pontiff preferred his family's residence—the grand Villa Montalto, near his beloved Basilica of Santa Maria Maggiore—and he also committed himself to the expansion of the Quirinal villa, the ownership of which was determined in 1587, and which was on the way to becoming an official residence next to the Vatican citadel and a symbol of papal power.[52]

The election of the next pope, Clement VIII (1595–1605) of the Aldobrandini family, opened a new period of splendor for Frascati and for its confirmation as a city of villas. After initially using Villa Mondragone for his sojourns, the pope allocated to the cardinal-nephew Pietro Aldobrandini a villa that had once belonged to the physician Contugi, then to Monsignor Capranica, then after the death of the latter to the Apostolic Camera. Giacomo della Porta transformed the villa into the magnificent, stately Villa Aldobrandini; its imposing structure and the splendid array of holm oaks along its access road still dominate the town of Frascati. The advent of the villa prompted substantial modifications to the appearance and character of the area: the importance of its agricultural functions diminished and leisure functions gained prevalence, as subsequent villas, constituting an exhibition of power by the families of the reigning popes and by members of the Curia, were constructed.[53] Villa Aldobrandini was completed in 1603, and

240. Mattheus Greuter, *True and New Drawing of Frascati with All of the Surrounding Villas*, c. 1620, etching.

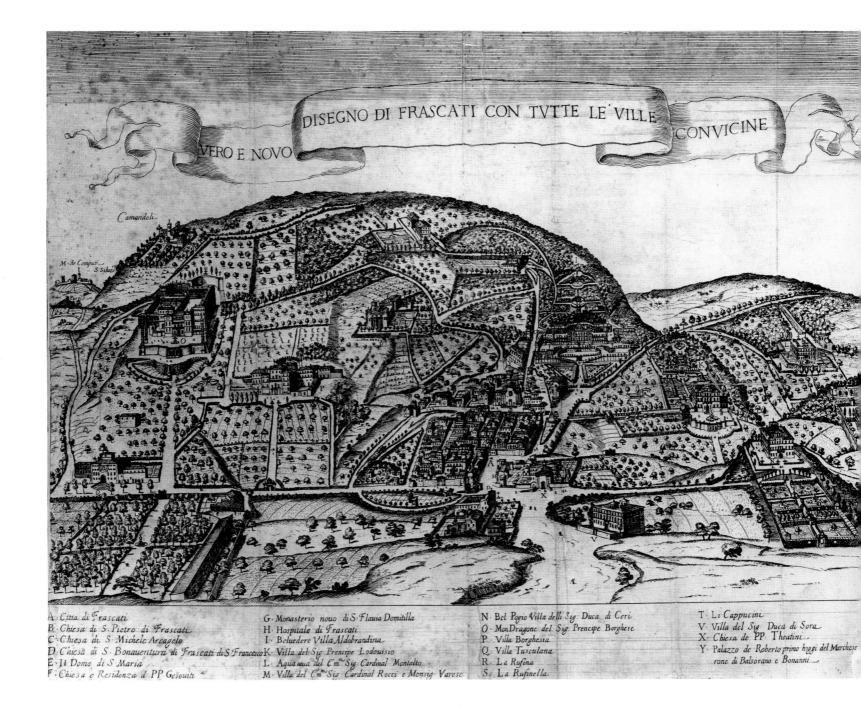

VERO E NOVO DISEGNO DI FRASCATI CON TVTTE LE VILLE CONVICINE

Camandoli

M. de Computi
S. Siluestro

A · Citta di Frascati
B · Chiesa di S. Pietro di Frascati
C · Chiesa di S. Michele Arcagelo
D · Chiesa di S. Bonauentura di Frascati di S. Francesco
E · Il Domo di S. Maria
F · Chiesa e Residenza d PP Gesouiti

G · Monasterio nouo di S. Flauia Domitilla
H · Hospitale di Frascati
I · Beluedere Villa Aldobrandina
K · Villa del Sig. Prencipe Lodouisio
L · Aqua iaua del Em.mo Sig. Cardinal Montalto
M · Villa del Em.mo Sig. Cardinal Rocci e Monsig. Varese

N · Bel Pogio Villa delli Sig. Duca di Ceri
O · MonDragone del Sig. Prencipe Borghese
P · Villa Borghesia
Q · Villa Tusculana
R · La Rufina
S · La Rufinella

T · Li Cappucini
V · Villa del Sig. Duca di Sora
X · Chiesa de PP. Theatini
Y · Palazzo de Roberto primo hoggi del Marchese rone di Balsorano e Bonanni

its majesty was evident. It had an incredible water supply, unscrupulously purloined from the surrounding area, that fed the grandiose waterfall and permitted the installation of enormously rich and complex gardens.[54] One contemporary description allows us to grasp fully the novelty of the complex, asserting that it was without precedent and set in the dominant position on the world's stage.[55] Clement VIII was able to enjoy this splendid residence only briefly; his death in 1605 paved the way for his successor and rival, Paul V Borghese (1605–21), who would steal the show of Frascati, transforming it into a true and proper Borghese city.

Through the cardinal-nephew Scipione Caffarelli Borghese, the pontiff had use of the splendid Villa Pinciana. Situated just outside the city walls of Rome, it had a fine view and was an ideal site for the exhibition of art collections as well as pleasant banquets.[56] The villa was constructed with great speed, and by 1609 the pope was attending musical performances there; at the same time work continued on the expansion of the Quirinal residence and the adjacent garden.[57] The pope's interest in the Roman villas did not, however, cause him to neglect Frascati, where he had already spent time as a cardinal in 1593, 1594, and 1602, as a guest of the Altemps family. In the first years of his papacy he convinced Cardinal Ottavio Acquaviva to grant him use of his Tuscolan villa, which was lovely but not adequate for a demanding court. Cardinal Scipione then acquired the nearby "Caravilla," celebrated for having belonged to poet Annibale Caro, and thus initiated a program of expansion on the Tuscolan hills that is depicted in a view by Mattheus Greuter (plate 240), painted in 1620, at the end of the Borghese pontificate. Visible in the natural amphitheater of the hills are the numerous villas that had been built, most prominently the three interconnecting Borghese properties: Villa Mondragone, Villa Taverna Belvedere, and Villa Tuscolana, all the fruit of costly if unscrupulous acquisitions.

When the pope went to Frascati, his court settled in at Villa Mondragone, the largest and most elaborate of the villas, while Cardinal Scipione resided at Villa Taverna and the attendants at Villa Tuscolana; thus the hierarchy was reflected even in the choice of residences. The three properties were linked by wide avenues, and the entire landscape was organized into a system of connecting axes. The monumental entrance to this true "Tuscolan state" was the majestic Portale delle Armi, so called for the Borghese coats of arms that still adorn it. Paul V went to Frascati in the spring and fall, often repeatedly and for long periods, and it seems

he intended to transform it into the permanent summer papal residence, even considering the idea of a tree-lined road to connect it directly with Rome.[58]

Under Paul V, the phenomenon of the popes' holidays reached its greatest splendor with the creation, at Frascati, of a system of residences capable of housing not only the papal court and its entourage but also illustrious guests, whose stays were enlivened by sumptuous banquets. The transfer of the court to the countryside required a complex organization that involved even the transportation of silverware and table linens, while the management of each day was meticulously regulated by weekly menus. For banquets various tables were set up and the seating arranged according to the hierarchy of the guests, who were entertained with music and theatrical performances.[59]

In the chronicles of the time there is no longer any mention of health needs as justification for the popes' holidays. On the contrary, emphasis was placed on the splendor and sophistication of the sites and their way of life. The papal holiday had by now become a status symbol, and the cardinals competed to offer the pontiff increasingly refined sojourns in their residences, as the visits were often occasions to obtain favors or concessions.

The rise to the papal throne of the humanist Maffeo Barberini, who adopted the name Urban VIII (1623–44), saw changes not in approach but in location. After sojourning several times in Mondragone, as the guest of his friend Cardinal Scipione Borghese, he chose for his holidays as pope another small nearby town: Castel Gandolfo, where the Barberini family owned a *casino*, or country house (plate 241), and where he would oversee the building of a true papal residence. His pontificate marked the beginning of the tradition of sojourns in this city, which, with its lake and surrounding woods, offered a magnificent setting. Even though they continued to spend time in the villas of the cardinals around Rome,[60] with the residence in Castel Gandolfo the popes at last had at their constant disposal a villa belonging to the Apostolic Camera, and not to a family member or prelate friend. The expansion and renovation of the original residence would transform it, over time, into the official summer seat of the pontificate, and it would be used—albeit with some long interruptions for political reasons—from 1626 until the present day.[61]

The Papal Villa in Castel Gandolfo

The Papal Villa in Castel Gandolfo,[62] in its present form, is the result of the integration of three separate properties that were joined over time: the original seventeenth-century papal villa; the Villa Cybo, acquired in 1773; and the Villa Barberini, added in 1929 following the Lateran Accords.

THE VILLA PONTIFICIA, OR PAPAL VILLA

In 1594, as a consequence of the indebtedness of the noble and powerful Savelli family of Rome, their property in Castel Gandolfo was forcibly acquired by the Apostolic Camera, and in 1604, via a consistorial decree by Clement VIII, it was incorporated into the temporal dominions of the Holy See. According to some sources, Paul v, enticed by the amenities of the site, its proximity to Rome, and the pleasantness of the lake, had expressed his intention to create a papal residence there but was distracted by the demands of the villas in Frascati. In fact, the only change the Borghese pope made in Castel Gandolfo was the piping in of water from the healthy springs of Palazzolo, which was undoubtedly beneficial, as the only previous water source was the lake. The catalyst behind the transformation of the Savelli property from a stronghold into a palace with a garden was Urban VIII,[63] who while still a cardinal had, on his doctor's advice, sojourned several times in Castel Gandolfo, even dedicating some verses to it.[64]

Work on the villa began in 1623 on the site of the ancient necropolis of Alba Longa, where the ducal Gandolfi family had once built the stronghold that later passed to the Savellis. Carlo Maderno, with the collaboration of Domenico Castelli and Bartolomeo Braccioli, was in charge of the construction. The project involved the expansion of the old fortress in the direction of the lake, thereby connecting it to the existing structures that faced the village piazza. The garden, of modest size, was sited to the northwest of the new complex, laid out in geometric divisions, and surrounded by a high wall.[65] The entrance portal, attributed to Gian Lorenzo Bernini, was demolished in 1933, following the unification of the properties, in order to make a new connecting road. Urban VIII paid attention to the accessibility of the complex as well, and ordered two new roads built, one toward Albano and the other toward the residential area of Castel Gandolfo. Both were lined with holm oaks to form covered avenues or *cocchi*. Urban VIII's contribution is commemorated on a medallion that depicts the complex along with the words SUBURBANO RECESSU (suburban retreat).[66] However, some sources relate that the pope never resided there, preferring the nearby family property, where he sojourned until his precarious state of health kept him from leaving Rome.

The new palace (plate 242), destined to become the pontifical residence, was simple and austere, with some frescoed rooms and others covered with *corami* (decorated-leather wall coverings), fine paintings, and antique-style furnishings.[67] The first pope to reside there in earnest was Alexander VII (1655–67), who further enlarged the palace of Urban VIII, completed its main facade, and commissioned Gian Lorenzo Bernini to build the west wing with the long gallery, according to an inscription still in place.[68] The project to "enlarge and beautify" the Apostolic Palace included the planned construction of an oven and two "pits for snow," as well as the demolition of some nearby houses.[69] The pope dearly loved Castel Gandolfo, where he would go in the spring and fall, sometimes for long periods, and where he organized spectacular events recorded in the chronicles; these included a mock naval battle, held in the lake, between Turks and Christians, ending with the inevitable victory of the latter and celebratory music and fireworks.[70] For sailing on the lake he had brought from Civitavecchia a felucca and a richly decorated brig, which were stored in the garden's nymphaeum when not in use. An image of the property (plate 244), dating to 1659 and therefore to the period of the Chigi papacy, was drawn up by Felice della Greca. In this plan, the papal palace is depicted with the small adjacent garden surrounded by the wall; next to it is the area of the future Villa Cybo, with a much larger park.

For some decades thereafter, and for various reasons, the popes did not visit the lakeside Castel Gandolfo, but we have evidence that the residence was looked after. In 1674, during the papacy of Clement x (1670–76), the espaliers of roses in the garden were carefully secured and, depending on the season, pots of citrus trees and jasmine were either sheltered or brought outdoors.[71] The following year "three squares were planted with tulip bulbs," many strawberry plants were planted, the paths were cleaned, and the high hedges that enclosed the beds, generally formed of low oaks, laurel, and boxwood, were regularly pruned.[72] The gardens' produce, although of modest value, served to supply the court of Rome, as is clear from an accounting of April 1676, when "flowers and fruit" were brought to Rome from Castel Gandolfo.[73] In the following decades there were no important changes, only ordinary maintenance,

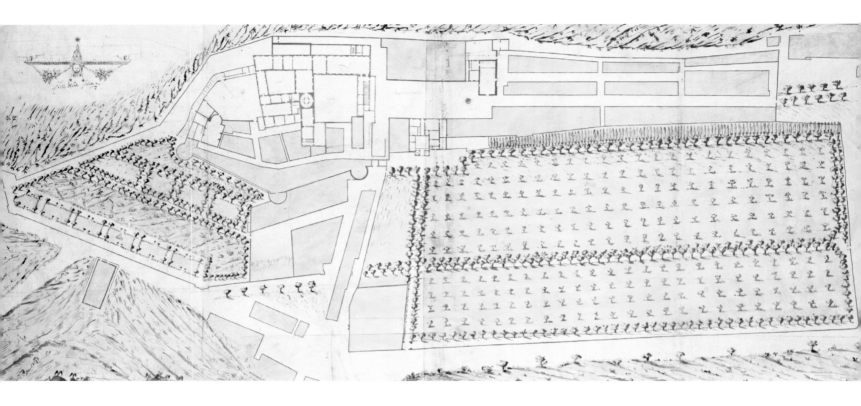

241. (*above*) Luigi Arrigucci, *Territory of Castel Gandolfo*,
1630, detail of the pen-and-ink drawing showing the Casino
of Pope Urban VIII. BAV, Chigi, Part VII, 12, sheet 2r.

242. (*opposite*) Giovan Battista Falda, *View of Castel Gandolfo
with the Papal Palace and the Church of San Tommaso di
Villanova*, before 1667, etching.

although Clement xi (1700–21) made repeated visits.[74] Of great interest, however, are the transformations and embellishments carried out under Benedict xiv (1740–58), primarily in the interiors,[75] but also including the construction of the benediction loggia, which was painted entirely by Pier Leone Ghezzi and furnished with chinoiserie.[76] Clement xiv (1769–74) was responsible for further expansion and the decoration of some rooms next to the gallery with views of the works completed during his papacy. More importantly, two events of great consequence for the residence occurred during his brief reign: a viaduct was built in 1773 to facilitate access to the portal of the complex for those arriving from Albano, and in the same year, the neighboring Villa Cybo was acquired, thereby permitting the construction of a garden worthy of a papal residence, as the space available in the original nucleus was very limited and the popes were forced to leave their property in order to take a stroll.[77] In fact, in a fresco in the Sala del Biliardo of the papal palace, Clement xiv himself is depicted on a white steed preparing to leave the hamlet, with the court in tow, for an excursion in the countryside.

THE VILLA CYBO

Cardinal Camillo Cybo (1681–1743) was the second son of the duke of Massa Carlo ii Cybo Malaspina and Teresa Pamphilj.[78] Thanks to the proceeds from the sale of the family palace in Piazza Navona to the Pamphiljs, he acquired various properties in Castel Gandolfo in order to make a luxurious residence there, as it was the "site of pleasure closest to Rome…of them all, the healthiest" and also "a site destined for the holidays of the supreme Popes," and thus a point of pride for the family.[79] To this end he picked out a *piccolo casino*, built by the architect Francesco Fontana (1668–1708)[80] for his personal use, and a nearby abandoned site belonging to the Bonelli family, which he intended to "outfit…later with a lovely structure for garden use."[81] On April 18, 1716, the acquisition of the Casino was stipulated between Francesco Fontana's son, Mauro,[82] and

243. *(pages 304–5)* Castel Gandolfo, view from above of the papal palace and of the district facing the lake.

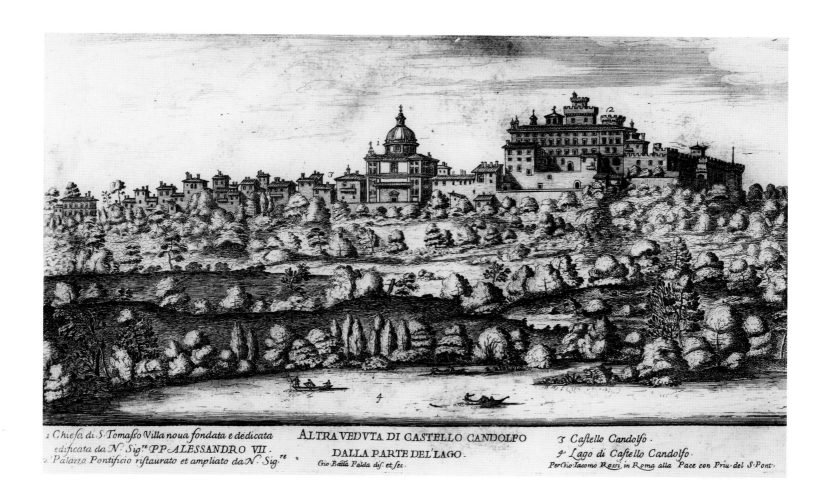

1 *Chiefa di S. Tomaffo Villa noua fondata e dedicata edificata da N. Sig.re PP ALESSANDRO VII.*
2 *Palazzo Pontificio riftaurato et ampliato da N. Sig.re*

ALTRA VEDVTA DI CASTELLO CANDOLFO
DALLA PARTE DEL LAGO.
Gio. Batta Falda dif. et fec.

3 *Caftello Candolfo.*
4 *Lago di Caftello Candolfo.*
Per Gio. Iacomo Roffi in Roma alla Pace con Priu. del S. Pont.

the cardinal[83] for the sum of 2,850 *scudi*, and soon there-after the Bonelli land was also purchased.[84]

Major work began on the property immediately: a "boundary wall to keep the animals in the park for hunting…and groves for thrush" were added,[85] and niches were made in the walls, probably to hold marble busts. Moreover, six statues, seven palms high, were set up facing the roads "at the heads of the roads of the Ragnaia,"[86] and another six in front of the casino; the fountain in the court-yard of the casino was decorated with two putti; and a new gate was made on the land formerly belonging to the Bonellis.[87] The work to expand the casino and embellish the site, directed by the architect Carlo Stefano Fontana (1703–40),[88] cost some 113,253.72 *scudi*[89] and is documented in some interesting drawings (plates 247–50).[90] The three-story casino had two adjacent chicken coops and a servants' hall, and twenty-four pots of citrus trees were dispersed all around.[91] In addition, there were a fruit orchard and a *parter*, or parterre.[92] There were in fact two gardens: a smaller, more private one, directly accessible from the log-gia of the casino, and a second, larger one beyond the road, toward the village. More substantial modifications followed this initial phase a few years later, again directed by Carlo Stefano Fontana and aimed primarily at embellishing the site with numerous sculptures from the Cybo properties in Massa Carrara, for a total value of 21,974.48 *scudi* for the statues situated in the garden and 14,732 *scudi* for those in the casino, according to the estimate of Fontana and the Carrara sculptor Francesco Pincellotti.[93]

Beginning in April 1724, numerous "boats" arrived in Fiumicino loaded with marble from Carrara, which was then transferred to wagons and brought to Castel Gan-dolfo. Registered until 1736 are substantial, repeated ship-ments of marble busts, including six lions, twenty-four pyramids, and the same number of little boats, as well as "large bases of *pietre mischie*, with their busts of *pietre mischie*," that is, colored marble such as antique yellow, Sicilian jasper, and gray from the Veneto region. Other marble was transported from the Roman properties, and when the work was completed the appearance of the Villa Cybo must have been truly splendid, the casino richly deco-rated and surrounded by a garden in which hedges and flowers formed elaborate arabesques peppered with statues and fountains. Beyond this was the park with its ordered roads, groves, and the hunting zone. There was also a lovely, precious fountain, again of *pietre mischie*. The casino, how-ever, was separate from the gardens and connected to them by means of two bridges at the height of the *piano nobile*.

This was a temporary solution, pending the realization of the cardinal's grandiose project—never carried out—to build a new, larger casino facing the town's principal road, with an entrance in the direction of the papal villa and the rear opening toward the gardens. There were many subse-quent modifications, especially in the 1930s, that largely changed the original layout of the villa, but some of the decorative elements of great interest are still in place: the entrance square in front of the casino with its dramatic, double-ramped staircase (plates 256, 257), dubbed "Teatro Grande" for its grandeur; the Fontana delle Lavandaie, so called for the two figures, unfortunately now headless, in the act of washing; the elegant balustrade topped by six large sculptures that reproduce the two-headed eagle of the Cybo crest; and, lower down, four pilasters supporting the statues of the *mattacini* (plate 245), typical folk figures from Massa Carrara, brought there from Villa della Rinchiostra. A painting (plate 246) that can be admired today in the palace's Sala del Biliardo shows the meeting between Pope Clement XIV and his cook, nicknamed "Setteminestre" (Seven Soups), in the garden, whose parterres—along with a fountain and the wood in the background—are visible.

The glorious period of the Villa Cybo was brief and ended with the death of the cardinal in 1743. Inherited by Maria Teresa Cybo, it was used by the French ambassador, Monsignor de Canillac, who, to facilitate the pope's strolls in the villa's gardens, had the stairway built at the entry to the property, where a monumental entrance was planned. A constant visitor to the villa, Benedict XIV established the habitual use of the property that would be emulated by his successors. In 1772 the villa was turned over to the duke of Bracciano, Livio Odescalchi,[94] but immediately, and under the same terms, acquired by Clement XIV to enlarge the pontifical residence. According to Bonomelli, he paid only 18,000 *scudi* for the property, but this sum is far smaller than the cost documented by the deeds mentioned above and must have referred to the furnishings alone.[95]

His successor, Pius VI (1775–99) never used the Castel Gandolfo residence during his long reign, in part because of the tragic historical events he was faced with, and the villa was rented for a number of years to third parties, who transformed the garden into a vegetable plot.[96] Pius VII (1800–23) went there on occasion, but the custom of rent-ing it out continued, and by 1815 the garden had become a "grazing pasture for cows" and an "artichoke patch" until the tenancy of Monsignor de Blocasse, minister of France, when it was revamped in the "English style" in vogue at the time.[97]

Even subsequently, the Casino Cybo was not used by the popes and continued to be rented out: in 1828 Leo XII (1823–29) granted use to the marchioness Orsola Macca-rani, and in 1840 it housed a school, in keeping with a custom documented in 1903.[98] During the nineteenth century, papal visits there were frequent, if brief, but many statues from the Villa Cybo were transported to Rome and installed in the Quirinal gardens. In 1869, for obvious reasons, the visits were interrupted, resuming only in 1934, after the pontifical residence had also acquired the adjacent Villa Barberini under the terms of the Lateran Accords and assumed its present-day parameters and function.[99]

THE VILLA BARBERINI

The Villa Barberini was built on the site of the ancient Villa di Domiziano, the vast and magnificent cryptoporti-

244. Felice della Greca, plan of the papal residence in Castel Gandolfo (palace and garden) with the adjacent site of the future Villa Cybo, c. 1659, pen-and-ink drawing with watercolor on parchment. BAV, Chigi, Part VII. 12, sheet 1r.

cus of which still exists (plates 251–54). Beginning in 1628, Taddeo Barberini, nephew of Pope Urban VIII, initiated the acquisition of tracts of land that culminated in 1631 with the purchase of the property of Monsignor Scipione Visconti, which also included a *casino*. This building was partly demolished and rebuilt in a more majestic and lavish form, albeit at a modest size, after a design attributed to Gian Lorenzo Bernini. To create the garden, a team of diggers from Aquila worked for months to deforest and level the terrain and remove the huge stones of the ancient ruins. The leveled area was then organized into regular roads and plantings bordered by boxwood hedges, with rows of holm oaks that shaded the garden on the side toward the sea.[100] Woods, pastures, and olive groves surrounded the formal gardens. The park was not filled with the customary statues and reliefs, but one work of great interest was installed: the personification of the Nile, in mulberry-colored marble, now held in the Villa Albani Torlonia. In 1635 work must have been completed, as we have documentation showing that furnishings and provisions for the first sojourn of the family were transported there. The casino was not situated in the center of the garden, as was customary, but was set

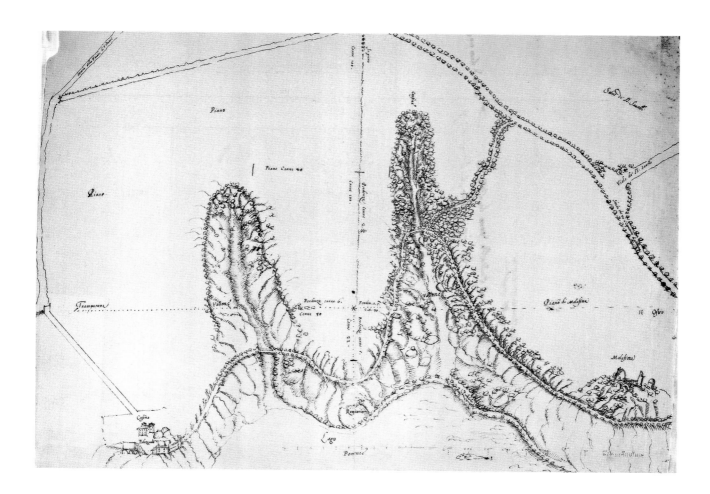

245. Villa Cybo, Statues of the *mattaccini*, folk figures from
the Villa Rinchiostra near Massa; above is the balustrade with
eagles, the emblem of Cardinal Cybo.

246. Detail of the Cybo garden with the parterres, from a
painting held in the papal palace.

at a distance and separated from it by a drop in the terrain. For this reason a kind of viaduct supported by walls was built to create a long avenue, called "la Catena."[101] Plans for a new garden next to the casino and for supplying the park with water and fountains remained unrealized, but Taddeo Barberini had the terrace over the cryptoporticus designed in a spectacular fashion, with paving in peperino and a beautiful balustrade. Subsequently, a lovely and original gate was added to the complex, but just after the death of Urban VIII and the fall from grace of the Barberinis, the villa became the object of legal diatribes by the Reformed Fathers, whose monastery bordered the garden. Only in 1791 was the dispute resolved in a formal agreement, although it seems that in the intervening decades the popes frequently went there to take walks during their holidays at Castel Gandolfo. After alternating periods of abandonment and recovery, the villa underwent a comprehensive renovation in 1912, fostered by Prince Luigi Barberini: the garden was redesigned into geometric beds, fountains were created, and the remains of the antique villa were restored.[102] A few years later, however, following the Lateran Accords of February 11, 1929, the villa was assigned to the Holy See and soon linked to the preexisting property as the permanent summer residence of the popes (plate 243).

Twentieth-Century Modifications

In June 1930 the job of transforming Villa Barberini began, and soon thereafter renovations were undertaken at Villa Pontificia and Villa Cybo as well. The three nuclei were interconnected with overpasses and new roads, the buildings renovated and furnished, the gardens put in order or created anew (plate 258), and an agricultural area annexed and equipped. On May 23, 1934, the work was completed and presented to Pope Pius XI (1922–29), who had followed the progress during two previous visits. The architect in charge of the building renovations was Giuseppo Momo (1875–1940), who was also active in the Vatican,[103] while the plan for the gardens and park was the work of Emilio Bonomelli (1890–1970), later named director of the papal villas. Formally organized areas alternated with natural zones in the fifty-five hectare park, and in the gardens fountains were built and an irrigation system installed at the behest of the pope's nephew, Franco Ratti.

The reorganization of the villa was designed to offer a variety of scenery and landscapes, including sweeping panoramas—an attempt to compensate for the popes' inability to leave the confines of the complex and stroll in the surrounding woods and valleys as they had in the past. To maximize the most panoramic part of the route, substantial areas of land were reclaimed and leveled: rises and drops were modified with embankments and trenches, and by cutting through banks of rock and then flattening the terrain. Through the most carefully tended part of the walk, which includes the gardens of Villa Barberini, one could now reach the agricultural area bordering the town of Albano, with its pastures, olive trees, vegetable gardens, and orchards. The effect was one of gradual transition from pleasure ground to agricultural activity. Created in the center of the estate was its most important feature, the Belvedere Gardens (plate 255), which were divided into three terraces (plate 260) and now frame the view of the surviving structures of the Villa di Domiziano. The flat area of the seventeenth-century garden was enlarged and laid out in various flowered parterres bordered by cypress trees (plate 259), which act as columns framing the landscape below. A citrus orchard was even planted (plate 261), harking back to the tradition of cultivating the "golden fruit." It is enclosed between a green espalier and the ruins of the cryptoporticus and recalls the layout of a secret garden. Antique sculptures, some of which were found during the renovation, were placed throughout the park, and the fountains once again spouted water. The impetus for the creation of the new gardens was the revival of the formal garden tradition that became widespread in the first decades of the twentieth century, and not just in Italy. Particular attention was paid to restoring the remains of the Villa di Domiziano, both the visible ruins and those found during the course of the work.[104] The result is a remarkable, harmonious ensemble of "flora et ruinae,"[105] with jasmine and roses scaling the ancient rocks and columns of cypresses positioned to re-create, through living architecture, the stone originals that had by then been lost.

247. *(opposite, top)* Carlo Stefano Fontana, design for the Casino Cybo with the planned expansion, first half of the eighteenth century, drawing with watercolor. ASR, Archivio Cybo.

248. *(opposite, bottom)* Carlo Stefano Fontana, design for the Casino Cybo, detail of the rear garden, with the adjacent district visible in the upper section, first half of the eighteenth century, drawing with watercolor. ASR, Archivio Cybo.

Scala di Cen to Palmi Romani

249. *(opposite)* Carlo Stefano Fontana, design for the Casino Cybo, detail of the parterre of the rear garden, first half of the eighteenth century, drawing with watercolor. ASR, Archivio Cybo.

250. *(above)* Carlo Stefano Fontana, design for the Casino Cybo, facade facing the rear garden, first half of the eighteenth century, drawing with watercolor. ASR, Archivio Cybo.

253. *(below)* The cryptoporticus of the Villa di Domiziano, exterior.

254. *(bottom)* The cryptoporticus of the Villa di Domiziano, interior.

255. *(overleaf)* The Belvedere Gardens, built in the 1930s, with the cryptoporticus of the Villa di Domiziano on the right.

256. (*above*) View of the Magnolia Garden from the *boschetto*.

257. *(above)* Villa Cybo's Garden of Mirrors, so called for its two reflecting pools.

258. *(overleaf)* Another view of the Garden of Mirrors.

259. *(pages 322–23)* The Square Piazza, bordered by espaliers of cypress and holm oaks pruned in geometric shapes.

260. *(pages 324–25)* View of the terraces rising from the Square Piazza to the Belvedere Gardens. In the foreground is the coat of arms with eagle and sphere of Pius XI, patron of the final modifications.

261. *(pages 326–27)* Detail of the citrus fruit orchard and its central fountain.

Notes

CHAPTER ONE: ORIGINS AND
FIRST DEVELOPMENTS

1. The sequence of building stages at the Vatican is reconstructed in A. Taka, *Descrizione dei Palazzi Apostolici Vaticani* (Rome, 1750); C. Cecchelli, *Il Vaticano: la basilica, i palazzi, i giardini*, (Milan-Rome: Tuminelli, 1926); J. S. Ackerman, *The Cortile del Belvedere* (Vatican City, 1954); D. Redig de Campos, *Il Belvedere di Innocent VIII in Vaticano* (Vatican City, 1958); D. Redig de Campos, *I Palazzi Vaticani* (Bologna: L. Cappelli, 1967). The numerous publications that have appeared since do not provide additional information, but at times contain splendid illustrations. See, for example, C. Pietrangeli (editor), *I Palazzi Apostolici Vaticani*, Nardini edizioni, Florence 1992. In general, treatment of the gardens is brief and not supported by references to archival material or sources from the period.

2. "...apud Sanctum Petrum palatium, cameras et turrim pulcherrimas hedificari et vineas ibi emi fecit." F. Ehrle and H. Egger, *Studi e documenti per la storia del Palazzo Apostolico Vaticano* (Vatican City: Biblioteca Apostolica Vaticana, 1935), with ample list of sources.

3. His brochure, *Thesaurus pauperumin*, was widely distributed; it indicated the least costly remedy for every disease, generally suggesting plants and herbal medicines.

4. All of the acquisitions are reconstructed and recorded in detail in F. Ehrle, H. Egger, *Studi*.

5. M. Fagiolo, *I giardini papali del Vaticano e del Quirinale*, in M. Amari, ed., *Giardini Regali* (Milan: Electa, 1998), p. 69.

6. The complex symbology of the garden and its elements, from the time of its origins, has been amply explored in the fascinating essay by M. Venturi Ferriolo, *Nel grembo della vita. Le origini dell'idea di giardino* (Milan: Guerini e Associati, 1989).

7. S. Piale, "Delle mura e porte del Vaticano" (diss.), Pontificia Accademia Romana di Archeologia, IV, Rome 1834.

8. A.P. Frutaz, *Il Torrione di Niccolò v in Vaticano* (Vatican City, 1956).

9. "ANNO SECONDO PONTIFICATUS SUI FIERI FECIT CIRCUITUM MURORUM POMERII HUIUS..." The lapidary, now in the Sala dei Capitani, was discovered unexpectedly in 1727 by Monsignor Francesco Bianchini in one of his villas along the via Aurelia and donated by him to the Capitoline collections.

10. M. Fagiolo, *I giardini papali*, p. 70.

11. "Hic palatium Sancti Petri multum augmentavit. Et plurima aedificia faciens, iuxta illud parvum pratum inclusit, & fontem, ibidem profluere paravit, moenibus & turribus

munivit: hortum magnum diversis arboribus decoratum includendo." M. Poloni, *Chronicon expeditissimum, ad fidem veterum manoscriptorum codicum emendatum et auctum* (Antwerp: ex officina Christophori Platini, Architypographi Regij, 1574), p. 421.

12. F. Cardini and M. Miglio, *Nostalgia del paradiso. Il giardino medievale* (Bari: Laterza, 2002), pp. 24–25.

13. Albertus Magnus, *Opera Omnia*, ed. A. and E. Borgnet (Paris, 1898), pp. 600–603.

14. The documents are published in L. Duchesne, ed., *Liber Pontificalis*, 3 vols. (Paris: E. de Boccard, 1910–52, II, pp. 43–60.

15. A. Cortonesi, "Il Giardino del papa. Pratiche agricole e lavoro salariato nella Roma di fine Duecento," in *Scritti in memoria di Giuseppe Marchetti Longhi*, "Biblioteca di Latium," Anagni, 1990, I, pp. 129–30.

16. The *pezza romana* was equal to 2,640.62 square meters, according to M. Dykmans, "Du Monte Mario à l'escalier de Saint Pierre de Rome," in *Mélanges d'Archéologie et d'Histoire*, 80 (1968), pp. 547–94.

17. A detailed and interesting reconstruction of the agricultural practices and of the substance and use of the Vatican grounds is in A. Cortonesi, *Il giardino del papa*, pp. 115–33.

18. *Liber Pontificalis*, doc. 7, p. 47: "...duas petias vinearum, vites tantum, cum arboribus fructiferis et infructiferis, vasca, vascali et tino" (two plots of vineyards, vines only, together with fruit-bearing and non-fruit-bearing trees, a basin, trough, and vat).

19. ASV, Camera Apostolica, Introitus et Exitus, I, June 1285–May 1286, sheet 34r.

20. ASV, Camera Apostolica, Introitus et Exitus, I, June 1285–May 1286, sheet 54r, sheet 55r; two men work "ad secandum herbam in iardino."

21. C. Pietrangeli, ed., *Guide del Vaticano, La città* (Rome: Fratelli Palombi Editore, 1989), p. 66.

22. Various authors, *Rome e il suo Orto Botanico. Storia ed eventi di un'istituzione scientifica* (Rome: Edizioni Borgia, 1984), pp. 12–13.

23. Ibid.

24. "...circa fabricam ipsius basilicae ac custodiam palatii et iardinarum papalium." Both letters are published in F. Ehrle, H. Egger, *Studi*, p. 55.

25. ASV, Camera Apostolica, Introitus et Exitus, b. 269, sheet 8, Innocent VI, 1353.

26. ASV, Camera Apostolica, Introitus et Exitus, b. 269, sheets 22, 27, 78, 93, Innocent VI, 1354.

27. ASV, Camera Apostolica, Collectoriae, b. 451, Expensae Palatii Apostoliciis 1363-1369, sheets 154ss.

28. A. Theiner, *Codex diplomaticus dominii temporalis S. Sedis: recueil de documents pour servir à l'histoire du gouvernement temporel des Etats du Saint Siège: extraits des archives du Vatican* (Frankfurt am Main: Unveranderter Nachdruck, 1964), II, p. 430. The Latin text specifically cites, with reference to the plants, the terms "fructiferis et amenis" as confirmation of the coexistence of the utilitarian and the ornamental.

29. ASV, Camera Apostolica, Manuale Introitum et Expensorum pro conficienda vinea et viridario, year 1368, sheet 379.

30. ASV, Camera Apostolica, Introituс et Exitus, b. 325, years 1367–1368, sheet 82v: "tribus hominibus de Portuveneris, qui asportaverunt per mare de Marsilia usque Romem quesdam arbores seu plantas arborum missas de portibus gaballicanis pro plantando in viridario palacii apostolici Romee" ("three men from Portovenere, who brought by sea from Marseilles to Rome certain trees or tree-plantings which were sent from the Gaballican harbor to be planted in the garden of the apostolic palace of Rome").

31. ASV, Camera Apostolica, Introitus et Exitus, b. 325, November 13, 1367, sheet 73r.

32. All of the payments and documents are cited in F. Ehrle, H. Egger, *Studi*, p. 75.

33. The document is cited in C. D'Onofrio, "Introduzione storica," in M. Catalano, E. Pellegrini, *L'Orto botanico di Roma* (Rome: Palombi Editore, 1975), p. XVI.

34. A. Theiner, *Codex*, II, p. 473.

35. M. C. Pozzana, *Il giardino dei frutti* (Florence: Ponte alle Grazie, 1990).

36. In 1299, for example, roe-deer were introduced to the park. See A. Cortonesi, *Il giardino*, note 61, p. 126.

37. ASV, Camera Apostolica, Introitus et Exitus, b. 329, sheets 93r–94rv.

38. ASV, Camera Apostolica, Introitus et Exitus, b. 329, sheets 93v–96r, where expenses are cited for "III centenara de iunczi per ligare la coperta de l'arbori" and the purchase of chestnut posts "pro copriendo arbores citronum."

39. On the relationship between Rome and Jerusalem and its symbolic values, see M. Fagiolo, "Il pellegrinaggio a Roma. Strutture e simboli nella città degli Anni Santi," in F. Paloscia, ed., *Roma dei grandi viaggiatori* (Rome: Edizioni Abete, 1987), pp. 40–45.

40. Vespasiano da Bisticci, *Vite di uomini illustri del xv secolo*, Paolo d'Ancona, Erhard

Aeschinann, ed. (Milano: Hoepli, 1951), p. 353.

41. E. Muntz, *Les Arts à la cour des papes pendant le XV et le XVI siècles* (Paris, 1878), pp. 275–77.

42. The personality and work of Nicholas V are well explored in the translation and critical edition of his life: G. Manetti, *Vita di Niccolò V*, Italian translation and commentary by A. Modigliani, introduction by M. Miglio (Rome: Roma nel Rinascimento, 1999). On his urbanistic work, see T. Magnuson, "The Project of Nicholaus V for the Rebuilding of the Borgo Leonino in Rome," in *The Art Bulletin*, 36, 1954, pp. 94–96.

43. G. Manetti, *Vita*, p. 138.

44. G. Manetti, *Vita*, p. 140: "From the upper part, toward the west, one could see another garden, where other residences were located, different from the preceding ones, for use by the same camerlengo." D. R. Coffin, *Gardens and Gardening in Papal Rome* (Princeton: Princeton University Press, 1991), p. 8.

45. G. Boccaccio, *Decameron*, trans. J. M. Rigg (London: A. H. Bullen, 1903), III, Introduction. The theme of the garden as paradise is treated amply in M. Fagiolo and M. A. Giusti, *Lo Specchio del Paradiso. L'immagine del Paradiso dall'antico al Novecento* (Cinisello Balsamo: Pizzi, 1996).

46. G. Manetti, *Vita*, p. 140.

47. *Archivio Società Romana Storia Patria*, 1881, p. 14.

48. M. Fagiolo, "Architettura e città nel 'piano' di Niccolò V," in M. Fagiolo, M. L. Madonna, ed., *Roma 1300–1875. La città degli anni santi. Atlante* (Milan: A. Mondadori Editore, 1985), p. 90. The reader is also referred to this book for a full picture of Roman city planning at the time of Nicholas V in preparation for the Jubilee of 1450.

49. F. Cardini and M. Miglio, *Nostalgia*, p. 96.

50. A. M. Corbo, *I mestieri nella vita quotidiana alla corte di Niccolò V (1447–1455)* (Rome: Edilizio, 1998). Care of the vineyard was entrusted to Brother Giacomo da Gaeta and then to vinedressers from Pescia and to one Bandino da Lucca (p. 18), while the gardeners cited are M.o Guglielmo and Pavolo Pac(i) one from Rome (p. 34).

51. M. G. Barberini. "Il palazzo di Venezia e il suo viridario: un edificio e le sue metamorfosi," in Ibid., ed., *Il '400 a Rome: la rinascita delle arti da Donatello a Pinturicchio*, exhibition catalogue (Milan: Skira, 2008), pp. 27–35.

52. The document is cited in E. Muntz, *Les Arts à la cour*, p. 39.

53. On the origins and meaning of "secret garden," the reader is referred to the essay by G. Venturi, "Origine e sviluppo del giardino 'segreto,'" in M. Mosser, P. Teyssot, *L'architettura dei giardini d'occidente dal Rinascimento al Novecento* (Milan: Electa, 1990), pp. 84–86.

54. E. Muntz, *Les Arts à la cour*, pp. 33, 40.

55. For overall considerations regarding the development of the area, see D. R. Coffin, *Gardens and Gardening*, in particular pp. 3–16 and documentary appendix.

56. On all aspects of the medieval garden, see the fine volume by F. Cardini and M. Miglio, *Nostalgia*.

57. The names of the various people responsible, such as Giovanni Chambaret, Giacomo Tedallini, Giovanni Bernardo, and Giacomo di Giovanni, often friars and from the popes' homelands, are cited in P. Pagliuchi, "I castellani di Castel Sant'Angelo di Roma," in *Miscellanea di Storia e di Cultura Ecclesiastica*, III, 1904, p. 278, and cited in many documents published by D. R. Coffin, *Gardens*, pp. 216, 264–267.

58. The reader is reminded of the previously cited garden created by Cardinal Pietro Barbo, later Pope Paul II, next to the Palazzetto in Piazza Venezia, beginning in 1455.

59. On the development of Roman gardens in the Renaissance period see D. R. Coffin, *The Villa in the Life of Renaissance Rome* (Princeton: Princeton University Press, 1979).

CHAPTER TWO: THE BELVEDERE OF INNOCENT VIII

1. ASV, Camera Apostolica, Introitus et Exitus, b. 511, sheet 196, in which a payment results "pro pretius unius vineae post Tribunama Apostolorum site," cited in E. Muntz, *Les Arts à la cour des papes Innocent VIII, Alexandre VI, Pio III*, (Paris: Ernest Leroux, 1898), p. 77.

2. ASV, Camera Apostolica, Introitus et Exitus, b. 512, sheet 135r, "Die 26 octobris soluit similiter de mandato facto die dicti florenos quingentos auri de camera magistro Thome Mataratio muratori in deductionem fabrice muri clausure vinearum palatii" (On the 26th of October, he paid out, likewise in accordance with the mandate made on the aforesaid day, five hundred gold florins from the treasury to the master mason Thomas Matarazzi for the construction of a wall to enclose the vineyards of the Palace). I thank my friend Jadranca Neralic for pointing this out to me.

3. G. Vasari, *Le vite de più eccellenti architetti, pittori, et scultori italiani*, 1568, critical edition

edited by C. L. Ragghianti, 4 vols. (Milan: Rizzoli, 1942–50), vol. II, pp. 64–65.

4. For the complete history, see E. Muntz, "L'architettura a Roma durante il pontificato di Innocent VIII," in *Archivio Storico dell'Arte*, 4 (1891), pp. 459ff. ; J. Ackerman, "The Belvedere as a Classical Villa," in *Journal of the Warburg and Courtauld Institutes*, 14 (1951), pp. 70–91; D. Redig de Campos, "Il Belvedere d'Innocent VIII in Vaticano," in *Triplice omaggio a Sua Santità Pio XII* (Vatican City, 1958), II, pp. 289–304; and finally, M. Azzi Visentini, *La villa in Italia. Quattrocento e Cinquecento*, (Milan: Electa, 1995), pp. 73–87, with ample bibliography.

5. D. R. Coffin, *The Villa in the Life of Renaissance Rome* (Princeton: Princeton University Press, 1979), p. 63.

6. P. Adinolfi, *Roma nell'età di mezzo* (Rome: Fratelli Bocca Editori, 1881–82).

7. S. Infessura, *Diario della città di Roma*, ed. O. Tommasini, (Rome: Forzoni & C, Tipografia del Senato, 1890), p. 279.

8. E. Muntz, *Les arts*; J. Ackerman, *The Cortile del Belvedere* (Vatican City, 1954), pp. 10ff., to which the reader is referred for the building's history. Ackerman, in particular, cites a payment to Pietrasanta, dated March 31, 1495, in which reference is also made to the "vinea."

9. G. Vasari, *La vita di Michelangelo*, ed. P. Barocchi IV (Milan, 1962), p. 158. The stair, begun by Bramante, was continued by Baldassarre Peruzzi and completed by Pirro Ligorio.

10. I. Belli Barsali, *Ville di Roma*, (Milan: Rusconi, 1982), pp. 205ff.

11. G. Morello and A. Piazzoni, *I giardini vaticani*, (Rome: Logart, 1991), p. 13.

12. D. R. Coffin, "Pope Innocent VIII and the Villa Belvedere," in *Studies in Late Medieval and Renaissance Painting in Honor of Millard Meiss*, ed. I. Lavin, J. Plummer (New York: New York University Press, 1977), pp. 96–97.

13. F. Serdonati, *Vita e fatti d'Innocent VIII*, ed. Vincenzo Ferrario (Milan, 1829), p. 81.

14. D. R. Coffin, *The Villa*, p. 81.

15. P. Tomei, *L'architettura a Roma nel Quattrocento* (Rome: Multigrafica, 1977), pp. 211, 214; T. Magnuson, *Studies in Roman Quattrocento Architecture*, (Stockholm: Almqvist & Wiksell, 1958), pp. 326–327.

16. On the architecture-garden relationship, see M. L. Gothein, *Storia dell'Arte dei Giardini* (Italian edition), ed. M. de Vico Fallani and M. Bencivenni (Florence: Leo Olschki, 2006), p. 306. In the following pages there are other interesting references to Bramante's work.

17. A. Tagliolini, *Storia del Giardino italiano* (Florence: La casa Usher, 1991), pp. 83–84.

18. G. Vasari, *Lives of the Painters, Sculptors and Architects*, trans. Gaston du C. de Vere, 1912. First published in Everyman's Library, 1927 (New York: Alfred A. Knopf), vol. I, p. 662.

19. For an analysis of Bramante's personality and rich documentation on the Cortile del Belvedere, see the fundamental monograph by A. Bruschi, *Bramante architetto* (Bari: Laterza, 1969).

20. On the Roman villas and their discovery, see the excellent reconstruction by M. Cima and E. Talamo, *Horti Romani* (Milan: Electa, 2008).

21. J. Ackerman, *The Cortile del Belvedere. Studi e documenti per la storia del Palazzo Apostolico Vaticano*, III (Vatican City, 1954).

22. Bramante's greatness and his ability to interpret the ancient world were recognized in his own time: see, for example, S. Serlio, *Il terzo libro nel quale si figurano e descrivono le Antichità di Roma* (Venice 1540), in *Tutte l'opere d'architettura di Sebastiano Serlio*, ed. G. D. Scamozzi (Venice, 1584; reprinted with introduction by F. Irace, S. Serlio, *I sette libri dell'architettura*, 2 vols., Bologna, 1984), l. III, sheet 120r.; A. Palladio, *I quattro libri dell'architettura* (Venice, 1570; facsimile edition, Milan, 1968), l. IV, pp. 64–66.

23. The fountain was buried at the time of Pius IV to make way for a theater, but restored under Paul V, whose dragons and eagles carved on the base are still visible, as are the two inscriptions that refer to the restoration. In addition to being restored, the fountain was modified with the addition of an incongruous upper basin, removed in 1987. See C. Pietrangeli, "La fontana del Cortile del Belvedere," in *Strenna dei Romanisti*, April 18, 1987, pp. 475–484. On the same subject, see Chapter 5.

24. On the painting see R. Leone, entry with full bibliography: Roman School, first half of the seventeenth century, "Torneo nel cortile del Belvedere," in M. Fagiolo, *La festa a Roma dal Rinascimento al 1870*, exhibition catalogue (Rome, 1997), (Turin: Allemandi, 1997), pp. 227–228. The tournament and the subsequent etchings by Lafrery were probably by order of Pius IV, in part to celebrate the completion of the courtyard by Pirro Ligorio.

25. A very similar fresco, without ships but with water and greater attention to the landscape, is in the Rocca di Subiaco. See M. Minasi, "I Colonna nella Rocca di Subiaco. La decorazione cinquecentesca," in C. Cieri Via, ed., *Lo Specchio dei Principi. Il sistema decorativo delle dimore storiche nel territorio romano* (Rome: De Luca, 2007), p. 176.

26. The space was closed off with a glass-panel wall to become the cafeteria and washrooms for the Vatican Library and the Secret Archive, both of which face the courtyard arranged in large geometric beds of grass and flowers.

27. V. Cazzato, M. A. Giusti, M. Fagiolo, ed., *Atlante delle grotte e dei ninfei in Italia. Toscana, Lazio, Italia meridionale e isole* (Milan: Electa, 2001).

28. C. Pietrangeli, *La fontana*, and Ibid., "La base della Colonna di Antonino Pio," in *L'Urbe*, 1–2 (1982), pp. 11–12.

29. On Bramante's work see the following: M. Winner, ed., "Il Cortile delle Statue: der Statuenhof des Belvedere im Vatikan," *Atti del Convegno internazionale in onore di R. Krautheime*, Rome, October 1992 (Mainz: von Zabern, 1998); C. L. Frommel, "Giulio II, Bramante e il Cortile di Belvedere," in M. Seidel, ed., *L'Europa e l'arte italiana* (Venice: Marsilio, 2000), pp. 210–219.

30. H. H. Brummer, *The Statue Court in the Vatican Belvedere* (Stockholm: Almqvist & Wiksell, 1970).

31. Michaelis, "Der Statuenhof des Belvedere," in *Jahrbuch der Arch. Inst.*, 5 (1890), pp. 5ff., reconstructs the development of the collection and identifies all of its pieces.

32. F. Colonna, *Hypnerotomachia Poliphili, ubi humana omnia non nisi somnium esse docet*, in *Aedibus Aldi Manutii* (Venice, 1499). The text was critically acclaimed and the bibliography is vast.

33. E. H. Gombrich, *Immagini simboliche. Studi sull'arte del Rinascimento* (Turin: Einaudi, 1978), pp. 146–155. The chapter of interest here is titled, in fact, "Il giardino del Belvedere come boschetto di Venere."

34. An anthology of the description of the Cortile delle Statue is in S. Maffei, "La fama del Laocoonte nei testi del Cinquecento," in S. Settis, *Laocoonte. Fama e stile* (Rome: Donzelli Editore, 1999), pp. 85–230.

35. On the Cortile, see also F. Buranelli, "La scoperta del Laocoonte e il Cortile delle Statue in Vaticano," in F. Buranelli, P. Liverani, and A. Nesselrath, *Laocoonte. Alle origini dei Musei Vaticani*, exhibition catalogue (Rome: L'Erma di Bretschneider, 2006), pp. 49–60.

36. On collecting, see the important recent work by A. Cavallaro, ed., *Collezioni di antichità a Roma fra '400 e '500* (Rome: De Luca editori d'Arte, 2007).

37. For the diffusion of the garden-museum type and the role of the Belvedere as a model, see E. Blair MacDougall, *Fountains, Statues, and Flowers. Studies in Italian Gardens of the Sixteenth and Seventeenth Centuries* (Washington, D.C.: Dumbarton Oaks Research Library and Collection), 1994, pp. 23–36.

38. A recent study attributes the rustic grotto to Vignola, present in Rome, in collaboration with Jacopo Meleghino. F. R. Liserre, *Grotte e Ninfei nel '500. Il modello dei giardini di Caprarola* (Rome: Gangemi Editore, 2008), pp. 47, 50.

39. An examination of the complex symbolic meanings of the "Sleeping Nymph" can be found in the interesting essay by E. Blair MacDougall, *Fountains*, pp. 37–55 and in D. R. Coffin, *Gardens*, pp. 28-57, which also examine the success of this model in the villas of the following centuries.

40. C. Frommel, "Raffaello e il teatro alla corte di Leone X," in *Bollettino del Centro Internazionale di Studi di architettura Andrea Palladio*, 16 (1974), pp. 173–188.

41. "Sunt ibi nemora ferarum et avium cum viridariis et hortulis." F. Albertini, *Opusculum de Mirabilibus novae Urbis Romae*, for Jacobium Mazochium (Rome, 1510), p. 39.

42. A. Luzio, *Federico Gonzaga ostaggio alla corte di Julius II*, in ASRSP, IX, 1886, pp. 513–514.

43. C. Pedretti, *A Chronology of Leonardo da Vinci's Architectural Studies after 1500*, (Geneva: Droz, 1962), p. 83.

44. B. Castiglione, *Lettere del conte Baldessar Castiglione*, ed. P. Serassi (Padua, 1769), cited in D. R. Coffin, *The Life*, pp. 84–85.

45. G. Vasari, *Lives*, 1927, vol. I, p. 663.

46. Ibid.

47. E. H. Gombrich, *Immagini*, p. 153, relates that the pope, on seeing the Cortile delle Statue, exclaimed: "Sunt idola antiquorum" ("They are the idols of the ancients!"). For the reconstruction of Adrian VI's position regarding the arts, see A. Chastel, *Il Sacco di Roma: 1527* (Turin: Einaudi, 1983), pp. 120–123.

48. "Sommario del Viaggio degli oratori Veneti che andarono a Roma a dar l'obbedienza a Papa Adriano VI, 11 maggio 1523," in *Relazioni degli Ambasciatori Veneti al Senato*, ed. E. Alberi (Florence: Società Editrice Fiorentina, 1846), series II, vol. III, pp. 114ff.; also in J. Ackerman, *The Cortile*, p. 145, and M. Azzi Visentini, *L'arte dei giardini. Scritti teorici e pratici dal XIV al XIX secolo* (Milan: Edizioni il Polifilo, 1999), pp. 217–221.

49. A. Fulvio, *Antiquitates Urbis* (Rome, 1527; repr. Florence: Silber, 1968), f. 36: "Excitavitque amoenissimum fontem cum nemore aurea poma producente parietibus undique circumsepto" ("And he erected a most pleas-

ant fountain with a grove bearing golden apples and enclosed by walls on all sides").

CHAPTER THREE: THE SECRET GARDEN OF PAUL III

1. On Villa Madama see R. Lefevre, *Villa Madama* (Rome: Editalia, 1973); I. Belli Barsali, *Ville di Roma*, (Milan: Rusconi, 1983), pp. 142–57; D. R. Coffin, *The Villa in the Life of Renaissance Rome*, (Princeton: Princeton University Press, 1979), pp. 245–56; C. L. Frommel, S. Ray, and M. Tafuri, *Raffaello architetto*, exhibition catalogue (Milan: Electa, 1984); M. Azzi Visentini, *La Villa in Italia. Quattrocento e Cinquecento* (Milan: Electa, 1998), with full bibliography; and finally, C. Napoleone, ed., *Villa Madama* (Turin: Allemandi, 2007).

2. The garden subsequently took on a freer composition than that shown in the plans, with groves in place of flowerbeds, but in the 1970s it was completely eliminated with the construction of the Museo Paolino of Sacred Art, commissioned by Pope Paul VI and designed by Studio Passarelli in the 1970s.

3. D. R. Coffin, *Gardens and Gardening in Papal Rome* (Princeton: Princeton University Press, 1991), p. 14.

4. See the essential study by A. Chastel, *Il sacco di Roma: 1527* (Turin: Einaudi, 1983).

5. On the Orti Farnesiani al Palatino see G. Morganti, ed., *Gli Orti Farnesiani*, study conference proceedings, Rome, 1985 (Rome: L'Erma di Bretschneider, 1990).

6. F. Aliberti Gaudioso, *Gli affreschi di Paolo III a Castel Sant'Angelo* (Rome: De Luca, 1981).

7. L. Pastor, *Storia dei Papi* (Rome 1922–34), vol. IV, 2, p. 739, n. 133, letter of Girolamo Cattaneo to the Duke of Milan, and p. 740, n. 134, letter of Francesco Gonzaga to Federico Gonzaga, Duke of Mantua, in which the event is described with great vividness, with reference to an imminent storm that prevented the pope from going out for his usual walk in the courtyard lest he get mired in the ruins of the loggias.

8. G. Vasari, *Lives of the Painters, Sculptors and Architects*, trans. Gaston du C. de Vere (1912; Everyman's Library, 1927; repr. Alfred A. Knopf: Everyman's Library, 1996), vol. I, pp. 663–64.

9. J. Ackerman, *The Cortile del Belvedere* (Vatican City, 1954), pp. 61–63, which also includes some payment orders for executed work.

10. The essential features of the garden, but without the pergola, are documented in many eighteenth- and nineteenth-century etchings and in early-twentieth-century photographic reproductions.

11. On the garden see A. Cremona, *Felices Procerum Villulae. Il giardino della "Farnesina" dai Chigi all'Accademia dei Lincei*, at press. I thank Dr. Cremona for allowing me to read the manuscript before publication.

12. The construction of the Pinacoteca building, designed by Luca Beltrami in 1929, took away an ample portion of the garden on the side toward Monte Mario and of the Garden of Clement VII, creating a barrier between the two spaces. Another portion, on the side toward Bramante's loggias, was used in recent times as the Museums' cafeteria. The residual space of the garden was then redesigned to reconstitute the lost symmetry, and the fountain originally situated in the Cortile della Pigna was placed in the center.

13. Meleghino was considered Peruzzi's successor. The latter, ill and near death, left Meleghino his drawings and papers, and upon the death of Antonio da Sangallo the Younger, was appointed architect of St. Peter's by Paul III.

14. On Meleghino see F. E. Keller, "Meleghino Jacopo," in *The Dictionary of Art* (London: Grove, 1996), vol. XXI, p. 79.

15. E. Guidoni, "La ricostruzione di Frascati voluta da Paolo III ad opera di Jacopo Meleghino," in *Il Tesoro delle Città*, Strenna dell'Associazione Storia della Città, Year II (Rome: Edizioni Kappa, 2004), pp. 296–306. The date of Meleghino's death was considered 1549 until the discovery by Christoph L. Frommel of a payment document dated 1550, and now the latter date is accepted.

16. On the villa, see, finally, M. B. Guerrieri Borsoi, *Villa Rufina Falconieri. La rinascita di Frascati e la più antica dimora tuscolana* (Rome: Gangemi Editore, 2008).

17. G. Vasari, *Lives*, vol. II, p. 619, writes: "Vignuola then went to Rome to work at painting, and to obtain from that art the means to assist his poor family; at first he was employed at the Belvedere with Jacopo Melighini of Ferrara, the architect of Pope Paul III, drawing some architectural designs for him." According to F. R. Liserre, *Grotte e ninfei nel '500. Il modello dei giardini di Caprarola* (Rome: Gangemi Editore, 2008), p. 65, in 1538 Vignola was paid along with Meleghino for work in the Vatican, but she does not cite the referenced document.

18. Ackerman, *The Cortile*, p. 63, argues that the conception of the garden should be attributed to Baldassarre Peruzzi, and that it was interrupted by his death in 1536, but he does not cite references.

19. L. Dorez, *La cour du pape Paul III d'après les registres de la Tesorerie secrète*, vol. 2, *Les déspenses privées* (Paris: Librerie Ernest Leroux, 1932), p. 4. Dorez's volume is fundamental, as it includes numerous archival documents from the time of Paul III, some now untraceable. The reconstruction of the realization of the garden of Paul III is obviously based on these documents, along with some published by Ackerman and those discovered in the course of this research. Many of these are unpublished and are cited case by case.

20. Dorez, *La cour*, documents published on p. 20 and p. 94.

21. Ackerman, *The Cortile*, p. 158, document 36 of April 9, 1536.

22. The two gardeners were both salaried by the pope. Lucerta, whose first name was Romolo, was Florentine, and had come to Rome after the Sack of 1527. C. De Dominicis, "Immigrazione a Roma dopo il sacco del 1527 (1531–1549)," in *Archivio della società romana di storia patria*, CIX, 1986, pp. 165 and 179.

23. Dorez, *La cour*, pp. 119, 124, 135, 140, 148, 161, 162, 169, 171.

24. Dorez, *La cour*, pp. 177, 183, 189, 194, 195, 249, 253.

25. Dorez, *La cour*, pp. 185 and 246.

26. ASP, Epistolario scelto, b.21, f. 36 "Meleghino Giacomo," letter of April 11, 1538.

27. Coffin, *Gardens*, p. 15, fig. 9.

28. ASR, Camerale I, Tesoreria Segreta, Reg. 8/1290, 1540–43, f. 11a.

29. ASR, Camerale I, Tesoreria Segreta, Reg. 8/1290, 1540–43, f. 36a.

30. Dorez, *La cour*, pp. 296, 304.

31. ASR, Camerale I, Tesoreria Segreta, Reg. 8/1290, 1540–43, f. 40 a, f. 40b, f. 43 a, f. 45 a, f. 50 a, f. 54b, f. 58 a, f. 61b, f. 77 a.

32. On Meleghino and his work in general, see A. Ronchini, *Jacopo Meleghino* (Modena: C. Vincenzi, 1867); L. Puppi, "Il problema dell'eredità di Baldassarre Peruzzi: Jacopo Meleghino, il mistero di Francesco Sanese e Sebastiano Serlio," in M. Fagiolo dell'Arco, *Baldassarre Peruzzi: pittura, scena e architettura nel Cinquecento* (Rome: Istituto dell'Enciclopedia Italiana, 1987), pp. 491–501; M. De Angelis, "La Torre di Paolo III in Campidoglio: un'opera demolita di Jacopo Meleghino, architetto alla corte del Papa Farnese," in *Edilizia Militare*, 8, 1987, nn.21–22. Some information on his activity can also be found in P. Portoghesi, *Roma nel Rinascimento* (Milan: Electa, 1971).

33. "Interdicebatur autem a Paolo III, qui rerum naturalium et herbarum amata erat ne venderetur alicubi propter raritatem." Coffin, *Gardens*, p. 211.

34. Coffin, *Gardens*, p. 217, reproduces documents that include mention of Scipione Perotto in the reports of two visiting botanists, the Spaniard Andres de Laguna and the Frenchman Pierre Belon.

35. The *cocchio* (pergola), in particular the kind formed with citrus trees, was destined for great popularity in the following century and was even lauded by Ferrari in his treatises as a distinctive element in the most refined gardens. See A. Campitelli, "I cocchi di agrumi nelle ville romane," in A. Tagliolini, M. A. Giusti, ed., *I giardini delle Esperidi*, study conference proceedings, Pietrasanta, 1995 (Florence: Edifir, 1997), pp. 175–95.

36. On the typology and diffusion of pergolas in the 1500s, see C. L. Frommel, "Villa Lante e Tommaso Ghinucci," in S. Frommel, ed., *Villa Lante a Bagnaia* (Milan: Electa, 2005), pp. 79–93.

37. F. Colonna, *Hypnerotomachia Poliphili* (Venice: Aldo Manuzio, 1499).

38. On Giardino Ghinucci at the Quirinal Palace, see Coffin, *The Villa*, pp. 190–91. The drawing by Giovanni Colonna is in BAV, Vat. Lat., 7721, sheets 15r and 15v. On Colonna, see M. E. Micheli, *Giovanni Colonna da Tivoli* (Rome: De Luca, 1982).

39. Coffin, *Gardens*, p. 15.

40. ASR, Camerale I, Tesoreria Segreta, Reg. 8/1290, 1540–43, f. 16a and f. 39a.

41. ASR, camerale I, Tesoreria Segreta, Reg. 8/1290, 1540–43, f. 39a, f. 40°, f. 40b.

42. ASR; Camerale I, Tesoreria Segreta, Reg. 8/1290, 1540–43, f. 46a, f. 47b, f. 48a, f. 49a, f. 49b, f. 50b, f. 52b, f. 53b, f. 54a, f. 66a.

43. The documents contain the citation *mortella*, which actually, in the area of Rome, is synonymous with boxwood, while in the 1500s and 1600s references are more frequent to myrtle, then more widely used for its scent. In the case of the espaliers in Clement VII's garden, we believe that myrtle must have been used, both in view of its height, which makes it more appropriate for the use in question, and because it was often used in combination with roses.

44. ASR, Camerale I, Tesoreria Segreta, Reg. 9/1291, f. 22b, f. 18b, and Reg. 11/1293, f. 51b.

45. ASR, Camerale I, Tesoreria Segreta, Reg. 11/1293, sheet 84b and Reg. 8/1290, 1540–43, f. 23a.

46. Dorez, *La cour*, pp. 21, 33, 34, 40, 42, 45, 54, 60, 61, 66, 67, 88, 124, and ASR, Camerale I, Tesoreria Segreta, Reg. 8/1290, 1540–43, f. 4, f. 20a, f. 50b; Reg. 9/1291, f. 15b.

47. On the subject, see A. Cavallaro, ed., *Collezioni di antichità a Roma fra '400 e '500* (Rome: De Luca Editori d'Arte, 2007).

48. "Ex palatio itur in hortos latissimos, post quos est locus ille Bellivider, qui aedificiis, ambulacris, fontibus, arboribus, statuis antiquis, positu et prospectu est ornatissimus et incomparabilis. Habet cochleam, per quam ascenditur ad summum usque, unde potissimum patet loci amoenitas et prospectus, qualem nusquam esse, puto amoeniorem." J. Von Fichard, *Italia* (Frankfurt am Meine: Gebhard & Korben, 1815), pp. 48–49.

49. In the first decades of the 1500s, the splendid season of the Roman villas began. It was destined to continue for the entire following century. The first villas built were Villa Farnesina, commissioned by Agostino Chigi in the first years of the century, Villa Madama, begun, as mentioned, in 1517, and Villa Lante, datable beginning in 1518. For a complete overview of the villas of Rome see Belli Barsali, *Ville*.

CHAPTER FOUR: THE CASINA OF PIUS IV

1. A complete study of the villa does not yet exist. For a general overview, see I. Belli Barsali, *Ville di Roma* (Milan: Rusconi, 1983), pp. 170–87; M. Azzi Visentini, *La villa in Italia. Quattrocento e Cinquecento* (Milan: Electa, 1999), pp. 159–72.

2. ASR, Camerale I, Giustificazioni di Tesoreria, b.2; Camera Apostolica, Diversa Cameralia, vol. 155, fascs. 141r-142v; Camerale I, Fabbriche, b.1519.

3. See J. Ackerman, *The Cortile del Belvedere* (Vatican City, 1954), pp. 163–68, in which many payment orders are transcribed.

4. The document was published by Ackerman, *The Cortile*, p. 165, doc. 75.

5. See Ackerman, *The Cortile*, p. 69, who argues that the nyphaeum dates back to Bramante but was transformed under Julius III and that its typology is close to that of the young architects of the time, in particular Vignola; M. Fagiolo, "Introduzione alle nuove scene e ai nuovi miti di Caprarola," in F. R. Liserre, *Grotte e ninfei nel '500. Il modello dei giardini di Caprarola* (Rome: Gangemi Editore, 2008), p. ix, who refers to a subsequent examination of the subject and hypothizes that the organization of the garden was also the work of two architects. In this volume, the figure of Maccarone, previously identified by Coffin, is reconstructed in relationship to his various clients and is extremely interesting.

6. D. R. Coffin, *Gardens and Gardening in Papal Rome* (Princeton: Princeton University Press, 1991), p. 218.

7. BAV, Urb. Lat. 1039, fasc. 320v.

8. W. Friedlaender, *Das Kasino Pio des Vierte* (Leipzig: Hiersemann, 1912), pp. 3, 123.

9. The works commissioned by Paul IV are discussed in D. R. Ancel, "Le Vatican sous Paul IV," in *Revue Benedectine*, XXV, 1908, pp. 47–71.

10. In reality the pope was not related to the Medicis of Florence, but had obtained authorization from Cosimo I to use the emblem, following his appointment as cardinal by Paul III. I thank Elisabetta Mori for this information.

11. Cited in E. Wharton, *Italian Villas and Their Gardens* (New York: The Century Co., 1907), p. 104. In this volume Wharton describes the Vatican Gardens as they appeared at the beginning of the twentieth century, with espaliered trees, flowerbeds, and the admirable coexistence of formal and naturalistic layouts.

12. The payment documents were published by Friedlaender, *Das Kasino*, and conserved in ASR, Camerale I, Fabbriche, b. 1520 and 1521. Other documents, referring mainly to the decorative elements, are in G. Smith, *The Casino of Pio IV* (Princeton: Princeton University Press, 1977). On the villa, see also C. Volpi, *Pirro Ligorio e i giardini a Roma nella seconda metà del Cinquecento* (Rome, Università degli Studi di Roma La Sapienza: Lithos Edizioni, 1996).

13. R. de Maio, *Alfonso Carafa, cardinale di Napoli (1540–1565)* (Vatican City, 1961), p. 286.

14. Studies on Ligorio are many and of various importance, examining the diverse aspects of his multifaceted personality, and so the reader is referred to the excellent comprehensive study by D. R. Coffin, *Pirro Ligorio: The Renaissance Artist, Architect and Antiquarian* (Philadelphia: Pennsylvania University Press, 2003), also for its earlier bibliography on the same subject.

15. The bibliography on the villa is vast, and so the reader is referred to the still essential work by D. R. Coffin, *The Villa d'Este* (Princeton: Princeton University Press, 1960), and to the publication by I. Barisi, M. Fagiolo, and M. L. Madonna, *Villa d'Este* (Rome: De Luca, 2004), with its earlier bibliography on the subject.

16. D. R. Coffin, *The Villa in the Life of Renaissance Rome* (Princeton: Princeton University Press, 1979), pp. 269ff.

17. The stairs were added later, probably in the late seventeenth century, as they are not present in the earliest depictions of the building.

18. M. Fagiolo, "La nave della Chiesa: dalla barca di Pietro alla Chiesa come nave," in A.

Mondadori, ed., *La preghiera del marinaio. La fede e il mare nei segni della Chiesa e nelle tradizioni marinare*, exhibition catalogue (Rome, 1992), pp. 267–80.

19. Belli Barsali, *Ville*, pp. 206–8, in which both the architecture and decoration of the complex are examined.

20. Coffin, *The Villa*, p. 269.

21. Coffin, *The Villa*, p. 273, notes that many antique marbles from Villa Giulia were expropriated to decorate the Casina.

22. The side and rear elevations of the main building did not have decorations, but rather a simple plaster treatment with stucco moldings, thus confirming the scant importance given to the sides facing the woods.

23. G. Smith, "The Stucco Decoration of the Casino of Pio IV," in *Zeitschrift fur Kunstgeschichte*, 37, 1974, p. 144.

24. Traditionally, the Hours are the daughters of Zeus and Themis, but in his writings and in the Casina, Pirro Ligorio followed an alternative version of the myth in which Apollo and Hegle are the parents.

25. G. Perin-Chattard, *Nuova descrizione del Vaticano o sia della Sacrosanta Basilica di San Pietro* (Rome: Barbiellini, 1762), p. 232.

26. M. Fagiolo, "Il significato dell'acqua e la dialettica del giardino. Pirro Ligorio e la 'filosofia' della villa cinquecentesca," in M. Fagiolo, ed., *Natura e artificio* (Rome: Officina edizioni, 1981), pp. 176–87.

27. Ligorio had a particular fondness for the figures of Flora and Pomona, which he described in detail in his writings. See BNN, mss. XIII. B. 3. pp. 408, 429.

28. Obviously Ligorio could not have been familiar with Pompeii, but in his time that style of decoration was widespread in many Roman buildings that are still extant.

29. For the interpretation of the many symbolic meanings of the Casina's iconographic program, see the relevant studies by M. Fagiolo and M. L. Madonna, "La Roma di Pio IV: La 'Civitas Pia,' la 'Salus Medica,' la 'Custodia Angelica,'" in *Arte Illustrata*, 51, 1972, pp. 384–85; M. Fagiolo and M. L. Madonna, "La Casina di Pio IV in Vaticano. Pirro Ligorio e l'architettura come geroglifico," in *Storia dell'arte*, 1972, 15–16, pp. 237ff.; G. Smith, "The Stucco." A new survey of the rich decorative apparatus in a recent publication adds nothing fresh to what has already been written on the subject; see M. Losito, *La Casina Pio IV in Vaticano* (Vatican City, 2005).

30. In a letter of 1560, Cardinal Borromeo was reminded to conduct his life in a more reserved way—dedicated, for example, to the honest pleasures of the garden—in keeping with his status. See Coffin, *The Life.*, p. 273.

31. On the academy, see L. Berra, *L'Accademia delle Notti Vaticane fondata da S. Carlo Borromeo. Con tre appendici di documenti* (Rome: M. Bretschneider, 1915).

32. C. Bragaglia Venuti, "L'antichità moralizzata di Pirro Logorio nella Loggia di Pio IV: quelle immagini 'profane di dei gentili' che 'havendole conosciute tutte possono essere tirate a gloria del Salvator nostro,'" in *Rivista di Storia della Chiesa in Italia*, 53, 1999, pp. 39–82.

33. M. Fagiolo, "Trionfi delle acque sacre nel Cinquecento," in M. Fagiolo and M. A. Giusti, *Lo Specchio del Paradiso. Il Giardino e il sacro dall'Antico all'Ottocento*, (Cinisello Balsamo: Silvana Editoriale, 1998), pp. 92–96; C. Volpi, "La favola moralizzata nella Roma della Controriforma: Pirro Ligorio e Federico Zuccari tra riflessioni teoriche e pratica artistica," in *Storia dell'Arte*, 9–10, 2004, pp. 131–60.

34. A. Michaelis, "Geschichte des Statuenhofes im Vaticanischen Belvedere," in *Jahrbuch des kaiserlich deutschen archaeologischen Instituts*, v, 1890, pp. 62–63; Friedlaender, *Das Kasino*, p. 10; Smith, *The Stucco*, pp. 120–121.

35. BNN, P. Ligorio, mss. XIII.B.5, sheet c.5v.

36. AST, P. Ligorio, mss. J.A.II.13.fasc.22.

37. Having lost the job, Pirro Ligorio left Rome and found refuge at the court of Ferrara.

38. Ackerman, *The Cortile*, p. 86.

39. A. Lafrery, *Speculum Romanae magnificentiae: omnia fere quaecunq. in Urbe monumenta extant partim iuxta antiquam partim iuxta hodiernam formam accuratiss. delineata repraesentans; accesserunt non paucae, tum antiquarum, tum modernarum rerum Urbis figurae nunquam antehac aeditae* (Mirror of Roman Magnificence: containing nearly all of the existing monuments of the City most carefully delineated, partly in their ancient form, and partly in their present one; to which have been added numerous portraits of things in the City, both ancient and modern, never before published) (Rome: mid-1570s).

40. The physician to Nicholas IV and then to Boniface VIII, he translated treatises from Arab to Latin, including writings by Avicenna, and wrote what is considered the first physics-botany dictionary, *Clavis sanationis*.

41. F. M. Renazzi, *Storia dell'Università degli Studi di Roma detta comunemente la Sapienza* (Rome: Stamperia Paglierini, 1803–6), vol. 4, contains the names of all of the custodians of the Orto Botanico Vaticano, and relates that Pius V conferred on Michele Mercati the role of *prefectus* of the Orto.

42. M. Zalum Cardon, *Passione e cultura dei fiori tra Firenze e Roma nel XVI e XVII secolo* (Florence: Leo S. Olschki, 2008), p. 5. This volume provides a most interesting frame of reference for the understanding of the cultural context in which the Vatican Giardino dei Semplici was created.

43. On the relationship between the Giardino dei Semplici and the Orto Botanico, see L. Tongiorgi Tomasi, "Gli Orti botanici nei secoli XVI e XVII," in M. Mosser and P. Teyssot, *L'architettura dei giardini d'Occidente dal Rinascimento al Novecento*, (Milan: Electa, 1990), pp. 77–79.

44. "…botanicam cathedram, hortumque simplicium sub Pio IV administravit." G. Bonelli, *Horti Romani Brevis Historia* (Rome, 1772), p. I.

45. *Instruttione sopra la Peste di M. Michele Mercati medico e filosofo* (Rome: vinc. Accolto, 1576), p. 8. In the booklet Mercati cites many plants to use as medicine against the plague, but does not specify where he cultivated them in the Vatican.

46. Some information about Mercati's role and the antiquity of the Orto dei Semplici in Vaticano can be found in G. Lais, "I due Orti botanici vaticani," in *Atti dell'Accademia Pontificia dei Nuovi Lincei*, volume XXXII, year XXXII (1878–79), pp. 63–78. According to the author, the Orto Botanico Vaticano already existed at the time of Nicholas V, since Manetti referred to a garden "cunctis herbarum atque omnium [fructuum] generibus refertus" (filled with every kind of herb and all sorts of [produce]) that could not have been anything but a botanical garden. This evidence supports, therefore, the earlier date of the botanical garden in Rome as compared to those in Padua and Pisa.

47. M. Mercati, *Considerazioni…intorno ad alcune cose scritte nel libro de gli Obelischi di Roma* (Rome: Domenico Basa, 1590), p. 68.

48. Some brief references are in R. Pirotta and E. Chiovenda, *Flora Romana* (Rome: Tipografia Voghera, 1900), p. 51. Mercati also wrote a book on Roman obelisks, further confirmation of his vast erudition and many interests.

49. Andrea Cesalpino (Arezzo, 1519–Rome, 1603) was a botanist, physician, and anatomist, director of the Orto Botanico of Pisa and author of a new system of plant classification.

50. G. Masson, "Italian Flower Collectors' Gardens in Seventeenth-Century Italy," in D. R. Coffin, ed., *The Italian Garden*, (Washington, D.C.: Dumbarton Oaks, 1972), pp. 61–80. As Margherita Zalum has shown in

her book on the subject, in the sixteenth century, in both Rome and Florence, there was already a tight network of flower enthusiasts and cultivators in contact with illustrious exponents in other European capitals. For a more in-depth examination of the topic, see Zalum, *Passione*, particularly the first two chapters.

51. Ulisse Aldrovandi (Bologna, 1522–1605) was a naturalist, botanist, and entomologist, professor at the University of Bologna, and director of the city's Orto Botanico beginning in 1568. His herbarium is famous. The letters between Mercati and Aldrovandi, conserved in the Archivio Aldrovandi in Bologna, were published in full by A. Neviani, "I primi documenti su l'Orto dei Semplici in Vaticano nella seconda metà del secolo XVI," in *Atti della Pontificia Accademia dei Nuovi Lincei*, year LXXXVI (1932–33), pp. 127–53, but apparently have not been widely read.

52. On the birth of botanical gardens and collecting, see L. Tongiorgi Tomasi, "'Extra' e 'Intus': progettualità degli orti botanici e collezionismo eclettico tra XVI e XVII secolo," in G. Pirrone, ed., *Il giardino come labirinto della storia*, conference proceedings, Palermo, 1984 (Palermo: Centro Studi di Storia e Arte dei Giardini, date unknown), pp. 277–89.

53. On Philip and his botanical interests, see C. Anon Feliu and J. L. Sancho, *Jardin y Naturalezza en el reinado de Felipe II* (Madrid: Doce Calles, 1998), in particular pp. 276–331 for the section on botany and Philip II's interest in natural history. The king's garden of medicinal plants was next to the Guadalupe monastery.

54. The physician was Francisco Hernandez, who from 1570 to 1577 carried out expeditions to the Americas to compile a book on natural history, published some decades later at the behest of Federico Cesi and the members of the Accademia dei Lincei, coordinated by Johannes Faber. On this undertaking, see D. Freedberg, *The Eye of the Lynx: Galileo, His Friends, and the Beginnings of Modern Natural History*, (Chicago and London: The University of Chicago Press, 2002), pp. 245–74.

55. For references on the timing of the introduction of various plants to Europe, see P. A. Saccardo, *Cronologia della Flora italiana* (Padua: Tipografia Seminario, 1909). See also G. Caneva, *Il Mondo di Cerere nella Loggia di Psiche* (Rome: Palombi, 1992).

56. I thank my friend Sofia Varoli Piazza, who gave me extremely useful indications for identifying the plants and their provenance.

57. The document, conserved in ASV, is cited in Neviani, *I primi*, pp. 128–129.

58. The pope had his own suburban residence, whose rigorous architecture expressed the culture in question. On the subject, see C. Benocci, "Il Casaletto di San Pio V sulla via Aurelia Antica, emblema romano della controriforma trasformato in delizia settecentesca chigiana," in C. Benocci, ed., *I giardini Chigi tra Siena e Roma dal Cinquecento agli inizi dell'Ottocento*, Fondazione Monte dei Paschi di Siena (Siena: Protagon Editori, 2005), pp. 317–50.

59. C. Durante, *Herbario Nuovo* (Rome: Bartholomeo Bonfadino & Tito Diani, 1585).

60. For the chronology of the curators of the Orto Vaticano, see Lais, *I due orti*, p. 69.

61. A. Bacci, *Tabula simplicium medicamentum*, Romae apud Josephum de Angelis, 1577.

62. On the villa, see I. Belli Barsali and M.G. Branchetti, *Ville della campagna romana* (Milan: Rusconi, 1975), pp. 164–77, and A. M. Tantillo, ed., *Villa e Paese. Dimore nobili del Tuscolo e di Marino* (Rome: De Luca, 1982).

63. M. Franceschini, E. Mori, and M. Vendittelli, *Torre in Pietra, vicende storiche, architettoniche, artistiche di un insediamento della campagna romana dal medioevo all'età moderna* (Rome: Viella, 1994).

64. Belli Barsali, *Ville*, pp. 30–38, 85–89, M. Quast, *Die Villa Montalto im Rom: Entstehung und Gestalt in Cinquecento* (Munich: Tuduv, 1991).

65. On the history of the papal residence at the Quirinal, see various authors, *Il Palazzo del Quirinale. La storia, le sale, le collezioni* (Bologna: Franco Maria Ricci Edizioni, 2006).

66. On the Library, see J. Hess, "La Biblioteca vaticana. Storia della costruzione," in *L'Illustrazione Vaticana*, 1938; J. Ruysschaert, "La Biblioteca Vaticana di Sisto V nelle testimonianze coeve," and S. Benedetti, "L'architettura di Domenico Fontana," both in M. Fagiolo and M. L. Madonna, *Sisto V, I, Roma e il Lazio* (Rome: Istituto Poligrafico e Zecca dello Stato, 1992), pp. 329–38 and pp. 397–417.

67. See Chapter Five.

68. Ruysschaert, *La Biblioteca*, p. 332.

69. Ruysschaert, *La Biblioteca*, p. 334.

70. ASR, Camerale I, Giustificazioni di Tesoreria, b.19, f. 16 and f. 18.

71. On the villa in Rome, see C. Benocci, *Villa Aldobrandini a Montemagnanapoli* (Rome: Argos, 1992); on the villa at Frascati, see C. D'Onofrio, *Villa Aldobrandini a Frascati* (Rome: Staderini, 1963); M. Fagiolo and M. Fagiolo dell'Arco, "Villa Aldobrandini tuscolana: percorso, allegoria, capricci,"

in *Quaderni Istituto di Storia dell'Architettura*, XI, 1964, pp. 61–92; L. Devoti, *La Villa Aldobrandini di Frascati* (Velletri: Edizioni Tra 8&9, 1990); Azzi Visentini, *La Villa*, pp. 164–77.

72. ASR, Camerale I, Giustificazioni di Tesoreria, b.18, c.30, c.39, c.81; b.19, c.23; b.22, c.1, c.3, c.7, c.9, c.11, c.29; b.24, c.4, b.25, c.24. The information given has been drawn from these succinct payment orders.

CHAPTER FIVE: THE FIRST DECADES OF THE SEVENTEENTH CENTURY

1. For the reconstruction of this singular and interesting period and its protagonists, see G. Masson, "Italian Flower Collectors' Gardens in Seventeenth-century Italy," in D. R. Coffin, ed., *The Italian Garden* (Washington, D.C.: Dumbarton Oaks, 1972), pp. 61–80 and also the important, rich, and original contribution by M. Zalum Cardon, *Passione e cultura dei fiori tra Firenze e Roma nel XVI e XVII secolo* (Florence: Leo S. Olschki, 2008).

2. I. Belli Barsali, *Ville di Roma* (Milan: Rusconi, 1983), pp. 296–307, and various authors, *Il Palazzo del Quirinale. La storia, le sale e le collezioni* (Bologna: Franco Maria Ricci, 2006).

3. A. Campitelli, *Villa Borghese. Da giardino del principe a parco dei romani* (Rome: Istituto Poligrafico e Zecca dello Stato, 2003).

4. On the Frascati villas, see I. Belli Barsali and M. G. Branchetti, *Ville della campagna romana* (Milan: Rusconi, 1975); A. M.Tantillo, ed., *Villa e Paese, dimore nobili del Tuscolo e di Marino* (Rome: De Luca, 1980), and A. Campitelli, "Il sistema residenziale del cardinale Scipione Borghese tra Roma e i colli tuscolani," in M. Bevilacqua and M. L. Madonna, ed., *Residenze nobiliari barocche* (Rome: De Luca, 2003), pp. 63–74.

5. "…qua Pontificio ex intimo cubiculo facilis descensus in imos hortos patet." F. Bonanni, *Numismata Summorum Pontificum Templi vaticani fabricam indicantia* (Rome: Typis Domenici Antonini Herculis, 1696), p. 221.

6. ASR, Camerale I, Fabbriche, b.1540, c.103.

7. Many archival documents have been published by A. M. Corbo and M. Pomponi, *Fonti per la storia artistica romana al tempo di Paolo V* (Rome: Istituto Poligrafico e Zecca dello Stato, 1995), but often only the title is transcribed. Other documents emerged during the course of research.

8. A. Bzovius (Brzowski), *Paulus Quintus Burghesius P.O.M.* (Rome: Ex Typographia Stephani Paulini, 1624).

9. "Vaticanum S. Petri Templum toto terrarum orbe celeberrimum cum adiunctis pontificum aedibus hortisque accurate delin-

eatum ea omnia Paulus V Pont. Max. multis partibus amplificavit ornavitque." The plan was published by F. Ehrle, *La grande veduta di Maggi e Mascardi, (1615) del Tempio e del Palazzo vaticano* (Rome: Tipografia Poliglotta Vaticana, 1914).

10. We have no evidence that, after the publication and commentary by Father Ehrle, this fine plan was used to reconstruct the history of the Vatican Gardens.

11. On the reactivation of the antique Acqua Traiana and the construction of the Traiana-Paolina aqueduct, see G. Pisani Sartorio, ed., *Il trionfo dell'acqua. Acqua e acquedotti a Roma dal IV sec. A.C. al XX secolo*, exhibition catalogue (Rome: Paleani, 1986).

12. Bzovius, *Paulus*, pp. 66–67.

13. The figure of Martino Ferrabosco remains to be explored. Among the few contributions, see L. Beltrami, "Martino Ferrabosco architetto," in *L'Arte*, 29, 1926, pp. 1–15.

14. ASR, Camerale I, Giustificazioni di Tesoreria, b.33, f. 5, f. 12, f. 17. In the last folder, for example, are payments from 1606–7 for "lead to repair the fountain of the Peschiera and the fountains of the Palazzina" or "to unblock and repair all of the fountains of the Palazzina and of the Peschiera [for] the woods…[to] repair the conduit of the wall and those of the Statues…" and the bill of Silvestro Amici, tinsmith, from November 1607, showing substantial payments for "having laid down the conduits in Belvedere…"

15. J. A. F. Orbaan, *Documenti sul barocco in Roma* (Perugia: Unione Tipografica Cooperativa, 1920), p. 158.

16. ASR, Camerale I, Giustificazioni di Tesoreria, b.33, p. 1, February 8, 1607.

17. "Sub Paulo V pontifice maximo, dum ad templi frontem erigendam pinea praedicta loco suo mota fuit et in hortos Vaticanos translata." G. Grimaldi, *Descrizione della basilica antica di San Pietro in Vaticano*, 1620, BAV, Barb. Lat. 2733, R. Niggl, ed. (Vatican City, 1972), p. 86.

18. Orban, *Documenti*, p. 158.

19. For the similarities between this niche-fountain and the one, also commissioned by the Borghese family, that can still be seen in what was formerly the court of the Casino dei Giuochi d'Acqua and is now a room in the Museo Carlo Bilotti nell'Aranciera in the Villa Borghese, see A. Arconti and A. Campitelli, ed., *Il Museo Carlo Bilotti nell'Aranciera di Villa Borghese* (Milan: Electa, 2006).

20. Bzovius, *Paulus*, pp. 66–67.

21. ASR, Camerale I, Giustificazioni di Tesoreria, b.33, p. 6, p. 12, p. 13, p. 16; Camerale I,

Fabbriche, b.1537, f. 100. A payment to Giovanni Bellucci for "work done to excavate the great basin of oriental granite in the theater of the Palace of Saint Peter," is cited, but without any indication of the source, in G. Morello and P. Silvan, *Vedute di Roma dai dipinti della Biblioteca Apostolica Vaticana* (Milan: Electa, 1997), p. 136.

22. ASR, Camerale I, Giustificazioni di Tesoreria, b.33, p. 13.

23. C. Pietrangeli, "La Fontana del Cortile del Belvedere," in *Strenna dei Romanisti*, April 18, 1987, pp. 475–84.

24. This very recent discovery was brought to light by M. A. San Mauro, "Le fabbriche di Paolo V tornano a splendere," in *Il Quirinale*, 3, March 2006, pp. 38–54. I thank the author and Dr. Francesco Colalucci for allowing me to observe the frieze and use the images.

25. Morello and Silvan, *Vedute*, pp. 114–15.

26. For this fountain, documented payments to the sculptor refer to work executed by Niccolò Cordier, between 1609 and 1610, on the creation of a "putto holding a round shell that spurts water into the air, set atop the tail of four sea dragons." The fountain itself is described as located "near the entrance of the Belvedere garden." The documents are referred to by C. D'Onofrio, *Le Fontane di Roma* (Rome: Romana Società Editrice, 1986), p. 515.

27. G. B. Falda, *Le Fontane di Roma e del Tuscolo* (1676; repr. Rome: Edizioni Editalia, 1965).

28. ASR, Camerale I, Giustificazioni di Tesoreria, b.33, p. 2, p. 3, p. 5.

29. ASR, Camerale I, Fabbriche, b.1540, c.40v.

30. For an overview of the history and evolution of the typology of fountains in Rome, fundamental resources remain the volumes of D'Onofrio: *Le Fontane* and *Acque e Fontane di Roma* (Rome: Staderini, 1977).

31. See Campitelli, *Villa Borghese*, pp. 88–90 for the Fontane Oscure, while for the fountains in general see D'Onofrio, *Le Fontane*.

32. Campitelli, *Villa Borghese*, pp. 86–88.

33. A. Caro, *De le Lettere familiari*, vol. 1 (Venice: Aldo Manuzio, 1572), p. 60.

34. The letter of July 26, 1543, addressed to Giambattista Grimaldi, is published in M. Azzi Visentini, *L'arte dei giardini*, vol. I (Milan: Edizioni Il Polifilo, 1999), pp. 241–45.

35. A very interesting repertory of the fountains existing in the first decades of the seventeenth century is in D. Parasacchi, *Raccolta delle principali fontane dell'inclita città di Roma* (1647; repr. Carlo Losi, ed., Rome,

1773), which also introduces some typologies with rocaille, for the most part no longer extant.

36. Some payment orders are cited in D'Onofrio, *Le Fontane*, pp. 514–15.

37. ASR, Camerale I, Giustificazioni di Tesoreria, b.33, p. 18, p. 19.

38. ASR, Camerale I, Fabbriche, b.1537, c.177, c.197, c.175 (this last payment pertains to transport from the house of Santi Solaro to the Belvedere garden "for service of the fountain" of a "dolphin.")

39. ASR, Camerale I, Fabbriche, b.1537, c.175, c.182.

40. ASR, Camerale I, Fabbriche, b.1537, c.270, c.98, c.105, c.157, c.250, c.253, c.255.

41. ASR, Camerale I, Fabbriche, b.1537, c.173, c.176, c.199.

42. For a repertory of this typology, see V. Cazzato, M. Fagiolo, M. Adriana Giusti, ed., *Atlante delle Grotte e dei Ninfei in Italia. Toscana, Lazio, Italia meridionale e Isole* (Milan: Electa, 2001).

43. Interpretation taken from Belli Barsali, *Ville*, p. 209.

44. ASR, Camerale I, Giustificazioni di Tesoreria, b.33, p. 20, p. 21; b.35, p. 3.

45. For the complete list of payments, see Corbo and Pomponi, *Fonti*.

46. In the 1684 etching by Giovan Francesco Venturini (1650–1710), the fountain is called "Architecture by Carlo Maderno."

47. D'Onofrio, *Le Fontane*, pp. 510–18.

48. Campitelli, *Villa Borghese*, pp. 134–35.

49. ASR, Camerale I, Giustificazioni di Tesoreria, b.34, p. 22.

50. D'Onofrio, *Le Fontane*, pp. 510–18.

51. We do not have any data that confirms the participation of Agostino Tassi in the conception of the Galera, but the similarities between the Galera for the fountain and the galleys represented in many of his works are astonishing. We know that Agostino Tassi lived for a long time in Livorno, and the time he spent in the city's port allowed him to gain detailed knowledge of the ships of the time.

52. Ferdinando Caroli, *De Vaticano Templo et palatio*, BAV, Cod. Vat. Lat. 10751, translated and cited in D'Onofrio, *Le Fontane*, p. 516.

53. On Barberini's verses and the fountain in general, see also D'Onofrio, *Acque e Fontane*, pp. 350–94 and *Roma vista da Roma* (Rome: Edizioni Liber, 1967), pp. 362–66.

54. A. Guglielmotti, *Storia della marina pontificia*, vol. 7 (Rome: Tipografia Vaticana, 1886–93), pp. 187ff. The new galley was not realized, however.

55. G. Perin Chattard, *Nuova descrizione del Vaticano o sia della Sacrosanta Basilica di San Pietro* (Rome: Barbiellini, 1762), pp. 227–28. Chattard took this view even when, as he wrote, the fountain appeared "quite abandoned."

56. Belli Barsali, *Ville*, p. 208.

57. On the two masons, see A. Campitelli, "Agostino e Bernardino Radi: due protagonisti dei cantieri berniniani," in O. Bonfait and A. Coliva, ed., *Bernini dai Borghese ai Barberini. La cultura a Roma intorno agli anni venti* (Rome: De Luca, 2004), pp. 105–13. It is not specified what the stonemasons might have carved, but we can assume they were heraldic emblems, which was their specialty.

58. ASR, Camerale I, Giustificazioni di Tesoreria, b.42, p. 5; b.43, p. 3; b.46, p. 14.

59. See A. Negro, *Il giardino dipinto del cardinale Borghese* (Rome: Argos, 2000).

60. A. Campitelli and A. Costamagna, *Villa Borghese. L'Uccelliera, la Meridiana, i Giardini Segreti* (Rome: Gebart, 2005).

61. ASR, Camerale I, Giustificazioni di Tesoreria, b.33, p. 8, November 19, 1608.

62. ASR, Camerale I, Giustificazioni di Tesoreria, b.45, p. 2, "Measurement and estimate of the work of mosaics, stucco, and gold ordered done by master Martino Ferraboschi on top of the fountain of Cleopatra," March 7, 1618.

63. This name derives from a lovely antique statue, made into a fountain, of a seated woman. This is the only "historic" reference still in place, as the whole is now occupied by the Museo Paolino built in the 1970s during the pontificate of Paul VI (1963–78).

64. A complete reconstruction of the figure of Faber is in S. De Renzi, "Storia naturale ed erudizione nella prima età moderna: Giovanni [Johannes] Faber (1574–1629) medico linceo," diss. in the history of science, university consortium Bari-Rome-Bologna, (VI cycle), academic year 1992–93. Some references to Faber's activity as curator of the Vatican Gardens can be found in Zalum, *Passione*, pp. 17–18.

65. On the history of the Accademia and the multitude of interests of its protagonists, see the study conference proceedings by various authors, *Federico Cesi: convegno celebrativo del IV centenario della nascita* (Rome: Accademia Nazionale dei Lincei, 1986); the study by G. Gabrielli, *Contributi alla storia dell'Accademia dei Lincei* (Rome: Accademia Nazionale dei Lincei, 1989); and the monumental and fundamental work by D. Freedberg, *The Eye of the Lynx: Galileo, His Friends and the Beginnings of Modern Natural History* (Chicago and London: The University of Chicago Press, 2002).

66. In a letter to Cardinal Scipione Borghese, nephew of pope Paul V, he refers to himself as "herbalist to our Lord and lecturer in the University of Rome"; see Biblioteca Corsiniana, Archivio della Pia Casa degli Orfani di Santa Maria in Aquiro, Fondo Faber, vol. 420, f. 61. Henceforward this work will be cited as the Fondo Faber.

67. The Aldobrandinis built a villa in Rome and one in Frascati; the Borgheses, the Pinciana in Rome and numerous villas in Frascati; the Ludovisis, a villa in Rome, unfortunately destroyed; the Barberinis, a villa-palazzo in Rome and one in Castel Gandolfo, later a papal residence. In addition, they all devoted themselves to the expansion and embellishment of the buildings and gardens of the other papal residence, the Quirinal.

68. "Cum tamen jam sub tertio Pontifice romano et Horti Pontificii vaticani curam geram." J. Faber, *De Nardo et Epithymo* (Rome: Facciotti, 1607), p. 10. This is a booklet that was widely distributed and made the expert botanist famous. We must also remember Faber's great involvement in the publication of the colossal work commissioned by Federico Cesi, the so-called *Tesoro Messicano* (Mexican Treasury), devoted to the flora and fauna of the New World, which the following authors drew from heavily: Freedberg, *The Eye*, pp. 245–74; I. Baldriga, *L'occhio della lince. I primi lincei tra arte, scienza e collezionismo (1603–1630)* (Rome: Accademia Nazionale dei Lincei, 2002), pp. 236–58.

69. Even in recent publications on the Vatican Gardens, such as the volume by G. Morello and A. Piazzoni, *I Giardini Vaticani* (Rome: Logart Press, 1991), Faber's name does not appear.

70. In the studies of the Academy of the Lynxes, Faber's interests in other fields have been brought to the fore, with just a few passing mentions of his botanical interests, while the reams of materials (lists of plants, letters exchanged with important scholars and experts of the time, etc.) that have come down to us deserve complete, thorough, and specific study.

71. Fondo Faber, vol. 413, f. 845.

72. On the use and fate of the citrus trees, see M. Azzi Visentini, and A. Tagliolini, *I Giardini delle Esperidi*, conference proceedings, Pietrasanta 1995 (Florence: Edifir, 1996).

73. ASR, Camerale I, Giustificazioni di Tesoreria, b.33, p. 3 ("work to lay down the conduit that brings water to the espalier of citron"), p. 13 ("for having laid down the conduit of the espalier in Belvedere in two places").

74. ASR, Camerale I, Giustificazioni di Tesoreria, b.34, p. 7.

75. ASR, Camerale I, Giustificazioni di Tesoreria, b.34, p. 2.

76. On the flower gardens, see A. V. Segre, "Le retour de Flore. Naissance et évolution des jardins de fleurs de 1550 à 1650" in S. Van Sprang, ed., *L'Empire de Flore*, (Brussels: La Renaissance du Livre, 1996), pp. 174–93.

77. Fondo Faber, vol. 413, f. 841.

78. F. Garbari and L. Tongiorgi Tomasi, *Il Giardiniere del Granduca. Storia ed immagini del Codice Casabona* (Pisa: ETS, 1995); F. Garbari, L. Tongiorgi Tomasi, and A. Tosi, *Giardino dei Semplici*, (Pisa: Edizioni Pless, University of Pisa, 2002). I thank Lucia Tongiorgi Tomasi for having shared this interpretation with me.

79. Masson, *Italian Flower*, pp. 61–80.

80. ASR, Camerale I, Fabbriche, b.1537 (1609–14). On pp. 85, 87, 88, 89, 91, 93, 95, 97, 99, 101, 103, 105, 107, 108, numerous payments to Martini Alberto are cited for expenses in making "compartments in the giardino de' semplici in Belvedere," b.1542 (1608–15); on pp. 6–11 other payments to the same gardener, again for the Giardino dei Semplici, are cited.

81. On Faber the botanist, and his contacts with Corvino, cf. Baldriga, *L'occhio*, in particular pp. 171–220.

82. Fondo Faber, vol. 413, f. 815 v. On Trachelio and the dedication to Cardinal Barberini, see E. Schettini Piazza, "I Barberini e i Lincei: dalla mirabil congiuntura alla fine della prima Accademia (1623–1630)," in L. Mochi Onori, S. Schultze, and F. Solinas, eds., *I Barberini e la cultura Europea del Seicento*, international conference proceedings, Rome, 2005 (Rome: De Luca Editori, 2007), p. 123.

83. Fondo Faber, vol. 413, f. 846 v.

84. The volumes cited contain letters in Faber's hand or by other people who wrote to him and are in no particular order, either chronological or thematic. Among these are numerous loose pages, generally undated and unsigned, including many lists of plants that deserve specific, systematic study.

85. Fondo Faber, vol. 420, f. 306ff.

86. See Chapter Four.

87. ASV, Fondo Borghese, Serie II, Tomo XII, f. 477, letter of September 10, 1610 from Guido Bentivoglio to Scipione Borghese.

88. ASR, Camerale I, Tesoreria Segreta, b.1542, p. 23, payment to Capriolo Marco for "bulbs from Flanders and Constantinople."

89. There is a vast bibliography on the subject. See W. Blunt, *Tulipomania*, (Harmondsworth: Penguin Books, 1950) and, among the most recent, L. Tongiorgi Tomasi, "Tulipomania. Addenda," in M. A. Giusti and A. Tagliolini, eds., *Il Giardino delle Muse*, conference proceedings (Florence: Edifir, 1995), pp. 79–95.

90. Fondo Faber, vol. 419, f. 659, cited in Baldriga, *L'occhio*, p. 198. The trip to Naples is described in a letter from Faber to Cassiano dal Pozzo, cited by Di Renzi, *Storia naturale*, p. 50. In Naples Faber met important figures in the field, such as Giovanni della Porta and Ferrante Imperato.

91. The expedition to Ostia by Giovanni Fabro had cost 5 *scudi*, and its objective was to "pick up various herbs to plant in the garden of the Belvedere." The document, conserved in the Archivio di Stato in Rome, was published by Orbaan, *Documenti*, pp. 302–303.

92. Fondo Faber, vol. 420, f. 304.

93. On Corvino see Baldriga, *L'occhio*, in particular pp. 211–15, and more especially M. B. Guerrieri Borsoi, *Gli Strozzi a Roma. Mecenati e collezionisti nel Sei e Settecento* (Rome: Editore Colombo, 2004), in particular pp. 121–40, in which the remarkable herb collection is reconstructed. Corvino had a garden in Rome, at the time highly appreciated for the incredible variety of flowers it contained. A letter from Corvino to Faber, undated, contains a list of plants that he is sending to him without specifying their destination, including hyacinths, varieties of tulip, fritillaries, anemones, muscaris, trachelii, martagon lilies, and narcissus in many varieties: all bulbs that were in vogue in those years and whose costs were extremely elevated. There are also plants with picturesque names such as "devil's bite," "goat's beard," and "serpent's tongue" that are impossible for us to identify.

94. On Imperato, see, lastly, E. Stendardo, *Ferrante Imperato: collezionismo e studio della natura a Napoli tra Cinque e Seicento* (Naples: Accademia Pontaiana, 2001). A letter by Imperato from 1610 contains his thanks for the plants that Faber had sent him, as well as scientific disquisitions on botany and appreciations of the work of P. Mattioli, *Commentarii in sex libros Pedacii Dioscoridis Anarzabei de medica materia* (Venice: Valgrisi, 1565), a publication that elicited great interest among enthusiasts. See Fondo Faber, vol. 420, f. 348.

95. Like Faber, Muller was a member of the Academy of the Lynxes. Among his letters to Faber is one of November 24, 1616, with a list of precious bulbs (see Fondo Faber, vol. 420, f. 1), while another from 1627 refers to bulbs sent from Bohemia (see Fondo Faber, vol. 413, f. 775).

96. Fondo Faber, vol. 413, f. 876; in a letter of April 2, 1624, Faber is called a friend of the cardinal, noted flower enthusiast, whose gardens at the Quirinal were among the most celebrated of the time. On Barberini and the gardens, see A. Campitelli, "Gli Horti di Flora nella Roma dei Barberini," in Mochi Onori, Schultze, and Solinas, ed., *I Barberini*, pp. 571–80.

97. On the garden and the figure of Alessandro Rondanini, see Zalum, *Passione*, pp. 88, 92, 119, 122.

98. Until now, studies of the villa have been partial and limited to individual aspects, but a comprehensive study with various contributors is under way, coordinated by Alessandro Cremona and scheduled to be published shortly in a stand-alone issue of *Ricerche di Storia dell'Arte*.

99. G. B. Ferrari, *Flora, overo cultura dei fiori* (Rome: Facciotti, 1638; edition in Latin, 1633; repr. L. Tongiorgi Tomasi, ed., Florence: Olschki, 2001, with critical introduction by the editor and essays by A. Campitelli and M. Zalum). The subsequent treatise by Ferrari, *Hesperides sive de malorum aereorum cultura et usu*, Rome: H. Scheus, 1646), is devoted to citrus trees, which, as we know, were present in the Vatican Gardens from the fifteenth century onward. Here, however, there is no mention of the gardens.

100. Ferrari, *Flora*, pp. 13–14 and p. 458.

101. Ferrari, *Flora*, pp. 89, 372.

102. Orban, *Documenti*, pp. 303, 350; BAV, Mss. Ruoli, 147, December 31, 1627, f. 18v.

103. There exists a well known description of the plants cultivated in the Farnese Gardens on the Palatine, signed by Tobia Aldini but unanimously attributed to Pietro Castelli. See *Exactissima descriptiorariorum quorandorum plantarum quae continentur Romae in Horto Farnesiano rariores plantae exactissimae descriptae* (Rome: Mascardi, 1625).

104. BAV, Mss. Ruoli 158, November 5, 1637, f. 12v.

105. "Io: quidam Faber non ausus mecum in aciem discendere." Cited in Baldriga, *L'occhio*, p. 196, note 62.

CHAPTER SIX: THE SEVENTEENTH AND EIGHTEENTH CENTURIES

1. On the Villa Ludovisi, see A. Schiavo, *Villa Ludovisi e Palazzo Margherita* (Rome: Editrice Roma Amor, 1981); I. Belli Barsali, *Ville di Roma* (Milan: Rusconi, 1983), pp. 236–47.

2. Urban VIII and the family residence were thoroughly investigated in a recent conference; see L. Mochi Onori, S. Schultze, and F. Solinas, eds., *I Barberini e la cultura del tempo*, international study conference proceedings, Rome, 2005 (Rome: De Luca, 2007).

3. On the Barberini gardens, in addition to the conference proceedings cited in the note above, the reader is referred to the important, pioneering study by E. Blair MacDougall, *Fountains, Statues, and Flowers* (Washington D.C.: Dumbarton Oaks Research Library and Collection, 1994), in particular the chapter "A Cardinal's Bulb Garden: A Giardino Segreto at the Palazzo Barberini in Rome," pp. 219–348.

4. On the Villa at Castel Gandolfo, see Chapter Nine.

5. A fundamental reference on the popes' summer sojourns outside the Vatican is E. Bonomelli, *I papi in campagna* (Rome: Gherardo Casini Editore, 1953), rich with curious and interesting bits of information. For the origins of the papal residence in Castel Gandolfo, see, in particular, chapter III, pp. 41–69.

6. This information is contained in G. Morello and A. Piazzoni, *I Giardini vaticani* (Rome: Logart, 1992), p. 42, but it does not indicate the source.

7. M. Del Piazzo, *Ragguagli borrominiani* (Rome: Stabilimento Arti Grafiche Palombi, 1968), p. 68.

8. The payment was published in H. Hibbard and I. Jaffe, "Bernini's Barcaccia," in *Burlington Magazine*, 106, 1964, p. 170. See also F. Buranelli and L. Vattuone, "I luoghi di riposo," in C. Pietrangeli, ed., *Il Palazzo Apostolico Vaticano* (Florence: Nardini, 1992), pp. 237–40.

9. "Quid miraris Apem, quae mel de floribus haurit? / Si tibi mellitam gutture fundit aquam." *The Diary of John Evelyn*, E. S. de Beer, ed. (Oxford: Clarendon Press, 1955), p. 405.

10. On Faber and his activity in the Vatican Gardens, see Chapter Five.

11. On the villa, see also C. Benocci, ed., *Villa Pamphilj* (Rome: publisher, 2005), with earlier bibliography.

12. See G. Petrucci, *San Martino al Cimino* (Rome: Multigrafica editrice, 1987).

13. Various authors, *Roma e il suo Orto Botanico. Storia ed eventi di una istituzione scientifica* (Rome: Borgia, 1984).

14. On the Academy of the Lynxes, see the monumental, foundational work by D. Freedberg, *The Eye of the Lynx: Galileo, His Friend, and the Beginnings of Modern Natural History* (Chicago and London: University of Chicago Press, 2002).

15. See C. Benocci, ed., *I giardini Chigi tra Siena e Roma dal Cinquecento agli inizi dell'Ottocento*, (Siena: Fondazione Monte dei Paschi di Siena, Protagon editore, 2005).

16. J. Connors and L. Rice, *Specchio di Roma barocca. Una guida inedita del XVII secolo* (Rome: Edizioni dell'Elefante, 1990), pp. 34–5. I thank Anna Maria de Strobel for telling me about this interesting document.

17. G. B. Falda, *Li giardini di Roma*, undated, but1676 (Rome: G. G. de Rossi).

18. On the representations of the gardens, see A. Tagliolini and R. Assunto, ed., *Ville e Giardini di Roma nelle incisioni di Giovan Battista Falda* (Milan: Il Polifilo, 1980).

19. Jan Martensz, a Dutch merchant born in Horn in 1574 and interested in botany, writes in a description dated 1600 that not only date palms but also the so-called traveler's palm, with its characteristic fan shape, grew there. The description is included in I. Baldriga, *L'occhio della Lince, I primi lincei tra arte, scienza e collezionismo (1603–1630)* (Rome: Accademia Nazionale dei Lincei, 2002), p. 237.

20. On the events of the occupation and the destiny of Pope Pius VI, see P. Baldassarri, *Relazione delle avversità e patimenti del glorioso papa Pio VI*, vols. 1–2 (Rome: Tipografia Poliglotta, 1889), p. 354, which relates how the French occupied the Vatican palaces on February 16.

21. ASV, S.P.A., Computisteria, Rincontro dei Giardini. The envelopes numbered 3205–3210 include news and payments from June 1677 to 1740, while envelope 3211 contains payments from the years 1795–98.

22. ASV, S.P.A., Computisteria, b.3211, p. 22. In 1795 an expense is registered during the winter for the coal used "to make a fire for the citrus plants."

23. See G. B. Ferrari, *Hesperides, sive de malorum aureorum cultura et usu* (Rome: H. Scheus, 1644). On the techniques used to cover citrus plants in the villas of Rome, see A. Campitelli, "I cocchi di agrumi nelle ville romane," in M. Azzi Visentini and A. Tagliolini, ed., *Gli orti delle Esperidi*, study conference proceedings, Pietrasanta, 1995 (Florence: Edifir, 1996), pp. 175–96.

24. ASV, S.P.A., Computisteria, b.5239, Palazzo, Giardini, Orti, Mola ed altre fabbriche adiacenti al Vaticano, letter L, 1679.

25. ASV, S.P.A., Computisteria, Registro dei Giardini, b.3205, p. 324 and b. 3209, p. 116, p. 125, and p. 132.

26. ASV, S.P.A., Computisteria, b.158, pp. 26–31. My heartfelt thanks to Anna Maria de Strobel for bringing this document to my attention.

27. The garden was closed at the time on three sides, and only in the next century, with the construction of the so-called "Braccio Nuovo" at the behest of Pius VII, would the fourth side also be closed, making it truly a "secret garden."

28. ASV, Fondo Albani, b.12, pp. 106–7. I thank Anna Maria de Strobel for bringing this document to my attention.

29. For the history of the complex, see P. Liverani, "La Pigna Vaticana: note storiche," in *Bollettino dei Monumenti, Musei e Gallerie Pontificie*, n. 6, 1986, pp. 51–63.

30. ASV, S.P.A., Computisteria, b.3207, p. 67.

31. ASV, S.P.A., Computisteria, b.3209, p. 148, payment of February 1727. Evidently the maintenance of the gardens was not interrupted by the successor to Clement XI.

32. ASV, S.P.A., Computisteria, b.5329, Palazzo, Giardini, Orti, Mola ed altre fabbriche adiacenti al Vaticano, letters H and L.

33. ASV, SPA, Computisteria, b. 3209, p. 133ff.

34. G. P. Chattard, *Nuova descrizione del Vaticano, o sia Della Sacrosanta Basilica di S. Pietro*, 3 vols., (Rome: Barbiellini, 1762–67), p. 412.

35. See A. Scardin, *Disegni dei perther dei più cospicui giardini posti in Roma*, ed. A. Tagliolini (Milan: Il Polifilo, 1995). On the title page of the collection, Scardin defines himself as "Gardener to the Pope," and drawing no. 16, titled garden "of His Holiness at the Vatican," presents a lovely rendering of a parterre bordered by buildings; it does, however, seem to correspond to any site within the Vatican Gardens.

36. On the plan, see the excellent study by M. Bevilacqua, *Roma nel secolo dei lumi. Architettura erudizione scienza nella pianta di G. B. Nolli "celebre geometra"* (Naples: Electa, 1998) and the critical edition, now at press, edited by C. Travaglini.

37. F. Buranelli, "La scoperta del Laocoonte e il Cortile delle Statue in Vaticano," in F. Buranelli, P. Liverani, and A. Nesselrath, ed., *Laocoonte. Alle origini dei Musei Vaticani*, exhibition catalogue (Rome: L'Erma di Bretschneider, 2006), p. 57.

38. ASV, S.P.A., Computisteria, b.3211, which contains the payments from 1795 to 1798.

39. R. Pirotta and E. Chiovenda, *Flora Romana* (Rome: Tipografia Voghera, 1900), p. 158; M. Catalano and E. Pellegrini, with historical introduction by C. D'Onofrio, *L'Orto Botanico di Roma* (Rome: Palombi, 1975).

40. On this subject the reader is referred to Chapters Four and Five.

41. Some information about Suarez and his experience in the Vatican Gardens can be found in Pirotta and Chiovenda, *Flora Romana*, pp. 257–58 and 262–63.

42. In 1753 Carl Linnaeus had published the *Species plantarum*, revolutionizing the classification system of the entire plant world.

43. F. L. Gilii and G. Suarez, *Osservazioni Fitologiche sopra alcune piante esotiche introdotte in Roma fatte nell'anno 1790* (Rome: Stamperia Giunchiana, 1792). On the work of the two botanists, see the paper by Sofia Varoli Piazza, "Il Giardino del lago a Villa Borghese a Roma: nuove specie arboree dal 1766," presented at the convention "Novae Plantae Antiquis Hortis," Aranjuez, 1992. I thank my friend Sofia for giving me a copy of her work and for allowing me to use her observations, which are centered on the Villa Borghese but also refer to Roman gardens in general.

44. G. Lais, "I due Orti Botanici vaticani," in *Atti della Pontificia Accademia dei Nuovi Lincei*, vol. 32, 1878–79, pp. 63–78.

45. Lais states that many documents in Gilii's hand that relate to the botanical garden are held in the Biblioteca Apostolica Vaticana. Unfortunately, we were unable to verify this information because the library was closed to the public for renovations.

46. *Annona squamosa*, commonly referred to as Cirimoja, and known in English as sugar apple or sweetsop, is native to the Peruvian Andes and, according to Gilii, was introduced in Rome for the first time by the Spanish envoy to the Holy See, Nicola de Azara.

47. On the introduction of plants from the Americas to the villas of Rome, see A. Campitelli, "Novae Plantae Antiquis Hortis: Continuity and Innovation in the Roman Villas in the Eighteenth and Nineteenth Centuries," in *Studies in the History of Gardens and Designed Landscapes*, vol. 23, no. 1, 2003, pp. 22–41.

48. On Francesco Bettini, a particularly interesting figure in the history of the villas of Rome, the essential study remains M. Heimburger Ravalli, *Disegni di giardini e opere minori di Francesco Bettini* (Florence: Leo Olschki, 1981).

49. Ibid. Bettini recounts that the precious *bignonia catalpa* were traded for figs and that the exotic plants were considered unjustified eccentricities.

50. He is responsible for a very interesting publication on South American plants, H. Ruiz Lopez, *Florae Peruvianae, et Chilensis prodromus sive novarum generum plantarum*

Peruvianorum et Chilensium descriptiones et icones (Rome: Typographia Paleariniano, 1797).

51. The herbarium is probably also preserved in the BAV but, as explained in note 45, it is not possible to verify this at the moment.

52. ASV, S.P.A., Amministrazione, Art. 48, f.I, VI.

53. The inscription reads: PIUS SEXTUS PONT. MAX. / FONTEM RUSTICO ANTEA OPERE / A PAULO V/EXTRUCTUM / IN ELEGANTIOREM HANC SPLENDIDIOREMQUE FORMAM / RESTITUIT / ANNO DOMINI MDCCLXXIX PONTIF. SUI V. (In the year of our Lord 1779, the fifth year of his pontificate, Pope Pius VI restored this fountain, built formerly by Paul V with rustic craft, to this more elegant and more splendid form.)

54. C. Percier and P. F. L. Fontaine, *Villas de Rome: choix des plus célèbres maisons de plaisance de Rome et des ses environs* (1809; Jean-Philippe Garric, ed. Wavre: Mardaga, 2007).

55. G. A. Sala, *Diario Romano degli anni 1798–1799*, Miscellanea della Società Romana di Storia Patria, anastatic reprint, Rome 1980, vol. I, p. 34.

56. Ibid., p. 156.

57. L. von Pastor, *Storia dei Papi* (Rome: Desclée & C Editori Pontifici, 1934), vol. 16, p. 637.

CHAPTER SEVEN: THE NINETEENTH CENTURY

1. ASV, Sacri Palazzi Apostolici, Computisteria, b.1439, 1806, p. 245.

2. ASV, Sacri Palazzi Apostolici, Computisteria, b.1438, 1803. The figures from the subsequent years were similar.

3. This is the Roman name for cardoons.

4. ASV, Sacri Palazzi Apostolici, Computisteria, b.1438, 1804, p. 249.

5. ASV, Sacri Palazzi Apostolici, Computisteria, b.1438, 1804, p. 252, and 1805, p. 451.

6. ASV, Sacri Palazzi Apostolici, Amministrazione, b.1056.

7. There are frequent descriptions in the document of wooden gates, which were often painted bright colors such as red or green.

8. G. Moroni, *Dizionario di erudizione storico-ecclesiastica da San Pietro sino ai nostri giorni*, 109 vols. (Venice: Tipografia Emiliana, 1840–1879), vol. 50, p. 268.

9. ASV, Sacri Palazzi Apostolici, Amministrazione, b.1056.

10. Ibid.

11. Ibid.

12. ASV, Sacri Palazzi Apostolici, Computisteria, bb.1438, 1439, 1440, 1441, 1442, which contain the accounts from 1803 to 1809.

13. ASV, Sacri Palazzi Apostolici, Computisteria, b.1442, 1809, p. 125.

14. ASV, Sacri Palazzi Apostolici, Computisteria, b.1445, 1815, p. 450. Pius VII was forced into exile from 1809 to 1814.

15. ASV, Sacri Palazzi Apostolici, Computisteria, b.1445, 1815, p. 450ff., with documents referring to 1812.

16. ASV, Sacri Palazzi Apostolici, Computisteria, b.1444, 1814, p. 138.

17. Ibid., p. 447.

18. ASV, Sacri Palazzi Apostolici, Computisteria, b.1446, 1816; b.1447, 1817–18; b.1448, 1819; b.1449, 1820–21; b.1450, 1822.

19. Cardinal Ercole Consalvi was secretary of state in twice, from 1800 to 1806 and from 1814 to 1823. We believe that the memorandum refers to the second period, because Gianicolo Antonio Sebastiani is mentioned as director of the Botanical Garden, a position he held from 1815 to 1820. Thus we can assume that the memorandum was written just after 1815.

20. ASV, Sacri Palazzi Apostolici, Amministrazione, Art. 48, f. I, VI, p. 89, folder titled, "General Dispositions, records, and various matters. Regulations for the Papal Gardens."

21. On Sebastiani, see various authors, *Roma e il suo Orto Botanico. Storia ed eventi di un'istituzione scientifica* (Rome: Ed. Borgia, 1984), p. 30.

22. Ibid., p. 32.

23. ASV, Sacri Palazzi Apostolici, Computisteria, b.1446, 1816, p. 180 and b.1447, 1817–18, payment without page number, dated September 1817.

24. ASR, Catasto Gregoriano Urbano, Map and Legend, Rione XIV Borgo.

25. ASV, Sacri Palazzi Apostolici, Amministrazione, Art. 48, f. I, VI, n.394.

26. ASR, Catasto Gregoriano Urbano, Map and Legend, Rione XIV Borgo.

27. This is the area occupied today by the tennis courts and playground.

28. Another "artichoke patch" was located just behind the basilica's apse.

29. M. Losito, *La Casina Pius IV in Vaticano* (Vatican City: Pontificia Accademia delle Scienze, 2005), pp. 22–23. A previous restoration had taken place under Pope Clement XI Albani, between 1702 and 1703, by the architects Carlo Fontana and Giovan Battista Contini, who had respected the original layout.

30. ASV, Palazzi Apostolici, art. 48, p. 105. The aviary, built by the company Pietro Fumaroli, cost some 1,067.16 *scudi*.

31. E. Bonomelli, *I papi in campagna* (Rome: Casini Editore, 1953), p. 199. The "Annual homage of twenty-four pheasants" that the Royal Court of Naples sent to the pope is annotated with regularity for the entire period 1825–58; see ASV, Sacri Palazzi Apostolici, Title 14, f. 2.

32. C. Pietrangeli, "Una veduta ottocentesca dei Giardini Vaticani," in *Strenna dei Romanisti*, no. 55, 1994, pp. 413–17.

33. The first English-style garden in Rome was in the Villetta Doria, property of Cardinal Giuseppe Doria (brother of Prince Andrea, who owned the much more grandiose villa in Porta San Pancrazio), which was situated in the area occupied today by the Galoppatoio of Villa Borghese, but it had a brief life: built in 1785, it was dismantled and sold in 1798 due to political upheaval. In the same years the lake garden was created at the Villa Borghese, and it is still visible today, although partially transformed. Finally, beginning in 1839, the great Veneto landscape architect Giuseppe Jappelli was in Rome, and charged with redesigning the park of Villa Torlonia in via Nomentana according to modern taste.

34. Moroni, *Dizionario*, vol. 50, p. 270.

35. Ibid., vol. 85, p. 28.

36. The inscription reads as follows: GREGORIUS XVI P.M. HORTOS VATICANOS / URBANIS CIRCUM MOENIBUS RESTAURATIS / AEDIFICIS ORNATIS NEMORIBUS CONSITIS / AMBULATIONIBUS PATEFACTIS FONTIBUS AUCTIS / IN VETEREM AMOENITATEM / RESTITUENDOS CURAVIT / ANNO SAL MDCCCXXXIV / SACRI PRINCIPATUS ANNO IV (In the year of Salvation 1834, the fourth year of his sacred principate, Pope Gregory XVI, by rebuilding the surrounding city walls, adorning buildings, planting groves, opening up promenades, and enlarging the fountains, took care to restore the Vatican Gardens to their erstwhile pleasantness).

37. The watercolor drawing is held in the director's office of the Vatican Museums.

38. A document dated 1841 recounts the attempt to make the coat of arms with leftover mosaic tiles supplied by the Reverenda Fabbrica of St. Peter's, in sky blue, red, yellow, black, and white, but does not say whether it was in fact executed; see ASV, Palazzi Apostolici, Tit. 269, 1841, ff. 47–56.

39. C. Pietrangeli, "La Fontana del Cortile del Belvedere," in *Strenna dei Romanisti*, 1987, pp. 475–84.

40. Moroni, *Dizionario*, vol. 50, p. 253.

41. Ibid., vol. 85, p. 28.

42. Ibid., vol. 50, p. 271. We recall that according to the Catasto Gregoriano Urbano of 1818 the site was used as an irrigated (vegetable) garden.

43. Ibid., vol. 50, p. 272.

44. Ibid., vol. 50, p. 271; G. De Fabris, Il piedistallo della Colonna Antonina per munificenza della Santità di Nostro Signore Papa Gregorio XVI felicemente regnante collocato nel giardino della Pigna al Vaticano / brevemente descritto e ristaurato (Rome: Monaldi, 1846).

45. Moroni, Dizionario, vol. 50, p. 290, and vol. 44, p. 103.

46. ASV, Palazzi Apostolici, Amministrazione, Tit. 6, "Inventory of all of the objects existing in the Papal Gardens of the Vatican as of January 1, 1841."

47. Moroni, Dizionario, vol. 82, p. 45.

48. ASV, Palazzi Apostolici, Tit. 259.

49. Moroni, Dizionario, vol. 50, p. 271.

50. ASV, Palazzi Apostolici, Art. 48, p. 136.

51. L. E. Audot, Notes sur les jardins du sud de l'Italie: recueillies pendant un voyage fait en 1839/40 (Paris: Bouchard-Huzard, 1840), p. 26.

52. These were the great Bramante fountain situated in the center of the Secret Garden of Paul III, the four smaller fountains on ground level at the intersection of the paths, and the two wall fountains in the same garden, all clearly shown in Rinaldi's drawing.

53. The account is a free translation from the French.

54. ASV, Palazzi Apostolici, Tit. 278, ff. 249–62 "Report on the damages to the palace and gardens in 1849 at the end of the government of the Roman Republic," July 28, 1849.

55. Bonomelli, I papi, pp. 259ff.

56. Ibid., pp. 327–29.

57. S. Negro, Vaticano minore (Milan: Hoepli, 1936), p. 188.

58. Ibid., p. 248.

59. Ibid., p. 267.

60. All of the papal stays at Castel Gandolfo, from 1626 to 1952, are precisely recorded by Bonomelli, I papi, pp. 481–83.

61. The citation is in the novel, Rome, and quoted in Bonomelli, I papi, p. 330.

62. Bonomelli, I papi, p. 330.

63. Negro, Vaticano, p. 249.

64. Ibid.

65. Bonomelli, I papi, p. 342.

66. Ibid., p. 329.

67. Ibid., p. 334.

68. Ibid., p. 356, note 8.

69. See E. Soderini, Il pontificato di Leone XIII (Milan: Mondadori, 1932–33), p. 266.

70. The micro-mosaic belongs to Gianni Giordani, whom I thank for allowing me to publish it. Biagio Barzotti was the mosaicist of the Reverenda Fabbrica of St. Peter's, and we know of another micro-mosaic by him, Piazza St. Peter during the Papal Benediction, datable to around 1879. The micro-mosaic shown here is cited in M. Alfieri, M. G. Branchetti, and G. Cornini, ed., Mosaici minuti romani del 700 e dell'800, exhibition catalogue, Vatican City, October–November 1986, (Rome, 1986); P. Levillain and J. W. O'Malley, The Papacy. An Encyclopedia, (New York and London: Routlege, 2002), p. 1022, entry on mosaics by H. Lavagne.

71. On the techniques of bird hunting and the roccolo in particular, see. L. Zangheri, "Ragnaie, Paretai e Uccelliere nelle Ville barocche," in A. Campitelli, ed., Villa Borghese. Storia e gestione, international conference proceedings, Rome, 2003, (Milan: Skira, 2005), pp. 57–66.

72. Bonomelli, I papi, p. 335.

73. Ibid., p. 329.

74. Sneider's activity is remembered in the obituary published in L'illustrazione Vaticana, year 3, no. 9, 1932, p. 435.

75. Bonomelli, I papi, pp. 340–41.

76. The viaduct is documented in various photographs of the time and was demolished in the 1930s.

CHAPTER EIGHT: THE NEW IMAGE OF THE CITY-STATE

1. S. Negro, Vaticano minore, (Milan: Hoepli, 1936), p. 271.

2. A brief description of the fountain can be found in F. Mastrigli, Acque, Acquedotti e Fontane di Roma, 2 vols. (Rome: Edizioni Pinci, 1928), vol. 2, p. 376.

3. This was a popular technique at the beginning of the twentieth century and involved the placement of small beds of diverse flowers within larger beds, in imitation of mosaic tiles.

4. ASV, Palazzi Apostolici, Titolo 170, art. 48 f. 1, pp. 177–88, "Traduzione di Giovanni Guacci di una relazione di Bechnick sui giardini vaticani (senza data)." We can deduce that this refers to the years of Benedict XV's papacy, as it cites the fountains that he had constructed in the woods. No identifying information has emerged about the author to date.

5. The inscription is immured in the Leonine Wall.

6. Both documents are held at the Archivio Storico dei Musei Vaticani. The description is titled: "Nuova pianta dei Giardini Vaticani con l'elenco dei monumenti ivi conservati eseguita dal conte Federico Paolozzi e da lui dedicata con filiale devozione al Santo Padre Pio P.P. XI felicemente regnante nell'anno di grazia MCMXXIIII." My thanks to Dr. Cristina Pantanella for helping me and for facilitating my research.

7. A similar image of the garden complex in the 1920s, by Victor L. S. Hafner, a fellow at the American Academy in Rome, was published by V. Cazzato, Ville e Giardini italiani. I disegni di architetti e paesaggisti dell'American Academy in Rome (Rome: Istituto Poligrafico e Zecca dello Stato, 2004), p. 488. Published in the same volume are numerous survey drawings of the Casina of Pius IV, also by Academy fellows.

8. A brief recounting of the history of the gardens and a summary of new modifications begun after 1929 are in an article by Giacomo Nicolini, "I giardini Vaticani," in L'Illustrazione Vaticana, year V, January 1934, pp. 61–66. Nicolini, originally from Bologna, moved to Rome in the 1930s. According to the text, he has a degree in pharmacy and was a botany scholar. His knowledge of the gardens leads one to believe that he may have had an important role in their conception, but as of this writing no document to support this hypothesis has surfaced. Itineraries for the exploration of the gardens as they are now are in C. Pietrangeli and F. Mancinelli, Vaticano. Città e giardini (Florence: Scala, 1985); G. Morello and A. Piazzoni, I Giardini Vaticani (Rome: Logart, 1992).

9. Nicolini, I giardini, p. 64.

10. The two plans are published in L'Illustrazione Vaticana, 1933, vol. 1, p. 237.

11. An entry on the architect by Alessandro Mazza is in V. Cazzato, ed., Atlante del giardino italiano 1750–1940. Dizionario biografico di architetti, giardinieri, botanici, committenti, letterati e altri protagonisti, vol. I: Italia settentrionale, vol. II: Italia centrale e meridionale (Rome: Istituto Poligrafico e Zecca Dello Stato, on press).

12. M. Losito, La Casina di Pio IV in Vaticano (Vatican City: Pontificia Accademia delle Scienze, 2005, pp. 175–83.

13. N. Del Re, ed., Mondo Vaticano. Passato e presente (Vatican City: Libreria Editrice Vaticana, 1995), p. 527. Roscioli also made a bust of Pope Pius XI. For other information, see A. Cremona, S. Gnisci, A. Ponente, Il Giardino della memoria. I busti dei grandi italiani

al Pincio, (Rome: Artemide, 1999), pp. 192–193.

14. On this subject, see the fine volume by V. Cazzato, ed., *La Memoria, il Tempo, la Storia nel giardino italiano fra '800 e '900* (Rome: Istituto Poligrafico e Zecca dello Stato, 1999). For the Roman situation see, in the same volume, the essay by A. Campitelli, "Eclettismo e revival nei giardini romani," pp. 369–92.

15. Nicolini, *I giardini*, pp. 65–66.

16. Ibid., p. 66.

17. Ibid., p. 66.

18. See *L'Illustrazione Vaticana*, vol. 3, no. 21, 1932, pp. 1037–38.

19. The bibliography by and on Luca Beltrami is boundless, but primarily concerns his Milanese activity. For his Roman activity see the essay by A. Bellini, "Luca Beltrami architetto della Fabbrica di San Pietro," in *Quaderni dell'Istituto di Storia dell'Architettura*, nos. 25–30, 1995–97, pp. 395–408; P. Innocenti, "La Pinacoteca vaticana nella storia della museografia: dalle origini al progetto di Luca Beltrami," in *Atti e Memorie dell'Accademia Clementina*, no. 40, 2000 (2001), pp. 95–183.

20. On the organization of the piazza, see *L'Illustrazione Vaticana*, vol. 3, 1932, p. 1127.

21. In the Villa Borghese, citrus trees were recently reintroduced as part of the restoration of the secret gardens, and they are now present in numerous varieties, both on espaliers against the retaining walls and in pots.

22. Evidence of the presence of citrus in the villa is the place name, Casale dei Cedrati, which identifies the fine seventeenth-century country house, near the Villa Vecchia, that was surrounded by a lovely garden with *cocchi* of citrus trees.

CHAPTER NINE: PAPAL HOLIDAYS AND THE VILLA IN CASTEL GANDOLFO

1. This topic has been addressed in various studies, including the fundamental references: D. R. Coffin, *The Villa in the Life of Renaissance Rome* (Princeton: Princeton University Press, 1979); A. Paravicini Bagliani, "La mobilità della Curia Romana nel secolo XIII: riflessi locali," in *Società e istituzioni dell'Italia Comunale: l'esempio di Perugia (secoli XII–XIV)*, International Historical Congress, Perugia, 1985, (Perugia: 1988), pp. 156–278; and the fine university thesis in Beni Culturali at the Università della Tuscia by S. Ciccolini, "La cultura della 'vita in villa' nel Quattrocento. Pratiche curiali e modelli pontifici," 1999–2000.

2. L. Duchesne, ed., *Liber Pontificalis* (Paris: E. de Boccard, 1886–92), vol. 2, p. 465.

3. Coffin, *The Villa*, p. 23.

4. Cited in E. Bonomelli, *I papi in campagna* (Rome: Gherardo Casini editore, 1953), p. 22.

5. L. Muratori, *Rerum Italicarum Scriptores* (Milan: Typographia Societatis Palatinae, 1723–51), vol. 3, p. 439; P. Jaffè, ed., *Regesta Pontificum Romanorum* (Berlin: Veit et Comp., 1851), p. 73ff., where documents relating to the papal sojourns in Segni are reprinted.

6. A. Paravicini Bagliani, *La vita quotidiana alla corte dei papi nel Duecento* (Bari: Laterza, 1996), p. 24.

7. The definition is by Magister Gregorius in his *De Mirabilibus Urbis Romae* and is reprinted in Paravicini Bagliani, "La mobilità," p. 170.

8. Ibid., pp. 170–71.

9. A. Paravicini Bagliani, *Il corpo del papa* (Turin: Einaudi, 1994), p. 288.

10. Ibid., p. 268.

11. On this important city magistrate, see E. Re, "Maestri di Strada," in *Archivio della Società Romana di Storia Patria*, 43, 1920, pp. 5ff.

12. Coffin, *The Life*, p. 25, which takes the information from the letters of Poggio Bracciolini, papal secretary and companion.

13. In 1299 the Aragon ambassadors recounted that the pope had gone to Anagni "ad castra sua," cited in Paravicini Bagliani, *La mobilità*, p. 157.

14. R. Ambrosi De Magistris, *Il viaggio di Innocenzo III nel Lazio e il primo ospedale di Anagni* (Rome: Tipografia Poliglotta De Propaganda Fide, 1898), p. 6, without indication of the source.

15. E.S. Piccolomini, *I Commentari*, ed. L. Totaro (Milan: Adelphi, 1984), vol. 5, p. 971: "in that way he could reinforce the loyalty of the uncertain city and at the same time avoid the toxic Roman air."

16. G. da Verona and M. Canensi, *Le vite di Paolo II*, ed. G. Zippel (Città di Castello: Editore S. Lapi, 1904–11), p. 107.

17. On the residence, see A. Vivit, "L'insigne viridario di Francesco Gonzaga in Roma," in *Bollettino del Centro Studi per la Storia dell'Architettura*, no. 34, 1987.

18. A broad treatment of the theme, with numerous references to the writings of the humanists, is in the previously cited thesis by Sara Ciccolini.

19. "IV mensis julii, fuerunt indicte vacationes generales ab hac die usque ad Kalendas octobris exclusive." J. Burchard, *Liber Notarum ab anno MCCCCLXXXIII usque ad annum MDVI*, ed. E. Celani (Città di Castello: Editore S. Lapi, 1910), part I, f. 2, p. 117, cited by Coffin, *The Life*, p. 24.

20. B. Platina, *Le vite de' sommi pontefici* (Venice: Presso Girolamo Savioni, 1730), p. 413, cited in Coffin, *The Life*, p. 23. Platina's poor relationship with Paul II is well known, so it is not surprising that he paints him in a negative light.

21. "Juro et promitto, quod unicuique dominorum Cardinalium, qui nunc sunt, et pro tempore fuerint, unam terram, seu castellum in locis propinquis, ut supra, cum illius arce, si eam habuerit, ac plena jurisdictione, et singulis reddititibus, et proventibus illius Cardinalis regendum, tenendum, et possidendum, ut etiam ipsi domini Cardinales locum aliquem specialem habeant, in quem libere, vel ad declinandam pestem, vel recreationis suae causa possint se recidere." Burchard, *Liber*, p. 185.

22. An excellent, comprehensive study has finally been made of this splendid complex, long semi-ignored. A. Cavallaro, *La Villa dei Papi alla Magliana* (Rome: Istituto Poligrafico e Zecca dello Stato, 2005).

23. Ibid., p. 5.

24. On the subject, the reader is referred to Chapter Two and to the essay by P. F. Bagatti Valsecchi and S. Langè, "La Villa. Cultura umanistica e nascita della villa come tipo codificato," in F. Zeri, ed., *Storia dell'arte italiana*, vol. 4, *Forme e modelli*, part 3, "Situazioni momenti indagini" (Turin: Einaudi, 1982), pp. 363–70.

25. See Chapter Two.

26. On the castle, see S. Danesi Squarzina and G. Borghini, *Il Borgo di Ostia da Sisto IV a Giulio II*, exhibition catalogue, June–September 1980 (Rome: De Luca Editori, 1980); U. Broccoli and A. Pellegrino, *Castello di Giulio II a Ostia antica* (Rome: Tipografia Centenari, n.d.).

27. This information, if not otherwise indicated, comes from Cavallaro, *La Villa*.

28. P. Grassi, *Il Diario di Leone X*, ed. P. Delicati and M. Armellini (Rome: Tipografia della Pace, 1884), p. 88, c.487r, reports that the pope's death on December 1, 1521, was caused "ex catharro concepto in villa Magliana."

29. Coffin, *The Life*, p. 26.

30. L. Dorez, *La cour du pape Paolo III d'après les registres de la Trésorerie secrète*, vol. 2: *Les déspenses privées* (Paris: Librairie Ernest Leroux, 1932).

31. F. E. Keller, "Residenze estive e 'ville' per la corte farnesiana nel viterbese nel '500," in *I Farnese dalla Tuscia Romana alle corti d'Europa*, conference proceedings (Caprarola, 1983), p. 69.

32. For an overview of the topic, see Keller, *Residenze estive*, pp. 67–104.

33. L. Pastor, *Storia dei papi* (Rome: Desclée & C editori, 1925), vol. 6.

34. The villa, the first in the Frascati territory, was built by Monsignor Alessandro Rufini beginning in 1548 as part of the reconstruction of the city promoted by Paul III Farnese. On the villa, see A. Tantillo Mignosi, ed., *Villa e Paese. Dimore nobili del Tuscolo e di Marino* (Rome: De Luca Editore, 1980), pp. 82–104; M. B. Guerrieri Borsoi, *Villa Rufina Falconieri. La rinascita di Frascati e la più antica dimora tuscolana* (Rome: Gangemi Editore, 2008).

35. There is no exhaustive study to date on the villa, so the reader is referred to the most interesting essays: Coffin, *The Life*, pp. 150–74; I. Belli Barsali, *Ville di Roma* (Milan: Rusconi, 1983), pp. 170–87; M. Azzi Visentini, *La Villa in Italia. Quattrocento e Cinquecento* (Milan: Electa, 1999), pp. 159–72, with extensive bibliography.

36. Both citations are in C. Zaccagnini, *Le Ville di Roma* (Rome: Newton Compton, 1976), pp. 94–96.

37. The fact that funds from the Reverenda Camera Apostolica were used to build the villa led to its immediate reacquisition on the part of the new pope, even though it had been put—albeit after construction—in the name of the pope's nephew, Baldovino dal Monte. Already during the construction of the Casina of Pius IV many precious marbles were taken from the villa and reused; subsequently, in the new climate of the Counter-Reformation, the villa seemed too overtly luxurious and pagan to be appreciated.

38. See Chapter Four.

39. B. Taegio, *La Villa* (Milan: Francesco Moscheni, 1559), pp. 53–54.

40. Coffin, *The Life*, p. 36.

41. Ibid.

42. Ibid.

43. On the building, see Coffin, *The Life*, pp. 38–40; Belli Barsali, *Ville*, pp. 375–77; and C. Benocci, "Il Casaletto di S. Pio V sulla via Aurelia Antica, emblema romano della cultura della controriforma trasformata in delizia settecentesca chigiana," in C. Benocci, ed., *I Giardini Chigi tra Siena e Roma dal Cinquecento agli inizi dell'Ottocento* (Siena: Fondazione Monte dei Paschi di Siena, Protagon Editori, 2005), pp. 317–50, which deals mostly with the subsequent transformations.

44. I.A.F. Orban, *Documenti sul barocco a Roma* (Perugia: Unione Tipografica Cooperativa, 1920), pp. 69, 72.

45. Tantillo Mignosi, *Villa e Paese*, pp. 11–14.

46. Tantillo Mignosi, *Villa e Paese*, pp. 15–16.

47. F. Grossi Gondi, *Le ville tuscolane nell'epoca classica e dopo il Rinascimento. La Villa dei Quintili e la Villa di Mondragone* (Rome: Unione Cooperativa Editrice, 1901), pp. 60, 215.

48. Tantillo Mignosi, *Villa e Paese*, pp. 14–15, 17.

49. Ibid., p. 109.

50. Coffin, *The Villa*, p. 58, reprints the "avvisi" previously published by Grossi Gondi.

51. Pastor, *Storia*, vol. 9, pp. 842–43.

52. For an overall picture of the events surrounding the development of the residence, see the volume AA.VV., *Il Palazzo del Quirinale. La storia, le sale e le collezioni* (Bologna: Franco Maria Ricci, 2006). For the history of the gardens, see Belli Barsali, *Ville*, pp. 296–307.

53. For a picture of the cardinals' residences see M. B. Guerrieri Borsoi, "Ville e Villeggiature a Frascati nel 1600," in *La corte pontificia nel Tuscolano*, Quaderni delle Scuderie Aldobrandini per l'Arte (Avellino: De Angelis Editore, 2002), pp. 23–34.

54. On the villa, see C. D'Onofrio, *La villa Aldobrandini a Frascati* (Rome: Staderini, 1963); I. Belli Barsali and M. G. Branchetti, *Ville della campagna romana* (Milan: Rusconi, 1975), pp. 178–95; Mignosi Tantillo, *Villa*, pp. 164–78.

55. Cited in Mignosi Tantillo, *Villa*, p. 21.

56. On the Villa Borghese, also called "Pinciana" because of its position on the Colle del Pincio, see A. Campitelli, *Villa Borghese. Da giardino del principe a parco dei Romani* (Rome: Istituto Poligrafico e Zecca dello Stato, 2003).

57. For an overall picture of the Borghese residences, see A. Campitelli, "Il sistema residenziale del cardinal Scipione Borghese tra Roma e i colli Tuscolani," in M. Bevilacqua and M. L. Madonna, *Residenze nobiliari. Stato Pontificio e Granducato di Toscana* (Rome: De Luca Editori d'arte, 2003), pp. 63–74.

58. F. Cancellieri, *Lettera sopra il tarantismo, l'aria di Roma, e della sua campagna, ed i palazzi pontifici entro, e fuori Roma, con le notizie di Castel Gandolfo, e de' paesi circonvicini* (Rome: Bourliè, 1817), p. 106; C. Fea, *Compendio di ragioni per l'illustrissima città di Frascati* (Rome: Stamperia della Reverenda Camera Apostolica, 1830), p. 6.

59. For a reconstruction of the banquets of Paul V in Frascati and, in general, of the banquets in the villas around Rome, see A. Campitelli, "Rinfreschi e delizie nel giardino," in J. Di Schino, ed., *I Fasti del Banch-*

etto Barocco (Rome: Diomeda, 2005), pp. 73–82.

60. An idea of the network of residences in the Roman area, commissioned by the popes and noblemen, is in the exhibition catalogue by A. Mignosi Tantillo, ed., *L'arte per i papi e per i principi nella campagna romana. Grande pittura del '600 e del '700* (Rome: Quasar, 1990).

61. All of the papal sojourns from 1626 to 1952 are accurately registered in the fine volume dedicated to Castel Gandolfo by E. Bonomelli, *I papi in campagna* (Rome: Gherardo Casini Editore, 1953). Bonomelli was the curator of the Villa Pontificia di Castel Gandolfo and therefore had full knowledge of the events.

62. This brief overview is a preview of a more comprehensive study of the complex, planned for a future, undetermined date. It is impossible to complete the study at the present time because the closure of the Biblioteca Apostolica Vaticana makes the Archivio Barberini, where many unpublished documents on the villa are held, inaccessible.

63. A complete study of the Villa Pontificia has not yet been done, and so the reader is referred to Bonomelli, *I papi*; Belli Barsali and Branchetti, *Ville*, 255–57; for the eighteenth-century history of the Palazzo, M. De Angelis, *Il Palazzo Apostolico di Castel Gandolfo al tempo di Benedetto XIV (1740–1758). Pitture e arredi* (Rome: De Luca, 2008), which contains an ample bibliography. On the sojourns of Urban VIII, see also G. Tomassetti, *La Campagna Romana antica, medievale e moderna*, updated edition, ed. L. Chiumenti and F. Bilancia (Florence: L. Olschki, 1979–1980), vol. 2, pp. 223–25.

64. Cancellieri, *Lettera*, p. 106.

65. G. Moroni, *Dizionario di erudizione storico-ecclesiastica da San Pietro sino ai nostri giorni* (Venice: Tipografia Emiliana, 1840–1879), vol. 10 (1841), p. 159.

66. F. Bonanni, *Numismata Summarum Pontificum Templi Vaticani fabricam indicantia, Typis Domenica Antonimi Herculis,* (Rome: 1696), vol. 2, p. 594.

67. On the decorative elements, see A. Lo Bianco, "Castel Gandolfo. Il Palazzo e la Villa Barberini," in Mignosi Tantillo, *Villa*, pp. 263–73.

68. M. Fagiolo and M. Fagiolo dell'Arco, *Bernini. Una introduzione al gran teatro del barocco* (Rome: Bulzoni, 1967), entry 186. The inscription reads: ALEXANDER VII PONTIFEX MAX. AEDES AB URBANO VIII / OB COELI SOLIQUE SALUBRITATEM AMOENITATAMQUE / ANIMI CORPORIQUE BREVI SECESSU REFICIENDIS / POSITAS AMPLIAVIT INSTRUXIT ABSOLVIT AN. S. MDCLX (In the year of Salva-

tion 1660, Pope Alexander VII expanded, built, and completed the palace set up by Urban VIII on account of the healthfulness and pleasantness of the sky and sun, and in order to restore the mind and body with a brief retreat). Alexander VII also commissioned Bernini to design the church of San Tommaso da Villanova in Castel Gandolfo.

69. ASV, Sacri Palazzi Apostolici, Amministrazione 6, b.1, f. 1, the document is dated December 30, 1660. The snow pits were underground. Pressed snow was accumulated in them during the winter and used to prepare sorbets in the summertime.

70. Bonomelli, *I papi*, pp. 72–73.

71. ASR, Sacri Palazzi Apostolici, Computisteria, b.496, year 1674, f. 114 and f. 365.

72. ASR, Sacri Palazzi Apostolici, Computisteria, b.497, year 1675, f. 25, f. 253, and f. 543.

73. ASR, Sacri Palazzi Apostolici, Computisteria, b.498, year 1676, f. 217.

74. Bonomelli, *I papi*, p. 481. The work carried out is documented in detail in De Angelis, *Il Palazzo*, pp. 26–32.

75. De Angelis, *Il Palazzo*.

76. Moroni, *Dizionario*, p. 165.

77. The undertakings of Pope Ganganelli are commemorated in a marble inscription set up in front of the main entrance of the Apostolic Palace, and reads: CLEMENS XIV P.M. / AD COMMODIOREM PONTIFICIAM RUSTICATIONEM / HAS AEDES NOVA ACCESSIONE AUXIT / PROXIMAM VILLAM HORTOSQUE AMOENISSIMOS COMPARAVIT / PER MONTIS CLIVUM LENIOREM VIAM APERUIT / ANNO MDCCXXIV PONTIFICATUS SUI QUINTO (In the year 1824, the fifth year of his pontificate, Pope Clement XIV, for a more comfortable papal country retreat, expanded this residence with a new entrance, purchased the nearby villa and most pleasant gardens, and opened a gentler road up the slope of the mountain).

78. On the cardinal, see the entry by A. Borromeo in *Dizionario Biografico degli Italiani*, vol. 25, 1981, pp. 233–37, based on his autobiography, held in the Biblioteca Nazionale Vittorio Emanuele II, Rome, mss. Gesuitici, 95–104.

79. ASV, Archivio Cybo, b. 1, Arm. C, prot. XIV, f. 3, p. 206v. The manuscript contains a summary of the events surrounding the acquisition and of the completed work.

80. For information about the architect, the son of the much more renowned Carlo (1638–1714), see C. Contardi and G. Curcio, *In Urbe architectus* (Rome: Argos, 1991), pp. 373–75.

81. ASV, Archivio Cybo, b. 1, Arm. C, prot. XIV, f. 3, p. 206v.

82. Mauro (1701–1776) was also an architect. See Contardi, Curcio, *In Urbe*, pp. 374–75.

83. ASV, Archivio Cybo, b. 21 f. 7, acquisition agreement of the Casino Fontana stipulated by the notaries Capitolini Mancinelli and Senapa.

84. ASV, Archivio Cybo, b. 1 Arm. C., prot. XIV, p. 388, acquisition agreement for the land stipulated by the notary Capitolino Mancinelli on June 2, 1718, with an estimate by the architect Carlo Stefano Fontana.

85. ASV, Archivio Cybo, b. 1 Arm. C, prot. XIV, p. 350.

86. The *ragnaia* was a structure for the hunt, very popular in Tuscany, consisting of a series of tunnels formed of oaks and other trees with berries, to which birds were attracted. The tunnels were then closed with nets (the *ragne*, or webs), so the birds could be captured easily.

87. Some information on the villa and the notary documents referred to are published in A. Antinori, "Francesco e Bartolomeo Pincellotti: una ricostruzione del catalogo con nuove attribuzione nel contesto di imprese architettoniche per Camillo Cybo (la Villa di Castel Gandolfo e lo scomparso Oratorio dei Santi Angeli Custodi)," in E. Debenedetti, ed., *Sculture romane del Settecento, III. La professione dello scultore* (Rome: Bonsignori Editore, 2003), pp. 233–70. See also the entry by A. Roca de Amicis in B. Azzaro, M. Bevilacqua, G. Coccioli, A. Roca de Amicis, ed., *Atlante del Barocco in Italia, Lazio, I, Provincia di Roma* (Rome: De Luca Editori, 2002), p. 100.

88. For information on the architect, nephew of Carlo Fontana, see Contardi, Curcio, *In Urbe*, p. 372, where, however, the work at Villa Cybo is not mentioned, because it remains unpublished to this day.

89. ASV, Archivio Cybo, b. 21, f. 8.

90. The drawings were published by A. Antinori in "Francesco e Bartolomeo Pincellotti," whom I thank for giving me the reproductions, as in the Archivio di Stato di Roma, where they are held, they cannot be accessed at this time.

91. ASV, Archivio Cybo, b. 1, Arm. C., prot. XIV, p. 360.

92. ASV, Archivio Cybo, b. 21, p. 209.

93. ASR, Archivio Cybo, b. 4, n. 5, "Estimate of all of the marbles taken from Massa Carrara and brought to Castel Gandolfo" dated August 7, 1733. On this topic, see P. Ceccopieri Maruffi, I marmi dei Cybo da Massa al Quirinale, Aedes Muratoriana, Modena, 1985, pp. 59–76.

94. The acquisition was stipulated by the notary Monti on December 22 , 1772, see Bonomelli, *I papi*, p. 169, note 56.

95. Ibid., p. 160.

96. Ibid., p. 163.

97. ASV, Amministrazione VI, b. 4, f. 3. Among the documents is a fine description that will be published in the future.

98. Ibid., b. 5, f. 1.

99. All of the papal sojourns in Castel Gandolfo until 1952 are listed in detail in Bonomelli, *I papi*, pp. 481–83 and updated through the year 2000 in S. Petrillo, *Le Ville pontificie di Castel Gandolfo* (Vatican City: Edizioni Musei Vaticani, 2000), pp. 116–23.

100. Bonomelli, *I papi*, pp. 372 ff., who bases his work on documents in the Archivio Barberini, held in the Biblioteca Apostolica Vaticana, which, as previously noted, is currently closed to the public.

101. Ibid.

102. Ibid.

103. On his activity in the Vatican, see Chapter Eight.

104. A summary of the work undertaken can be found in Bonomelli, *I papi*, pp. 390–96, and there is a fine photo essay in Petrillo, *Le Ville*.

105. This is the theory of Giacomo Boni, the archaeologist and author of the reorganization of the Palatine in Rome, whose work was inspired by this concept. On the same subject, see V. Cazzato, "Giacomo Boni: flora e 'ruine,'" in G. Morganti, ed., *Gli Orti Farnesiani sul Palatino* (Rome: L'Erma di Bretschneider, 1990), pp. 605–26.

Bibliography

[Various authors.] *Federico Cesi: convegno celebrativo del IV centenario della nascita.* Rome: Accademia Nazionale dei Lincei, 1986.

———. *Il Palazzo del Quirinale. La storia, le sale e le collezioni.* Bologna, Italy: Franco Maria Ricci, 2006.

———. *Roma e il suo Orto Botanico. Storia ed eventi di un'istituzione scientifica.* Rome: Ed. Borgia, 1984.

Ackerman, J., "The Belvedere as a Classical Villa." *Journal of the Warburg and Courtald Institutes,* 14 (1951): 71–91.

———. *The Cortile del Belvedere.* Vatican City: Biblioteca Apostolica Vaticana, 1954.

———. *La Villa. Forma e ideologia.* Turin, Italy: Einaudi, 1992.

Adinolfi, P. *Roma nell'età di mezzo.* Rome: Fratelli Bocca Editori, 1881–82.

Aksamija, N., "Defining the Counter-Reformation Villa: Landscape and Sacredness in Late Renaissance 'Villeggiatura,'" in G. Venturi and F. Ceccarelli, *Delizie in Villa: il giardino rinascimentale e I suoi committenti,* pp. 33–63. Florence: Olschki, 2008.

Alberi, E., ed. *Relazioni degli Ambasciatori Veneti al Senato.* Florence: Società Editrice Fiorentina, 1858.

Albertini, F. *Opusculum de Mirabilibus novae Urbis Romae.* Rome: Jacobium Mazochium, 1510.

Aliberti Gaudioso, F., ed. *Gli affreschi di Paolo III a Castel Sant'Angelo.* Rome: De Luca, 1981.

Ambrosi De Magistris, R. *Il viaggio di Innocenzo III nel Lazio e il primo ospedale di Anagni.* Rome: *Tipografia* Poliglotta De Propaganda Fide, 1898.

Ancel, D. L. "Le Vatican sous Paul IV." *Revue Benedectine* 25 (1908): 47–71.

Anon Feliu, C., and J. L. Sancho. *Jardin y Naturaleza en el reinado de Felipe II.* Madrid: Ed. Doce Calles, 1998.

Arconti, A., and A. Campitelli, eds. *Il Museo Carlo Bilotti nell'Aranciera di Villa Borghese.* Milan: Electa, 2006.

Audot, L. E. *Notes sur les jardins du sud de l'Italie: recueillies pendant un voyage fait en 1839/40.* Paris: Bouchard-Huzard, 1840.

Azzi Visentini, M. *L'arte dei giardini. Scritti teorici e pratici dal XIV al XIX secolo.* Milan: Edizioni il Polifilo, 1999.

———. *La villa in Italia. Quattrocento e Cinquecento.* Milan: Electa, 1995.

Azzi Visentini, M., and A. Tagliolini, eds. *I Giardini delle Esperidi,* conference proceedings, Pietrasanta, 1995. Florence: Edifir, 1996.

Bacci, A. *Tabula simplicium medicamentum.* Rome: Josephum de Angelis, 1577.

Bagatti Valsecchi, P. F., and S. Langè. "La Villa. Cultura umanistica e nascita della villa come tipo codificato." In *Storia dell'arte italiana,* vol. 4 *Forme e modelli.* Part 3: *Situazioni momenti indagini,* edited by F. Zeri, pp. 363–70. Turin, Italy: Einaudi, 1982.

Bagliani, A. Paravicini. *Il corpo del papa.* Turin: Einaudi, 1994.

———. "La mobilità della Curia Romana nel secolo XIII: riflessi locali." In *Società e istituzioni dell'Italia Comunale: l'esempio di Perugia (secoli XII–XIV),* international historical convention, Perugia, 1985. Perugia: 1988.

———. *La vita quotidiana alla corte dei papi nel Duecento.* Bari: Laterza, 1996.

Baldassarri, P. *Relazione delle avversità e patimenti del glorioso papa Pio VI,* 2 vols. Rome: Tipografia Poliglotta, 1889.

Baldriga, I. *L'occhio della Lince, I primi lincei tra arte, scienza e collezionismo (1603–1630).* Rome: Accademia Nazionale dei Lincei, 2002.

Barberini, M. G. "Il palazzo di Venezia e il suo viridario: un edificio e le sue metamorfosi." In *Il '400 a Roma: la rinascita delle arti da Donatello a Pinturicchio,* exhibition catalogue, edited by M. G. Bernardini, pp. 27–35. Milan: Skira, 2008.

Barisi, I., M. Fagiolo, and M. L. Madonna. *Villa d'Este.* Rome: De Luca, 2004.

Belli Barsali, I. *Ville di Roma.* Milan: Rusconi, 1982.

Belli Barsali, I., and M. G. Branchetti. *Ville della campagna romana.* Milan: Rusconi, 1975.

Bellini, A. "Luca Beltrami architetto della Fabbrica di San Pietro." In *Quaderni dell'Istituto di Storia dell'Architettura,* 25–30 (1995–97): 395–408.

Beltrami, L. "Martino Ferrabosco architetto." In *L'Arte* 29 (1926): 1–15.

Benedetti, S. "L'architettura di Domenico Fontana." In *Sisto V, vol. 1: Roma e il Lazio,* edited by M. Fagiolo and M. L. Madonna, pp. 397–417. Rome: Istituto Poligrafico e Zecca dello Stato, 1992.

Benocci, C. "Il Casaletto di S. Pio V sulla via Aurelia Antica, emblema romano della cultura della controriforma trasformata in delizia settecentesca chigiana." In *I Giardini Chigi tra Siena e Roma dal Cinquecento agli inizi dell'Ottocento,* edited by C. Benocci, pp. 317–35. Fondazione Monte dei Paschi di Siena. Siena, Italy: Protagon Editori, 2005.

———. *Villa Aldobrandini a Montemagnanapoli.* Rome: Argos, 1992.

Benocci, C., ed. *I giardini Chigi tra Siena e Roma dal Cinquecento agli inizi dell'Ottocento.* Fondazione Monte dei Paschi di Siena. Siena: Protagon Editori, 2005.

———. *Villa Pamphilj.* Rome: Art Color Printing, 2005.

Berra, L. *L'Accademia delle Notti Vaticane fondata da S. Carlo Borromeo. Con tre appendici di documenti.* Rome: M. Bretschneider, 1915.

Bevilacqua, M. *Roma nel secolo dei lumi. Architettura erudizione scienza nella pianta di G. B. Nolli "celebre geometra."* Naples: Electa, 1998.

Biancastella, A. *L'Erbario di Ulisse Aldrovandi. Natura arte e scienza in un tesoro del Rinascimento.* Milan: Federico Motta Editore, 2003.

Blair MacDougall, E. *Fountains, Statues, and Flowers: Studies in Italian Gardens of the Sixteenth and Seventeenth Centuries.* Washington, D.C.: Dumbarton Oaks Research Library and Collection, 1994.

Boccaccio, Giovanni. *Decameron,* edited by E. Branca. Turin: Einaudi, 1980.

Bonanni, F. *Numismata Summarum Pontificum Templi vaticani fabricam indicantia.* Rome: Typis Domenici Antonini Herculis, 1696.

Bonomelli, Emilio. *I papi in campagna.* Rome: Gherardo Casini Editore, 1953.

Bouchet, J. *La villa Pia des jardins du Vatican.* Paris: Cousin, 1837.

Bracci Fratadocchi, M., ed. *Erbe e speziali. I laboratori della salute,* exhibition catalogue. Sansepolcro: Aboca Museum, 2007.

Bragaglia Venuti, C. "L'antichità moralizzata di Pirro Logorio nella Loggia di Pio IV: quelle immagini 'profane di dei gentili' che 'havendole conosciute tutte possono essere tirate a gloria del Salvator nostro.'" In *Rivista di Storia della Chiesa in Italia* 53 (1999): 39–82.

Branchetti, M. G., and G. Cornini, eds. *Mosaici minuti romani del '700 e dell '800,* exhibition catalogue. Rome: L'Accademia Nazionale di San Luca, 1986.

Broccoli, U., and A. Pellegrino. *Castello di Giulio II a Ostia antica.* Rome: Tipografia Centenari, Rome, n.d.

Brummer, H. H. *The Statue Court in the Vatican Belvedere.* Stockholm: Almqvist & Wiksell, 1970.

Bruschi, A. *Bramante architetto.* Bari: Laterza, 1969.

Buranelli, F., P. Liverani, and A. Nesselrath. *Laocoonte. Alle origini dei Musei Vaticani,* exhibition catalogue. Rome: L'Erma di Bretschneider, 2006.

Burchard, J. *Liber Notarum ab anno MCCCCLXXXIII usque ad annum MDVI*, edited by E. Celani. Città di Castello, Italy: Editore S. Lapi, 1910.

Bzovius (Brzowski), A. *Paulus Quintus Burghesius P.O.M.* Rome: Stephani Paulini, 1624.

Campitelli, A. "Agostino e Bernardino Radi: due protagonisti dei cantieri berniniani." In *Bernini dai Borghese ai Barberini. La cultura a Roma intorno agli anni venti*, edited by O. Bonfait and A. Coliva, pp. 105–13. Rome: De Luca, 2004.

———. I cocchi di agrumi nelle ville romane." In *Gli orti delle Esperidi*, conference proceedings, Pietrasanta, 1995, edited by M. Azzi Visentini and A. Tagliolini, pp. 175–96. Florence: Edifir, 1996.

———. "Gli Horti di Flora nella Roma dei Barberini." In *I Barberini e la cultura del tempo*, international study conference proceedings, Rome, 2005, edited by Mochi Onori, Schultze, and Solinas, pp. 571–80. Rome: De Luca, 2007.

———. "Novae Plantae Antiquis Hortis: Continuity and Innovation in the Roman Villas in the Eighteenth and Nineteenth Centuries." In *Studies in the History of Gardens and Designed Landscapes* 23, no. 1 (2003): 22–41.

———. "Il sistema residenziale del cardinale Scipione Borghese tra Roma e i colli tuscolani." In *Residenze nobiliari barocche*, edited by M. Bevilacqua and M. L. Madonna, pp. 63–74. Rome: De Luca, 2003.

———. *Villa Borghese. Da giardino del principe a parco dei Romani*. Rome: Istituto Poligrafico e Zecca dello Stato, 2003.

Campitelli, A., and A. Costamagna. *Villa Borghese. L'Uccelliera, la Meridiana, i Giardini Segreti*. Rome: Gebart, 2005.

Cancellieri, F. *Lettera sopra il tarantismo, l'aria di Roma, e della sua campagna, ed i palazzi pontifici entro, e fuori Roma, con le notizie di Castel Gandolfo, e de' paesi circonvicini*. Rome: Bourliè, 1817.

Canensi, M. *Le vite di Paolo II*, edited by G. Zippel. Città di Castello, Italy: Editore S. Lapi, 1904–11.

Caneva, G. *Il Mondo di Cerere nella Loggia di Psiche*. Rome: Palombi, 1992.

Cardini, F., and M. Miglio. *Nostalgia del paradiso. Il giardino medievale*. Bari: Laterza, 2002.

Caro, A. *De le Lettere familiari*, vol. I. Venice: Giunti, 1581.

Castelli, P. *Exactissima descriptio rariorum quorandorum plantarum quae continentur Romae in Horto Farnesiano rariores plantae*

exactissimae descriptae. Rome: Mascardi, 1625.

Castiglione, B. *Lettere del conte Baldessar Castiglione*, edited by P. Serassi. Padua: G. Comino, 1769.

Catalano, M., and E. Pellegrini. *L'Orto Botanico di Roma*, with historical introduction by C. D'Onofrio. Rome: Palombi, 1975.

Cavallaro, A. *La Villa dei Papi alla Magliana*. Rome: Istituto Poligrafico e Zecca dello Stato, 2005.

Cavallaro, A., ed. *Collezioni di antichità a Roma fra '400 e '500*. Rome: De Luca Editori d'Arte, 2007.

Cazzato, V. "Giacomo Boni: flora e 'ruine.'" In *Gli Orti Farnesiani sul Palatino*, edited by G. Morganti, pp. 605–26. Rome: L'Erma di Bretschneider, 1990.

———. *Atlante del giardino italiano 1750–1940. Dizionario biografico di architetti, giardinieri, botanici, committenti, letterati e altri protagonisti*, vol. I: *Northern Italy*, vol. II: *Central and Southern Italy*. Rome: Istituto Poligrafico e Zecca Dello Stato, 2009.

———. *Ville e Giardini italiani. I disegni di architetti e paesaggisti dell'American Academy in Rome*. Rome: Istituto Poligrafico e Zecca dello Stato, 2004.

———. *La Memoria, il Tempo, la Storia nel giardino italiano fra '800 e '900*. Rome: Istituto Poligrafico e Zecca dello Stato, 1999.

Cazzato, V., M. A. Giusti, and M. Fagiolo, eds. *Atlante delle grotte e dei ninfei in Italia. Toscana, Lazio, Italia meridionale e isole*. Milan: Electa, 2001.

Cecchelli, C. *Il Vaticano: la basilica, i palazzi, i giardini*. Milan and Rome: Tuminelli, 1926.

Chastel, A. *Il Sacco di Roma. 1527*. Turin: Einaudi, 1983.

Chattard, G. P. *Nuova descrizione del Vaticano, o sia Della Sacrosanta Basilica di S. Pietro*, 3 vols. Rome: Barbiellini, 1762–67.

Cima, M., and E. Talamo. *Horti Romani*. Milan: Electa, 2008.

Coffin, D. R. *Gardens and Gardening in Papal Rome*. Princeton: Princeton University Press, 1991.

———. *Pirro Ligorio: The Renaissance Artist, Architect and Antiquarian*. Philadelphia: University of Pennsylvania Press, 2003.

———. "Pope Innocent VIII and the Villa Belvedere." In *Studies in Late Medieval and Renaissance Painting in Honor of Millard Meiss*, edited by I. Lavin and J. Plummer. New York: New York University Press, 1977.

———. *The Villa in the Life of Renaissance Rome*. Princeton: Princeton University Press, 1979.

Colonna, F. *Hypnerotomachia Poliphili, ubi humana omnia non nisi somnium esse docet*. In *Aedibus Aldi Manutii*. Venice, 1499.

Connors, J., and L. Rice. *Specchio di Roma barocca. Una guida inedita del XVII secolo*. Rome: Edizioni dell'Elefante, 1990.

Contardi, B., and G. Curcio, eds. *In Urbe architectus: modelli, disegni, misure; la professione dell'architetto, Roma 1680–1750*. Rome: Argos, 1991.

Corbo, A. M. *I mestieri nella vita quotidiana alla corte di Niccolò V (1447–1455)*. Rome: Edilazio, 1998.

Corbo, A. M., and M. Pomponi. *Fonti per la storia artistica romana al tempo di Paolo V*. Rome: Istituto Poligrafico e Zecca dello Stato, 1995.

Cortonesi, A., "Il Giardino del papa. Pratiche agricole e lavoro salariato nella Roma di fine Duecento." In *Scritti in memoria di Giuseppe Marchetti Longhi*, vol. I, pp. 129–30. Anagni, Italy: "Biblioteca di Latium," 1990.

Danesi Squarzina, S., and G. Borghini. *Il Borgo di Ostia da Sisto IV a Giulio II*, exhibition catalogue. Rome: De Luca Editori, 1980.

De Angelis, M. *Il Palazzo Apostolico di Castel Gandolfo al tempo di Benedetto XIV (1740–1758). Pitture e arredi*. Rome: De Luca, 2008.

Danesi Squarzina, S., ed., *Roma centro ideale della cultura dell'antico nei secoli XV e XVI: da Martino V al Sacco di Roma 1417–1527*, conference proceedings. Milan: Electa, 1989.

De Angelis, M. "La Torre di Paolo III in Campidoglio: un'opera demolita di Jacopo Meleghino, architetto alla corte del Papa Farnese." In *Edilizia Militare* 8 (1987), nos. 21–22.

De Beer, E. S., ed. *The Diary of John Evelyn*. Oxford: Clarendon Press, 1955.

De Fabris, G. *Il piedistallo della Colonna Antonina per munificenza della Santità di Nostro Signore Papa Gregorio XVI felicemente regnante collocato nel giardino della Pigna al Vaticano / brevemente descritto e ristaurato*. Rome: Monaldi, 1846.

De Dominicis, C. "Immigrazione a Roma dopo il sacco del 1527 (1531–1549)." *Archivio della società romana di storia patria* 109 (1986).

Delfini Filippi, G. *Pontificia Accademia delle Scienze. La sede*, Introduction by C. Pietrangeli. Vatican City: Pontificia Accademia delle Scienze, 1986.

Del Piazzo, M. *Ragguagli borrominiani*. Rome: Stabilimento Arti Grafiche Palombi, 1968.

De Maio, R. *Alfonso Carafa, cardinale di Napoli (1540–1565)*. Vatican City: Biblioteca Apostolica Vaticana, 1961.

Devoti, L. *La Villa Aldobrandini di Frascati.* Velletri: Edizioni Tra 8 & 9, 1990.

Di Schino, J., ed. *I Fasti del Banchetto Barocco.* Rome: Diomeda, 2005.

D'Onofrio, C. *Acque e Fontane di Roma.* Rome: Staderini, 1977.

———. *Le Fontane di Roma.* Rome: Romana Società Editrice, 1986.

———. *Roma vista da Roma.* Rome: Edizioni Liber, 1967.

———. *La villa Aldobrandini a Frascati.* Rome: Staderini, 1963.

Dorez, L. *La cour du pape Paul III d'après les registres de la Tesorerie secrète*, vol. 2. Paris: Les déspenses privées, Librerie Ernest Leroux, 1932.

Duchesne, L., ed. *Liber Pontificalis.* Paris: E. de Boccard, 1886–92.

Durante, C. *Herbario Nuovo.* Rome: Stamperia di Bartholomeo Bonfadino & Tito Diani, 1585.

Dykmans, M. "Du Monte Mario à l'escalier de Saint Pierre de Rome." *Mélanges d'archéologie et d'histoire 80* (1968): 547–94.

Ehrle, F. *La grande veduta di Maggi e Mascardi, (1615) del Tempio e del Palazzo vaticano.* Rome: Tipografia Poliglotta Vaticana, 1914.

Ehrle, F., and H. Egger. *Studi e documenti per la storia del Palazzo Apostolico Vaticano.* Vatican City: Biblioteca Apostolica Vaticana, 1935.

Faber, J. *De Nardo et Epithymo.* Rome: Facciotti, 1607.

Fagiolo dell'Arco, M., ed., *L'arte dei papi.* Milan: Mondadori, 1982.

Fagiolo, M. *La festa a Roma dal Rinascimento al 1870*, exhibition catalogue. Turin: Allemandi, 1997.

———. "I giardini papali del Vaticano e del Quirinale." In *Giardini Regali*, edited by M. Amari, pp. 67–80. Milan: Electa, 1998.

———. "La nave della Chiesa: dalla barca di Pietro alla Chiesa come nave." In *La preghiera del marinaio. La fede e il mare nei segni della Chiesa e nelle tradizioni marinare*, exhibition catalogue, edited by A. Mondadori, pp. 267–80. Rome: Mondadori, 1992.

———. "Il pellegrinaggio a Roma. Strutture e simboli nella città degli Anni Santi." In *Roma dei grandi viaggiatori*, edited by F. Paloscia, pp. 40–45. Rome: Edizioni Abete, 1987.

———. *Roma delle delizie. I teatri dell'acqua, grotte, ninfei, fontane.* Milan: Franco Maria Ricci, 1990.

———. "Il significato dell'acqua e la dialettica del giardino. Pirro Ligorio e la 'filosofia' della villa cinquecentesca." In *Natura e artificio*, edited by M. Fagiolo, pp. 176–87. Rome: Officina edizioni, 1981.

———. "Trionfi delle acque sacre nel Cinquecento." In *Lo Specchio del Paradiso. Il Giardino e il sacro dall'Antico all'Ottocento.* M. Fagiolo, and M. A. Giusti, pp. 92–96. Cinisello Balsamo, Italy: Silvana Editoriale, 1998.

———. *Vignola. L'architettura dei principi.* Rome: Gangemi Editore, 2007.

Fagiolo, M., and M. Fagiolo dell'Arco. *Bernini. Una introduzione al gran teatro del barocco.* Rome: Bulzoni, 1967.

———. "Villa Aldobrandini tuscolana: percorso, allegoria, capricci." In *Quaderni Istituto di Storia dell'Architettura* 11 (1964): 61–92.

Fagiolo, M., and M. A. Giusti. *Lo specchio del paradiso. Il giardino e il sacro dall'antico al Novecento.* Cinisello Balsamo: Silvana editoriale, 1998.

Fagiolo, M., and M. A. Giusti. *Lo specchio del paradiso. L'immagine del giardino dall'antico al Novecento.* Cinisello Balsamo, Italy: Silvana Editoriale, 1996.

Fagiolo, M., and M. L. Madonna. "La Casina di Pio IV in Vaticano. Pirro Ligorio e l'architettura come geroglifico." In *Storia dell'arte* nos.15–16 (1972): 237 ff.

———. "La contesa dell'Aria e dell'Acqua: il tema degli elementi nel teatro e nel giardino fra manierismo e barocco." In *Les éléments et les métamorphoses de la nature: imaginaire et symboliques des arts dans la culture européenne du XVIe au XVIIIe siècle*, vol. 4 of *Annales du Centre Ledoux.* Bourdeaux: William Blake & Co., 1994.

———. "La Roma di Pio IV: La 'Civitas Pia,' la 'Salus medica,' la 'Custodia angelica.'" In *Arte Illustrata* no. 51 (1972): 384–85.

———. *Baldassarre Peruzzi: pittura, scena e architettura nel Cinquecento.* Rome: Istituto della Enciclopedia Italiana, 1987.

———. *Roma 1300–1875: la città degli anni santi.* Milan: Mondadori, 1984.

Falda, G. B. *Le Fontane di Roma e del Tuscolo*, 1676. Reprint, Rome: Edizioni Editalia, 1965.

———. *Li giardini di Roma.* Rome: G. G. de Rossi, 1676.

Fea, C. *Compendio di ragioni per l'illustrissima città di Frascati.* Rome: Stamperia della Reverenda Camera Apostolica, 1830.

Ferrari, G. B. *Flora, overo cultura dei fiori.* Rome: Facciotti, 1638.

———. *Hesperides, sive de malorum aureorum cultura et usu.* Rome: H. Scheus, 1644.

Fanceschini, M., E. Mori, and M. Vendittelli. *Torre in Pietra, vicende storiche, architettoniche, artistiche di un insediamento della campagna romana dal medioevo all'età moderna.* Rome: Viella, 1994.

Freedberg, D. *The Eye of the Lynx: Galileo, His Friend, and the Beginnings of Modern Natural History.* Chicago and London: University of Chicago Press, 2002.

Friedlaender, W. *Das Kasino Pius des Vierte.* Leipzig: Hiersemann, 1912.

Frommel, C. L. *Architettura alla corte papale nel Rinascimento.* Milan: Electa, 2003.

———. "Giulio II, Bramante e il Cortile di Belvedere." In *L'Europa e l'arte italiana*, edited by M. Seidel, pp. 210–19. Venice: Marsilio, 2000.

———. "Raffaello e il teatro alla corte di Leone X." In *Bollettino del Centro Internazionale di Studi di architettura Andrea Palladio* 16 (1974): 173–88.

———. "I tre progetti bramanteschi per il Cortile del Belvedere." In *Il Cortile delle Statue: der statuenhof des Belvedere im Vatikan*, edited by M. Winner, B. Andree, and C. Pietrangeli, pp. 16–66. Mainz, Germany: von Zabern, 1998.

———. "La Villa e i Giardini del Quirinale nel Cinquecento." In *Restauri al Quirinale*, special volume of the *Bollettino d'Arte* (1999): 15–62.

———. "Villa Lante e Tommaso Ghinucci." In *Villa Lante a Bagnaia*, edited by S. Frommel, pp. 79–93. Milan: Electa, 2005.

Frommel, C. L., S. Ray, and M. Tafuri. *Raffaello architetto*, exhibition catalogue. Milan: Electa, 1984.

Frutaz, A. P. *Le Piante di Roma.* Rome: Istituto di Studi Romani, 1962.

———. *Piante e vedute di Roma e del Vaticano dal 1300 al 1676.* Vatican City: Biblioteca Apostolica Vaticana, 1956.

———. *Il Torrione di Niccolò V in Vaticano.* Vatican City: Tipografia Poliglotta Vaticana, 1956.

Fulvio, A. *Antiquitates Urbis*, 1527. Reprint, Florence: Silber, 1968.

Gabrieli, G. *Contributi alla storia dell'Accademia dei Lincei.* Rome: Accademia Nazionale dei Lincei, 1989.

Garbari, F., L. Tongiorgi Tomasi, and A. Tosi. *Giardino dei Semplici.* Pisa: Edizioni Press, Università di Pisa, 2002.

Gilii, F. L., and G. Suarez. *Osservazioni Fitologiche sopra alcune piante esotiche introdotte in Roma fatte nell'anno 1790.* Rome: Stamperia Giunchiana, 1792.

Giusti, M. A., Tagliolini, A., ed., *Il giardino delle muse: arti e artifici nel barocco europeo*, conference proceedings. Florence: Edifir, 1995.

Giustiniani, V., *Discorsi sulle arti e sui mestieri*, A. Banti, ed. Florence: Sansoni, 1981.

Goldgar, A., *Tulipmania: Money, Honor, and Knowledge in the Dutch Golden Age*. Chicago: University of Chicago Press, 2007.

Gombrich, E. H. *Immagini simboliche. Studi sull'arte del Rinascimento*. Turin: Einaudi, 1978.

Gothein, M. L. *Storia dell'Arte dei Giardini*. Italian edition edited by M. de Vico Fallani and M. Bencivenni. Florence: Leo S. Olschki, 2006.

Grassi, P. *Il Diario di Leone x*, edited by P. Delicati and M. Armellini. Rome: Tipografia della Pace, 1884.

Grossi Gondi, F. *Le ville tuscolane nell'epoca classica e dopo il Rinascimento. La Villa dei Quintili e la Villa di Mondragone*. Rome: Unione Cooperativa Editrice, 1901.

Guerrieri Borsoi, M. B. *Gli Strozzi a Roma. Mecenati e collezionisti nel Sei e Settecento*. Rome: Editore Colombo, 2004.

———. "Ville e Villeggiature a Frascati nel 1600." In *La corte pontificia nel Tuscolano*. Quaderni delle Scuderie Aldobrandini per l'Arte, pp. 23–34. Avellino, Italy: De Angelis Editore, 2002.

———. *Villa Rufina Falconieri. La rinascita di Frascati e la più antica dimora tuscolana*. Rome: Gangemi Editore, 2008.

Guglielmotti, A. *Storia della marina pontificia*. Rome: Tipografia Vaticana, 1886–93.

Guidoni, E. "La ricostruzione di Frascati voluta da Paolo III ad opera di Jacopo Meleghino." In *Il Tesoro delle Città*. Strenna dell'Associazione Storia della Città, Year 2, pp. 296–306. Rome: Edizioni Kappa, 2004.

Heimburger Ravalli, M. *Disegni di giardini e opere minori di Francesco Bettini*. Florence: Leo S. Olschki, 1981.

Hess, J. "La Biblioteca vaticana. Storia della costruzione." In *L'Illustrazione Vaticana*, 1938.

Hibbard, H., and I. Jaffe. "Bernini's Barcaccia." *Burlington Magazine*, no. 106 (1964), 159–60.

Impelluso, L. *Giardini orti labirinti*. Volume in Dizionari dell'arte series. Milan: Electa, 2005.

Infessura, S. *Diario della città di Roma*, edited by O. Tommasini. Rome: Tipografia del Senato, Forzani & C., 1890.

Innocenti, P. "La Pinacoteca vaticana nella storia della museografia: dalle origini al progetto di Luca Beltrami." In *Atti e Memorie dell'Accademia Clementina*, no. 40 (2000 [2001]), pp. 95–183.

Keller, F. E. "Meleghino Jacopo." In *The Dictionary of Art*, vol. 21. London: Grove, 1996.

———. "Residenze estive e 'ville' per la corte farnesiana nel viterbese nel '500." In *I Farnese dalla Tuscia Romana alle corti d'Europa*, congress proceedings, Caprarola, 1983.

Lafreri, A. *Speculum Romanae Magnificentiae*. 1559–1602. Reprint, Königstein im Taunus, Germany: Reiss & Sohn, 2002.

Lais, G. "I due Orti Botanici vaticani." In *Atti della Pontificia Accademia dei Nuovi Lincei* 32 (1878–79): 63–78.

Lanciani, R., *Storia degli scavi di Roma e notizie intorno le collezioni romane di antichità* (1902–1912), edited by L. Malvezzi Campeggi, 7 vols. Rome: Quasar, 1989–2002.

Lazzaro Bruno, C., *The Italian Renaissance Garden*. New Haven and London: Yale University Press, 1990.

Lefevre, R. *Villa Madama*. Rome: Editalia, 1973.

Letarouilly, P. M. *Edifices de Rome moderne*. London: Tiranti, 1929.

Levi D'Ancona, M., *The Garden of the Renaissance: Botanical Symbolism in Italian Paintings*. Florence: Olschki, 1977.

———. *L'Hortus conclusus nel Medioevo e nel Rinascimento*, in "Miniatura", 2, 1989, pp. 121-130

Levillain, P., and J. W. O'Malley. Entry on the mosaics of H. Lavagne. *The Papacy: An Encyclopedia*, p. 1022. New York and London: Routlege, 2002.

Liserre, F. R. *Grotte e Ninfei nel '500. Il modello dei giardini di Caprarola*. Rome: Gangemi Editore, 2008.

Liverani, P. "La Pigna Vaticana: note storiche." In *Bollettino dei Monumenti, Musei e Gallerie Pontificie*, no. 6 (1986): 51–63.

Losito, M. *La Casina Pio IV in Vaticano*. Vatican City: Pontificia Accademia delle Scienze, 2005.

Luzio, A. "Federico Gonzaga ostaggio alla corte di Giulio II." In *Archivio della Società Romana di Storia Patria* 9 (1886): 513–14.

Madonna, M. L. "Pirro Ligorio e l'Enciclopedia del Mondo Antico." In *Atti del I Convegno Nazionale di Storia dell'Arte*, Rome, 1978, pp. 257–71. Rome: CNR, 1980.

Maffei, S. "La fama del Laocoonte nei testi del Cinquecento." In *Laocoonte. Fama e stile*, edited by S. Settis, pp. 85–230. Rome: Donzelli Editore, 1999.

Magnus, A. *Opera Omnia*, vol. 36, edited by A. Borgnet and E. Borgnet. Paris: Ludovicum Vives, 1898.

Magnuson, T. "The Project of Nicholaus V for the Rebuilding the Borgo Leonino in Rome." In *The Art Bulletin*, 36 (1954): 94–96.

———. *Studies in Roman Quattrocento Architecture*. Stockholm: Almqvist & Wiksell, 1958.

Manetti, G. *Vita di Nicolò V*. Italian translation and commentary by A. Modigliani with a preface by M. Miglio. Rome: Roma nel Rinascimento, 1999.

Masson, G. "Italian Flower Collectors' Gardens in Seventeenth-Century Italy." In *The Italian Garden*, edited by D. R. Coffin, pp. 61–80. Washington, D.C.: Dumbarton Oaks, 1972.

———. *Italian Villas and Palaces*. New York: Harry N. Abrams, 1959.

Mastrigli, F. *Acque, Acquedotti e Fontane di Roma*, 2 vols. Rome: Edizioni Pinci, 1928.

Mattioli, P. *Commentarii in sex libros Pedacii Dioscoridis Anarzabei de medica materia*. Venice: Valgrisi, 1565.

Mercati, M. *Considerazioni…intorno ad alcune cose scritte nel libro de gli Obelischi di Roma*. Rome: Domenico Basa, 1590.

———. *Instruttione sopra la Peste di M. Michele Mercati medico e filosofo*. Rome: Vinc. Accolto, 1576.

Michaelis, A. "Geschichte des Statuenhofes im Vaticanischen Belvedere." In *Jahrbuch des kaiserlich deutschen archaologischen Instituts*, 5 (1890): 62–63.

———. "Der Statuenhof des Belvedere." *Jahrbuch der Arch. Inst.*, 5 (1890): 5 ff.

Micheli, M. E. *Giovanni Colonna da Tivoli*. Rome: De Luca, 1982.

Mignosi Tantillo, A. M., ed. *L'arte per i papi e per i principi nella campagna romana. Grande pittura del '600 e del '700*. Rome: Quasar, 1990.

———. *Villa e Paese, dimore nobili del Tuscolo e di Marino*. Rome: De Luca, 1980.

Minasi, M. "I Colonna nella Rocca di Subiaco. La decorazione cinquecentesca." In *Lo Specchio dei Principi. Il sistema decorativo delle dimore storiche nel territorio romano*, edited by C. Cieri Via, p. 176. Rome: De Luca, 2007.

Mochi Onori, L., S. Schultze, and F. Solinas, eds. *I Barberini e la cultura del tempo*, international study conference proceedings, Rome, 2005. Rome: De Luca, 2007.

Morel, P., *Les grottes maniéristes en Italie au XVI siècle: théatre et alchimie de la nature*. Paris: Macula, 1998.

Morello, G., and A. Piazzoni. *I giardini vaticani*. Rome: Logart, 1991.

Morello, G., and P. Silvan. *Vedute di Roma dai dipinti della Biblioteca Apostolica Vaticana*. Milan: Electa, 1997.

Moretti Sgubini, A. M., ed., *Villa Giulia dalle origini al 2000*. Rome: L'Erma di Bretschneider, 2000.

Morganti, G., ed. *Gli Orti Farnesiani*, study conference proceedings, Rome, 1985. Rome: L'Erma di Bretschneider, 1990.

Moroni, G. *Dizionario di erudizione storico-ecclesiastica da San Pietro sino ai nostri giorni*. Venice: Tipografia Emiliana, 1840–79.

Mosser, M., and G. Teyssot. *L'architettura dei giardini d'Occidente dal Rinascimento al Novecento*. Milan: Electa, 1990.

Muntz, E. "L'architettura a Roma durante il pontificato di Innocenzo VIII." In *Archivio Storico dell'Arte* 4 (1891): 459ff.

———. *Les arts à la cour de papes Innocent VIII, Alexandre VI, Pio III*. Paris: Ernest Leroux, 1898.

Muratori, L. *Rerum Italicarum Scriptores*. Milan: Typographia Societatis Palatinae, 1723–51.

Napoleone, C., ed. *Villa Madama*. Turin: Allemandi, 2007.

Negro, A. *Il giardino dipinto del cardinale Borghese*. Rome: Argos, 2000.

Negro, S. *Vaticano minore*. Milan: Hoepli, 1936.

Neviani, A. "I primi documenti su l'Orto dei Semplici in Vaticano nella seconda metà del secolo XVI." In *Atti della Pontificia Accademia dei Nuovi Lincei* 86 (1932–33): 127–53.

Nicolini, G. "I giardini Vaticani." In *L'Illustrazione Vaticana*, vol. 5, January 1934, pp. 61–66.

Orbaan, J. A. F. *Documenti sul barocco in Roma*. Perugia: Unione Tipografica Cooperativa, 1920.

Pagliuchi, P. "I castellani di Castel Sant'Angelo di Roma." In *Miscellanea di Storia e di Cultura Ecclesiastica*, 3 (1904), pp. 129ff.

Parasacchi, D. *Raccolta delle principali fontane dell'inclita città di Roma*, 1647. Reprint, Rome: Carlo Losi, 1773.

Pedretti, C. *A Chronology of Leonardo da Vinci's Architectural Studies after 1500*. Geneva: Droz, 1962.

Percier, C., and P.F.L. Fontaine. *Villas de Rome: choix des plus célèbres maisons de plaisance de Rome et des ses environs*, 1809. Reprint, edited by Jean-Philippe Garric. Wavre, Belgium: Mardaga, 2007.

Petrillo, S. *Le Ville pontificie di Castel Gandolfo*. Vatican City: Edizioni Musei Vaticani, 2000.

Petrucci, G. *San Martino al Cimino*. Rome: Multigrafica Editrice, 1987.

Piale, S. *Delle mura e porte del Vaticano*. Dissertation. Rome: Pontificia Accademia Romana di Archeologia, IV, 1834.

Piccolomini, E. S. *I Commentari*, edited by L. Totaro. Milan: Adelphi, 1984.

Pietrangeli, C. "La base della Colonna di Antonino Pio." In *L'Urbe*, 1–2 (1982): 11–12.

———. "La Fontana del Cortile del Belvedere." In *Strenna dei Romanisti*, April 18, 1987, XLVIII, pp. 475–84.

———. "Una veduta ottocentesca dei Giardini Vaticani." In *Strenna dei Romanisti*, no. 55 (1994): 413–17.

———. *Guide del Vaticano, La città*. Rome: Fratelli Palombi Editore, 1989.

———. *Il Palazzo Apostolico Vaticano*, Florence: Nardini, 1992.

Pietrangeli, C., and F. Mancinelli. *Vaticano. Città e giardini*. Florence: Scala, 1985.

Pinelli, A., and L. Gambi, ed., *La Galleria delle Carte Geografiche in Vaticano*. Modena: C. Pannini, 1994.

Pirotta, R., and E. Chiovenda. *Flora Romana*. Rome: Tipografia Voghera, 1900.

Pisani Sartorio, G., ed. *Il trionfo dell'acqua. Acqua e acquedotti a Roma dal IV sec. A.C. al XX secolo*, exhibition catalogue. Rome: Paleani, 1986.

Platina, B. *Le vite de' sommi pontefici*. Venice: Girolamo Savioni, 1730.

Polono, M. *Chronicon expeditissimum, ad fidem veterum manoscriptorum codicum emendatum et auctum*. Antwerp: ex officina Christophori Platini, Architypographi Regij, 1574.

Portoghesi, P. *Roma nel Rinascimento*. Milan: Electa, 1971.

Pozzana, M. C. *Il giardino dei frutti*. Florence: Ponte alle Grazie, 1990.

Puppi, L. "Il problema dell'eredità di Baldassarre Peruzzi: Jacopo Meleghino, il mistero di Francesco Sanese e Sebastiano Serlio." In *Baldassarre Peruzzi: pittura, scena e architettura nel Cinquecento*, edited by M. Fagiolo dell'Arco, pp. 491–501. Rome: Istituto dell'Enciclopedia Italiana, 1987.

Quast, M. *Die Villa Montalto im Rom: Entstehung und Gestalt in Cinquecento*. Munich: Tuduv, 1991.

Re, E. "Maestri di Strada." In *Archivio della Società Romana di Storia Patria* 63 (1920): 5ff.

Redig de Campos, D. "Il Belvedere d'Innocenzo VIII in Vaticano." In *Triplice omaggio a Sua Santità Pio XII*, vol. 2, pp. 289–304. Vatican City: Tipografia Poliglotta Vaticana, 1958.

———. "Les constructions d'Innocent III et de Nicolas III sur la colline Vaticane." In *Mélanges d'archéologie et d'histoire* 71 (1959): 359–76.

———. *I Palazzi vaticani*. Bologna, Italy: Cappelli, 1967.

Renazzi, F. M. *Storia dell'Università degli Studi di Roma detta comunemente la Sapienza*, vol.4. Rome: Stamperia Paglierini, 1803–6.

Ronchini, A. *Jacopo Meleghino*. Modena: C. Vincenzi, 1867.

Ruiz Lopez, H. *Florae Peruvianae, et Chilensis prodromus sive novarum generum plantarum Peruvianorum et Chilensium descriptiones et icones*. Rome: Typographia Paleariniano, 1797.

Ruysschaert, J. "La Biblioteca Vaticana di Sisto V nelle testimonianze coeve." In *Sisto V, vol. 1: Roma e il Lazio*, edited by M. Fagiolo, M. L. Madonna, pp. 329–38. Rome: Istituto Poligrafico e Zecca dello Stato, 1992.

Saccardo, P. A. *Cronologia della Flora italiana*. Padua: Tipografia Seminario, 1909.

Sala, G. A. *Diario Romano degli anni 1798–1799*. Reprint, Rome: Miscellanea della Società Romana di Storia Patria, 1980.

San Mauro, M. A. "Le fabbriche di Paolo V tornano a splendere." *Il Quirinale*, no.2 (March 2006): 38–54.

Scardin, A. *Disegni dei perther dei più cospicui giardini posti in Roma*. Edited by A. Tagliolini. Milan: Editore Il Polifilo, 1995.

Schettini Piazza, E. "I Barberini e i Lincei: dalla mirabil congiuntura alla fine della prima Accademia (1623–1630)." In *I Barberini e la cultura Europea del Seicento*, international conference proceedings (Rome, 2005), edited by L. Mochi Onori, S. Schultze, and F. Solinas, pp. 117–26. Rome: De Luca, 2007.

Schiavo, A. *Villa Ludovisi e Palazzo Margherita*. Rome: Editrice Roma Amor, 1981.

Segre, A. V. "Le retour de Flore. Naissance et évolution des jardins de fleurs de 1550 à 1650." In *L'Empire de Flore*, edited by S. Van Sprang, pp. 174–93. Brussels: La Renaissance du Livre, 1996.

Serdonati, F. *Vita e fatti d'Innocenzo VIII*. Milan: Edizione Vincenzo Ferrario, 1829.

Smith, G. *The Casino of Pius IV*. Princeton: Princeton University Press, 1977.

Smith, G. "The Stucco Decoration of the Casino of Pio IV." *Zeitschrift fur Kunstgeschichte* 37, (1974): 116–56.

Soderini, E. *Il pontificato di Leone XIII*. Milan: Mondadori, 1932–33.

Taegio, B. *La Villa*. Milan: Francesco Moscheni, 1559.

Tagliolini, A. *Storia del Giardino italiano*. Florence: La Casa Usher, 1991.

Tagliolini, A., and R. Assunto, eds. *Ville e Giardini di Roma nelle incisioni di Giovan Battista Falda*. Milan: Il Polifilo, 1980.

Taja, A. *Descrizione del Palazzo Apostolico Vaticano*. Rome: Pagliarini, 1750.

Theiner, A. *Codex diplomaticus dominii temporalis S. Sedis: recueil de documents pour servir à l'histoire du gouvernement temporel des Etats du Saint Siege: extraits des archives du Vatican*. Frankfurt am Main: Unveranderter Nachdruch, 1964.

Tomassetti, G. *La Campagna Romana antica, medievale e moderna*, new updated edition edited by L. Chiumenti and F. Bilancia. Florence: Leo S. Olschki, 1979–80.

Tomei, T. *L'architettura a Roma nel Quattrocento*. Rome: Multigrafica, 1977.

Tongiorgi Tomasi, L., *An Oak Spring Flora: Flower Illustration from the Fifteenth Century to the Present Time*. Upperville: Oak Spring Garden Library, 1997.

———. "'Extra' e 'Intus': progettualità degli orti botanici e collezionismo eclettico tra XVI e XVII secolo." In *Il giardino come labirinto della storia*, conference proceedings, Palermo, 1984, edited by G. Pirrone, pp. 277–89. Palermo: Centro Studi di Storia e Arte dei Giardini, n.d.

———. "Gli Orti botanici nei secoli XVI e XVII." In *L'architettura dei giardini d'Occidente dal Rinascimento al Novecento*, edited by M. Mosser, P. Teyssot, pp. 77–79. Milan: Electa, 1990.

———. "Tulipomania. Addenda." In *Il Giardino delle Muse*, conference proceedings, edited by M. A. Giusti, and A. Tagliolini, pp. 79–95. Florence: Edifir, 1995.

Tongiorgi Tomasi, L., and F. Garbari, *Il giardiniere del Granduca: storia e immagini del Codice Casabona*. Pisa: Edizione ETS, 1995.

Varoli-Piazza, S. *Paesaggi e giardini della Tuscia*. Rome: De Luca, 2007.

Vasari, G. *Le vite*, 1568. Critical edition edited by C. L. Ragghianti, 4 vols. Milan and Rome, 1942–49.

Vasari, G. *Lives of the Painters, Sculptors and Architects*. Trans. Gaston du C. de Vere. 1912. New York: Alfred A. Knopf, first published in Everyman's Library, 1927.

Venturi, G. "Origine e sviluppo del giardino 'segreto.'" In *L'architettura dei giardini d'occidente dal Rinascimento al Novecento*, edited by M. Mosser and P. Teyssot, pp. 84–86. Milan: Electa, 1990.

———. "Picta poesis: ricerca sulla poesia e il giardino dalle origini al Seicento," in C. De Seta, ed., *Storia d'Italia*. Annali, v, *Il Paesaggio*, pp. 663-749. Turin, Italy: Einaudi, 1982.

Venturi Ferriolo, M. *Nel grembo della vita. Le origini dell'idea di giardino*. Milan: Guerini e Associati, 1989.

Vespasiano da Bisticci. *Vite di uomini illustri del 15° secolo, rivedute sui manoscritti da Ludovico Frati*. Bologna, Italy: Romagnoli dell'Acqua Editori, 1892.

Vivit, A. "L'insigne viridario di Francesco Gonzaga in Roma." In *Bollettino del Centro Studi per la Storia dell'Architettura*, no. 34 (1987): 5–33.

Volpi, C., "La favola moralizzata nella Roma della Controriforma: Pirro Ligorio e Federico Zuccari tra riflessioni teoriche e pratica artistica." *Storia dell'Arte*, nos. 9–10 (2004): 131–60.

———. *Pirro Ligorio e i giardini a Roma nella seconda metà del Cinquecento*. Rome: Università degli Studi di Roma La Sapienza, Lithos Edizioni, 1996.

———. "Il teatro del mondo: Pirro Ligorio (1513-1573) architetto papale in Vaticano," *Bollettino d'Arte*, 107, 1999, pp. 83-102.

Von Fichard, J. *Italia*. Frankfurt am Main: Gebhard & Korben, 1815.

von Pastor, L. *Storia dei Papi*. Rome: Desclée & C Editori Pontifici, 1934.

Wharton, E. *Italian Villas and Their Gardens*. New York: The Century Co., 1907.

Wharton, E. *Ville italiane e loro giardini*. Florence: Passigli, 1991.

Winner, M., B. Andree, and C. Pietrangeli, eds. *Il Cortile delle Statue: der Statuenhof des Belvedere im Vatikan*, international conference proceedings in honor of R. Krautheimer, Rome, October 1992. Mainz, Germany: von Zabern, 1998.

Zaccagnini, C. *Le Ville di Roma*. Rome: Newton Compton, 1976.

Zalum Cardon, M. *Passione e cultura dei fiori tra Firenze e Roma nel XVI e XVII secolo*. Florence: Leo S. Olschki, 2008.

Zangheri, L. "Naturalia e curiosa nei giardini del Cinquecento," in M. Mosser and G. Teyssot, *L'architettura dei giardini d'Occidente dal Rinascimento al Novecento*, pp. 92–101. Milan: Electa, 1990.

———. "Ragnaie, Paretai e Uccelliere nelle Ville barocche." In *Villa Borghese. Storia e gestione*, international conference proceedings, Rome, 2003, edited by A. Campitelli, pp. 57–66. Milan: Skira, 2005.

———. *Storia del giardino e del paesaggio: il verde nella cultura occidentale*. Florence: Olschki, 2003.

Index